Chemistry 141

Study Guide

Paul W. Hunter | Amy M. Pollock

CENGAGE
Learning™

Australia • Brazil • Japan • Korea • Mexico • Singapore • Spain • United Kingdom • United States

CENGAGE
Learning™

Chemistry 141: Study Guide

Paul W. Hunter | Amy M. Pollock

Executive Editors:
Michele Baird
Maureen Staudt
Michael Stranz

Project Development Manager:
Linda deStefano

Senior Marketing Coordinators:
Sara Mercurio
Lindsay Shapiro

Senior Production / Manufacturing Manager: ➕
Donna M. Brown

PreMedia Services Supervisor:
Rebecca A. Walker

Rights & Permissions Specialist:
Kalina Hintz

Cover Image:
Getty Images*

* Unless otherwise noted, all cover images used by Custom Solutions, a part of Cengage Learning, have been supplied courtesy of Getty Images with the exception of the Earthview cover image, which has been supplied by the National Aeronautics and Space Administration (NASA).

For product information and technology assistance, contact us at
Cengage Learning Customer & Sales Support, 1-800-354-9706

For permission to use material from this text or product,
submit all requests online at **cengage.com/permissions**
Further permissions questions can be emailed to
permissionrequest@cengage.com

ISBN-13: 978-0-7593-5456-2

ISBN-10: 0-7593-5456-1

Cengage Learning
5191 Natorp Boulevard
Mason, Ohio 45040
USA

Cengage Learning is a leading provider of customized learning solutions with office locations around the globe, including Singapore, the United Kingdom, Australia, Mexico, Brazil, and Japan. Locate your local office at:
international.cengage.com/region

Cengage Learning products are represented in Canada by Nelson Education, Ltd.

For your lifelong learning solutions, visit **custom.cengage.com**

Visit our corporate website at **cengage.com**

CONTENTS

Part 1:   The Basic Tools of Chemistry

1. Matter and Measurement   1
2. Atoms and Elements   13
3. Molecules, Ions, and Their Compounds   29
4. Chemical Equations and Stoichiometry   45
5. Reactions in Aqueous Solution   61
6. Principles of Reactivity: Energy and Chemical Reactions   79
   Examination 1   95

Part 2:   The Structure of Atoms and Molecules

7. Atomic Structure   101
8. Atomic Electron Configurations and Chemical Periodicity   113
9. Bonding and Molecular Structure: Fundamental Concepts   125
10. Bonding and Molecular Structure: Orbital Hybridization
    and Molecular Orbitals   143
    Examination 2   151

Part 3:   States of Matter

11. Gases and Their Properties   157
12. Intermolecular Forces, Liquids, and Solids   171
13. Solutions and Their Behavior   185
    Examination 3   199

Part 4:   Introduction to Chemical Equilibria

15. Chemical Kinetics   205
16. Chemical Equilibria   213
17. Acids and Bases   229

Solutions   251

Changes for this Edition

These study guides have been revised and reorganized to match the syllabus of CEM 141 and CEM 142 at Michigan State University. The format and style of the fifth edition appeared to work well for many students and has been kept the same.

The study guides have been divided into two separate books. This, the first book, accompanies CEM 141.

Although care has been taken to avoid new errors in this edition, undoubtedly some have slipped through. So any corrections, criticisms, or comments are very welcome and may be emailed to us. Please do not hesitate to do so.

Paul Hunter
Amy Pollock

A Note on the Organization of these Study Guides

There is a study guide for section of the syllabus. After a brief introduction and list of topics, each study guide begins with a section-by-section summary of the material. This summary outlines the essential points—the content to learn and understand. Key points and comments are noted in the margins and important words or phases are written in boldface.

After the summary your knowledge and understanding of the material is tested through a series of short review questions. Answers follow these review questions.

At the end of each study guide a limited number of problems are presented. These vary in difficulty and again they test and reinforce your mastery of the subject. It is important to try *all* these problems, either by yourself or with your friends, before looking through the solutions that follow. Key points and comments are again noted in the margins.

Crossword puzzles are provided in some chapters—for both your entertainment and learning. Solutions to these puzzles are provided at the end of the book.

Three sample examinations are presented at various stages through this book corresponding approximately to the three examinations in CEM 141. The questions on these sample exams are intended to prepare you for your own examinations. The answers are again provided at the end of the book.

Introduction to the 4th Edition

The study of chemistry is required by almost all science majors at college. However, chemistry has the reputation of being a subject difficult to master. Introductory courses in chemistry are universally regarded by students as hard—a rite of passage that must be endured. Why is this?

Chemistry presents a considerable amount of material that needs to be mastered early in the course. It is for many students an almost overwhelming amount of material: names to be learned, formulas to write, equations to balance, stoichiometric calculations to perform, concepts to understand. And then, after the introductory topics have been dealt with, the pace never lets up; it just seems that the chemistry gets more and more difficult.

This study guide is intended to help you organize your study of chemistry so that you can learn more efficiently, understand the subject better, and ultimately achieve success in the course.

Our experience has shown that one study habit is essential for success, and another study habit helps enormously. The essential habit is a regular, preferably daily, study and *active* practice of the subject. Be prepared for the lectures and be an active participant in them; take notes and review and *rewrite* them afterward. Solve problems and answer the questions assigned as homework and *never* look at the solutions or answers until you have tried the problems yourself.

What helps in your study is a collaboration and cooperation with your fellow students. Never underestimate the power of your peers! Talking about the chemistry with other students, explaining concepts to others, reading about the chemistry in your textbook, and practicing the problems is the way to success. Chemistry is like a foreign language to many students. Like any other language, the more you use it, the easier it will become. In this study guide we hope to make your learning of chemistry easier.

We will provide suggestions on how to use and learn from the textbook, summarize and point out the important features within each chapter, and provide supplementary problems, and their solutions, on each topic.

Benjamin Franklin (1706-1790) once said that education is what remains after the information that has been taught has been forgotten. This is true of chemistry. You will probably have forgotten many of the facts you memorize in this course by the time you graduate in four years' time. However, the concepts, ideas, and principles of chemistry that you have *understood* will remain with you. You will apply this knowledge time and time again in your major studies. Let's begin.

CHAPTER 1

Introduction

This first chapter starts with an introduction of some fundamental properties of matter. Elements and compounds, and atoms and molecules, are described. Physical properties of matter (such as density and temperature), and chemical and physical changes are discussed. The chapter presents a scheme for the classification of matter with a description of the three states of matter. At the end of the chapter some of the mathematics essential to introductory chemistry—the International System of units, dimensional analysis, scientific notation, significant figures, and problem-solving strategies—are introduced.

Contents

Elements and Atoms
Compounds and Molecules
Physical Properties
Physical and Chemical Change
Classifying Matter
Units of Measurement
Using Numerical Information
Problem Solving

Elements and Atoms

A **substance** that cannot be decomposed further by chemical means is called an **element**. At present 116 different elements are known, but only about 90 are found in nature. Some of these, for example, copper (Cu), gold (Au), and lead (Pb), have been known for more than two thousand years. Others, for example aluminum (Al), germanium (Ge), and helium (He), have been discovered and isolated only within the last two hundred years. In relatively recent years many new elements have been created artificially by nuclear reaction.

Each element has a name and a **symbol**, for example hydrogen (H), iodine (I), chlorine (Cl), tin (Sn), and silver (Ag). The symbol may consist of one or two letters. Each element has its own place in the **Periodic Table of Elements**. The smallest particle of an element is called an **atom** of that element.

Learn the symbols and names of the first 18 elements. When you have mastered these extend the range to the first 38. These are the elements you will encounter most frequently.

The first (or only) letter of the symbol is capitalized; the second letter is always lower case.

There is a Periodic Table on the inside front cover of this study guide.

Compounds and Molecules

A substance may be a **compound** of two or more elements. When two or more elements combine to form a compound, the compound has properties quite distinct from the properties of the original elements. Just as elements have symbols, so compounds have **formulas**.

There are two major classes of compounds: molecular and ionic. **Molecules** are discrete groups of atoms bonded together. They are the smallest units that exhibit the chemical characteristics of the substance. An example is the water molecule H_2O, composed of two hydrogen atoms and one oxygen atom. The formula for a **molecular compound** like water is composed of the symbols for the elements in the molecule, with subscripts indicating the number of atoms of each element present. The subscript 1 is always omitted. Water has chemical and physical properties quite unlike those of its constituent elements hydrogen and oxygen.

Ionic compounds and their formulas are described in Chapter 3.

Ionic compounds are composed of **ions**—these are electrically charged atoms or groups of atoms. Examples are common salt (sodium chloride $NaCl$), and baking soda (sodium bicarbonate $NaHCO_3$). Sodium chloride is a compound of sodium and chlorine in which the sodium is present as positive sodium ions Na^+ and chlorine is present as negative chloride ions Cl^-.

Mixture of two elements:
Variable composition
Properties of elements evident
Decomposed by physical means

Compound of two elements:
Fixed composition
Distinctly different properties
Decomposed only by chemical means

Compounds are quite different from mixtures of elements. Individual elements can be identified in mixtures since they will show their characteristic properties; they may be present in any proportion; and they can be separated by physical means. A compound, on the other hand, can be decomposed only by chemical means and the elements are always present in the same definite proportions by mass (the law of constant composition).

Physical Properties

All matter possesses physical properties such as melting point, boiling point, density, solubility, conductivity, viscosity, heat of fusion, and color. Physical properties enable the classification and identification of substances.

Density = mass/volume.
See study question #1.

Density is a physical property that relates the mass of an object to its volume. If two of the three variables density, mass, and volume are known, the third can always be calculated.

Temperature is the property of matter that measures how hot a substance is. Since heat travels from a hotter region to a colder one, temperature determines the direction of heat flow.

Know how to convert a temperature on one scale into a temperature on another scale. Although the size of one °F is 5/9 the size of one °C, you cannot convert from one to the other by simply multiplying or dividing by 5/9. The zero points are different!
See study questions #2, 3, & 4.

Human body temperature is now recognized to be 98.6°F not 100°F.

Any temperature scale can be established by assigning numbers to two reproducible events: Anders Celsius (1701-1744) chose 0° for melting ice and 100° for boiling water—the **Celsius** scale; Gabriel Fahrenheit (1686–1736) chose 0° for an ice/salt/water mixture and 100° for the body temperature of a human being—the **Fahrenheit** scale. The Fahrenheit scale is now established using 32° for melting ice and 212° for boiling water. The size of a Fahrenheit degree (one division on the scale) is 5/9 of the size of a Celsius degree and this relationship can be used to convert from one scale to the other. On the **Kelvin** (or absolute) temperature scale a value of 0° is assigned to the lowest temperature attainable with a degree size the same as the Celsius degree. Zero on the Celsius scale (0°C) is equal to 273.15K. (Note the absence of the °degree symbol for Kelvin temperature.)

The Kelvin scale is named after William Thompson, Lord Kelvin, whose title, in turn, derived from the River Kelvin, Glasgow, Scotland.

Physical properties are often affected by a change in temperature; density, for example, decreases as temperature increases. There are two types of physical property: extensive and intensive. **Extensive** properties, like mass and volume, depend upon the amount of substance present. **Intensive** properties, like color and density, are independent of the amount of substance.

Be able to classify properties as either extensive or intensive.
See study question #5.

Physical and Chemical Change

In a **physical change**, the identity of a substance remains unchanged. Examples are the conversion of liquid water into water vapor, and dissolving salt in water to make a solution. In both cases the identity of the substance remains the same.

Be able to classify a change as either chemical or physical.
See study question #6.

The conversion of one or more substances into other substances is referred to as a chemical change or **chemical reaction**. For example, the two substances hydrogen and oxygen react to form water, another substance. Atoms of the elements involved are neither created nor destroyed, they are simply rearranged. A chemical reaction is represented by a **chemical equation**.

Both chemical and physical changes are almost always accompanied by a transfer of energy.

Classifying Matter

Matter normally exists in one of three states—solid, liquid, or gas. A **solid** has a rigid shape and a volume that changes very little as the temperature and pressure change. A **liquid** is fluid—it takes on the shape of the lower part of its container and has a well-defined surface. It also changes little in volume with change in temperature or pressure. A **gas** expands to fill its container and its volume varies considerably with change in temperature or pressure.

Both solids and liquids are referred to as condensed states of matter—the molecules touch one another.

Physical properties of matter can be understood by the **kinetic molecular theory**—the idea that matter consists of tiny particles called molecules or atoms that are in constant motion. In a solid these particles are packed tightly in a regular pattern. In a liquid the particles are in constant motion and are not held in place. The particles interact constantly, continually making and breaking bonds between themselves. In a gas the particles are far apart and are independent of each other; they move rapidly between collisions with each other and the container in which the gas is confined. As the temperature is increased the kinetic energy of the particles increases—a solid will eventually melt and a liquid will vaporize.

Kinetic energy is the energy of motion.

At room temperature, molecules in the air are moving around at average speeds of 1000 mph.

Some physical properties can be observed by unaided human senses—these are macroscopic properties. Some matter is too small to be seen without a microscope and is called **microscopic**. The structure of matter at the atomic scale is called sub-microscopic or **particulate**.

Chemistry has three main components:

the macroscopic—
    tangible, visible

Most naturally occurring samples of matter are mixtures. There are two types of mixtures: heterogeneous and homogeneous. In a **heterogeneous mixture** the properties of the mixture vary throughout. Often the individual components of the mixture are observable (for example in a mixture of salt and pepper) but sometimes closer examination or magnification is necessary. A **homogeneous mixture** is called a **solution**—this is a mixture of components at a molecular level. No amount of optical magnification can reveal different properties in different regions of a solution.

the particulate—
    atoms, ions, & molecules

the symbolic—
    formulas & equations.

Recognize two types of mixtures: homogeneous and heterogeneous.

Purification is the separation of a mixture into its components. The purity of a component can be determined by examination of its physical properties such as its color or melting point. A substance is considered pure when no observable change in its physical properties occurs with further purification.

A (pure) substance can be identified by a characteristic set of properties.

The separation of mixtures can be quite difficult; the methods used to isolate the components of a mixture take advantage of the different physical properties of the components.

Units of Measurement

Learn the six base SI units of interest to chemists:

Mass	kilogram	kg
Length	meter	m
Time	second	s
Temperature	kelvin	K
Amount	mole	mol
Current	ampere	A

Common prefixes for SI units and conversion factors for changing from non SI to SI units are listed on the inside back cover of this study guide.

See study question #10 for other examples.

Quantitative measurements are essential in most chemical reactions. Most measurements in science are based upon the **International System of Units** (abbreviated SI). In SI all units are derived from seven base units (of which six are of interest to chemists). Often a prefix is added to indicate a power of ten (or order of magnitude). For example, highway distances are given in kilometers where the kilo prefix indicates an order of 10^3 (i.e. 1000 meters = 1 kilometer). The kilogram is the only base unit with a prefix.

Scientific notation, combining decimal and **exponential notation,** is explained in Appendix A of the text. To use this notation a number is written as a decimal value between 1 and 10 (but not including 10) multiplied by 10 raised to a whole number power (which may be positive, negative, or zero). For example, 0.08206 would be written as 8.206×10^{-2}.

Using Numerical Information

See study question #9.

Manipulating numerical data is an everyday part of experimental chemistry. **Dimensional analysis** is a particularly useful approach to solving many problems in chemistry. The method involves the use of appropriate conversion factors to obtain the desired result. If the units cancel correctly, then the numerical result will be correct.

Understand the difference between accuracy and precision.

See study question #11.

The **precision** of a measurement indicates how well several determinations of a quantity agree with one another (the reproducibility of the measurement). Precision can be expressed in terms of the **average deviation** within an experimental data set. **Accuracy** on the other hand indicates how close the determinations are to the actual value. A precise series of measurements does not guarantee an accurate determination—there may be a systematic error in the experimental method.

The result of an experimental measurement is written as precisely as possible. The final digit in a number is assumed to be no more certain than ±1. For example, the thickness of a tabletop written as 23 mm means that the thickness might be 23±1 mm, that is, somewhere between 22 and 24 mm. Error is often reported as **percent error**, which is the difference between the experimental value and the accepted or true value, multiplied by 100.

Be able to do calculations with proper regard for the precision of the measurements involved.

See study question #13.

When manipulating numbers and their units in calculations, care must be taken to retain all digits until the end of the calculation and then to write the result with no more significant digits than is warranted. In short, when adding or subtracting numbers, line up the decimal points and round the answer to no more decimal places than the number with the fewest places. When multiplying or dividing numbers, the number of significant figures in the answer should be the same as in the number with the fewest significant figures. Use common sense!

Percent (%) means *per centum*, or the fraction of one hundred. Usually the percent is w/w or mass per mass. For example, a 6% solution of sugar in water means that in 100 g of solution there are 6 grams of sugar (and 94 g of water).

Problem Solving

Knowing how to interpret a question, and how to solve the problem, is often more difficult than the actual solution. If you misunderstand the problem, the chances of a successful solution are remote. Logical steps are:

1. Define the problem (understand the question!)
2. Develop a plan.
3. Execute the plan.
4. Check the answer: is it reasonable? are the units correct?

Review Questions

1. What is an element? What is a compound?

2. What is a molecule?

3. Do compounds always contain molecules?

4. Is a molecule always a compound?

5. What is the difference between a chemical and a physical property?

6. What is the relationship between density, volume, and mass?

7. What is the difference between the Fahrenheit and Celsius temperature scales?

8. What is the significance of zero degrees kelvin (0K)?

9. What is the difference between an extensive property and an intensive property?

10. How do atoms or molecules behave differently in the three states of matter?

11. What are the two different kinds of mixtures and what is the difference between them?

12. What is the base SI unit for mass?

13. Describe the six base SI units of interest to chemists.

14. What is the SI unit for volume? How does it compare to the liter?

Key terms:

substance
element
atom
molecule
ion
compound
molecular compound
ionic compound
formula
density
temperature
extensive property
intensive property
physical change
chemical reaction
chemical equation
states of matter
solid
liquid
gas
kinetic molecular theory
mixture
heterogeneous
homogeneous
solution
SI
exponential notation
dimensional analysis
precision
average deviation
accuracy
percent error
conversion factor
significant figures

15. Are the values of the exponents in scientific notation always positive? Can the value of the exponent be zero?

16. What is dimensional analysis? Explain what a conversion factor is and give an example.

17. Is it possible for a series of measurements to be accurate but not very precise?

18. What is the average deviation of a set of experimental results and how is it calculated?

Answers to Review Questions

1. An element is a substance that cannot be decomposed further by chemical means. Only 116 different elements are known, and only about 90 of these are found in nature. Each element has its own name, symbol, and place in the Periodic Table. A compound is a combination of elements.

Molecules and compounds are discussed in more detail in Chapter 3.

2. A molecule is a discrete group of atoms that behaves as a single unit and has the composition and chemical characteristics of the compound.

3. A compound can be molecular, but it can also be an ionic compound like salt (sodium chloride).

4. A molecule can be a compound, like water H_2O, or it can be an element, like oxygen O_2. Other examples of elements that exist as molecules are H_2, N_2, I_2, S_8, P_4, and C_{60}. Most molecules, however, are compounds.

5. A chemical change is the conversion of one or more substances into other substances. Atoms of the elements involved are neither created nor destroyed, they are simply rearranged. In a physical change, the identities of the substances remain unchanged.

Remember this relationship; you will use it often.

6. Density = mass/volume.

Zero K is the temperature at which an ideal gas would have zero volume. An absolute temperature scale had been proposed by French scientists Amontons, Charles, and Gay-Lussac based upon the expansion of gases. In 1854 Kelvin based his absolute temperature scale on what is called the Joule-Thompson effect.

7. Celsius chose the numbers 0° for melting ice and 100° for boiling water for his temperature scale. Fahrenheit chose 0° for an ice/salt/water mixture and 100° for the body temperature of a human being. An identical event has a different number (°degrees) on the two scales. The size of a Fahrenheit degree is 5/9 of the size of a Celsius degree. However, the zero points are different for the two scales—0°C equals 32°F. The only temperature at which both scales have the same value is −40°.

8. Zero degrees kelvin is theoretically the lowest temperature possible.

9.   An extensive property depends upon the amount of substance present; an obvious example is the mass of the substance. An intensive property is independent of the amount present; color is an example.

10.   In a solid, atoms or molecules are packed tightly in a regular array. In a liquid the atoms or molecules are in constant random motion although they interact constantly with each other. Bonds between molecules are continually broken and reformed. In a gas the particles are far apart, independent of each other; and move rapidly between collisions with each other and the container.

11.   There are two types of mixtures: heterogeneous and homogeneous. In a heterogeneous mixture the properties of the mixture vary throughout (although this may be difficult to see). A homogeneous mixture is called a solution—this is a mixture of components at a particulate level and the properties of a solution are constant throughout.

12.   The base SI unit for mass is the kilogram (kg)—not the gram.

SI is derived from the French: système international d'unites.

13.   The six base SI units are: mass(kg); length(m); time(s); temperature(K); current(A); amount(mol).

The 7th base SI unit is the candela—the unit for luminous intensity.

14.   The derived SI unit for volume is the m^3 (not the liter!). There are 1000 liters in one m^3. 1 liter = 1 dm^3.

15.   No, the exponent in scientific notation can be positive (for numbers 10 or greater) or negative (for numbers less than 1) and it can be zero—although 10^0 equals 1 and is usually omitted.

16.   Dimensional analysis, sometimes called the factor label method, is a procedure in which a quantity described in one unit is converted to an equivalent quantity in a different unit. This is done by multiplying by a conversion factor that relates one unit to the other.

The conversion factor is always written as 'the new units divided by the original units'.

See study question #9.

17.   Yes, if there is considerable random error in the series of measurements, the precision will be poor. However, providing the errors are truly random, the average will be accurate.

18.   The average deviation of a set of experimental data is calculated as follows: The average of the values is calculated; the deviation of each value from the average is calculated (all as positive or absolute values); and then these deviations are averaged.

See study question #11.

Le nouveau système de poids et mesures sera un sujet d'embarras et de difficultés pour plusieurs générations... C'est tourmenter le peuple par des vétilles!!!

The new system of weights and measures will be a stumbling block and source of difficulty for several generations...It's just tormenting people with trivia!!!

Napoléon I, Emperor 1804-1815 (1769-1821)

Study Questions and Problems

1. a. Calculate the density of lead if a 10 kg block has a volume of 885 cm^3.
    b. What is the volume of a 100 g bar of aluminum if its density is 2.70 g cm^{-3}?
    c. Calculate the mass of 100 cm^3 of uranium (density 19.07 g cm^{-3}).

2. At what temperature do the Fahrenheit and Celsius scales have the same value?

3. Convert
    a. 12°F to °C
    b. 300K to °F
    c. 25°C to K

4. Which of the following physical properties are extensive?

    a. heat of fusion
    b. viscosity
    c. melting point
    d. conductivity
    e. color
    f. density

You can develop any temperature scale you wish. Many scientists had their own scale: Newton, Rankine, and Réamur, for example.

5. It is possible to use any convenient substance as the basis of a temperature scale. For example, benzene freezes at 5°C and boils at 80°C. Suppose you assign the freezing point of benzene as the zero point on a new temperature scale (0°B) and assign the boiling point of benzene as 100°B on your new scale.
    a. Which is smaller, one °B or one °C?
    b. What is the boiling point of ammonia (–33°C) on the new scale?
    c. What is the melting point of sulfur (115°C) on the new scale?

6. Identify the following changes as physical or chemical changes:

    a. Baking soda reacts with vinegar to produce carbon dioxide.
    b. Iron metal rusts in the shipyard.
    c. Addition of salt melts ice on the highway.
    d. Steam condenses on the bathroom mirror.
    e. Milk turns sour.
    f. Sugar dissolves in a cup of tea.
    g. Natural gas burns in a furnace.

7. Look up the following symbols in the Periodic Table and write the names of the elements:

a. F	d. B	g. Cu
b. K	e. S	h. Ni
c. P	f. Ar	i. Sn

8. Write the symbols for the following elements:
    a. silicon
    b. calcium
    c. sodium
    d. zinc
    e. carbon
    f. iron
    g. tungsten
    h. nitrogen
    i. chlorine
    j. gold
    k. silver
    l. magnesium

    The symbols for some elements that have been known for a long time are based upon names other than their English names.

9. Using dimensional analysis, convert
    a. 1342 mL into L
    b. 3.26 km into mm
    c. 87.68 mg into g
    d. 400 cm^3 into m^3
    e. 3600 sq.in. into sq.ft.

10. Write the following numbers in scientific notation with the correct number of significant figures:
    a. 1,327
    b. 0.00562
    c. 2.76
    d. 0.166
    e. 0.09911

11. Measurements of the boiling point of a liquid were taken by two laboratory technicians (A and B). The actual boiling point was 92.3°C. Which technician achieved the most accurate result and which technician was most precise? Calculate the average deviation within each set.
    A: 92.0   92.1   92.4   92.2 °C
    B: 91.9   92.5   92.6   92.0 °C

12. Match the SI prefix with the correct multiplier:

milli	10^3	kilo	10^{-12}
centi	10^{-3}	micro	10^6
mega	10^{-6}	pico	10^{-2}

13. Evaluate the following expressions. Express the answers in scientific notation with the correct number of significant figures and the correct units.

    a. 0.0045 in + 1.0098 in + 0.987 in + 23.08 in

    b. (3.45 cm^3 × 2.70 g cm^{-3}) + (7.433 cm^3 × 1.677 g cm^{-3})

    c. 2.703 g/(1.376 cm × 2.45 cm × 3.78 cm)

14. A 12.3 g block of an unknown metal is immersed in water in a graduated cylinder. The level of water in the cylinder rose. The level of water in the cylinder rose exactly the same distance when 17.4 grams of aluminum (density 2.70 g cm^{-3}) was added to the same cylinder. What is the density of the unknown metal?

15.   Use the outline described in the "Problem Solving" section of this study guide to plan your approach to solving the following problem. Describe the strategy you use.
       The level of water in a graduated cylinder is at the 100 mL mark. When a platinum crucible floats on the surface of the water, the level reads 157.9 mL. When the crucible is totally immersed in the same cylinder, the level reads 102.70 mL. What is the density of platinum? The density of water is 0.997 g/mL at 25°C.

16.   If one pound is 453.59 grams, how many grams are there in one ounce? How many ounces are there in one kilogram?

17.   A sample of a gold alloy contains 5.6% silver by mass. How many grams of silver are there in 1 kilogram of the alloy?

Answers to Study Questions and Problems

1.   a.   Density = mass/volume = 10,000g/885cm^3 = 11.3 g cm^{-3}

These expressions are all equivalent representations of

Density = mass/volume.

If two of the variables are known, the third can always be calculated.

      b.   Volume = mass/density = 100g/2.70 g cm^{-3} = 37.0 cm^3

      c.   Mass = volume × density = 100 cm^3 × 19.07 g cm^{-3} = 1910 g.

9 Fahrenheit degrees
= 5 Celsius degrees

2.   The gradients of the two scales are different. The Fahrenheit scale rises 180° between the melting point of ice and the boiling point of water. The Celsius scale rises only 100°. The ratio between the gradients is 180/100 or 9/5. Using the conversion method presented in the text:
      If the value on the two scales is equal, and x is that value, then
      x°C = (5/9)(x°F −32), so 9x = 5x − 160, and x = −40°F or −40°C.

This is because the temperature at which both scales have the same value is –40°, so add 40 to bring the common point to 0°, multiply by 9/5 or 5/9, then subtract the 40°.

Multiply by 5/9 because a Fahrenheit degree is smaller than a Celsius degree.

3.   A convenient method for converting °F to °C and *vice versa* is to add 40; multiply by 5/9 (or 9/5); and then subtract 40. To convert °F to K, first convert to °C, and then convert °C to K.

      a.   *add 40°*   12°F + 40° = 52°
            × 5/9   52° × 5/9 = 28.9°
            subtract 40° 28.9° − 40° = −11°C

      b.   300K = 300° − 273.15° = 26.9°C
            add 40°   26.9°C + 40° = 66.9°
            × 9/5   66.9° × 9/5 = 120.33°
            subtract 40° 120.33° − 40° = 80°F

      c.   25°C + 273.15° = 298K

The heat of fusion is usually expressed in units of kJ/mol or J/g which is an intensive property.
It does however take more heat to melt more material.

4.   None; all are intensive (see note at left).

5. a. One °B is a smaller interval than one °C (100°B = 75°C)

    b. It is useful to draw a diagram illustrating the relationship between the two different scales. A common error is to neglect the different zero points. Ammonia boils at –33°C, i.e. 38°C below 5°C. In °B, this corresponds to (38 × 100/75)°B = 51°B below 5°C. Note that 5°C is zero°B on the benzene scale; so the boiling point of ammonia on the benzene scale is –51°B.

    c. The melting point of sulfur (115°C) is 35°C above the boiling point of benzene; this corresponds to 47°B. So the melting point is 147°B.

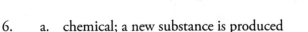

6. a. chemical; a new substance is produced
    b. chemical; iron combines with oxygen
    c. physical; no chemical change takes place
    d. physical
    e. chemical
    f. physical; the sugar is still sugar
    g. chemical

7. a. F   fluorine   d. B   boron   g. Cu copper
    b. K   potassium   e. S   sulfur   h. Ni nickel
    c. P   phosphorus   f. Ar argon   i. Sn tin

8. a. silicon   Si   e. carbon   C   i. chlorine Cl
    b. calcium   Ca   f. iron   Fe   j. gold   Au
    c. sodium   Na   g. tungsten W   k. silver   Ag
    d. zinc   Zn   h. nitrogen N   l. magnesium Mg

9. a. $1342 \text{ mL} \times (1L/1000\text{mL}) = 1.342 \text{ L}$
    b. $3.26 \text{ km} \times (10^6\text{mm}/1\text{km}) = 3.26 \times 10^6 \text{ mm}$
    c. $87.68 \text{ mg} \times (1g/10^3\text{mg}) = 8.768 \times 10^{-2} \text{ g}$
    d. $400 \text{ cm}^3 \times (1\text{m}/100\text{cm})^3 = 4 \times 10^{-4} \text{ m}^3$
    e. $3600 \text{ sq.in.} \times (1\text{ft}/12\text{in})^2 = 25 \text{ sq.ft.}$

Note that the 1 is exactly 1; it is an integer and has infinite precision (so has the 1000). There are 4 significant figures in the answer.

The number of significant figures in numbers like 400 and 3600 is often in doubt. They could be exactly 400 and 3600 or just approximately 400 or 3600—the context indicates which is correct.

10. a. 1,327 $= 1.327 \times 10^3$ d. 0.166 $= 1.66 \times 10^{-1}$
     b. 0.00562 $= 5.62 \times 10^{-3}$ e. 0.09911 $= 9.911 \times 10^{-2}$
     c. 2.76 $= 2.76$

The 8 written as a subscript is not significant. It is retained to maintain precision in subsequent calculations of deviation.

11. A: more precise   average $= 368.7/4 = 92.1_8°C$
         deviations are 0.18, 0.08, 0.22, 0.02°C; average deviation $= 0.1_3°C$

Note that all deviations are positive quantities.

     B: less precise   average $= 369.0/4 = 92.2_5°C$ slightly more accurate
         deviations are 0.35, 0.25, 0.35, 0.25°C; average deviation $= 0.3_0°C$

12. pico 10^{-12} micro 10^{-6} milli 10^{-3}
     centi 10^{-2} kilo 10^{3} mega 10^{6}

The first measurement (0.0045) is insignificant but must be included in the sum.

13. a. 0.0045 in + 1.0098 in + 0.987 in + 23.08 in $= 2.508 \times 10^1$ in

Note the answer has 4 sig. fig. even though some numbers have only 3 sig. fig.

     b. $(3.45 \text{ cm}^3 \times 2.70 \text{ g cm}^{-3}) + (7.433 \text{ cm}^3 \times 1.677 \text{ g cm}^{-3})$
         $= 9.32 \text{ g} + 12.47 \text{ g} = 2.178 \times 10^1 \text{ g}$

     c. 2.703 g/(1.376 cm × 2.45 cm × 3.78 cm) $= 2.12 \times 10^{-1}$ g cm^{-3}

14. The 17.4 grams of aluminum (density 2.70 g cm^{-3}) has a volume of 6.44 cm^3. The 12.3 g block of the unknown metal has the same volume, so its density must be 12.3 g/6.44 cm^3 = 1.91 g cm^{-3}.

Density = mass/volume.

15. *Define the problem:* Need to calculate the density of platinum.

     Develop a plan: Density is mass/volume; so determine the mass and the volume perhaps? But how can they be determined? When something floats on the surface of the water, it displaces a mass of water equal to its own mass. So the mass can be determined by the quantity of water displaced when the crucible floats. When an object is totally immersed, it displaces a volume of water equal to its own volume, so the volume can be determined by the change in the volume when the crucible is totally immersed.

     Execute the plan: The mass of the crucible equals the volume of water displaced × the density of water = 57.9mL × 0.997g/mL = 57.7 g. The volume of the crucible equals 2.70 cm^3. The density of the platinum metal is therefore 57.7g/2.70cm^3 = 21.4 g cm^{-3}.

     Check the answer: The magnitude of the density is about right and the units are correct. *Always check the units!*

16. One pound is equal to 16 ounces:
     (453.59 grams/1 lb) × (1 lb/16 oz) = 28.35 g/oz
     (16 oz/1 lb) × (1 lb/453.59 grams) × (1000 grams/1 kg) = 35.27 oz/kg

17. The 5.6% indicates that in every 100 grams of alloy, there are 5.6 grams of silver. The % is usually a mass/mass percent. In 1000 grams of alloy there are 56 grams of silver.

CHAPTER 2

Introduction

The history of the way in which our view of matter at the atomic level has developed is fascinating. In some cases simple experiments with rudimentary apparatus led to startling results and great steps forward in our understanding of things too small to see. This chapter describes the origins of atomic theory. The mole and Avogadro's number are introduced and the Periodic Table of the Elements is described.

Contents

Protons, Electrons, and Neutrons; Atomic Structure
Atomic Number and Atomic Mass
Isotopes
Atomic Weight
Atoms and the Mole
The Periodic Table
The Elements, Their Chemistry, and the Periodic Table
Essential Elements

Protons, Electrons, and Neutrons; Atomic Structure

In 1803, an English mathematics teacher called John Dalton (1766–1844) revived the idea that the fundamental particle of all matter is the atom—a particle he thought to be indivisible.

The existence of electric charge was one of the first indications that particles smaller than atoms existed. Benjamin Franklin (1706–1790) had already suggested the terms positive and negative for the two types of electric charge. In 1834, Michael Faraday (1791–1867) published accounts of his experiments in electrolysis that led to the idea of a fundamental particle of electricity associated with atoms. This fundamental particle was called an **electron** by Johnstone Stoney (1826–1911) in 1891. In 1897 Joseph J. Thomson (1856–1940) announced experiments using cathode ray tubes and the existence of charged particles considerably smaller than atoms.

Early experiments in **radioactivity** and the discovery of three types of radiation, α, ß, and γ, led Marie Curie (1867–1934) to suggest in 1899 that atoms could indeed disintegrate into smaller particles. The actual electrical charge on an electron, and its mass, were finally established by Robert Millikan (1868–1953) in his oil-drop experiment.

The **proton**, the fundamental positive particle, was observed in cathode ray tubes containing hydrogen gas. The **neutron**, the third subatomic particle, was discovered by James Chadwick (1891–1974) in 1932. This particle, as the name suggests, has no charge. It has a mass slightly greater than a proton. Because negative

Democritus (460-370 BC) and Leucippus (96-55 BC) proposed the idea of a fundamental indivisible particle. The word atom means indivisible.

The word electricity is derived from the Greek ηλεκτρον meaning amber. When amber is rubbed it gains a static electric charge.

See study question #5.

Some knowledge of the history of the development of atomic theory will help you understand it.

An α particle is a helium nucleus. A helium nucleus contains 2 protons and 2 neutrons.

Learn the characteristics (mass and charge) of the three primary subatomic particles.

proton:
mass 1.673×10^{-24} gram
charge $+1$

neutron:
mass 1.675×10^{-24} gram
no charge

electron:
mass 9.109×10^{-28} gram
charge -1

Originally, atomic masses were based upon a mass of exactly 1.000 for hydrogen. Then upon a mass of exactly 16.000 for oxygen. Unfortunately, this meant the mass of oxygen–16 for physicists, but the atomic mass of oxygen (weighted average of all isotopes) for chemists. To resolve the conflict, the new standard, carbon–12 was chosen in 1961.

One amu equals 1.6606×10^{-24}g.

The symbol for carbon–12 is $^{12}_{6}C$.

Strictly speaking, just as the fundametal particle of an element is called an atom, the fundamental particle of a particular isotope is called a nuclide.

Some isotope masses are:

^{12}C 12.000000 amu

^{58}Ni 57.935346 amu
^{60}Ni 59.930788 amu

^{238}U 238.050784 amu

and positive charges attract one another, and like charges repel each other, Thomson envisioned the atom as a homogeneous mix of positive and negative matter. Ernest Rutherford (1871–1937) tested this model by directing a beam of α particles at a thin sheet of gold. Some α particles bounced back—which could only mean that they had encountered something in the atom more massive than themselves. So he proposed a **nuclear model** for the atom: a very small positively charged nucleus at the center, containing protons and neutrons, responsible for virtually the entire mass of the atom surrounded by the negative electrons taking up almost the entire volume of the atom. These three primary particles, the proton, the neutron, and the electron, make up all atoms.

Atomic Number and Atomic Mass

All atoms of an element have the same number of protons in the nucleus. This number is called the **atomic number** (Z). It is the atomic number that identifies an element. For example, an atom that has 6 protons in its nucleus, and therefore an atomic number Z of 6, is always an atom of carbon.

Historically, the relative masses of the atoms of the elements were determined by careful experiments. For example, a nitrogen atom is fourteen times heavier than a hydrogen atom. To develop an absolute mass scale, an arbitrary standard is required. This standard has been chosen to be an atom of carbon with six protons, six neutrons, and six electrons—it is assigned a mass of exactly 12 units.

One **atomic mass unit** (one amu or one dalton) is therefore defined as $1/12^{th}$ the mass of a carbon atom with six protons, six neutrons, and six electrons.

The sum of the number of protons and the number of neutrons in the nucleus of an atom is called the **mass number** (A). For example the mass number of a carbon atom with six protons, six neutrons, and six electrons is 12. This atom of carbon is often referred to as carbon–12.

Isotopes

Although atoms of the same element must, by definition, have the same number of protons in the nucleus, they may have different numbers of neutrons. Therefore the atomic number for an element is always the same, but the mass number may vary. Atoms of the same element with differing numbers of neutrons are called **isotopes**.

Some elements have only one stable (nonradioactive) isotope, other elements have many isotopes. Hydrogen has two stable isotopes (protium and deuterium) and one radioactive isotope (tritium). These three isotopes have mass numbers 1, 2, and 3 respectively. When deuterium is substituted for hydrogen in water, the result is "heavy water", a molecule with a mass of 20 amu instead of 18 amu.

The masses and the relative abundances of the various isotopes of an element can be obtained from a mass spectrometer. For example, boron has two isotopes: boron-10 with a mass of 10.0129 amu and an abundance of 19.91% and boron-11 with a mass of 11.0093 amu and an abundance of 80.09%.

Note that the masses of isotopes are not integers (except for carbon–12), they are numbers close to, but not equal to, the mass numbers. Nor do the mass numbers equal the sum of the masses of all the protons, neutrons, and electrons present. The mass is always less than this sum; the difference is called the **mass defect**.

Atomic Weight

The **atomic mass** (or more commonly **atomic weight**) of an element is a weighted average of all naturally occurring isotopes of that element. For example, boron has an atomic mass of 10.81 amu. This is between 10.0129 and 11.0093 amu, but nearer to 11.0093 because the boron-11 isotope is the more abundant.

Know how to calculate the atomic mass from the masses of the isotopes and their abundances, and vice versa. E.g., for boron:

$(19.91/100) \times 10.0129 +$
$(80.09/100) \times 11.0093 = 10.81$

See study questions #3 & 4.

Atoms and the Mole

Atoms are extremely small—far too small to be seen. The number of atoms or molecules within a relatively small amount of matter, a few grams, is unimaginably large. So, although chemists often think in terms of individual atoms and molecules, their experiments usually involve vastly larger numbers. The particulate world of individual atoms is related to the world we see through the **mole**.

The mole is the SI unit for an **amount of substance**. It is defined as the amount of substance that contains as many elementary entities (atoms or molecules, for example) as there are atoms in exactly 12 grams of carbon–12.

Eggs are counted by the dozen, pencils by the gross, shoes by the pair, sheets of paper by the ream, and substances by the mole. What do these terms represent? One dozen eggs means 12 eggs; one gross of pencils means 144 pencils; one pair of shoes means 2 shoes; one ream of paper means 500 sheets; one mole of a substance means 6.022×10^{23} particles of that substance—they are counting units.

There are two differences between terms such as dozen or score and the mole. The mole is a far larger number and it is not an integer. The number of particles in a mole is determined experimentally, not by counting! The actual number is given a name; it is called **Avogadro's Number**. The reason it has a name is that it's not so easy to say "six point zero two two one four one....times ten to the twenty third" as it is to say "twelve". However, the relationship between one dozen and twelve is exactly the same as the relationship between one mole and Avogadro's Number.

The actual value of Avogadro's Number depends upon the definition chosen for one mole. If a standard other than carbon–12 had been chosen, the value would be different.

The convenience of the mole as a unit results from the fact that the number of entities in one mole of anything is always the same—Avogadro's Number. Similarly, the number of entities—eggs, donuts, cans of Guinness®, etc.—in one dozen is always 12. Thus, a pile of 23 grams of sodium contains just as many atoms as a pile of 207 grams of lead.

The mass in grams of one mole (1 mol) of atoms of any element is called the **molar mass** of that element. It is numerically equal to the atomic mass in amu. For example, the atomic mass of sulfur is 32.07 amu. This is the average mass of one atom. The molar mass of sulfur atoms is 32.07 grams. This is the mass of one mole of sulfur atoms.

The mole is the cornerstone of quantitative chemistry. The number of moles of a substance within a sample is the mass of the sample divided by the molar mass of

Chemistry has three components:

— the particulate (individual atoms, molecules and ions,
— the macroscopic (the real world that can be touched and seen)
— the symbolic (the symbols, formulas, and equations used to represent substances and their reactions).

More precisely, the number is $6.02214199 \times 10^{23}$.

Although it's simple enough to determine the value of a dozen by counting, it is impossible to use a counting method for a mole—it would take too long. A reliable method for establishing the value of Avogadro's number involves determining the density of a crystal, its molar mass, and the interatomic spacing by X-ray crystallography.

See study question #7.

The atomic mass of an element can therefore be expressed in amu or in g mol^{-1}.

You must be able to convert between mass and moles with ease; practice!

mass/molar mass = #moles

9.0 g/26.98 g mol^{-1} = 0.33 mol

See study questions #8 & 9.

the substance. For example, an aluminum can weighs 9.0 grams. How many moles of aluminum are there in the can? The molar mass of aluminum is 26.98 g/mol. Dividing the mass (9.0 grams) by the molar mass (26.98 g/mol) yields 0.33 mol. Notice how the units cancel to produce the correct answer.

The Periodic Table

The **Periodic Table of Elements** is an arrangement of the elements so that those with similar properties lie in vertical columns called groups. The **groups** are numbered 1 through 8, with a letter A or B. The A groups are called the main groups and the B groups contain the transition elements. The horizontal rows are called **periods**.

A proposed scheme for renumbering the groups in the Periodic Table starts with 1 at the left and then numbers each group (including the transition elements) sequentially through to 18 for the noble gases.

See study question #11.

The Periodic Table is divided into two main regions: the **metals** (to the left) and the **nonmetals** (to the upper right). On the boundary between these two regions lie the **metalloids**. Most of the elements are metals. All metals except mercury are solid at room temperature. Some nonmetals (e.g. carbon, phosphorus, sulfur, iodine) are solids; one (bromine) is a liquid; and several (e.g. hydrogen, helium, oxygen, nitrogen, chlorine, xenon) are gases. The metalloids are the elements silicon, germanium, arsenic, antimony, and tellurium that lie on the diagonal line separating the metals and nonmetals.

Note that the elements in the Periodic Table are not always in order of increasing mass. For example:

Argon and potassium

Cobalt and nickel

Tellurium and iodine

Dmitri Mendeleev (1834–1907) was the first to develop the Periodic Table (1869) as it is known today. He noticed a **periodicity** in the chemical and physical properties of the elements as their atomic weights increased and arranged the elements so that those elements with similar properties lay in the same group. He left spaces for unknown elements and predicted their existence. Many (e.g. gallium, germanium, scandium) were soon discovered.

Henry G. J. Moseley (1888–1915) determined that it is not the atomic mass that governs periodicity in properties but in fact the atomic number. The atomic number of an element was unknown to Mendeleev.

The Elements, Their Chemistry, and the Periodic Table.

The Periodic Table is the chemist's most valuable reference. Become familiar with the arrangement of the elements in the Periodic Table. You will quickly associate a different chemical behavior of an element with its position in the table.

See study question #12.

Group 1A elements are called the **alkali metals**. Below hydrogen, all these elements are very reactive and are found in nature only in compounds. They react with water to produce alkaline solutions and they form compounds A_2O with oxygen (where A is the alkali metal). Hydrogen is often placed in Group 1A although in most of its properties it is quite unlike the alkali metals.

Group 2A elements are called the **alkaline earth metals**. Not quite as reactive as the alkali metals, they still are found in nature only in compounds. They too form alkaline solutions. The general formula of their oxides (compounds with oxygen) is EO, where E is the alkaline earth metal.

Group 3A contains one nonmetal at the top (boron). The next element (aluminum) is the third most abundant element in the earth's crust.

Group 4A contains one nonmetal at the top (carbon), two metalloids (silicon and germanium), and two metals (tin and lead). Carbon is the basis for the great variety of compounds (called organic compounds) that make up living things. The element exists in three forms (called **allotropes**): graphite, diamond, and the

Allotropes are different forms of the same element that exist in the same physical state.

fullerenes. Silicon is the second most abundant element on earth and occurs with aluminum and oxygen in many minerals (aluminosilicates). An alloy of tin and copper is called bronze—after which an entire age was named. Lead, at the bottom, is a toxic metal.

Group 5A contains a gas (nitrogen N_2) at the top, followed by phosphorus, (another nonmetal), arsenic and antimony (two metalloids), and finally bismuth (a metal). Nitrogen gas consists of diatomic molecules and is essential to life. Fixing nitrogen (forming compounds of the element) is difficult. Phosphorus is also essential to life. It exists as several allotropes, two principal forms being red and white. The white form consists of P_4 molecules. In the red form these P_4 tetrahedra are joined together. Bismuth is the last element in the Periodic Table that is not radioactive.

Group 6A begins with oxygen, a diatomic gas like nitrogen. Unlike nitrogen, oxygen readily combines with most other elements. Ozone O_3 is an allotrope of oxygen. Sulfur exists commonly as S_8 molecules and can be found in its elemental form. It is used primarily in the manufacture of sulfuric acid—a chemical manufactured in greater quantity than any other (largely for use in the agricultural fertilizer industry). Polonium at the bottom of the group is radioactive. It was isolated by Marie Curie in 1898.

Group 7A are the **halogens**; they are all nonmetals and are all diatomic molecules. They are all reactive; they form salts with metals and they form molecular compounds with most nonmetals including themselves. The reactivity decreases down the group. Fluorine and chlorine are gases, bromine is a liquid, and iodine is a solid.

Group 8A consists of the monatomic **noble gases**; these are the least reactive of all the elements. It is, however, possible to make compounds of xenon and fluorine relatively easily. Compounds of krypton and argon are known. Radon is radioactive.

The **transition elements** lie between groups 2A and 3A. This block of elements is ten columns wide and contains many common elements (e.g. iron, titanium, and manganese). Some transition metals that are less reactive occur in nature as the element (e.g. silver, copper, gold, platinum). Many of the transition metals have commercial uses.

The **lanthanides** and **actinides** are usually drawn at the bottom of the table to save space. These two rows are fourteen elements wide.

Essential Elements

99% of all atoms present in humans are either oxygen, carbon, hydrogen, or nitrogen—these are the most essential elements. Another seven elements contribute the next 0.9% of the total: calcium, phosphorus, potassium, sulfur, chlorine, sodium, and magnesium. These are also essential to life. Note that all eleven elements have atomic numbers 17 or less. Several biologically important elements are also required; deficiencies can cause serious defects. Examples are iron, cobalt, zinc, copper, and selenium. These elements however are present in minute amounts.

Key terms:

subatomic particle
nucleus
proton
neutron
electron
atomic number
mass number
isotope
nuclide
abundance
atomic mass
mole
Avogadro's number
molar mass
Periodic Table
periodicity
group
period
allotrope

Review Questions

1.   List the three primary subatomic particles, their masses, and their charges.

2.   What is the atomic number of an element? What is the mass number?

3.   What is an isotope? What is a nuclide?

4.   List the three isotopes of hydrogen and describe how they differ.

5.   Define the atomic mass unit.

6.   Identify the isotope with twenty protons, twenty neutrons, and twenty electrons. Write its symbol.

7.   What is SI unit for the amount of substance?

8.   What is the difference between "one mole" and "Avogadro's Number"?

9.   Do one dozen donuts have the same mass as one dozen eggs? Do one mole of sodium atoms have the same mass as one mole of oxygen atoms? What then is the same in these two pairs of samples?

10.   Why isn't Avogadro's number an integer, like 12 (dozen) or 20 (score)?

11.   What is the molar mass of a substance?

12.   Compare the definition of an atomic mass unit and the definition of one mole. What is the relationship between them?

13.   In what ways, and why, was Mendeleev's Periodic Table different from the present-day table?

14.   What is a group in the Periodic Table? What is a period?

15.   What is periodicity? What is the law of chemical periodicity?

16.   Sketch the Periodic Table without looking at a printed copy. Fill in the table with as much detail as you can remember or deduce. Concentrate on elements at the top of the table.

17.   What are allotropes? Describe the three allotropes of carbon.

18.   List the nonmetals; state whether each is a solid, liquid, or gas.

19.   List the elements essential to life. Which four are required in abundance? Which seven are next in importance?

Answers to Review Questions

1. The three primary subatomic particles are:

proton	mass 1.672622×10^{-24} gram	charge +1
neutron	mass 1.674927×10^{-24} gram	no charge
electron	mass 9.109382×10^{-28} gram	charge −1

2. The atomic number of an element is the number of protons in the nucleus of an atom of the element. It also equals the number of electrons in a neutral atom.

    The mass number of an element is the total number of nucleons (protons and neutrons) in the nucleus of an atom of a particular isotope of the element.

3. An isotope of an element consists of atoms with a specific number of neutrons (a specific mass number). For example, three isotopes of carbon are:

    carbon-12 with 6 protons and 6 neutrons,
    carbon-13 with 6 protons and 7 neutrons,
    carbon-14 with 6 protons and 8 neutrons.

    A nuclide is an atom of a particular isotope.

4. The three isotopes of hydrogen (all have an atomic number = 1) are:

hydrogen (protium):	$^{1}_{1}\text{H}$	1 proton	0 neutrons	mass number 1
deuterium:	$^{2}_{1}\text{H}$	1 proton	1 neutron	mass number 2
tritium:	$^{3}_{1}\text{H}$	1 proton	2 neutrons	mass number 3

    Tritium is radioactive.

5. The atomic mass unit (amu) is the mass unit of a scale in which one amu is equal to $1/12^{\text{th}}$ of the mass of a carbon-12 atom.

6. There are 20 protons—the atomic number Z is equal to 20. There are 20 neutrons—the mass number must be 40. The atomic number identifies the element as calcium. The mass number identifies the isotope. The symbol is $^{40}_{20}\text{Ca}$. The number of electrons equals the number of protons, so the atom has no charge.

    Note that the subscript $_{20}$ can be omitted from the symbol ^{40}Ca. The element is calcium (symbol Ca) so the subscript $_{20}$ is in fact redundant.

    The subscript is included in nuclear reactions to make balancing the equations easier.

7. The SI unit for the amount of substance is the mole.

8. One mole is an amount of substance, and Avogadro's number is the number of entities (6.022×10^{23}) within that amount. By analogy, one dozen is an amount of donuts, eggs, or cans of Coca Cola® and twelve is the number of entities (12) within that amount.

9. No, one dozen donuts do not have the same mass as one dozen eggs, nor does one mole of sodium atoms have the same mass as one mole of oxygen atoms. What is the same is the number of eggs or donuts, or the number of sodium atoms or oxygen atoms.

10.   Avogadro's number is so large that it cannot be determined by counting. It would take far too long. If it could be determined by counting then it would indeed be useful to set it equal to a simple integer (for example 1×10^{23}). The basis for Avogadro's number is arbitrary. It is currently equal to the number of atoms of carbon in exactly 12 grams of carbon–12.

11.   The molar mass of a substance is the mass that contains one mole of that substance, that is, Avogadro's number of items of that substance.

12.   The atomic mass unit is defined as 1/12th the mass of a single atom of carbon–12. The mole is defined as the amount of substance that contains the same number of particles as there are atoms in exactly 12 grams of carbon–12. The amu is the mass unit used at the particulate level; the gram is the mass unit used at the macroscopic (real world) level. The relationship between them is Avogadro's number. For example:

> One carbon–12 atom has a mass of 12 amu (exactly).
> One mole of carbon–12 atoms has a mass of 12 grams (exactly).
> One gram = 6.022×10^{23} amu
> One amu = 1.6606×10^{-24} gram.

13.   Mendeleev arranged the elements in order of increasing atomic mass and sorted them into groups by comparing their chemical properties. Mendeleev left gaps for missing elements and predicted their properties. Elements in the current table are arranged in order of increasing atomic number and are sorted into groups having the same valence shell electron configurations.

Valence shell electron configurations are described in Chapter 8.

14.   A group in the Periodic Table is a column of elements having similar chemical properties. A period is a horizontal row in the table.

15.   Periodicity is a regular and repetitive cycling of similar chemical and physical properties as the atomic number of the elements increase. The law of chemical periodicity states that the properties of the elements are periodic functions of their atomic numbers. Note that Mendeleev originally stated the law as a function of atomic mass.

16.   As your course in chemistry progresses, you will learn more and more about the Periodic Table. Some features of the table may already be familiar. For example,

There is no need to memorize atomic numbers or atomic masses; a Periodic Table will almost always be provided for you.

   • the two groups on the left containing the alkali and alkaline earth metals,
   • the six-column block on the right with the diagonal line running through it that separates the metals and nonmetals,
   • the 4 × 10 block of transition elements with the last row occupied by elements only recently formed in nuclear reactions,
   • and the two rows at the bottom of the table.

You should perhaps, at this stage, be able to place 20 or 30 elements at the top of the table.

17. Allotropes are different forms of the same element that exist in the same physical state. There are three allotropes of carbon: diamond with a three-dimensional structure, graphite consisting of two-dimensional sheets of carbon atoms, and the fullerenes of which the most common is the C_{60} molecule shaped like a soccer ball.

18. There are 19 nonmetals, including two that are *radioactive*:

    Group 3A: boron*(s)*
    Group 4A: carbon*(s)*, silicon*(s)*
    Group 5A: nitrogen*(g)*, phosphorus*(s)*
    Group 6A: oxygen*(g)*, sulfur*(s)*, selenium*(s)*
    Group 7A: fluorine*(g)*, chlorine*(g)*, bromine*(l)*, iodine*(s)*, *astatine(s)*
    Group 8A: helium*(g)*, neon*(g)*, argon*(g)*, krypton*(g)*, xenon*(g)*, *radon(g)*

    Abbreviations are:
    (s) solid
    (l) liquid
    (g) gas

19. Of the 113 elements, only about 20 are essential to life. The four most essential (99%) are oxygen, carbon, hydrogen, and nitrogen. The next seven in importance (0.9%) are calcium, phosphorus, potassium, sulfur, chlorine, sodium, and magnesium.

Study Questions and Problems

1. Explain, at an atomic or molecular level, what happens when

    a. water freezes to form ice
    b. copper and tin combine to form bronze
    c. rainwater evaporates from the pavement

The one quality which sets one man apart from another—the key which lifts one to every aspiration while others are caught up in the mire of mediocrity—is not talent, formal education, nor brightness —it is self-discipline. With self-discipline, all things are possible. Without it, even the simplest goal can seem like the impossible dream.

Theodore Roosevelt
(1858-1919)

2. Which of the following atoms are isotopes of the same element? Identify the elements of these isotopes and describe the number of protons and neutrons in the nucleus of them all.

    $^{15}_{7}X$ $^{12}_{6}X$ $^{13}_{7}X$ $^{18}_{8}X$ $^{14}_{7}X$ $^{14}_{6}X$ $^{16}_{8}X$ $^{13}_{6}X$ $^{17}_{8}X$

3. There are three naturally occurring isotopes of neon:

    neon–20   mass 19.9924 amu   abundance 90.48%
    neon–21   mass 20.9938 amu   abundance 0.27%
    neon–22   mass 21.9914 amu   abundance 9.25%

    a. Without calculation, what is the approximate atomic mass of neon?
    b. Calculate the actual atomic mass.

4. Uranium has an atomic mass of 238.0289. It consists of two isotopes: uranium–235 with an isotopic mass of 235.044 amu and uranium–238 with an isotopic mass of 238.051. Calculate the % abundance of the uranium–235 isotope.

A small quantity (0.005%) of uranium–234 also occurs in nature.

5.   To illustrate Robert Millikan's determination of the charge on an electron, suppose that you were given the task of determining the mass of a single jelly bean given the following experimental data:

Various scoops of jelly beans were weighed and the following masses determined. The number of jelly beans in each scoop was not known.

Masses (in grams) of ten different scoops:
4.96, 8.68, 13.64, 7.44, 21.08, 16.12, 9.92, 19.84, 6.20, 12.40.

6.   Reorder this list to match the name of the scientist with his or her contribution to our understanding of the nature of matter:

Joseph Thompson   developed the idea of the atomic nature of matter
James Chadwick   established the law of conservation of matter
Robert Millikan   characterized positive and negative electrical charges
Henry Moseley   suggested that atoms could disintegrate
Michael Faraday   experimented with electrolysis
Dmitri Mendeleev   proved the existence of the electron
John Dalton   developed the idea of a nuclear atom
Henri Becquerel   discovered the neutron
Democritus   developed the first periodic table of elements
Joseph Proust   showed that periodicity depends upon atomic number
Antoine Lavoisier   formulated the law of constant composition
Ernest Rutherford   determined the charge on a single electron
Marie Curie   revived the atomic theory in the early 1800s
Benjamin Franklin   discovered radioactivity

Instead of 1/12th the mass of a carbon–12 atom.

7.   Suppose the atomic mass unit had been defined as 1/10th of the average mass of an atom of phosphorus. What would the atomic mass of carbon be on this scale? What would Avogadro's number be?

8.   A sample of copper metal wire has a mass of 21.18 grams. How many moles of copper atoms are present in the sample? How many atoms of copper are present?

9.   Which has the greater mass, four moles of helium atoms or one mole of fluorine atoms. What are the masses of these samples?

10.   What mass of lead has the same number of atoms as 50 grams of oxygen?

11.   From amongst the elements sodium, chlorine, nickel, argon, calcium, uranium, and oxygen, select the alkali metal, the alkaline earth metal, the transition metal, the actinide, the halogen, the noble gas, and the chalcogen (Group 6A).

12. If the formulas of magnesium chloride, sodium oxide, and lithium nitride are $MgCl_2$, Na_2O, and Li_3N respectively, predict the formulas of calcium bromide, potassium sulfide, and sodium phosphide.

13. Identify the following elements:
     a. The most abundant metal in the earth's crust.
     b. Combined with chlorine, it produces a compound essential to life.
     c. A metal that occurs in vast limestone deposits and combines with oxygen to form an oxide with a formula MO.
     d. The transition element at the center of hemoglobin.
     e. Used in smoke detectors and named for the United States.
     f. A component of washing powder mined in Death Valley.
     g. The basis for the compounds that make up all living things.
     h. Primary constituent of pencil lead.
     i. The last element in the Periodic Table that is not radioactive.
     j. Exists as X_4 molecules.
     k. The element named after the sun, where it was first detected.

Answers to Study Questions and Problems

1. a. In the liquid state the water molecules are in constant motion and are not restricted to specific locations. The molecules collide and interact with each other constantly. When the water freezes to form ice, the water molecules become locked in place in a regular crystalline lattice. Their translational motion ceases. The water molecules are held together by a relatively strong intermolecular attraction.

    b. A solution (alloy) of copper and tin is a mixture at the atomic level. No amount of optical magnification can reveal the different metals in the alloy. The mixture is a random arrangement of copper and tin atoms.

    c. In a liquid there is a distribution of molecular energies—some molecules moving quite fast with high kinetic energies and others moving slowly with low kinetic energies. Those molecules with high energies may have enough energy to overcome the intermolecular attraction and escape into the vapor state. They evaporate. As the rainwater absorbs more energy, so more molecules are able to escape. Eventually all the rainwater evaporates.

2. $^{12}_{6}X$ $^{13}_{6}X$ $^{14}_{6}X$ — all have an atomic number = 6
        carbon, with 6, 7, and 8 neutrons respectively.

    $^{13}_{7}X$ $^{14}_{7}X$ $^{15}_{7}X$ — all have an atomic number = 7
        nitrogen, with 6, 7, and 8 neutrons respectively.

    $^{16}_{8}X$ $^{17}_{8}X$ $^{18}_{8}X$ — all have an atomic number = 8
        oxygen, with 8, 9, and 10 neutrons respectively.

Nothing exists except atoms and empty space; everything else is opinion.

Democritus of Abdera (460–370BC)

Energy is removed to cause the water to freeze.

These intermolecular forces of attraction are called hydrogen bonds—see page 172 in this study guide.

3.   neon–20   mass 19.9924 amu   abundance 90.48%
      neon–21   mass 20.9938 amu   abundance 0.27%
      neon–22   mass 21.9914 amu   abundance 9.25%

a.   The most abundant isotope is neon–20 (90.84%) so the atomic mass
     will be near to the mass of this isotope, i.e. about 20 amu.

b.   The actual atomic mass is a weighted average:
     [90.48 (19.9924) + 0.27 (20.9938) + 9.25 (21.9914)]/100
     = 20.18 amu.

Divide by 100 because the abundances are expressed as percentages not fractions.

4.   The atomic mass (238.0289) is a weighted average of the two isotopes:
      uranium–235 with an isotopic mass of 235.044 amu and uranium–238
      with an isotopic mass of 238.051. Let x = the fractional abundance of the
      uranium–235 isotope.

Uranium–235 is the isotope used in nuclear fission reactors. It must be separated from the uranium–238.

      [235.044x + 238.051(1–x)] = 238.0289
      235.044x + 238.051 – 238.051x = 238.0289   therefore x = 0.0073
      % abundance of uranium–235 = 0.73%

5.   The difference in mass between two scoops, and the masses of the scoops
      themselves, must be a whole number multiple of the mass of one bean.
      In the data provided, the smallest difference is 1.24g (e.g. 8.68–7.44 or
      21.08–19.84). If this was indeed the mass of one bean, the numbers of beans
      in each scoop would be: 4, 7, 11, 6, 17, 13, 8, 16, 5, and 10.

      But perhaps 1.24g could be the mass of 2 beans, or 3 beans? Unlikely—the
      chances of random scoops all being a multiple of 2 (or 3) beans is remote.

6.   John Dalton   revived the atomic theory
      Democritus   developed the idea of the atomic nature of matter
      Antoine Lavoisier   established the law of conservation of matter
      Joseph Proust   formulated the law of constant composition
      Benjamin Franklin   characterized positive and negative electrical charges
      Henri Becquerel   discovered radioactivity
      Marie Curie   suggested that atoms could disintegrate
      Michael Faraday   experimented with electrolysis
      Joseph Thompson   proved the existence of the electron
      Robert Millikan   determined the charge on a single electron
      Ernest Rutherford   developed the idea of a nuclear atom
      James Chadwick   discovered the neutron
      Dmitri Mendeleev   developed the first periodic table of elements
      Henry Moseley   showed that periodicity depends upon atomic
                           number

7.   If the new mass unit is the nmu, then the atomic mass of phosphorus would
      be, by definition, 10 nmu. The nmu is defined as 1/10th the mass of phos-
      phorus.

The relationship between the mass of carbon–12 and the mass of phosphorus is 12.00 to 30.97 (on the old amu scale). It must be the same on the new nmu scale.

Therefore the mass of carbon on the new scale equals 10 nmu × (12.00/30.97) = 3.87 nmu.

Avogadro's number would become the number of phosphorus atoms in 10 grams of phosphorus (or 3.87 grams of carbon–12). It would therefore be $6.022 \times 10^{23} \times (10/30.97) = 1.945 \times 10^{23}$.

8.   If the sample of copper metal wire has a mass of 21.18 grams, divide by the molar mass to obtain the number of moles.

Number of moles of copper = 21.18 g/63.55 g mol^{-1} = 0.333 mol

Number of atoms of copper = 0.333 mol × 6.022×10^{23} atoms mol^{-1} = 2.00×10^{23} atoms

9.   Four moles of helium atoms = 4 mol × 4.003 g mol^{-1} = 16.01 grams

One mole of fluorine atoms = 1 mol × 19.00 g mol^{-1} = 19.00 grams

The one mole of fluorine atoms has the greater mass.

10.   50 grams of oxygen contains 50/16.00 moles of oxygen atoms = 3.125 mol

3.125 moles of lead has a mass of 3.125 mol × 207.19 g mol^{-1} = 647 grams.

11.   sodium   alkali metal
       chlorine   halogen
       nickel   transition element
       argon   noble gas
       calcium   alkaline earth metal
       uranium   actinide
       oxygen   chalcogen

12.   Note that the elements are in the same groups

Calcium bromide is $CaBr_2$ analogous to   magnesium chloride $MgCl_2$
Potassium sulfide K_2S analogous to   sodium oxide Na_2O
Sodium phosphide Na_3P analogous to   lithium nitride Li_3N

13.   a.   aluminum Al
       b.   sodium Na
       c.   calcium Ca
       d.   iron Fe
       e.   americium Am
       f.   boron B
       g.   carbon C
       h.   carbon (graphite) C
       i.   bismuth Bi
       j.   phosphorus (white) P
       k.   helium He

80 Elements

—a crossword puzzle

Across:

3. Its oxide is pitchblende, and radioactive.
6. A penny from Cyprus.
7. Named for Vanadis, the Norse goddess of beauty.
8. It plumbs the depths, this heavy metal.
10. Its oxide emits brilliant white light when heated.
13. Named for Greek stone.
14. Make a meal of it to see inside.
16. Brimstone...
19. ...and the element below.
20. ...and old lace, Capra's macabre farce.
24. Discovered by Priestley, but named by Lavoisier.
26. Its plate is shiny.
28. Discovered in 1839 in Sweden by Mosander.
29. Filled the first vacant space in Mendeleev's Table.
30. From a mineral hauled by 20 mules.
33. Dark red emission led to its discovery.
36. This one melts in your hand.
37. Beneath *13 across*, its lamps are yellow.
38. Argentum.
41. Noble origin of the man of steel?
43. A rose by this name would be as red.
44. The metal on galvanized iron.
45. The liquid halogen.
46. Produces iridescent colors.
49. But there's no W anywhere in the name!
50. Albert's in his element.
52. The most abundant metal in the earth's crust.
53. For the originator of the table.
55. For the German goblin.
57. America's element for smoke detectors.
59. With *6 across* it's bronze.
63. The most abundant gas in the atmosphere.
64. For the thief of fire.
65. Symbol from latin kalium, arabic al-kali.
67. Moisson received the Nobel Prize for isolating this.
68. A colored sign.
70. Halfway across the Lanthanides.
71. For the daughter of *23 down*.
72. For the Latin name for Copenhagen.
73. Its disulfide is slippery.

Down:

1. Its allotropes are white, red, and black.
2. For Madame Marie, two Nobel Prizes...
4. ...one for the discovery of this element.
5. Not alone, according to its name in Greek.
9. Is it the first of the actinides?
10. With or without the T, it's found where *42 down* is.
11. Its silicate is diamond–like.
12. Discovered with *46 across* and named for its smell.
15. Quicksilver, winged messenger.
17. Radioactive alkali metal.
18. A silent basement killer.
21. A semiconductor from the valley in California.
22. Between *59 across* and *66 down*.
23. Tantalizing element.
25. The goal of the alchemists.
27. A transition metal sometimes mistaken for *56 down*.
30. For the site of Seaborg's laboratory.
31. Named for the 8th planet from the sun.
32. The metal in cisplatin, the antitumor drug.
33. So many R's: Ra, Rb, Re, Rf, Rh, Rn, this one's Ru.
34. Its tincture is antiseptic.
35. Essential for bones...
38. ...and below, Dalton's symbol for it was ⊙.
39. For Lise, who explained nuclear fission in 1939.
40. The last of the nonradioactive elements.
42. Source and symbol initially Ytterby in Sweden.
47. A ferrous metal first cast as pigs.
48. Named for the Titans, symbolic of strength.
51. An essential element of living things.
54. Isolated from *58 down* and named for Europe.
55. Halogen used in water purification.
56. The milk of its hydroxide settles the stomach.
58. Isolated from a mineral named for Col. Samarskite.
60. Idle gas...
61. ...and the stranger below.
62. The largest Group 3 metal.
65. Named for the native land of *2 down*.
66. Its sulfide is an artist's yellow pigment.
69. Named for the old devil himself.
72. Its isotopes are protium, deuterium, or tritium.

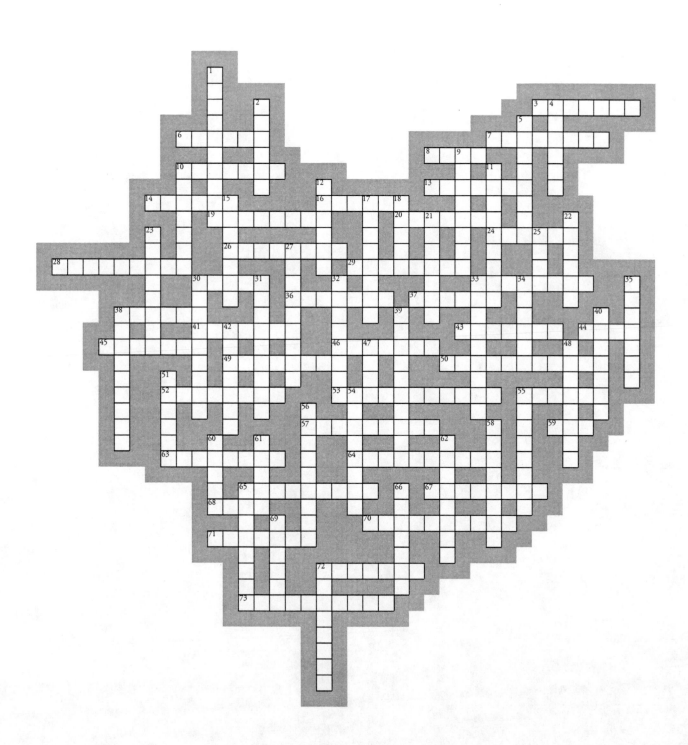

CHAPTER 3

Introduction

In this chapter chemical compounds and their properties are examined. There are two major classes of compounds: molecular and ionic—you will learn how to distinguish them, write formulas for them, and name them. The concept of the mole will be applied to molecules and ionic compounds. Finally, calculations to determine the formula of a compound will be described.

Contents

Molecules, Compounds, and Formulas
Molecular Models
Ionic Compounds: Formulas, Names, and Properties
Molecular Compounds: Formulas, Names, and Properties
Formulas, Compounds, and the Mole
Determining Compound Formulas
Hydrated Compounds

Molecules, Compounds, and Formulas

A **molecule** is the smallest identifiable unit of a substance that still retains the composition and properties of the substance. Molecules are discrete combinations of atoms bonded together so that the unit behaves as a whole and usually has properties quite unlike those of the individual atoms. For example, aluminum, a silver colored metal, reacts with bromine, a red-orange liquid, to produce the compound aluminum bromide, a white powder.

> Equations for chemical reactions will be examined in Chapter 4.

The **chemical formula** for a compound expresses the number, or relative number, of atoms of each element present in the compound. For example, the formula for aluminum bromide is Al_2Br_6. A molecule of sucrose has the formula $C_{12}H_{22}O_{11}$ indicating that one molecule of sucrose contains 12 carbon atoms, 22 hydrogen atoms, and 11 oxygen atoms.

> Be able to write the molecular formula for a compound.

There are different ways to write a chemical formula. An **empirical formula** indicates the simplest possible integer ratio of elements in a compound. For example, the empirical formula for aluminum bromide is $AlBr_3$—indicating that there are three bromine atoms for each aluminum atom. A **molecular formula** simply expresses the composition of the molecule—how many, and what, elements are present. A **condensed structural formula** (or, more simply, a **condensed formula**) provides additional information about the way in which the atoms of the molecule are grouped together. For example, ethanol has the molecular formula C_2H_6O and a condensed formula CH_3CH_2OH. The **structural formula** can be drawn in even greater detail showing how the atoms are connected together.

> Empirical formulas will be discussed later in this chapter.

> Two different substances may have the same molecular formula but will have different structural formulas.

> The structural formula of ethanol is
>
> $$\begin{array}{ccc} H & H & \\ | & | & \\ H-C-C-O-H \\ | & | & \\ H & H & \end{array}$$

Molecular Models

The purchase of a molecular model set and/or the use of modelling software is highly recommended. Computer resources for molecular modelling are now readily available.

Knowledge of the molecular structure of a substance is often essential in explaining its physical and chemical properties. It is, however, difficult to draw three-dimensional structures on paper even though certain conventions have been developed to help. Molecular models are able to give a better sense of three-dimensional structure. Molecular vizualization software permits the easy construction and manipulation of three-dimensional images of molecules on a computer.

Ionic Compounds: Formulas, Names, and Properties

There is no such thing as an ionic molecule. Ions do, under certain circumstances pair up—to form ion pairs.

See study question #2.

There are two major classes of compounds: **molecular compounds** and **ionic compounds**. They are quite different. Molecular compounds, like ethanol (CH_3CH_2OH) mentioned earlier, consist of discrete groups of atoms bonded together at the particulate level. These groups of atoms act together as a unit. Ionic compounds, as the name suggests, consist of ions. These ions may be single atoms (monatomic) or groups of atoms (polyatomic) with negative or positive charges.

Metal atoms generally lose electrons and form positive ions (**cations**). The positive charge on the ion depends upon the number of electrons lost. Nonmetals generally gain electrons and form negative ions (**anions**). The negative charge on the ion depends upon the number of electrons gained.

Group 1A metals form +1 ions. Group 2A metals form +2 ions. Group 3A metals form +3 ions.

Group 5A elements from −3 ions. Group 6A elements form −2 ions. Group 7A elements form −1 ions.

For example, a sodium atom, in virtually all its reactions, loses one electron. This loss results in an imbalance in the number of protons and electrons in the ion (11 protons but now only 10 electrons). The sodium ion therefore has a charge of +1. Magnesium, in Group 2A, loses two electrons and forms the Mg^{2+} ion.

Transition metals characteristically lose a variable number of electrons to form different ions. For example, iron commonly forms Fe^{2+} or Fe^{3+} by the loss of 2 electrons or 3 electrons respectively.

Nonmetals often form ions with a negative charge equal to 8 minus the group number. For example, the halogens form −1 anions, oxygen and sulfur form −2 anions, nitrogen and phosphorus form −3 anions. In the formation of ionic compounds, hydrogen either loses its electron to form the H^+ ion with nonmetals, or gains an additional electron to form the H^- ion with metals.

The outermost shell of electrons in an atom is called the valence shell. The electrons in the valence shell are called the valence electrons. It is these electrons that determine the chemical properties of the element.

The loss or gain of electrons by the main group elements results in the number of electrons remaining on the ions being equal to the number of electrons on the nearest noble gas. For example, by gaining two electrons, oxygen attains the same number of electrons as neon. By losing two electrons, calcium is left with the same number of electrons as argon. Noble gas electron configurations are particularly stable.

Do not confuse the ammonium ion NH_4^+ with the ammonia molecule NH_3.

A **polyatomic ion** is a group of atoms bonded together, just as in a molecule, with the entire unit bearing a charge. A common positive polyatomic ion is the ammonium ion NH_4^+. A common negative polyatomic ion is the carbonate ion CO_3^{2-}.

Commit to memory the 21 poly-atomic ions listed in the margin opposite. See study questions #3 & 4.

Ionic compounds are compounds in which the component particles are ions (monatomic or polyatomic). The net charge of the compound is neutral; the positive and negative charges must balance. For example, in the ionic compound aluminum nitrate, the charge on the aluminum ion is 3+ and the charge on the polyatomic nitrate ion is 1–. The formula requires three nitrate ions for every aluminum ion: $Al(NO_3)_3$. Note that the positive ion (the cation) is written first in the formula.

The name of an ionic compound is built from the names of the positive and negative ions in the compound. The positive ion, often a metal ion, is simply the name of the metal. For example, Na^+ is called the sodium ion. If the metal can form more than one ion, the charge is indicated by a Roman numeral in parentheses following the name of the metal. For example, iron forms two common ions, Fe^{2+} and Fe^{3+} that are referred to as iron(II) and iron(III). There are some nonmetallic positive ions. The example you will encounter most often is the ammonium ion NH_4^+.

A monatomic negative ion is named by changing the ending of the name of the element to –ide. For example the anion of chlorine Cl is called the chloride ion Cl^-. Polyatomic negative ions have their own names. Some are listed in the margin. Many of the polyatomic ions contain oxygen and their names are derived systematically. Note the use of the endings –ite and –ate, and the prefixes hypo– and per– shown for the chloro oxoanions in the margin.

In naming an ionic compound, the positive ion is named first, followed by the negative ion. The charge on the cation is specified only if more than one exists. For example, copper(I) bromide *vs.* copper(II) bromide. Likewise, prefixes denoting the stoichiometry are not necessary; $CaCl_2$ is calcium chloride, not calcium dichloride.

Ions are held together in ionic compounds by the electrostatic force of attraction between opposite charges. The magnitude of the force is determined by **Coulomb's Law** and depends upon the charges and the distance between them. The higher the charges, and the smaller the ions, the greater the force of attraction.

Formulas for ionic compounds are empirical formulas; they represent the simplest ratio of cations to anions in an almost infinite three-dimensional crystal lattice. Each cation is surrounded by anions and each anion is surrounded by cations.

Molecular Compounds: Formulas, Names, and Properties

Many compounds consist of molecules. Water, H_2O, is an example. Water is a **binary compound**—a compound of just two elements.

Binary compounds are named as follows. When the molecule contains hydrogen and an element from Groups 6A or 7A, the hydrogen is named first, followed by the other element with the ending -ide. For example, H_2S hydrogen sulfide, or HF hydrogen fluoride. When the molecule contains hydrogen and an element from Groups 4A or 5A, the molecules have special names. For example, CH_4 methane, SiH_4 silane, GeH_4 germane, SnH_4 stannane (note the ending –ane), NH_3 ammonia, PH_3 phosphine, AsH_3 arsine (note the ending –ine).

The names of other binary compounds are more straightforward: The elements are named in order of increasing group number and the number of atoms is indicated with a prefix such as mono–, di–, tri–, tetra–, penta–, hexa–... For example: CO_2 carbon dioxide, SO_3 sulfur trioxide, or N_2O_4 dinitrogen tetroxide.

See study question #6.

Note that the formula for the polyatomic ion is placed in parentheses when more than one occurs in the formula.

Note that the charge on the cation equals the subscript of the anion in the formula (and vice versa).

See study question #7.

21 polyatomic ions:

NH_4^+	ammonium ion
CN^-	cyanide
$CH_3CO_2^-$	acetate
CO_3^{2-}	carbonate
HCO_3^-	bicarbonate
NO_2^-	nitrite
NO_3^-	nitrate
PO_4^{3-}	phosphate
HPO_4^{2-}	hydrogen phosphate
$H_2PO_4^-$	dihydrogen phosphate
OH^-	hydroxide
SO_3^{2-}	sulfite
SO_4^{2-}	sulfate
HSO_4^-	bisulfate
ClO^-	hypochlorite
ClO_2^-	chlorite
ClO_3^-	chlorate
ClO_4^-	perchlorate
CrO_4^{2-}	chromate
$Cr_2O_7^{2-}$	dichromate
MnO_4^-	permanganate

The strength of the force of attraction between the ions in an ionic compound determines its physical properties. The stronger the force, the higher the melting point for example.

A binary compound is a compound containing just two elements. It more often than not contains more than two atoms.

Note that the -a- preceding the -o- of oxide is often omitted to make pronunciation easier. For example, dinitrogen tetroxide instead of dinitrogen tetraoxide.

Note that the mono– prefix is omitted for the first element in a name.

See study questions #8 & 9.

Formulas, Compounds, and the Mole

Recall that the mole is the SI unit for an **amount of substance**. It is defined as the amount of substance that contains as many elementary entities (molecules, for example) as there are atoms in exactly 12 grams of carbon–12. The number is 6.022×10^{23} and is called **Avogadro's Number**.

See study question #10.

As described in Chapter 2, the convenience of the mole as a unit results from the fact that the number of entities in one mole of anything is always the same—Avogadro's Number. Thus, just as there are two hydrogen atoms and one oxygen atom in one molecule of water, so there are two moles of hydrogen atoms and one mole of oxygen atoms in one mole of water molecules.

The mole applies to compounds just as it does to elements. The **molar mass of a compound** is the sum of the molar masses of the constituent elements. For example, ammonia has the formula NH_3. This means that in one molecule of ammonia there is one nitrogen atom and three hydrogen atoms. It also means that in one mole of ammonia molecules, there is one mole of nitrogen atoms and three moles of hydrogen atoms. The molar mass of ammonia is $14.01 + (3 \times 1.008) = 17.03$ g/mol. Remembering the relationship between one mole and Avogadro's Number, this means that in 17.03 grams (one mole) of ammonia, there are 6.022×10^{23} molecules of ammonia composed of 6.022×10^{23} atoms of nitrogen and $3 \times 6.022 \times 10^{23}$ atoms of hydrogen.

The molar mass of a molecular compound is often referred to as the **molecular mass** of the compound.

An old term for molecular mass is gram molecular weight.

Since ionic compounds do not exist as molecules, they cannot have a molecular mass. Instead, the simplest (empirical) formula is written and the molar mass calculated for that formula. This is referred to as the **formula mass** or **formula weight**.

Determining Compound Formulas

You should be able to convert mass data (ratio of elements present by mass) into mole data (ratio of elements present by mole—the formula).

According to the Law of Constant Composition, a pure compound always contains the same elements in the same proportion by mass. This is because the compound has the fixed composition described by its formula. How can the formula be obtained from data describing the mass composition, and *vice versa*?

The **percent composition** is the way by which the mass composition of a substance is often stated. It is the fraction of one hundred grams of a compound that is a particular element.

See study questions 13, 14, & 17.

For example, the mass percent of nitrogen in ammonia (NH_3) is the molar mass of nitrogen (14.007g) divided by the molar mass of ammonia (17.030g) multiplied by 100. This equals 82.25%.

If the percent composition data for a substance is known, then the formula for the substance can be calculated. For example, suppose a compound of copper and chlorine is analyzed and found to contain 47.26% copper by mass. In other words, 100 grams of the substance contains 47.26 grams of copper. The remainder is chlorine (52.74 grams).

Conversion from a mass ratio to a mole ratio requires dividing by the molar mass:

mass ratio:	47.26 g Cu	52.74 g Cl
divide by molar mass:	/63.546	/35.453
	= 0.7437	= 1.488
convert to integers by dividing by the smaller:	= 1	= 2

therefore $CuCl_2$

#moles = mass/molar mass

If the computed ratio at the end is not a whole number ratio, then multiply through by a whole number. For example, suppose the result is the ratio 2 to 1.33. Multiply by 3 to convert to a whole number ratio: 6 to 4. And then divide by 2 to obtain the simplest ratio: 3 to 2.

Only the ratio of elements in the compound can be established. This is called the **empirical formula**. To determine the molecular formula for a compound, the molecular mass must be obtained by further experiment. One method used is mass spectral analysis. The mass spectrum indicates the molecular mass directly and it can also be used to determine structures based upon the fragmentation pattern and the isotopic abundances of the elements present.

An empirical formula indicates the simplest possible integer ratio of elements in a compound.

Hydrated Compounds

Very often ionic salts crystallize with molecules of water included in the crystal lattice. The water molecules are often associated with ions in the crystal. These compounds are called **hydrated compounds**. When a hydrated salt is heated, it loses the water to form the **anhydrous** salt.

See study questions #15 & 16.

Anhydrous means "without water".

Review Questions

Key Terms

empirical formula
molecular formula
condensed formula
structural formula
molecular compound
molecular models
ionic compound
cation
anion
monatomic ion
polyatomic ion
oxoanion
Coulomb's Law
electrostatic force
crystal lattice
binary compound
molecular mass or weight
formula mass or weight
percent composition
mass spectrum
hydrated compound
anhydrous compound

1. What is the difference between a molecular formula, a condensed formula, and a structural formula?

2. What is the difference between molecular and ionic compounds?

3. Draw representations of water at the particulate, the macroscopic, and the symbolic levels.

4. How can you determine whether a compound is ionic or molecular?

5. How can you predict the charge on the monatomic ion of a main group element?

6. What is a polyatomic ion? Is the central atom in a polyatomic ion always a nonmetal?

7. Explain the naming procedure for the polyatomic oxoanions.

8. Summarize what you know about the procedure for naming binary compounds of the nonmetals.

9. Why is the formula of methane written CH_4, and phosphine written PH_3, whereas the formula of hydrogen sulfide is written H_2S, and hydrogen chloride written HCl? (i.e. why does the hydrogen follow the C or P, but precede the S or Cl?)

10.   What does the formula H_2O represent? What does the formula NaCl represent?

11.   What is the molar mass of a molecule? What is the molar mass of an ionic compound?

12.   How can mass composition data be converted into a mole ratio? In other words, how can the formula of a compound be established from knowledge of the percent masses of each element present in the compound?

13.   How does an empirical formula differ from a molecular formula?

14.   What is a hydrated compound? What does anhydrous mean?

Answers to Review Questions

1.   The molecular formula simply lists how many atoms of which elements are present in one molecule of the substance. The condensed formula goes one step further and indicates to some extent the arrangement of atoms in the molecule. The structural formula indicates, in complete detail, how the atoms are bonded to one another in the molecule. An example is the molecular formula for methanol (CH_4O), its condensed formula (CH_3OH), and its structural formula:

$$H-\overset{\overset{\displaystyle H}{|}}{\underset{\underset{\displaystyle H}{|}}{C}}-O-H$$

2.   There are two major classes of compounds: molecular compounds and ionic compounds. They are quite different. Molecular compounds, like water (H_2O) consist of discrete groups of atoms bonded together at the particulate level. Ionic compounds, as the name suggests, consist of monatomic or polyatomic ions arrayed in an almost infinite three-dimensional lattice.

3.   Particulate: macroscopic: symbolic: H_2O

        vapor

        liquid

        individual molecules cannot be seen

4.   In order to recognize ionic compounds, it is necessary to know the formulas and names of the common ions. In general, an ionic compound will consist of a metal cation with either a monatomic nonmetal anion or a polyatomic anion. If the compound contains no metal then it is usually molecular—but there are exceptions, for example NH_4NO_3.

Group 1A metals form +1 ions.
Group 2A metals form +2 ions.
Group 3A metals form +3 ions.

Group 5A elements from –3 ions.
Group 6A elements form –2 ions.
Group 7A elements form –1 ions.

5.   The positive charge on a metal ion from the left of the Periodic Table is equal to the group number. For example, 1+ for sodium in Group 1. The negative charge on the nonmetals from the right side of the Periodic Table is equal to the group number minus 8. For example, 2– for sulfur from Group 6A.

6. A polyatomic ion is a molecule with a charge; it is an ion with two or more atoms. The central atom is very often a nonmetal, but need not be. For example, permanganate MnO_4^- or chromate CrO_4^{2-}.

7. Although the names of some polyatomic ions just have to be memorized (for example, dichromate $Cr_2O_7^{2-}$, acetate $CH_3CO_2^-$, cyanide CN^-), it is possible to derive the names of many other oxygen containing anions logically. There are two suffixes, −ate and −ite. The oxoanion with the greater number of oxygen atoms has the suffix −ate. There are two prefixes per− and hypo− that are used when there are more than just two oxoanions. The stem of the name is derived from the central atom, for example: nitr− for nitrogen, sulf− for sulfur, phosph− for phosphorus, etc.

    For example:

BrO^-	hypobromite
BrO_2^-	bromite
BrO_3^-	bromate
BrO_4^-	perbromate

8. The elements are named in order of increasing group number and the number of atoms is indicated with a prefix such as di−, tri−, tetra−, penta−, hexa−... Examples are: SO_2 sulfur dioxide, SiO_2 silicon dioxide, N_2O dinitrogen monoxide, SF_4 sulfur tetrafluoride, CCl_4 carbon tetrachloride. When the binary compound contains hydrogen and an element from Groups 6A or 7A, the hydrogen is named first, followed by the other element with the ending −ide. For example, H_2S hydrogen sulfide, HBr hydrogen bromide. When the molecule contains hydrogen and an element from Groups 4A or 5A, the molecules have other names. For example, CH_4 methane, SiH_4 silane (note the ending −ane), PH_3 phosphine, AsH_3 arsine (note the ending −ine).

    Within the same group, elements are named lower to higher. For example, SiC is silicon carbide, not carbon silicide, and ICl is iodine monochloride, not chlorine monoiodide.

9. The position of hydrogen in the Periodic Table is a problem. Very often it will be placed at the top of Group 1A, or at the top of Group 7A, or as in the front of the text, in both places. In some respects, hydrogen behaves as if it belongs somewhere above carbon. The convention is that binary compounds are named with the element further to the lower left in the Periodic Table first, followed by the element further to the upper right. The same applies to the way the formula is written. For example: LiH, CaH_2, BH_3, but H_2O, HCl. Where does the change-over take place? Between Groups 5A and 6A. So CH_4, SiH_4, NH_3 and PH_3 but H_2O, H_2S, HF, and HCl.

    The order of elements in the name, and the order of the symbols in the formula, is in fact a reflection of the relative electronegativities of the elements.

10. The formula H_2O represents either one molecule of water, or one mole of water molecules. The context determines which. The formula NaCl represents the composition of the salt sodium chloride. There is no molecule of sodium chloride; there is one sodium ion for each chloride ion however. NaCl represents one formula unit or one mole of formula units.

11. The molar mass of a molecule is the sum of the molar masses of the atoms making up the molecule. For example, the molecule sulfur dioxide SO_2 contains one sulfur atom (molar mass 32 g mol^{-1}) and two oxygen atoms (molar mass 16 g mol^{-1}). So the molar mass of sulfur dioxide is $32 + 2 \times 16 = 64$ g mol^{-1}. Alternatively, the molar mass of a molecule is the mass of one mole of the molecules.

The molar mass of an ionic compound refers to the mass of one mole of formula units (the empirical formula of the ionic compound). Again, the molar mass is obtained by adding together the molar masses of all the constituent atoms. For example, sodium chloride $NaCl$ has the molar mass $22.99 + 35.45 = 58.44$ g mol^{-1}.

12. The relationship between the mass of a substance and the number of moles of the substance is fundamental. The two are related by the molar mass of the substance:

Number of moles = mass of the substance / molar mass of the substance.

If the mass composition data (mass ratio) is known, then dividing by the molar masses of the constituent elements will produce the mole ratio. The mole ratio reveals the formula of the substance.

13. An empirical formula indicates the simplest possible integer ratio of elements in a compound. The molecular formula indicates how many atoms of which elements there are in one molecule of the compound. For example, the molecular formula of ethylene is C_2H_4, but the empirical formula is CH_2—a ratio of 1 atom of C to 2 atoms of H.

14. Hydrated compounds are ionic salts with molecules of water included in the crystal lattice. When a hydrated salt is heated, it loses the water to form the anhydrous salt.

Study Questions and Problems

Matter exists in the form of atoms and combinations of atoms. Void and matter are mutually exclusive; matter is solid and eternal. No void exists in the atom; hence it is both indestructible and indivisible. It does consist of least parts, however; but these have never existed separately.

Lucretius
(c.94-55BC)

1. a. The condensed formula for acetic acid is CH_3CO_2H. What is its empirical formula; what is its molecular formula; what is its structural formula?
    b. The molecular formula of acrylonitrile is C_3H_3N. Look up and draw its condensed formula and its structural formula.
    c. The molecular formula of aspartame (nutrasweet) is $C_{14}H_{18}O_5N_2$. Look up and draw its condensed formula and its structural formula.

2. The formulas for ethanol and ammonium nitrate are C_2H_5OH and NH_4NO_3. In what respects are these formulas and compounds different?

3. The molecular formula for both butanol and diethylether is $C_4H_{10}O$. Write structural formulas for both and show how they are different. Are any other structures possible?

4. Name the polyatomic ions:

$CH_3CO_2^-$	HCO_3^-	CN^-
$H_2PO_4^-$	$Cr_2O_7^{2-}$	BrO^-
SO_3^{2-}	ClO_4^-	OH^-

5. What are the formulas of the polyatomic ions:

phosphate	nitrite
sulfate	cyanide
bisulfite	chlorite

6. Write the ions present in the following salts and predict their formulas:

   potassium bromide
   calcium carbonate
   magnesium iodide
   → lithium oxide
   aluminum sulfate
   ammonium chlorate
   beryllium phosphate

7. Name the following ionic salts:

$(NH_4)_2SO_4$	→ $Co_2(SO_4)_3$
$KHCO_3$	→ $NiSO_4$
$Ca(NO_3)_2$	$AlPO_4$

8. Name the following binary compounds of the nonmetals:

CS_2	$SiCl_4$
SF_6	GeH_4
IF_5	P_4O_{10}
N_2H_4	S_4N_4
PCl_5	OF_2
Cl_2O_7	IF_7

9. What are the formulas for the following binary compounds?

silicon dioxide	boron trifluoride
xenon tetroxide	dinitrogen pentoxide
bromine trifluoride	carbon tetrachloride
phosphine	silicon carbide
phosphorus tribromide	disulfur dichloride
hydrogen selenide	sulfur trioxide

10. a. How many moles are present in 128 grams of sulfur dioxide?
    b. What is the molar mass of methane CH_4?
    c. What is the mass of 9 moles of fluorine molecules?
    d. 102 grams of a gas contains 6 moles. What is its molar mass?
    e. How many grams are there in one mole of benzene C_6H_6?
    f. How many moles of nitrogen atoms are there in 6 moles of TNT (trinitrotoluene $CH_3C_6H_2(NO_2)_3$)?
    g. What is the molar mass of TNT?

A hydrocarbon is a binary compound of carbon and hydrogen.

11. What is the percent by mass of nitrogen in ammonium nitrate?
     What is the percent by mass of phosphorus in calcium phosphate?

12. The hydrocarbons ethylene (molar mass 28 g/mol), cyclobutane (molar mass 56 g/mol), pentene (molar mass 70 g/mol), and cyclohexane (molar mass 84 g/mol), all have the same empirical formula. What is it? Write the molecular formulas for these four compounds.

13. A compound was analyzed and found to contain 76.57% carbon, 6.43% hydrogen, and 17.00% oxygen by mass. Calculate the empirical formula of the compound. If the molar mass of the compound is 94.11 g/mol, what is the molecular formula of the compound?

14. A compound was analyzed and found to contain 53.30% carbon, 11.19% hydrogen, and 35.51% oxygen by mass. Calculate the empirical formula of the compound. If the molar mass of the compound is 90.12 g/mol, what is the molecular formula of the compound?

15. A 15.67 g sample of a hydrate of magnesium carbonate was carefully heated, without decomposing the carbonate, to drive off the water. The mass was reduced to 7.58 g. What is the formula of the hydrate?

16. Anhydrous lithium perchlorate (4.78 g) was dissolved in water and recrystallized. Care was taken to isolate all the lithium perchlorate as its hydrate. The mass of the hydrated salt obtained was 7.21 g. What hydrate is it?

17. An oxide of copper was analyzed and found to contain 88.82% copper. What is the name and formula of this oxide?

Answers to Study Questions and Problems

Education is an admirable thing, but it is well to remember from time to time that nothing that is worth knowing can be taught.

Oscar Wilde
(1854–1900)

1. a. The empirical formula for acetic acid is CH_2O.
        The molecular formula is $C_2H_4O_2$.
        The structural formula is

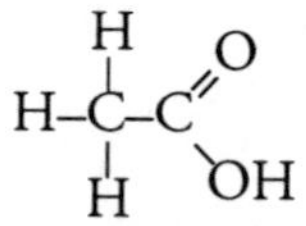

    b. The condensed formula of acrylonitrile is $CH_2{=}CHCN$.
        The structural formula is

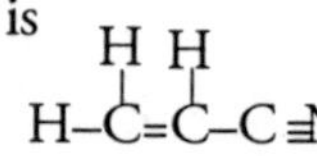

    c. The condensed formula of aspartame is
        $NH_2CH(CH_2CO_2H)CONHCH(CH_2C_6H_5)CO_2CH_3$

        The structural formula is

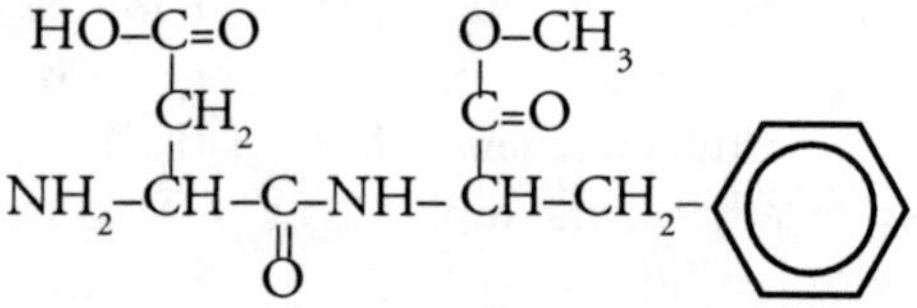

2. The formula for ethanol, C_2H_5OH, is the formula for one molecule of ethanol. One molecule of ethanol contains two carbon atoms, six hydrogen atoms, and one oxygen atom. Ammonium nitrate, NH_4NO_3, on the other hand, is an ionic compound. It consists of the ions NH_4^+ and NO_3^- in the 1:1 ratio indicated by the formula.

The formula can also represent one mole of ethanol molecules.

3. Butanol is an alcohol; it contains the $-OH$ functional group. Diethylether is an ether; it contains the $-O-$ functional group.
Butanol is $CH_3CH_2CH_2CH_2OH$.
Diethylether is $CH_3CH_2OCH_2CH_3$.
Both have the molecular formula $C_4H_{10}O$.

There are other structural isomers of butanol: one, for example, is $CH_3CH_2CH(OH)CH_3$. And another ether with the same molecular formula is methylpropylether $CH_3CH_2CH_2OCH_3$, and this ether itself has two structural possibilities.

There are two possible structures for the propyl group $CH_3CH_2CH_2-$ and $(CH_3)_2CH-$.

4.
$CH_3CO_2^-$	acetate		ClO_4^-	perchlorate
HCO_3^-	bicarbonate		CN^-	cyanide
$H_2PO_4^-$	dihydrogen phosphate		BrO^-	hypobromite
$Cr_2O_7^{2-}$	dichromate		OH^-	hydroxide
SO_3^{2-}	sulfite			

Hypobromite is not an ion that you should memorize; you can derive the name by analogy to the hypochlorite ClO^-.

Bicarbonate is sometime referred to as hydrogen carbonate.

5.
phosphate	PO_4^{3-}
sulfate	SO_4^{2-}
bisulfite	HSO_3^-
nitrite	NO_2^-
cyanide	CN^-
chlorite	ClO_2^-

6.
potassium bromide	K^+	Br^-	ratio 1:1	KBr
calcium carbonate	Ca^{2+}	CO_3^{2-}	1:1	$CaCO_3$
magnesium iodide	Mg^{2+}	I^-	1:2	MgI_2
lithium oxide	Li^+	O^{2-}	2:1	Li_2O
aluminum sulfate	Al^{3+}	SO_4^{2-}	2:3	$Al_2(SO_4)_3$
ammonium chlorate	NH_4^+	ClO_3^-	1:1	NH_4ClO_3
beryllium phosphate	Be^{2+}	PO_4^{3-}	3:2	$Be_3(PO_4)_2$

The ratio is such that the positive and negative charges balance. For example, for beryllium phosphate:
$|3 \times 2+|$ (for the cation) $= |2 \times 3-|$ (for the anion).

7.
$(NH_4)_2SO_4$	ammonium sulfate
$KHCO_3$	potassium bicarbonate
$Ca(NO_3)_2$	calcium nitrate
$Co_2(SO_4)_3$	cobalt(III) sulfate
$NiSO_4$	nickel(II) sulfate
$AlPO_4$	aluminum phosphate

8. | | | | |
   |---|---|---|---|
   | CS_2 | carbon disulfide | $SiCl_4$ | silicon tetrachloride |
   | SF_6 | sulfur hexafluoride | GeH_4 | germane |
   | IF_5 | iodine pentafluoride | P_4O_{10} | tetraphosphorus decoxide |
   | N_2H_4 | hydrazine | S_4N_4 | tetrasulfur tetranitride |
   | PCl_5 | phosphorus pentachloride | OF_2 | oxygen difluoride |
   | Cl_2O_7 | dichlorine heptoxide | IF_7 | iodine heptafluoride |

9. | | | |
   |---|---|---|
   | silicon dioxide | SiO_2 | |
   | boron trifluoride | BF_3 | |
   | xenon tetroxide | XeO_4 | |
   | dinitrogen pentoxide | N_2O_5 | |
   | bromine trifluoride | BrF_3 | |
   | carbon tetrachloride | CCl_4 | |
   | phosphine | PH_3 | |
   | silicon carbide | SiC | (note the absence of the prefix mono–) |
   | phosphorus tribromide | PBr_3 | |
   | disulfur dichloride | S_2Cl_2 | (sometimes called sulfur monochloride) |
   | hydrogen selenide | H_2Se | (note the absence of the prefix di-) |
   | sulfur trioxide | SO_3 | |

These are all equivalent expressions:

#moles = mass/molar mass

10. a. The molar mass of sulfur dioxide SO_2 is 64.06 g/mol.
   In 128 g there must be 128/64.06 moles = 2.00 moles.

   b. Methane (CH_4) has a molar mass = 12.011 + (4 ×1.008)
   = 16.04 g/mol.

mass = #moles × molar mass

   c. Fluorine is diatomic; its molar mass is 2 × 19.00 = 38.00 g/mol.
   The mass of 9 moles of fluorine = 9 moles × 38.00 g/mol = 342
   grams.

molar mass = mass/# moles

   d. The mass is 102 grams; the number of moles is 6.
   So the molar mass is 102 g / 6 mol = 17 g/mol (ammonia NH_3).

   e. One mole of benzene C_6H_6 has a molar mass = (6 × 12.011) + (6 ×
   1.008) = 78.11 g/mol.

   f. The number of nitrogen atoms in one molecule of trinitrotoluene
   $CH_3C_6H_2(NO_2)_3$ is 3, one in each NO_2 group. In 6 moles of TNT
   there must be 6 × 3 = 18 moles of nitrogen atoms.

carbon: 7 × 12.011 = 84.08 g
hydrogen: 5 × 1.008 = 5.04 g
nitrogen: 3 × 14.007 = 42.02 g
oxygen: 6 × 16.00 = 96.00 g

   g. The molar mass of TNT ($CH_3C_6H_2(NO_2)_3$)=
   84.08 g + 5.04 g + 42.02 g + 96.00 g = 227.14 g/mol

11. Ammonium nitrate, NH_4NO_3, has a molar mass of 80.04 g/mol. There are
   2 nitrogen atoms for every formula unit of ammonium nitrate; so the mass
   of nitrogen in every mole of ammonium nitrate is 2 × 14.007 g.
   The percent mass of nitrogen is (28.01 g / 80.04 g) × 100% = 35.00%.

12. The highest common factor is 14, which corresponds to one carbon atom and two hydrogen atoms. The empirical formula of all these hydrocarbons is therefore CH_2. The hydrocarbons are:

All of these hydrocarbons contain a ratio of two hydrogen atoms for every carbon atom.

ethylene molar mass 28 g/mol molecular formula C_2H_4
cyclobutane molar mass 56 g/mol molecular formula C_4H_8
pentene molar mass 70 g/mol molecular formula C_5H_{10}
cyclohexane molar mass 84 g/mol molecular formula C_6H_{12}

13. The data provided is mass composition data. A formula for a compound is a mole ratio—the relative numbers of the various constituent elements. To convert from mass to moles divide by the molar mass. So the mass percent for each element is divided by its molar mass as follows:

Setting up the problem in a table like this is highly recommended. The same format is used in questions 14 through 17.

	carbon	hydrogen	oxygen
mass % ratio:	76.57%	6.43%	17.00%
divide by molar mass:	/12.011	/1.008	/16.00
convert to integers by dividing by the smallest:	= 6.37	= 6.38	= 1.06
	= 6	= 6	= 1

The empirical formula is C_6H_6O
The empirical mass (the mass of this formula) is 94.11 g
This equals the molar mass, so this empirical formula is also the molecular formula.

14. Again, to convert from mass to moles divide by the molar mass. So divide the mass percent for each element by its molar mass:

	carbon	hydrogen	oxygen
mass % ratio:	53.30%	11.19%	35.51%
divide by molar mass:	/12.011	/1.008	/16.00
convert to integers by dividing by the smallest:	= 4.44	= 11.1	= 2.22
	= 2	= 5	= 1

The empirical formula is C_2H_5O
The empirical mass is 45.06 g
This is only one-half of the molar mass (90.12 g/mol), so this empirical formula is one-half the molecular formula.
The molecular formula is $C_4H_{10}O_2$.

15. The molar mass of magnesium carbonate $MgCO_3$ is 84.31 g/mol. Set up the problem as in the previous two questions. Again, to convert from mass to moles divide by the molar mass. The mass of water lost is the original mass (15.67 g) – the final mass (7.58 g) = 8.09 g.

	MgCO$_3$	H$_2$O
mass ratio:	7.58 g	8.09 g
divide by molar mass:	/84.31	/18.02
convert to integers by dividing by the smaller:	= 0.0899	= 0.449
	= 1	= 5

The formula of the hydrate is MgCO$_3$.5H$_2$O.

16.   The molar mass of lithium perchlorate LiClO$_4$ is 106.39 g/mol. Set up the problem as in the previous problem. To convert from mass to moles divide by the molar mass. The mass of water gained is 2.43 g.

	LiClO$_4$	H$_2$O
mass ratio:	4.78 g	2.43 g
divide by molar mass:	/106.39	/18.02
convert to integers by dividing by the smaller:	= 0.0449	= 0.135
	= 1	= 3

The formula of the hydrate is LiClO$_4$.3H$_2$O.

17.   The mass of oxygen can be obtained by subtracting 88.82 g from 100 g. Then set up the problem in the same way.

	Cu	O
mass ratio:	88.82 g	11.18 g
divide by molar mass:	/63.55	/16.00
convert to integers by dividing by the smaller:	= 1.398	= 0.699
	= 2	= 1

The oxide is copper(I) oxide (or cuprous oxide), formula Cu$_2$O.

Numbers

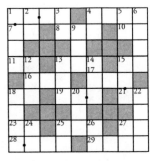

Across:

1.   Molar mass of copper.
4.   The year Antoine Lavoisier lost his head.
7   Neptune's number.
8.   The most recently detected element (Jan '99).
10.   The exponent of Avogadro's number.
11.   The number of inches in one foot...
13.   ...and the number of sq. in in one sq.ft.
15.   The molar mass of oxygen atoms.
16.   One atmosphere pressure in torr.
17.   273°C in K.
18.   The mass of the empirical formula for 9 down.
19.   The volume of one mole of a gas at 0°C and 1 atm.
21.   Niobe's number.
23.   Three moles of carbon.
25.   The ignition temperature of paper in °F.
27.   The molar mass of methane CH_4.
28.   The first four digits of Avogadro's number.
29.   The year John Dalton announced his atomic theory.

Down:

1.   Lithium's mass.
2.   The atomic number of arsenic...
3.   ...and that of the element under it.
4.   Radioactive carbon isotope used in dating.
5.   The atomic number of 20 down.
6.   The group numbers of silicon, aluminum, nitrogen, and sulfur, respectively.
9.   The mass of four moles of acetylene C_2H_2.
12.   It's freezing in K.
13.   A number for the prize-giver.
14.   The number of grams in one pound.
15.   The number of cubic cm in one cubic inch.
18.   The mass of a proton divided by the mass of an electron.
20.   The isotope of uranium used in nuclear reactors.
22.   The year Linus Pauling won his second Nobel Prize.
24.   The number of carbon atoms in a common fullerene.
25.   The number of neutrons in 2 down's isotope–75.
26.   The number of electrons in a sodium atom...
27.   ...and after it has lost one to form the sodium ion.

CHAPTER 4

Introduction

The objective in this chapter is to begin a study of reaction stoichiometry—the quantitative treatment of chemical reactions. You will learn how to write chemical equations, balance them, and use them to determine the mass relationships in a chemical reaction. The concept of a limiting reactant and the calculation of the yield of a reaction are introduced.

Contents

Chemical Equations
Balancing Chemical Equations
Mass Relationships in Chemical Reactions: Stoichiometry
Reactions in which One Reactant is Present in Limited Supply
Percent Yield
Chemical Equations and Chemical Analysis

Chemical Equations

A **chemical equation** is a representation of a chemical reaction. Symbols and formulas for the **reactants** (the substances that are going to react) are written on the left and symbols and formulas for the **products** (the substances that are produced) are written on the right. The arrow ($\rightarrow$) represents the reaction.

$$\text{Reactants} \quad \rightarrow \quad \text{Products}$$

A **chemical reaction** is only a rearrangement of atoms—atoms are neither created nor destroyed. Therefore, in a balanced chemical equation, the number of atoms on both sides of the arrow must be the same.

> This is the law of conservation of matter (Lavoisier) later incorporated into the atomic theory of matter (Dalton).

In a chemical reaction, bonds between atoms are broken, new bonds between atoms are formed, and new substances are produced. If necessary, the physical states of the reactants and products are denoted by *(s)* solid, *(l)* liquid, *(g)* gas, and *(aq)* solution. For example:

> The symbol (aq) is used for substances in solution.

$$P_4(s) \ + \ 6Cl_2(g) \ \rightarrow \ 4PCl_3(l)$$

The numbers in front of the formulas in the equation are called **coefficients** and are required to balance the equation. They reflect the principle of conservation of matter: four phosphorus atoms in one molecule of P_4 on the left are balanced by the four phosphorus atoms in the four molecules of PCl_3 on the right.

> The coefficients are more properly called stoichiometric coefficients.
>
> The number of phosphorus atoms and chlorine atoms on each side of the equation are the same.

The equation can be interpreted equally well in terms of moles. Thus one mole of P_4 molecules produces four moles of PCl_3 molecules. This ratio of one to four molecules, or one to four moles of molecules, is called the **mole ratio** or **stoichiometry** of the reaction.

Learn how to balance chemical equations. Note that, by definition, an equation must be balanced—an unbalanced equation is an oxymoron or contradiction in terms.

For a combustion of a hydrocarbon:

1:    Write the correct formulas
2:    Balance the C atoms
3:    Balance the H atoms
4:    Balance the O atoms

See study questions #1, 3, & 4.

Given quantitative data in mass (grams), always convert this to moles for stoichiometric calculations.

See study question #2.

You must be able to convert between mass and moles!

#moles = mass/molar mass

The molar mass of benzene C_6H_6 is 78 g/mol.

39g / 78 g mol^{-1} = 0.50 mol.

Notice how the units cancel to give moles of H_2O.

Balancing Chemical Equations

Using chemical equations for quantitative calculations requires that the equations be balanced. This balancing can often be done by trial and error although a systematic approach is useful:

Step 1: Write the correct formulas for the reactants and products.
Step 2: Look for the most complicated looking formula and balance the atoms in that formula first.
Step 3: Balance atoms that occur only in one reactant and one product.
Step 4: Balance the remaining atoms.

Remember that you cannot change the formulas for the reactants and the products in an equation in order to balance the equation. Doing so would change the identity of the substances involved in the reaction.

Mass Relationships in Chemical Reactions: Stoichiometry

A balanced chemical reaction illustrates the quantitative relationship between the reactants and products in a chemical reaction. The equation expresses this quantitative relationship in terms of **moles**—it expresses the mole ratio, or stoichiometry, required. There are four steps in a typical quantitative calculation for a chemical reaction:

Step 1: Write the balanced chemical equation.
Step 2: Convert mass data to moles.
Step 3: Use the stoichiometric relationship illustrated by the equation.
Step 4: If required, convert mole data back to mass data.

Any stoichiometric relationship of the chemical reaction is represented by a **stoichiometric factor** or mole ratio. This is an application of the dimensional analysis discussed in Chapter 1. For example, consider the combustion of benzene:

$$2C_6H_6(l) \ + \ 15O_2(g) \ \rightarrow \ 12CO_2(g) \ + \ 6H_2O(l)$$

The stoichiometric coefficients in the equation indicate that 2 moles of benzene C_6H_6 require 15 moles of O_2 to produce 12 moles of CO_2 and 6 moles of H_2O. What mass of water is produced when 39 grams of benzene is burned?

Step 1: The balanced chemical equation is already written.
Step 2: 39 grams of benzene is 0.50 mole of benzene.
Step 3: The equation provides the stoichiometric relationship between the moles of benzene burned and the moles of water produced:

The mole ratio, or stoichiometric factor, is ($6H_2O/2C_6H_6$)

So 0.5 mol C_6H_6 × (6 mol H_2O/2 mol C_6H_6) = 1.5 mol H_2O

Step 4: 1.5 moles of water = 1.5 mol × 18 g/mol = 27 grams.

Reactions in which One Reactant is Present in Limited Supply

In practice, reactants are rarely present in the correct stoichiometric ratio. This is often intentional; it can, for example, be done to ensure that the more expensive of two reactants is completely used. The reactant that is *not* in excess determines the amount of product that can be made and is, for that reason, called the **limiting reactant**. Some of the non-limiting reactant (the reactant in excess) will remain unused at the end of the reaction.

Suppose zinc metal is to be oxidized by hydrochloric acid according to the chemical equation:

$$Zn(s) \ + \ 2HCl(aq) \ \rightarrow \ ZnCl_2(aq) \ + \ H_2(g)$$

Suppose further that the mass of zinc is 6.54 grams and the mass of hydrochloric acid the solution is 5.47 grams. What mass of hydrogen gas will be produced? Approach the problem as before:

Step 1: Write the balanced chemical equation—done.

Step 2: Convert mass data to moles:
6.54 g of Zn = 6.54g / 65.39g mol^{-1} = 0.100 mol
5.47 g of HCl = 5.47g / 36.46g mol^{-1} = 0.150 mol

Step 3: Determine the limiting reactant:
0.100 mol of Zn requires 0.200 mol of HCl; but there is only 0.150 mol of HCl. So HCl is the limiting reactant.

Step 4: Use the stoichiometric relationship illustrated by the equation to determine the amount of product that can be formed:
0.150 mol HCl × (1 mol H$_2$/2 mol HCl) = 0.075 mol H$_2$

Step 5: Change back to mass data:
0.075 mol H$_2$ = 0.075 mol × 2.016 g/mol = 0.15 grams.

A useful analogy is the production of bicycles from frames and wheels. Each bicycle requires one frame and two wheels. How many bicycles can you produce from 7 frames and 10 wheels and which component is the limiting reactant?
You have enough frames for 7 bicycles, but only enough wheels for 5 bicycles; thus the wheels limit the number of bicycles that can be made. Two frames remain unused at the end.

The limiting reactant can often be established using common sense as in this example. The stoichiometry of the equation must be taken into account! Even though there are more moles of HCl than Zn, the HCl is the limiting reactant.

The limiting reactant can be established more formally by dividing the number of moles of each reactant present by its stoichiometric coefficient. The reactant with the lowest result is the limiting reactant.

For example, in this case, for Zn, 0.100 divided by 1 = 0.100; and for HCl, 0.150 divided by 2 = 0.075; so the HCl is the limiting reactant.

See study questions # 5, 6, 7, 13, & 14 for other examples.

Percent Yield

The maximum quantity of product that can be obtained in a chemical reaction is called the **theoretical yield**. In practice some waste occurs, other products may be formed, or the reaction may not even go to completion. The quantity of the desired product obtained is often less than the theoretical yield. The ratio of the **actual yield** to the theoretical yield multiplied by 100 is called the **percent yield**.

You should be able to calculate the % yield in a chemical reaction.

% yield = $\dfrac{\text{actual}}{\text{theoretical}}$ × 100%

See study questions #16 & 17.

Chemical Equations and Chemical Analysis

Chemical analysis depends upon the idea that the quantity of product obtained in a reaction is related exactly to an unknown quantity of the reactant. This relationship is the stoichiometric factor derived from the stoichiometry of the appropriate balanced chemical equation.

For example, nickel is often determined by precipitating it as a very insoluble red salt of dimethylglyoxime. If the mass of the salt is determined, the mass of nickel originally present can be calculated. This type of analysis is called **gravimetric**

See study question #8.

analysis and the stoichiometric factor in this case is called the gravimetric factor. Other methods of chemical analysis depend upon the same principle.

Another method of analysis often used for organic compounds is **combustion analysis**. In this method the substance is burned in oxygen and the quantity of carbon dioxide and water produced is measured:

Every carbon atom produces one molecule of carbon dioxide.
Every two hydrogen atoms produce one molecule of water.

For example, suppose 0.290 gram of a carbohydrate is analyzed by combustion. The analysis produces 0.440 gram of carbon dioxide and 0.090 gram of water. What is the empirical formula of the compound?

Step 1: What is the stoichiometry? —this is described above.

Step 2: Convert mass data to moles:
0.440 g of CO_2 = 0.440g / 44.01g mol^{-1} = 0.0100 mol
0.090 g of H_2O = 0.090g / 18.02g mol^{-1} = 0.0050 mol

Step 3: Use the stoichiometric relationships above:
Number of moles of carbon C = 0.0100 mol CO_2 = 0.0100 mol
Number of moles of hydrogen H = 2×0.005 mol H_2O = 0.0100 mol

There are an equal number of moles of carbon and hydrogen in the compound:

Mass of hydrogen = 0.0100 mol × 1.008 g/mol = 0.010 g
Mass of carbon = 0.0100 mol × 12.01 g/mol = 0.120 g
Total mass of carbon and hydrogen = 0.130 g

Remainder must be oxygen = 0.290 − 0.130 = 0.160 g
Moles of oxygen = 0.160g / 16.0g mol^{-1} = 0.0100 mol

Step 4: Write the empirical formula:
The number of moles of carbon, hydrogen, and oxygen are all the same; the empirical formula is CHO.

An organic compound is a compound of carbon and hydrogen, often with oxygen and nitrogen, and sometimes with other elements such as the halogens, sulfur, and phosphorus.

A carbohydrate is a compound of carbon, hydrogen, and oxygen.

It's useful to set up a table to organize these calculations. See study questions #9 & 10.

You must be able to convert between mass and moles!

#moles = mass/molar mass

An empirical formula indicates the simplest possible integer ratio of elements in a compound.

Review Questions

Key terms:

chemical equation
conservation of matter
reactants
products
coefficients
stoichiometry
mole ratio
stoichiometric factor
limiting reactant
actual yield
theoretical yield
percent yield
gravimetric analysis
combustion analysis

1.   What is the difference between a chemical reaction and a chemical equation?

2.   Why must a chemical equation be balanced?

3.   Why must you *not* change the subscripts of a formula to balance an equation?

4.   List the steps in a systematic approach to balancing a chemical equation.

5.   What is the stoichiometry of a reaction?

6.   What is a stoichiometric factor or mole ratio?

7.   What is a limiting reactant and how can you establish which reactant is the limiting reactant?

8.   How is the percent yield for a reaction calculated?

9.   Explain how a mixture can be analyzed to determine what, and how much, of a substance is in the mixture.

10.   Summarize the procedure used to establish the formula of a carbohydrate by combustion analysis.

11.   How can a molecular formula be established once the empirical formula is known?

Answers to Review Questions

1.   A chemical reaction is a process in which substances are changed into other substances by a rearrangement of atoms. A chemical equation is a symbolic representation of a chemical reaction. The substances involved in the chemical reaction are represented by symbols and formulas. The physical states of the substances are defined by symbols and the direction of the reaction is denoted by an arrow.

2.   A chemical equation must be balanced because of the law of conservation of mass. Atoms cannot be created nor destroyed in a chemical reaction. Therefore there have to be equal numbers of atoms on the two sides of an equation.

3.   Changing the subscript in a formula changes the substance. For example, carbon monoxide CO is not carbon dioxide CO_2. Changing the subscript in a chemical equation therefore misrepresents the actual reaction.

Practice balancing equations; see study question #1.

4. *Step 1:* Write the correct formulas for the reactants and products.
    Step 2: Look for the most complicated looking formula and balance the atoms in that formula first. Leave simple molecules to the end.
    Step 3: Balance atoms that occur only in one reactant and one product.
    Step 4: Balance the remaining atoms.

5. The stoichiometry of a reaction is the quantitative relationship between the amounts of reactants and products in the reaction. Note that the principles of stoichiometry are also applied to the composition of compounds and the formulas used to represent them.

See study question #2.

6. A stoichiometric factor is the mole ratio relating the number of moles of one reactant to the number of moles of another reactant or to the number of moles of product. The factor is obtained directly from the coefficients of the balanced chemical equation.

7. The limiting reactant is the reactant that is used up first and therefore is the reactant that determines, or limits, the amount of product that can be formed. The limiting reactant can often be established using common sense although it can be established more formally by dividing the number of moles of each reactant present by its stoichiometric coefficient. The reactant with the lowest result is the limiting reactant.

Dividing by the stoichiometric coefficients takes account of the stoichiometry of the reaction automatically.

8. The theoretical yield is calculated from the stoichiometry of the balanced chemical equation. The actual yield is the amount of product obtained experimentally. The actual yield divided by the theoretical yield multiplied by 100 is the percent yield.

$$\% \text{ yield} = \frac{\text{actual}}{\text{theoretical}} \times 100\%$$

9. Chemical analysis involves a chemical reaction. (There are other ways to analyze matter—for example spectroscopic analysis.) A reaction is chosen for the component (the analyte) within the mixture that needs to be determined; the other components in the mixture are supposed not to react. A positive reaction is all that is necessary for a qualitative test. For a quantitative determination, the quantity of product from the chemical reaction is measured, which in turn allows the quantity of the analyte in the original mixture to be determined.

10. If a compound burns in oxygen (typically an organic molecule containing carbon and hydrogen) then each element (except oxygen) in the compound will combine with oxygen to produce the appropriate oxide. The quantity of carbon dioxide is determined by absorbing it in sodium hydroxide. The quantity of water produced is determined by absorbing it in anhydrous magnesium perchlorate. The mass changes in the absorbents yield the amounts of carbon dioxide and water produced for a known mass of compound. Every mole of carbon in the original material yields one mole of carbon dioxide. Every two moles of hydrogen in the original material yields one mole of water.

11. To establish the molecular formula from the empirical formula, a determination of the molecular mass of the compound must be done. This could be achieved, for example, by mass spectrometry.

Study Questions and Problems

Most people would sooner die than think; in fact, they do so.

Bertrand Russell (1872-1970)

With practice, you will develop an instinctive approach to balancing a chemical equation.

1. Balance the following equations:

a. $_C_4H_6(g) + _O_2(g) \rightarrow _CO_2(g) + _H_2O(l)$

b. $_NH_3(g) + _O_2(g) \rightarrow _NO_2(g) + _H_2O(l)$

c. $_PCl_3(l) + _H_2O(l) \rightarrow _H_3PO_3(aq) + _HCl(aq)$

d. $_Ca_3P_2(s) + _H_2O(l) \rightarrow _Ca(OH)_2(aq) + _PH_3(g)$

e. $_C_4H_8(OH)_2(l) + _O_2(g) \rightarrow _CO_2(g) + _H_2O(l)$

f. $_NH_3(g) + _NO(g) \rightarrow _N_2(g) + _H_2O(l)$

g. $_KClO_3(s) \rightarrow _KCl(s) + _O_2(g)$

h. $_Ca(OH)_2(s) + _H_3PO_4(aq) \rightarrow _Ca_3(PO_4)_2(s) + _H_2O(l)$

i. $_C_3H_8(g) + _O_2(g) \rightarrow _CO_2(g) + _H_2O(l)$

j. $_N_2O(g) + _O_2(g) \rightarrow _NO_2(g)$

k. $_Al_4C_3(s) + _H_2O(l) \rightarrow _Al(OH)_3(aq) + _CH_4(g)$

l. $_CS_2(l) + _Cl_2(g) \rightarrow _CCl_4(l) + _S_2Cl_2(l)$

m. $_C_2H_5OH(l) + _PCl_3(l) \rightarrow _C_2H_5Cl(l) + _H_3PO_3(l)$

n. $_ZnS(s) + _O_2(g) \rightarrow _ZnO(s) + _SO_2(g)$

o. $_Ag(s) + _H_2S(g) + _O_2(g) \rightarrow _Ag_2S(s) + _H_2O(l)$

2. What are the stoichiometric factors between the first product and first reactant written in the equations in question 1?

3. Write balanced chemical equations for the following reactions:

a. the decomposition of ammonium nitrate to nitrogen gas, oxygen gas, and water vapor.
b. the reaction of sodium bicarbonate with sulfuric acid to produce sodium sulfate, water, and carbon dioxide.
c. the treatment of phosphorus pentachloride with water to produce phosphoric acid and hydrogen chloride.

4.   When asked to balance the equation:

$$C_2H_6(g) + O_2(g) \rightarrow CO_2(g) + H_2O(l)$$

the following suggestions were made:

$$C_2H_6(g) + 5O_2(g) \rightarrow 2CO_2(g) + 3H_2O(l)$$

$$C_2H_6(g) + 5O(g) \rightarrow 2CO(g) + 3H_2O(l)$$

$$2C_2H_6(g) + 7O_2(g) \rightarrow 4CO_2(g) + 6H_2O(l)$$

Which answer is correct and what is wrong with the others?

5.   If the maximum amount of product possible is formed in the following reactions, what mass of the specified product would you obtain?

a.   10 grams of sodium chloride is treated with excess silver nitrate:

$$AgNO_3(aq) + NaCl(aq) \rightarrow AgCl(s) + NaNO_3(aq)$$

How much silver chloride is precipitated?

b.   12 grams copper metal is treated with excess dilute nitric acid:

$$3Cu(s) + 8HNO_3(aq) \rightarrow 3Cu(NO_3)_2(aq) + 2NO(g) + 4H_2O(l)$$

How much nitric oxide gas (NO) is produced?

c.   60 grams propane gas is burned in excess oxygen:

$$C_3H_8(g) + 5O_2(g) \rightarrow 3CO_2(g) + 4H_2O(l)$$

How much water is produced?

6.   A furniture dealer put together a special deal for the annual sale—an entire dining room set comprising a table, six dining chairs, two bookshelves, a china cabinet, and a sideboard for $999. The dealer had in stock 280 tables, 1750 chairs, 550 bookshelves, 300 china cabinets, and 325 sideboards. He asked his assistant to figure out how many dining room sets they could sell, how much money they would make if they sold all the sets possible, and what they would have left that could not be sold as part of the deal.

7.   Hydrazine reacts with dinitrogen tetroxide according to the equation:

$$2N_2H_4(g) + N_2O_4(g) \rightarrow 3N_2(g) + 4H_2O(g)$$

50.0 grams of hydrazine is mixed with 100.0 grams of dinitrogen tetroxide. How much nitrogen gas was produced?

8.   A nickel(II) ammonia compound was prepared in the laboratory. Its formula was supposed to be $[Ni(NH_3)_6](NO_3)_2$. In order to verify the composition of the compound, a solution of the compound was treated with the reagent dimethylglyoxime. This reagent reacts with nickel(II) to produce an insoluble red compound $Ni(DMG)_2$.

0.1324 gram of the nickel ammonia compound was dissolved in water and treated with an excess of the dimethylglyoxime reagent. The mass of red $Ni(DMG)_2$ produced was 0.1343 gram.

a. Calculate the mass of nickel in the nickel(II) ammonia compound.

b. Calculate the %mass of nickel in the compound.

c. What %mass of nickel was expected?

d. What is the gravimetric factor for this analysis?

Molar mass of $[Ni(NH_3)_6](NO_3)_2$ is 284.887 g/mol.

Molar mass of $[Ni(DMG)_2]$ is 288.917 g/mol.

Molar mass of Ni is 58.693 g/mol.

9. 7.321 mg of an organic compound containing carbon, hydrogen, and oxygen was analyzed by combustion. The amount of carbon dioxide produced was 17.873 mg and the amount of water produced was 7.316 mg. Determine the empirical formula of the compound.

10. 0.1101 gram of an organic compound containing carbon, hydrogen, and oxygen was analyzed by combustion. The amount of carbon dioxide produced was 0.2503 gram and the amount of water produced was 0.1025 gram. A determination of the molar mass of the compound indicated a value of approximately 115 grams/mol. Determine the empirical formula, and the molecular formula, of the compound.

11. The reaction of hydrogen iodide and potassium bicarbonate produces potassium iodide according to the equation:

$$HI(aq) + KHCO_3(s) \rightarrow KI(aq) + H_2O + CO_2(g)$$

If 32 grams of potassium bicarbonate is treated with 48 grams of hydrogen iodide, what is the maximum amount of potassium iodide that can be produced?

12. A compound of boron and hydrogen is burned completely in oxygen to produce water and boron oxide B_2O_3. The number of moles of water formed is twice the number of moles of B_2O_3 formed. What is a possible formula for the boron–hydrogen compound?

a. B_2H_6 c. B_4H_9 e. B_6H_{12}
b. B_3H_8 d. B_3H_9 f. $B_{12}H_{12}$

13. TNT (trinitrotoluene) is prepared by treating toluene with nitric acid according to the equation:

$$C_7H_8(l) + 3HNO_3(aq) \rightarrow C_7H_5(NO_2)_3(s) + 3H_2O(l)$$

What mass of TNT can be made when 450 grams of toluene is treated with 1000 grams of nitric acid?

14. Sodium metal reacts vigorously with water to produce a solution of sodium hydroxide and hydrogen gas:

$$2Na(s) + 2H_2O(l) \rightarrow 2NaOH(aq) + H_2(g)$$

What mass of hydrogen gas can be produced when 10 grams of sodium is added to 15 grams of water?

15. Nitrous oxide reacts with oxygen to produce nitrogen dioxide according to the equation:

$$2N_2O(g) + 3O_2(g) \rightarrow 4NO_2(g)$$

What mass of nitrogen dioxide can be made from 42 grams of nitrous oxide and 42 grams of oxygen?

16. If only 75 grams of nitrogen dioxide was produced in the reaction described in the previous question, what was the %yield?

17. When copper was treated with dilute nitric acid as described in question 5b, the quantity of nitric oxide gas (NO) collected was only 3.0 grams. What was the %yield of this product?

Answers to Study Questions and Problems

...Nil posse creari de nilo.

...Nothing can be created out of nothing.

Lucretius
(c.94-55BC)

1. Follow the logical procedure outlined earlier. Examine the equation for any obvious stoichiometric relationships between the reactants and products. Remember that the number of atoms of each element on each side of the equation must be the same. For example, one C_4H_6 on the reactant side requires four CO_2 on the product side, or one Ca_3P_2 on the reactant side requires three $Ca(OH)_2$ on the product side—such relationships are not a bad place to start.

   a. $2C_4H_6(g) + 11O_2(g) \rightarrow 8CO_2(g) + 6H_2O(l)$

   b. $4NH_3(g) + 7O_2(g) \rightarrow 4NO_2(g) + 6H_2O(l)$

   c. $PCl_3(l) + 3H_2O(l) \rightarrow H_3PO_3(aq) + 3HCl(aq)$

   d. $Ca_3P_2(s) + 6H_2O(l) \rightarrow 3Ca(OH)_2(s) + 2PH_3(g)$

   e. $2C_4H_8(OH)_2(l) + 11O_2(g) \rightarrow 8CO_2(g) + 10H_2O(l)$

   f. $4NH_3(g) + 6NO(g) \rightarrow 5N_2(g) + 6H_2O(l)$

   g. $2KClO_3(s) \rightarrow 2KCl(s) + 3O_2(g)$

   h. $3Ca(OH)_2(s) + 2H_3PO_4(aq) \rightarrow Ca_3(PO_4)_2(s) + 6H_2O(l)$

   i. $C_3H_8(g) + 5O_2(g) \rightarrow 3CO_2(g) + 4H_2O(l)$

j. $2N_2O(g) + 3O_2(g) \rightarrow 4NO_2(g)$

k. $Al_4C_3(s) + 12H_2O(l) \rightarrow 4Al(OH)_3(aq) + 3CH_4(g)$

l. $CS_2(l) + 3Cl_2(g) \rightarrow CCl_4(l) + S_2Cl_2(l)$

m. $3C_2H_5OH(l) + PCl_3(l) \rightarrow 3C_2H_5Cl(l) + H_3PO_3(l)$

n. $2ZnS(s) + 3O_2(g) \rightarrow 2ZnO(s) + 2SO_2(g)$

o. $4Ag(s) + 2H_2S(g) + O_2(g) \rightarrow 2Ag_2S(s) + 2H_2O(l)$

2. Knowledge of the stoichiometric factors derived from a balanced chemical equation (often referred to as the mole ratios) is essential in quantitative (stoichiometric) calculations.

a. 2 moles C_4H_6 / 8 moles CO_2

b. 4 moles NH_3 / 4 moles NO_2

c. 1 mole PCl_3 / 1 mole H_3PO_3

d. 1 mole Ca_3P_2 / 3 moles $Ca(OH)_2$

e. 2 moles $C_4H_8(OH)_2$ / 8 moles CO_2

f. 4 moles NH_3 / 5 moles N_2

g. 2 moles $KClO_3$ / 2 moles KCl

h. 3 moles $Ca(OH)_2$ / 1 mole $Ca_3(PO_4)_2$

i. 1 mole C_3H_8 / 3 moles CO_2

j. 2 moles N_2O / 4 moles NO_2

k. 1 mole Al_4C_3 / 4 moles $Al(OH)_3$

l. 1 mole CS_2 / 1 mole CCl_4

m. 3 moles C_2H_5OH / 3 moles C_2H_5Cl

n. 2 moles ZnS / 2 moles ZnO

o. 4 moles Ag / 2 moles Ag_2S

Write the formulas for all the reactants and products and then balance the equation.

3. a. the decomposition of ammonium nitrate to nitrogen gas, oxygen gas, and water vapor.

$$2NH_4NO_3(s) \rightarrow 2N_2(g) + O_2(g) + 4H_2O(g)$$

b. the reaction of sodium bicarbonate with sulfuric acid to produce sodium sulfate, water, and carbon dioxide.

$$2NaHCO_3(s) + H_2SO_4(aq) \rightarrow Na_2SO_4(aq) + 2H_2O + 2CO_2(g)$$

c. the treatment of phosphorus pentachloride with water to produce phosphoric acid and hydrogen chloride.

$$PCl_5(s) + 4H_2O(l) \rightarrow H_3PO_4(aq) + 5HCl(g)$$

4. $$C_2H_6(g) + 5O_2(g) \rightarrow 2CO_2(g) + 3H_2O(l)$$

Not balanced—check the oxygen atoms.

$$C_2H_6(g) + 5O(g) \rightarrow 2CO(g) + 3H_2O(l)$$

Cannot change the formulas! Oxygen is O_2 and carbon dioxide is CO_2.

$$2C_2H_6(g) + 7O_2(g) \rightarrow 4CO_2(g) + 6H_2O(l)$$

This answer is correct.

5. a. 10 grams of sodium chloride is treated with excess silver nitrate:

$$AgNO_3(aq) + NaCl(aq) \rightarrow AgCl(s) + NaNO_3(aq)$$

Notice the procedure in these problems:

1. Convert mass to moles.
2. Use the stoichiometric factor.
3. Convert from moles back to mass.

Convert mass quantities to moles:
10 grams of NaCl is $10g/58.44$ g mol^{-1} = 0.171 mole.

The stoichiometric factor (mole ratio) is 1 mol AgCl/1 mol NaCl. One silver chloride unit is produced for every sodium chloride used. So the number of moles of silver chloride precipitated = 0.171 mole.

Convert back to mass:
0.171 mole of AgCl = 0.171 mole × 143.3 g mol^{-1} = 24.5 grams.

b. 12 grams copper metal is treated with excess dilute nitric acid:

$$3Cu(s) + 8HNO_3(aq) \rightarrow 3Cu(NO_3)_2(aq) + 2NO(g) + 4H_2O$$

Convert mass quantities to moles:
12 grams of copper is $12g/63.546$ g mol^{-1} = 0.189 mole.

Notice how the units cancel to give moles of NO.

The stoichiometric factor (mole ratio) is 2 mol NO/3 mol Cu.
2 moles NO are produced for every 3 moles copper used.
So the NO produced = 0.189 mol Cu × (2 mol NO/3 mol Cu)
= 0.126 mol NO .

Convert back to mass:
0.126 mole of nitric oxide = 0.126 mole × 30.0 g mol^{-1} = 3.8 grams.

c. 60 grams of propane gas is burned in excess oxygen:

$$C_3H_8(g) \; + \; 5O_2(g) \; \rightarrow \; 3CO_2(g) \; + \; 4H_2O(l)$$

Convert mass quantities to moles:
60 grams of propane is 60g/44.097 g mol^{-1} = 1.36 moles.

The stoichiometric factor (mole ratio) is 4 mol H_2O/1 mol C_3H_8.
4 moles of water are produced for every mole of propane burned.
So the water produced   = 1.36 mol C_3H_8 × (4 mol H_2O/1 mol C_3H_8)
                 = 5.44 moles water.

Convert back to mass:
5.44 moles water = 5.44 mole × 18.015 g mol^{-1} = 98 grams.

Intermediate calculations should be done with sufficient precision to ensure no loss of information. The final answer should be quoted with no greater precision (in this case 2 significant figures) than the the initial data.

6. An alternative way to determine the limiting reactant in a reaction is to calculate the quantity of product each reactant can make. The reactant that produces the least product is the limiting reactant.

tables:	280 tables	→ 280 sets	
chairs:	1750 chairs	→ 291 sets	
bookshelves:	550 shelves	→ 275 sets	— limiting reactant
china cabinets:	300 cabinets	→ 300 sets	
sideboards:	325 sideboards	→ 325 sets	

The bookshelves are the limiting reactant; the amounts of other items left unused are:

tables:	280 − 275 = 5 remaining
chair sets:	1750 − (6 × 275) = 100 remaining
bookshelves:	all used; this is the limiting reactant; none left
china cabinets:	300 − 275 = 25 remaining
sideboards:	325 − 275 = 50 remaining

At $999 per set, the total sale is 275 × $999 = $274,725.

This procedure is essentially the same as dividing the number of moles of each reactant by its stoichiometric coefficient. The reactant with the lowest result is the limiting reactant. This is the reactant that can produce the least amount of product. For example:

1750 chairs × ($\frac{1\ set}{6\ chairs}$) = 291 sets

7. Hydrazine reacts with dinitrogen tetroxide according to the equation:

$$2N_2H_4(g) \; + \; N_2O_4(g) \; \rightarrow \; 3N_2(g) \; + \; 4H_2O(g)$$

Convert mass quantities to moles:
50.0 grams of hydrazine is 50.0g/32.045 g mol^{-1} = 1.56 moles.
100.0 grams of N_2O_4 is 100.0g/92.011 g mol^{-1} = 1.087 moles.
The limiting reactant is hydrazine (it is used up first).
The quantity of N_2 formed will depend upon the amount of N_2H_4 used.

The stoichiometric factor is (3 mol N_2/2 mol N_2H_4).
3 moles N_2 are produced for every 2 moles hydrazine used.
So the N_2 produced   = 1.56 moles hydrazine × (3N_2/2N_2H_4)
                = 2.34 moles N_2.

Convert back to mass:
   2.34 moles of nitrogen = 2.34 mol × 28.01 g mol^{-1} = 65.6 grams.

8. a. The mass of red $Ni(DMG)_2$ produced was 0.1343 gram.
        The number of moles = 0.1343 g/288.917 g mol^{-1} = 4.648 × 10^{-4} mole.

        The number of moles of nickel must be the same, therefore the mass of nickel = 4.648 × 10^{-4} mole × 58.693 g mol^{-1} = 0.02728 g.

    b. The %mass of nickel = (0.02728g/0.1324) × 100% = 20.61%

    c. The %mass expected = (58.693/284.887) × 100% = 20.60%

    d. In terms of moles, the gravimetric factor is 1:1. There is one mole of Ni in every mole of $[Ni(NH_3)_6](NO_3)_2$ and every mole of $Ni(DMG)_2$. What is useful in gravimetric analysis is to calculate a gravimetric factor in terms of mass, so that from a mass of $Ni(DMG)_2$ the mass of nickel can be calculated directly. The mass gravimetric factor in this case is simply the ratio of the molar masses of the nickel and the $Ni(DMG)_2$.

Molar mass of $[Ni(DMG)_2]$ is 288.917 g/mol.

Molar mass of Ni is 58.693 g/mol.

Molar mass of $[Ni(NH_3)_6](NO_3)_2$ is 284.887 g/mol.

9. Setting up a systematic table for the various steps is a useful way to keep track of the calculations:

	carbon	hydrogen	oxygen
mass in mg:	17.873 mg CO_2	7.316 mg H_2O	?
divide by molar masses to get mmol CO_2 & H_2O:	/44.010 = 0.406	/18.015 = 0.406	?
	0.406 mmol C	0.812 mmol H	?
multiply by molar masses to get masses of C and H:	4.876 mg C	0.818 mg H	1.622 mg O
back to mmol:	0.406 mmol C	0.812 mmol H	0.101 mmol O
convert to integers:	4C	8H	1O

The molar mass of carbon dioxide is 44.010 g/mol. The molar mass of water is 18.015 g/mol.

Sometimes it is more convenient to work in millimoles (mmol) rather than moles.

There are 2 moles of H in every mole of water.

The only reason to convert to mass is to calculate the mass of oxygen in the compound by difference. The mass of oxygen is the mass of the compound less the mass of carbon and the mass of hydrogen.

The empirical formula of the compound is C_4H_8O.

10. A similar problem:

	carbon	hydrogen	oxygen
mass in mg:	250.3 mg CO_2	102.5 mg H_2O	?
divide by molar masses to get mmol CO_2 & H_2O:	/44.010 = 5.69	/18.015 = 5.69	?
	5.69 mmol C	11.38 mmol H	?
multiply by molar masses to get masses of C and H:	68.31 mg C	11.47 mg H	30.32 mg O
back to mmol:	5.69 mmol C	11.38 mmol H	1.89 mmol O
convert to integers:	3C	6H	1O

The empirical formula of the compound is C_3H_6O. The empirical mass (the molar mass of this empirical formula) is 58 g mol^{-1}. This is one-half the experimentally determined molecular mass which means that there must be two empirical units in one molecular unit. The molecular formula of the compound is therefore $C_6H_{12}O_2$.

11. The reaction of hydrogen iodide and potassium bicarbonate:

$$HI + KHCO_3 \rightarrow KI + H_2O + CO_2$$

Convert mass quantities to moles:
32 grams of $KHCO_3$ is $32g/100.12$ g mol^{-1} = 0.320 mole.
48 grams of HI is $48g/127.9$ g mol^{-1} = 0.375 mole.
The potassium bicarbonate is the limiting reactant.

The stoichiometric factor (mole ratio) is 1 mol KI/1 mol $KHCO_3$.
One KI unit is produced for every $KHCO_3$ used.
So the number of moles KI produced = 0.320 mole.

Convert back to mass:
0.320 mole of KI = 0.320 mole × 166.0 g mol^{-1} = 53 grams.

12. The equation for the reaction is:

$$\text{boron-hydrogen compound} \rightarrow B_2O_3 + 2 H_2O$$

The mole ratio of H_2O to B_2O_3 stated in the question is 2 to 1—the number of moles of water formed is twice the number of moles of B_2O_3 formed. The ratio of B to H on the right side of the equation is 2:4, or 1:2. So the empirical formula of the boron-hydrogen compound must be the same, that is BH_2. The only answer that fits is B_6H_{12}.

13. Trinitrotoluene is prepared by treating toluene with nitric acid:

$$C_7H_8(l) + 3HNO_3(aq) \rightarrow C_7H_5(NO_2)_3(s) + 3H_2O(l)$$

Convert mass quantities to moles:
450 grams of toluene is $450g/92.14$ g mol^{-1} = 4.884 moles.
1000 grams of nitric acid is $1000g/63.013$ g mol^{-1} = 15.87 moles.
The toluene is the limiting reactant.

The stoichiometric factor (mole ratio) is 1 mol TNT/1 mol toluene.
One TNT molecule is produced for every toluene molecule used.
So the number of moles TNT produced = 4.884 moles.

Remember that the limiting reactant can be established by dividing the number of moles of each reactant by its stoichiometric coefficient. The reactant with the lowest result is the limiting reactant.

Convert back to mass:
4.884 moles of TNT = 4.884 moles × 227.1 g mol^{-1} = 1109 grams.

14. Sodium metal reacts vigorously with water:

$$2Na(s) + 2H_2O(l) \rightarrow 2NaOH(aq) + H_2(g)$$

Convert mass quantities to moles:
10 grams of sodium is $10g/23$ g mol^{-1} = 0.435 mole.
15 grams of water is $15g/18.02$ g mol^{-1} = 0.833 mole.
The sodium is the limiting reactant.

The stoichiometric factor (mole ratio) is 1 mol H_2/2 mol Na.
One hydrogen molecule is produced for every 2 atoms of sodium used.
So the number of moles H_2 produced = $(1H_2/2Na)$ × 0.435 mole.

Convert back to mass:
    0.217 mole of hydrogen = 0.217 mole × 2.016 g mol^{-1} = 0.44 gram.

15. Nitrous oxide reacts with oxygen to produce nitrogen dioxide according to the equation:

$$2N_2O(g) + 3O_2(g) \rightarrow 4NO_2(g)$$

Convert mass quantities to moles:
    42 grams of N_2O is 42g/44.01 g mol^{-1} = 0.954 mole.
    42 grams of O_2 is 42g/32.0 g mol^{-1} = 1.313 mole.
    The oxygen is the limiting reactant.

0.954 divided by 2 = 0.477
1.313 divided by 3 = 0.438

—so oxygen is the limiting reactant.

The stoichiometric factor (mole ratio) is 4 mol NO_2/3 mol O_2.
    The number of moles NO_2 produced = (4NO_2/3O_2) × 1.313 mol O_2.
                                                    = 1.75 mol NO_2.
Convert back to mass:
    1.75 mole of nitrogen dioxide = 1.75 mol × 46.0 g mol^{-1} = 81 grams.

16. Actual yield = 75 grams
    Theoretical yield = 81 grams
    Percent yield = (75 grams / 81 grams) × 100% = 93% yield of NO_2.

17. Actual yield = 3.0 grams
    Theoretical yield = 3.8 grams
    Percent yield = (3.0 grams / 3.8 grams) × 100% = 79% yield of NO.

CHAPTER 5

Introduction

Many reactions occur in solution, especially in water (aqueous) solution. In solution, the molecules and ions are free to move about and interact. So in this chapter we will examine aqueous solutions to understand the behavior of ions in solution, to understand why some salts dissolve and others don't, to classify the types of reactions that occur in solution, and to determine the quantitative mass relationships for these reactions.

Contents

Properties of Compounds in Aqueous Solution
Precipitation Reactions
Acids and Bases
Reactions of Acids and Bases
Gas-forming Reactions
Classifying Reactions in Aqueous Solution
Oxidation-Reduction Reactions
Measuring Concentrations of Compounds in Solution
pH, a Concentration Scale for Acids and Bases
Stoichiometry of Reactions in Aqueous Solution

Properties of Compounds in Aqueous Solution

A **solution** is a homogeneous mixture of two or more substances. The substance that determines the state of the solution is the **solvent**. The substance that dissolves in the solvent is called the **solute**. Solutions in which the solvent is water are called **aqueous solutions**.

When an ionic solid dissolves in water, the solid breaks up and the individual ions become surrounded by water molecules. Positive ions attract the negative (oxygen) end of the water molecule; negative ions attract the positive (hydrogen) end of the water molecule. This process is called **solvation**. The solvated ions are free to move about in solution—and carry an electrical current. Solutes whose solutions conduct electricity are called **electrolytes**.

Electrolytes are strong or weak. A **strong electrolyte** is essentially completely ionized in solution and is a good conductor of electricity. A **weak electrolyte** produces relatively few ions in solution and conducts poorly. Most molecules of a weak electrolyte remain molecules—only a few break up to form ions. Some solutes do not ionize at all—these are called **nonelectrolytes**.

Not all ionic compounds dissolve in water; the interaction between the ions in the solid is too strong to break. Some solubility rules offer guidelines for determining the solubility of a salt. For example, almost all salts of sodium, potassium,

Common salt NaCl is an example of a strong electrolyte. It dissociates almost completely in solution.

Acetic acid (in vinegar) is an example of a weak electrolyte. Only a few acetic acid molecules break up to form ions.

Sugar is an example of a non-electrolyte.

See study question #1.

Solubility Guidelines:

Soluble salts:

Almost all Na^+, K^+, & NH_4^+
All NO_3^-, ClO_3^-, ClO_4^-, & $CH_3CO_2^-$
All SO_4^{2-}
except Sr^{2+}, Ba^{2+}, Pb^{2+}
All F^-
except Mg^{2+}, Ca^{2+}, Sr^{2+}, Ba^{2+}, Pb^{2+}
All Cl^-, Br^-, & I^-
except Ag^+, Hg_2^{2+}, Pb^{2+}

Insoluble salts:

CO_3^{2-}, PO_4^{3-}, $C_2O_4^{2-}$, CrO_4^{2-}, S^{2-}
Almost all OH^- and O^{2-}

See study questions #2, 3, & 4.

The (aq) symbols are omitted to make the equation clearer; all ions are in solution.

When writing a detailed ionic equation, write all species in the form in which they predominantly exist in solution. Solids, gases, non and weak electrolytes should be written in the molecular form. Strong electrolytes should be written in the ionic form.

See study question #5.

The net-ionic equation is still balanced.

Strong acids:

hydrochloric acid HCl
nitric acid HNO_3
perchloric acid $HClO_4$
sulfuric acid H_2SO_4
also HBr, HI, and $HClO_3$

Polyprotic acids:

sulfuric acid H_2SO_4 (strong)
phosphoric acid H_3PO_4 (weak)
carbonic acid H_2CO_3 (weak)

Some weak acids:

acetic acid CH_3CO_2H
bisulfate ion HSO_4^-
carbonic acid H_2CO_3
formic acid HCO_2H
hydrocyanic acid HCN
hypochlorous acid HOCl
lactic acid $CH_3CH(OH)CO_2H$
nitrous acid HNO_2
phosphoric acid H_3PO_4

and ammonia are soluble and all nitrates, acetates, chlorates, and perchlorates are soluble. Most carbonates, sulfides, hydroxides, and chromates are insoluble.

Precipitation Reactions

A **precipitation reaction** produces a product that precipitates from solution—it is insoluble. Two reactants may well be soluble, but the combination of the cation of one with the anion of the other is insoluble. An example is the precipitation of silver chloride when solutions of silver nitrate and sodium chloride are mixed:

$$AgNO_3(aq) \; + \; NaCl(aq) \;\; \rightarrow \;\; AgCl(s) \; + \; NaNO_3(aq)$$

It is useful to write **net-ionic equations** for reactions in aqueous solution because these equations present the essential process. Consider, for example, the precipitation reaction above. The silver nitrate, sodium chloride, and sodium nitrate are all salts; they exist in solution completely ionized:

$$Ag^+ \; + \; NO_3^- \; + \; Na^+ \; + \; Cl^- \;\; \rightarrow \;\; AgCl(s) \; + \; Na^+ \; + \; NO_3^-$$

This type of equation is sometimes referred to as a **detailed ionic equation**. Notice that nothing happens to the sodium ion in this reaction; likewise, nothing happens to the nitrate ion. They are not involved in the reaction and are called **spectator ions**. If these spectator ions are cancelled from both sides, the net-ionic equation results:

$$Ag^+ \; + \; Cl^- \;\; \rightarrow \;\; AgCl(s)$$

The net ionic equation more clearly illustrates what is happening in the reaction. In this case, silver ions (from any soluble silver salt) combine with chloride ions (from any soluble chloride salt) to produce the insoluble silver chloride.

Acids and Bases

Acids and bases are two important classes of compounds. An **acid** is a substance that, when dissolved in water, increases the concentration of hydrogen ions $H^+(aq)$. For example, hydrochloric acid ionizes in water to produce hydrogen ions and chloride ions. This acid is a **strong acid** because it is completely ionized in solution:

$$HCl(aq) \;\; \rightarrow \;\; H^+(aq) \; + \; Cl^-(aq) \qquad \text{complete ionization}$$

An acid may produce more than one hydrogen ion per molecule, in which case it is called a **polyprotic acid**. An example is sulfuric acid (a diprotic acid):

$$H_2SO_4(aq) \;\; \rightarrow \;\; H^+(aq) \; + \; HSO_4^-(aq) \;\; \text{complete ionization}$$

$$HSO_4^-(aq) \;\; \rightarrow \;\; H^+(aq) \; + \; SO_4^{2-}(aq) \qquad \text{only partial ionization}$$

Loss of the first hydrogen ion is virtually complete. So sulfuric acid is classified as strong. The second hydrogen ion is more difficult to remove and the bisulfate ion is only partially ionized. The bisulfate ion is a **weak acid**.

A **base** is a substance that, when dissolved in water, increases the concentration of hydroxide ions $OH^-(aq)$. Hydroxides of the Group 1A and 2A metals are common **strong bases**. These bases dissociate completely in water to produce metal cations and the hydroxide anions:

$$NaOH(aq) \rightarrow Na^+(aq) + OH^-(aq)$$

Ammonia, NH_3, is a **weak base**. It ionizes very little in solution and produces relatively few hydroxide ions. Most ammonia in solution remains as NH_3:

$$NH_3(aq) + H_2O(l) \rightarrow NH_4^+(aq) + OH^-(aq)$$

Some nonmetal oxides dissolve in water to form acidic solutions. For example:

$$CO_2(g) + H_2O(l) \rightarrow H_2CO_3(aq) \qquad [\rightarrow H_3O^+(aq) + HCO_3^-(aq)]$$

$$SO_3(g) + H_2O(l) \rightarrow H_2SO_4(aq) \qquad [\rightarrow H_3O^+(aq) + HSO_4^-(aq)]$$

$$P_4O_{10}(s) + 6H_2O(l) \rightarrow 4H_3PO_4(aq) \quad [\rightarrow H_3O^+(aq) + H_2PO_4^-(aq)]$$

Some metal oxides, if they dissolve in water, form basic solutions. For example:

$$CaO(s) + H_2O(l) \rightarrow Ca(OH)_2(s) \rightarrow Ca^+(aq) + 2OH^-(aq)$$

Reactions of Acids and Bases

Acids react with bases to produce a salt and water. The reaction is called **neutralization**:

$$HCl(aq) + NaOH(aq) \rightarrow NaCl(aq) + H_2O(l)$$

The anion (Cl^-) of the salt comes from the acid, and the cation (Na^+) of the salt comes from the base. Both hydrochloric acid and sodium hydroxide are strong electrolytes so the detailed ionic equation for the neutralization reaction is:

$$H^+(aq) + Cl^-(aq) + Na^+(aq) + OH^-(aq) \rightarrow Na^+(aq) + Cl^-(aq) + H_2O(l)$$

When the spectator ions are deleted, the net ionic equation becomes:

$$H^+(aq) + OH^-(aq) \rightarrow H_2O(l)$$

This is the net ionic equation for the neutralization of any strong acid by any strong base. The only change when the acid or base is different is the salt that is formed in the reaction. Weak acids and weak bases also undergo neutralization reactions. The difference is that, being weak electrolytes, the acids or bases exist predominantly in the molecular form. For example, consider the reaction of ammonia (a weak base) with nitric acid (a strong acid):

$$HNO_3(aq) + NH_3(aq) \rightarrow NH_4NO_3(aq) \qquad \text{overall}$$

$$H^+(aq) + NO_3^-(aq) + NH_3(aq) \rightarrow NH_4^+(aq) + NO_3^-(aq) \qquad \text{detailed}$$

$$H^+(aq) + NH_3(aq) \rightarrow NH_4^+(aq) \qquad \text{net ionic}$$

Some common strong bases:

sodium hydroxide NaOH
potassium hydroxide KOH
calcium hydroxide $Ca(OH)_2$

although Group 2A hydroxides are only slightly soluble.

The common weak base:

ammonia NH_3

Notice that the hydrogen ion H^+ is often, and better, written as H_3O^+, the hydronium ion. This indicates that the H^+ has attached itself to a water molecule.

The nonmetal oxides that produce acidic solutions are called acidic oxides.

The metal oxides that produce basic solutions are called basic oxides.

Even though the solution at the end of the reaction may not be neutral.

Gas-forming Reactions

A carbonate or bicarbonate salt reacts with acid to produce carbon dioxide gas. Similarly, sulfite salts react with acid to produce sulfur dioxide gas. Other salts react similarly. For example, nitric acid reacts with magnesium carbonate:

$$2\ HNO_3(aq)\ +\ MgCO_3(s)\ \rightarrow\ Mg(NO_3)_2(aq)\ +\ H_2CO_3(aq)$$

$$\rightarrow\ Mg^+(aq)\ +\ NO_3^-(aq)\ +\ H_2O(l)\ +\ CO_2(g)$$

The reaction is driven by the formation of the weak electrolyte, carbonic acid, which decomposes rapidly to form carbon dioxide and water.

Classifying Reactions in Aqueous Solution

See study questions #6 & 9.

Chemical reactions in aqueous solution maybe described as exchange reactions. They can be summarized as follows:

Precipitation—the formation of an insoluble product
Acid-Base—the formation of water (and a salt)
Gas-forming—the formation of a gas
In each case a weak electrolyte or insoluble compound is formed.

A fourth reaction type is called **oxidation-reduction** or **redox** and involves electron transfer. These reactions are described in the next section.

Oxidation-Reduction Reactions

The production of metals from their ores was an art developed by ancient civilizations.

When iron rusts, it combines with oxygen to form iron(III) oxide. This is a process called **oxidation**. If a metal oxide or sulfide ore is heated with carbon, it is converted into the metal. In this case the metal is said to be **reduced**. These are examples of a huge class of reactions called oxidation and reduction reactions, or **redox reactions**.

The oxidizing agent is always reduced. The reducing agent is always oxidized.

In every redox reaction, some substance is oxidized and another substance is reduced. One cannot occur without the other. The substance that is reduced is by definition the substance that oxidizes the other—it is called the **oxidizing agent**. Likewise, the substance that is oxidized must reduce the other substance—it is called the **reducing agent**. For example, consider the reaction of iron(III) oxide with carbon monoxide:

$$Fe_2O_3(s)\ +\ 3CO(g)\ \rightarrow\ 2Fe(s)\ +\ 3CO_2(g)$$

The carbon monoxide is the reducing agent: it removes oxygen from the iron(III) oxide. It therefore must be oxidized—it is, to carbon dioxide. The iron(III) oxide is the oxidizing agent—it is responsible for oxidizing the carbon monoxide to carbon dioxide. It must be reduced, and it is, to iron metal.

However, not all redox reactions involve oxygen. What is common to all redox reactions is a transfer of electrons between substances:

Reduction—the addition of electron(s)
Oxidation—the removal or loss of electron(s)
Reducing agent—supplies electrons
Oxidizing agent—removes electrons

Two popular mnemonics:

OIL   oxidation is loss of electrons
RIG   reduction is gain of electrons

LEO   loss of electrons is oxidation
GER   gain of electrons is reduction

When a substance loses electrons (when it is oxidized), the positive charge on an atom of the substance increases. When a substance gains electrons (when it is reduced), the positive charge on an atom of the substance decreases (or the negative charge increases).

Consider the oxidation of magnesium by oxygen:

$$2Mg(s) \ + \ O_2(g) \ \rightarrow \ 2Mg^{2+} \ + \ 2O^{2-} \ \textit{(as } MgO \textit{ solid)}$$

The magnesium is oxidized; it loses two electrons.
The oxygen is reduced; it gains two electrons per atom.
The magnesium is the reducing agent; it supplies the electrons.
The oxygen is the oxidizing agent; it gains the electrons.

Recognition of a redox reaction is easier if oxidation numbers are assigned to the elements in the reactants and products. If there is a change in the oxidation number of an element, then the reaction is a redox reaction. The assignment of oxidation numbers is a very useful bookkeeping device. However, it is important to understand that the numbers do not represent (except for monatomic ions) the actual charges on the atoms. For example, the oxidation number of manganese in the permanganate ion MnO_4^- is +7—a number much higher than the actual charge on the manganese atom.

Common oxidizing agents include oxygen itself, the halogens, nitric acid, permanganate and dichromate, and other reactants in which an element is in a high oxidation state. Common reducing agents are hydrogen, the alkali and alkaline earth metals, and carbon.

Measuring Concentrations of Compounds in Solution

Most reactions done in the lab are reactions in solution. In solution the reactant molecules are able to move about and interact with one another. When dealing with solutions, it is often more convenient to measure volumes of solution rather than masses or moles of reactants. The relationship between the amount of solute and the volume of solution is the **concentration**. If the amount of solute is expressed in moles, the concentration is the **molarity**.

$$\text{Molarity} = \frac{\text{moles of solute}}{\text{liters of solution}}$$

If the molarity of a solution is known, then the number of moles of solute can be determined from the volume of solution.

$$\text{Number of moles of solute} = \text{molarity} \times \text{volume of solution}$$

When a salt dissolves in water, the salt dissociates into its separate ions. The concentration of the individual ions depends upon the stoichiometry of the salt. For example, if one mole of magnesium nitrate $Mg(NO_3)_2$ is dissolved in water to make 1 liter of solution, the concentration of magnesium ions is one molar (1M) but the concentration of the nitrate ions is 2 molar (2M). This is because one magnesium nitrate formula unit produces one magnesium ion but two nitrate ions.

Guidelines for determining oxidation numbers:

Any element by itself = zero.

Monatomic ions = the charge of the ion.

Fluorine = always -1 in its compounds.

Oxygen = -2 except when combined with F alone, and in peroxides -1, and superoxides -½.

Halogens = -1 except when combined with O or F.

Hydrogen = +1 when combined with nonmetals, -1 when combined with a metal in a binary compound.

Alkali metals = +1 always.

Alkaline earth metals = +2 always.

Sum of oxidation numbers in a polyatomic ion = the charge on the ion (zero for a molecule).

See study questions #7 & 8.

$$\text{Concentration} = \frac{\text{amnt of solute}}{\text{vol of solution}}$$

This is the second fundamental relationship in stoichiometry that you must know. The first, if you recall, was:

moles = mass/molar mass

This is the same equation rearranged.

See study questions #10 & 12.

Molar means moles per liter. The symbol M means moles per liter or mol/L.

The extent to which salts actually dissociate varies considerably. In dilute solutions of the alkali metal salts the dissociation is virtually 100%. However, in more concentrated solutions of the salts of divalent alkaline earth metals (and other metals), the association between ions can be quite high. For example, there are ions such as $MgCl^+$ in a solution of magnesium chloride.

To prepare a solution of a known concentration (molarity) the required quantity of solute is dissolved in sufficient water to make the required volume of solution. The two relationships are required:

$$\text{\# moles} = \text{molarity} \times \text{volume}$$
$$\text{mass} = \text{\# moles} \times \text{molar mass}$$

Another method used to prepare a solution of a known concentration is to dilute a more concentrated solution. The key to such dilution tasks is to realize that the number of moles of solute remains unchanged when water is added. Therefore the molarity of the dilute solution × its volume must equal the molarity of the concentrated solution × its volume:

See study question #11.

dilute solution		*concentrated solution*
molarity × volume	=	molarity × volume

pH, a Concentration Scale for Acids and Bases

Acids produce H^+ ions (hydronium ions H_3O^+) in solution. The concentration of the hydrogen ions depends upon the acid and its concentration but it lies typically within the range from 1 to 1×10^{-7} M. An example is vinegar with a hydrogen ion concentration equal to 1.6×10^{-3} M. Small values like these are conveniently expressed by the logarithmic **pH scale**.

See study question #13.

The pH is defined as $-\log_{10}[H^+]$.

Acids have pH values less than 7 at 25°C. The lower the pH the higher the H^+ concentration. The pH of basic solutions is greater than 7 at 25°C. The pH of a solution can be determined using an **indicator**. This is a compound like litmus or phenolphthalein that changes color as the pH changes. Alternatively a **pH meter** can be used.

Stoichiometry of Reactions in Aqueous Solution

The stoichiometry of a chemical reaction is described by the coefficients in the balanced equation. These coefficients represent the mole ratio of reactants required and products formed. Because the number of moles can be expressed as the molarity of a solution multiplied by the volume of solution, stoichiometric calculations can be done equally well using molarity and volume information. There is just one additional step added to the series of calculations described earlier.

See study questions 14 & 15.

When a solution of an acid reacts with a solution of a base in a neutralization reaction the experiment is called a **titration**. An unknown quantity of an acid, or an unknown quantity of a base, can be determined in a titration provided that all other variables are known. For example:

The actual relationship between the number of moles of acid and the number of moles of base is determined by the stoichiometry of the neutralization reaction. Often simply 1:1, the stoichiometry is, for example, 1:2 for a diprotic acid such as H_2SO_4 titrated against NaOH, or 2:1 for HCl titrated against $Mg(OH)_2$.

solution of acid		*solution of base*
number of moles of acid	=	number of moles of base
molarity × volume of acid	=	molarity × volume of base

See study question #16.

In a titration, when the number of hydrogen ions supplied by the acid exactly equals the number of hydroxide ions supplied by the base, the **equivalence point** has been reached. Experimentally the equivalence point is recognized by the use of a pH meter or an acid-base **indicator**. The precise concentration of the acid or base used in the titration is determined by a process called **standardization**. The standardization is usually another titration in which the acid or base is titrated against a **primary standard**—the amount of which is known very accurately.

The other major type of titration involves a redox reaction. These titrations are particularly convenient when one of the reactants changes color when it is oxidized or reduced. An example is the reaction of permanganate against oxalate in which the permanganate ion is reduced. The color of the permanganate solution is an intense purple and a very slight excess of permanganate at the equivalence point imparts a faint pink color to the solution.

The stoichiometry of redox reactions is often more complicated than acid-base reactions.

Review Questions

1.   Define solute, solvent, and solution.

2.   Classify solutes in terms of their ability to conduct electricity in aqueous solution.

3.   Summarize the guidelines for determining the solubility of a salt in water.

4.   Explain why some reactions lead to the formation of a precipitate.

5.   What is the difference between a detailed ionic equation and a net ionic equation?

6.   Why are net ionic equations useful?

7.   Describe what substances must be written in an ionic form, and which must be written in the molecular form, when writing a detailed ionic equation.

8.   What is a neutralization reaction? Does neutralization result in a neutral solution?

9.   Summarize the different types of reactions that can occur in aqueous solution. What drives these reactions to form the products?

10.   Define oxidation and reduction in terms of electron transfer.

11.   What is a reducing agent; what is a oxidizing agent?

12.   How could you predict whether or not a substance is a good oxidizing agent?

13.   How can you recognize whether a reaction is a redox reaction or not?

Key terms:

solution
solvent
solute
aqueous solution
electrolyte
nonelectrolyte
strong electrolyte
weak electrolyte
precipitation
detailed ionic equation
net ionic equation
spectator ion
strong acid
weak acid
polyprotic acid
strong base
weak base
acidic oxide
basic oxide
redox
oxidation
reduction
oxidizing agent
reducing agent
concentration
molarity
dilution
hydrogen ion
hydronium ion
pH scale
titration
equivalence point
indicator
pH meter
primary standard

14.   What is an oxidation number?

15.   What is the molarity of a solution and how is it calculated?

16.   How are the concentrations of individual ions in a solution of a salt related to the stoichiometry of the salt?

17.   Describe the process you would use to calculate the mass of solute required to make 5.0 liters of a 3.0 M solution.

18.   Describe how a solution of particular molarity can be prepared from a more concentrated solution.

19.   What is the pH scale? How is the pH of an aqueous solution calculated?

20.   Quantitative chemical analysis often involves volumetric titration. Describe two major kinds of titration.

21.   What is the equivalence point in a titration?

22.   Explain why calculations based upon an acid-base titration, or a redox titration, depend upon a knowledge of the stoichiometry of the reaction.

23.   What is a primary standard?

Answers to Review Questions

1.   The solute is the substance that dissolves in the solvent to make the solution. The solvent is the component of the solution that determines the state of the solution. The solution is a homogeneous mixture of two or more substances.

2.   A solute that dissolves to form ions in solution is called an electrolyte. The ions carry the electrical current through the solution. A high concentration of ions means that the solution can carry a high current. Solutes such as salts dissociate almost completely in solution and produce a high concentration of ions —they are strong electrolytes. Other solutes, like acetic acid, ionize only slightly in solution and conduct poorly —these solutes are weak electrolytes. Some solutes produce no ions at all when they dissolve. These solutions do not conduct an electrical current. The solutes are nonelectrolytes.

3.   Check the margin notes on page 62 of this study guide. You are not required to memorize these rules.

4. When a salt dissolves in water, it dissociates completely. Once the ions are released from the salt in the solution process, the origin of the ions is immaterial. Any combination of cation and anion that is insoluble will precipitate from solution. For example, silver nitrate and sodium chloride solutions lead to a precipitate of silver chloride when mixed. The net ionic reaction is the reaction between the silver ions and the chloride ions. The reaction of potassium chloride and silver acetate leads to exactly the same precipitate.

There is actually considerable association between ions in solution. We will assume that the dissociation is complete.

5. A detailed ionic equation is derived from the initial chemical equation by writing all the strong electrolytes in their ionic form. All strong acids, strong bases, and all salts are written as ions because that is the form in which they predominantly exist in solution. A net ionic equation is then derived from the detailed ionic equation by cancelling all the spectator ions from the two sides of the equation.

6. The net ionic equation is particularly useful because it represents exactly what happens in the solution. For example, the reaction of a strong acid with a strong base is always:

$$H^+(aq) \ + \ OH^-(aq) \ \rightarrow \ H_2O(l)$$

7. When writing a detailed ionic equation, all strong electrolytes (in other words, all strong acids, all strong bases, and all salts) are written in the ionic form. Other solutes are weak electrolytes (weak acids and weak bases) and these are written in the molecular form because this is the form in which they predominantly exist.

Other substances that are not in solution are also written in the molecular form (gases that bubble out of the solution) or as formula units (salts that precipitate out of the solution).

8. A neutralization reaction is the reaction of an acid with a base; the base neutralizes the acid and *vice versa*. However the process does not necessarily result in a neutral solution. For example the reaction of equimolar quantities of a weak acid and a strong base leads to a solution that is slightly basic.

9. **Precipitation**—the formation of an insoluble product.
   Acid-Base—the formation of water (and a salt).
   Gas-forming—the formation of a gas.
   Redox—oxidation and reduction.

   These reactions are all driven to completion because the products are thermodynamically more stable than the reactants—the reactions are product-favored.

10. Oxidation—the loss of electron(s).
    Reduction—the gain of electron(s).

11.   The reducing agent reduces some other reactant; it supplies electrons; and therefore is itself oxidized.
      The oxidizing agent oxidizes some other reactant; it removes electrons; and therefore is itself reduced.

12.   An oxidizing agent often contains an element in a high oxidation state (for example: $KMnO_4$ or $K_2Cr_2O_7$). It is a substance that is readily reduced; it readily accepts electrons (for example: F_2 or O_2).

13.   Look for a change in the oxidation number of any one of the reactants.

Oxidation numbers can be assigned following a set of simple rules; see the margin of page 65 in this study guide.

14.   The oxidation number is a number assigned to an atom in a compound in order to keep account of the movement of electrons in a chemical reaction.

15.   The molarity of a solution is a measure of the concentration of the solute in the solution. Specifically, the amount of solute is expressed in moles and the amount of solution is expressed in liters. The molarity is the number of moles of solute per liter of solution.

16.   When a salt dissolves it dissociates into ions. The concentrations of the ions produced depends upon how many ions are present in one formula unit of the salt. For example, when one mole of sodium chloride $NaCl$ dissolves, it produces one mole of sodium ions and one mole of chloride ions. However, when one mole of magnesium nitrate $Mg(NO_3)_2$ dissolves, it produces one mole of magnesium ions and two moles of nitrate ions. The concentration of nitrate ions is twice the concentration of magnesium ions.

17.   There are two relationships that you will use over and over again. The first relates the mass of a substance and the number of moles:

$$mass \ = \ \# \ moles \ \times \ molar \ mass$$

      The second relates the number of moles and the molarity and volume:

$$\# \ moles \ = \ molarity \ \times \ volume$$

      It is the number of moles that is common to both relationships and in all stoichiometric calculations it is the number of moles that is important. Always work in moles!

      For example, the number of moles in 5.0 liters of a 3.0 M solution
         = 5.0L × 3.0 moles/L = 15 moles.

      The mass of substance required
         = number of moles (15 moles) × molar mass of the substance.

18.   The key to all dilution problems like this is to realize that the number of moles of solute does not change in a dilution. Only additional solvent (water) is added to the solution:

> *dilute solution*   *concentrated solution*
> molarity × volume   =   molarity × volume

The volume of concentrated solution required equals the molarity x volume of the dilute solution divided by the molarity of the concentrated solution.

19.   The pH scale is a logarithmic expression of the hydrogen ion H^+ concentration. It is a convenient way of expressing such low concentrations. The pH is defined as $-\log_{10}[H^+]$. So, for example, a hydrogen ion concentration equal to 1.0×10^{-6} M is described as having a pH of 6.0.

20.   Quantitative chemical analysis can be achieved by the volumetric titration of two reactants when the equivalence point is characterized by an observable change in a physical property of the solution. This is very often a change in color monitored directly or through the use of an indicator, but it could, for example, be a change in conductivity. Two major types of titration are acid-base and oxidation-reduction.

21.   The equivalence point in an acid-base titration is reached when the number of moles of H^+ (from the acid) exactly equals the number of moles of OH^- (from the base). The equivalence point in a redox titration is reached when the reactants have been added in the quantities indicated by the redox equation—one reactant has been exactly consumed by the other.

22.   All stoichiometric calculations depend upon the mole ratio of reactants and products in a balanced equation. In an acid-base reaction, the balanced equation indicates the number of moles of acid and the number of moles of base required to reach the equivalence point. The same is true for a redox reaction.

23.   A primary standard is a pure substance used to standardize a solution of reactant (acid, base, oxidizing or reducing agent) that will be subsequently used in a titration. The amount and purity of the primary standard is known precisely. A primary standard frequently used in acid-base titrations is potassium hydrogen phthalate (KHP).

Study Questions and Problems

1.   Classify each of the following solutes as a strong electrolyte, weak electrolyte, or nonelectrolyte:

sugar
common salt (NaCl)
alcohol
acetic acid
potassium chloride
sodium bicarbonate

sodium hydroxide
hydrochloric acid
copper sulfate
carbonic acid
hydrocyanic acid
citric acid

A life spent making mistakes is not only more honorable but more useful than a life spent doing nothing.

George Bernard Shaw (1856–1950)

2.   Predict the solubility of the following salts:

        sodium sulfate   aluminum nitrate
        potassium chromate   barium sulfide
        silver bromide   ammonium acetate
        nickel(II) hydroxide   strontium iodide

3.   Write the ions that are produced when the following substances dissolve in
        water:

        $Mg(OH)_2$ $(NH_4)_3PO_4$
        K_2SO_4 $NaClO$
        $NaHCO_3$ $Ca(CH_3CO_2)_2$

4.   Predict whether or not the following reactions will lead to a precipitate. Write
        detailed and net ionic equations for all the reactions.

        a. potassium chromate and lead acetate
        b. silver perchlorate and ammonium chloride
        c. potassium carbonate and copper acetate
        d. sodium fluoride and magnesium iodide
        e. barium nitrate and potassium sulfate

5.   Write the overall chemical reaction, the detailed ionic equation, and the net
        ionic equation, for the following acid-base reactions:

        a. acetic acid and potassium hydroxide
        b. hydrocyanic acid and ammonia
        c. nitric acid and sodium hydroxide
        d. sulfuric acid and ammonia (1:1 mole ratio)
        e. carbonic acid and sodium hydroxide (1:2 mole ratio)

6.   Write equations for, and classify, the following reactions:

        a. nitric acid and cobalt(II) carbonate
        b. ammonia and acetic acid
        c. hydrochloric acid and calcium carbonate
        d. sodium hydroxide and nickel carbonate
        e. lead acetate and hydrochloric acid
        f. iron(III) nitrate and sodium hydroxide

7.   Assign oxidation numbers to the underlined atoms in the following com-
        pounds:

        a. $\underline{N}O_3{}^-$ g. $\underline{S}O_2$
        b. $\underline{Cl}F_3$ h. $K_2\underline{Cr}_2O_7$
        c. $NaH_2\underline{P}O_4$ i. $\underline{Cu}(NO_3)_2$
        d. $Na\underline{Cl}O_4$ j. $K_2\underline{S}_2O_3$
        e. $\underline{O}F_2$ k. $\underline{P}_4O_{10}$
        f. $Na_2\underline{C}_2O_4$ l. $Na\underline{Mn}O_4$

8. In the following reactions determine which element is oxidized, which element is reduced, which reactant is the reducing agent, and which reactant is the oxidizing agent:

   a. $N_2H_4(aq) + 2O_2(g) \rightarrow N_2(g) + 2H_2O(g)$

   b. $3Cu(s) + 8HNO_3(aq) \rightarrow 3Cu(NO_3)_2(aq) + 2NO(g) + H_2O(l)$

   c. $3Cl_2(g) + NaI(aq) + 3H_2O(l) \rightarrow 6HCl(aq) + NaIO_3(aq)$

9. Determine whether the following reactions are acid-base reactions or oxidation-reduction reactions:

   a. $2N_2O(g) + 3O_2(g) \rightarrow 4NO_2(g)$

   b. $2NO_2(g) + H_2O(l) \rightarrow HNO_2(aq) + HNO_3(aq)$

   c. $MgCO_3(s) + H_2SO_4(aq) \rightarrow MgSO_4(s) + H_2O(l) + CO_2(g)$

   d. $Cu(s) + CuCl_2(aq) + 2Cl^-(aq) \rightarrow 2[CuCl_2]^-(s)$

   e. $HNO_3(aq) + KOH(aq) \rightarrow KNO_3(aq) + H_2O(l)$

10. a. If 5.00 grams of sodium hydroxide is dissolved to make 600 mL of solution, what is its molarity?

    b. How much potassium chloride has to be dissolved in water to produce 2.0 liters of a 2.45 M solution.

    c. If 24.63 grams of magnesium chloride is dissolved to make exactly 3 liters of solution, calculate the concentrations of the ions in the solution (in moles/liter).

11. a. What is the molarity of the solution that results from adding 25 mL of a 0.15 M solution of sodium hydroxide to sufficient water to make 500 mL of solution?

    b. What volume of a 2.50 M solution of hydrochloric acid is required to prepare 2.0 liters of a 0.30 M solution?

12. When excess silver nitrate was added to a 25.0 mL sample of a solution of calcium chloride, 0.9256 gram of silver chloride precipitated. What is the concentration of the calcium chloride solution?

13. What is the pH of a solution with a hydrogen ion concentration $[H^+]$ equal to 5.6×10^{-4} M?

14. What volume of a 0.291 M solution of NaOH is required to reach the equivalence point in a titration against 25.0 mL of 0.350 M HCl?

15. KHP (potassium hydrogen phthalate $KHC_8H_4O_4$) is often used as a primary standard for sodium hydroxide standardization:

$$HC_8H_4O_4^-(aq) \ + \ OH^-(aq) \ \rightarrow \ C_8H_4O_4^{2-}(aq) \ + \ H_2O(l)$$

The molar mass of KHP is 204.224 g/mol.

If a 0.4856 gram sample of KHP is dissolved in sufficient water to prepare 250 mL of solution, and 25 mL of the solution requires 18.76 mL of sodium hydroxide solution to reach the equivalence point, what is the molarity of the sodium hydroxide?

16. How would you modify the relationship

number of moles of acid	=	number of moles of base
molarity × volume of acid	=	molarity × volume of base

if the acid is a diprotic acid such as sulfuric acid in the reaction:
$$H_2SO_4(aq) \ + \ 2NaOH(aq) \ \rightarrow \ Na_2SO_4(aq) \ + \ 2H_2O(l)$$

Answers to Study Questions and Problems

They teach in academies far too many things, and far too much that is useless.

Johann Wolfgang van Goethe (1749-1832)

1.
sugar	nonelectrolyte	
common salt (NaCl)	strong electrolyte	(salt)
alcohol	nonelectrolyte	
acetic acid	weak electrolyte	(weak acid)
potassium chloride	strong electrolyte	(salt)
sodium bicarbonate	strong electrolyte	(salt)
sodium hydroxide	strong electrolyte	(strong base)
hydrochloric acid	strong electrolyte	(strong acid)
copper sulfate	strong electrolyte	(salt)
carbonic acid	weak electrolyte	(weak acid)
hydrocyanic acid	weak electrolyte	(weak acid)
citric acid	weak electrolyte	(weak acid)

2.
sodium sulfate	soluble	alkali metal salt
potassium chromate	soluble	alkali metal salt
silver bromide	insoluble	one of the 3 exceptions
nickel(II) hydroxide	insoluble	metal hydroxide
aluminum nitrate	soluble	nitrate
barium sulfide	insoluble	metal sulfide
ammonium acetate	soluble	both NH_4^+ and $CH_3CO_2^-$ confer solubility
strontium iodide	soluble	almost all iodides are soluble

3.
$Mg(OH)_2$	→	1 Mg^{2+} and 2 OH^-
K_2SO_4	→	2 K^+ and 1 SO_4^{2-}
$NaHCO_3$	→	1 Na^+ and 1 HCO_3^-
$(NH_4)_3PO_4$	→	3 NH_4^+ and 1 PO_4^{3-}
$NaClO$	→	1 Na^+ and 1 ClO^-
$Ca(CH_3CO_2)_2$	→	1 Ca^{2+} and 2 $CH_3CO_2^-$

4.   a.   potassium chromate + lead acetate → insoluble lead chromate

$$K_2CrO_4 + Pb(CH_3CO_2)_2 \rightarrow PbCrO_4(s) + 2KCH_3CO_2$$

$$2K^+ + CrO_4^{2-} + Pb^{2+} + 2CH_3CO_2^- \rightarrow PbCrO_4(s) + 2K^+ + 2CH_3CO_2^-$$

$$CrO_4^{2-} + Pb^{2+} \rightarrow PbCrO_4(s)$$

The (aq) have been omitted to simplify the equations. Normally, all species dissolved in water would have the notation (aq).

  b.   silver perchlorate + ammonium chloride → insoluble silver chloride

$$AgClO_4 + NH_4Cl \rightarrow AgCl(s) + NH_4ClO_4$$

$$Ag^+ + ClO_4^- + NH_4^+ + Cl^- \rightarrow AgCl(s) + NH_4^+ + ClO_4^-$$

$$Ag^+ + Cl^- \rightarrow AgCl(s)$$

  c.   potassium carbonate + copper acetate → insoluble copper carbonate

$$K_2CO_3 + Cu(CH_3CO_2)_2 \rightarrow CuCO_3(s) + 2KCH_3CO_2$$

$$2K^+ + CO_3^{2-} + Cu^{2+} + 2CH_3CO_2^- \rightarrow CuCO_3(s) + 2K^+ + 2CH_3CO_2^-$$

$$CO_3^{2-} + Cu^{2+} \rightarrow CuCO_3(s)$$

  d.   sodium fluoride + magnesium iodide → insoluble magnesium fluoride

$$2NaF + MgI_2 \rightarrow MgF_2(s) + 2NaI$$

$$2Na^+ + 2F^- + Mg^{2+} + 2I^- \rightarrow MgF_2(s) + 2Na^+ + 2I^-$$

$$2F^- + Mg^{2+} \rightarrow MgF_2(s)$$

  e.   barium nitrate + potassium sulfate → insoluble barium sulfate

$$Ba(NO_3)_2 + K_2SO_4 \rightarrow BaSO_4(s) + 2KNO_3$$

$$Ba^{2+} + 2NO_3^- + 2K^+ + SO_4^{2-} \rightarrow BaSO_4(s) + 2K^+ + 2NO_3^-$$

$$Ba^{2+} + SO_4^{2-} \rightarrow BaSO_4(s)$$

5.   a.   acetic acid and potassium hydroxide:

$$CH_3CO_2H + KOH \rightarrow KCH_3CO_2 + H_2O$$

$$CH_3CO_2H + K^+ + OH^- \rightarrow K^+ + CH_3CO_2^- + H_2O$$

$$CH_3CO_2H + OH^- \rightarrow CH_3CO_2^- + H_2O$$

  b.   hydrocyanic acid and ammonia:

$$HCN + NH_3 \rightarrow NH_4CN$$

$$HCN + NH_3 \rightarrow NH_4^+ + CN^- \quad \text{(detailed; no change for the net)}$$

  c.   nitric acid and sodium hydroxide:

$$HNO_3 + NaOH \rightarrow NaNO_3 + H_2O$$

$$H^+ + NO_3^- + Na^+ + OH^- \rightarrow Na^+ + NO_3^- + H_2O$$

$$H^+ + OH^- \rightarrow H_2O \text{ (for any strong acid-strong base reaction)}$$

d. sulfuric acid and ammonia (1:1 mole ratio):

$$H_2SO_4 + NH_3 \rightarrow NH_4HSO_4$$

$$H^+ + HSO_4^- + NH_3 \rightarrow NH_4^+ + HSO_4^-$$

$$H^+ + NH_3 \rightarrow NH_4^+$$

e. carbonic acid and sodium hydroxide (1:2 mole ratio):

$$H_2CO_3 + 2NaOH \rightarrow Na_2CO_3 + 2H_2O$$

$$H_2CO_3 + 2Na+ + 2OH^- \rightarrow 2Na^+ + CO_3^{2-} + 2H_2O$$

$$H_2CO_3 + 2OH^- \rightarrow CO_3^{2-} + 2H_2O$$

6. a. nitric acid and cobalt(II) carbonate:

$$2HNO_3 + CoCO_3 \rightarrow Co(NO_3)_2 + H_2O + CO_2(g)$$

gas-forming reaction

b. ammonia and acetic acid:

$$CH_3CO_2H + NH_3 \rightarrow NH_4CH_3CO_2$$

acid-base reaction

c. hydrochloric acid and calcium carbonate:

$$2HCl + CaCO_3 \rightarrow CaCl_2 + H_2O + CO_2(g)$$

gas-forming reaction

d. sodium hydroxide and nickel carbonate:

$$2NaOH + NiCO_3(s) \rightarrow Ni(OH)_2(s) + Na_2CO_3$$

both nickel(II) carbonate and nickel(II) hydroxide are insoluble.

e lead acetate and hydrochloric acid:

$$Pb(CH_3CO_2)_2 + 2HCl \rightarrow 2CH_3CO_2H + PbCl_2(s)$$

precipitation; $PbCl_2$ is one of three common insoluble chlorides

f. iron(III) nitrate and sodium hydroxide:

$$Fe(NO_3)_3 + 3NaOH \rightarrow Fe(OH)_3(s) + 3NaNO_3$$

precipitation; $Fe(OH)_3$ is insoluble.

7.

a.	$\underline{N}O_3^-$	+5	g.	$\underline{S}O_2$	+4
b.	$\underline{Cl}F_3$	+3	h.	$K_2\underline{Cr}_2O_7$	+6 (each)
c.	$NaH_2\underline{P}O_4$	+5	i.	$\underline{Cu}(NO_3)_2$	+2
d.	$Na\underline{Cl}O_4$	+7	j.	$K_2\underline{S}_2O_3$	+2 (average)
e.	$O\underline{F}_2$	+2	k.	$\underline{P}_4O_{10}$	+5
f.	$Na_2\underline{C}_2O_4$	+3 (each)	l.	$Na\underline{Mn}O_4$	+7

8.   a. $N_2H_4(aq) + 2O_2(g) \rightarrow N_2(g) + 2H_2O(g)$

nitrogen: –2 in N_2H_4 to zero in N_2 loses electrons, is oxidized, is the reducing agent.

oxygen: zero in O_2 to –2 in H_2O gains electrons, is reduced, is the oxidizing agent.

    b. $3Cu(s) + 8HNO_3(aq) \rightarrow 3Cu(NO_3)_2(aq) + 2NO(g) + 4H_2O(l)$

copper: zero in Cu to +2 in $Cu(NO_3)_2$ loses electrons, is oxidized, is the reducing agent.

nitrogen: +5 in HNO_3 to +2 in NO   gains electrons, is reduced, is the oxidizing agent.

    c. $3Cl_2(g) + NaI(aq) + 3H_2O(l) \rightarrow 6HCl(aq) + NaIO_3(aq)$

chlorine: zero in Cl_2 to –1 in HCl   gains electrons, is reduced, is the oxidizing agent.

iodine: –1 in NaI to +5 in $NaIO_3$ loses electrons, is oxidized, is the reducing agent.

9.   a. $2N_2O(g) + 3O_2(g) \rightarrow 4NO_2(g)$
redox; observe the change in oxidation state of the O for example: in O_2 it is zero and in NO_2 it is –2.

    b. $2NO_2(g) + H_2O(l) \rightarrow HNO_2(aq) + HNO_3(aq)$
redox; a disproportionation reaction; observe the change in oxidation state of the nitrogen, it is both oxidized and reduced.

> This reaction could equally well be interpreted as an acid-base reaction. There is no net change in the oxidation state of the N and it is an example of an acidic oxide dissolving in water to produce an acid.

    c. $MgCO_3(s) + H_2SO_4(aq) \rightarrow MgSO_4(s) + H_2O(l) + CO_2(g)$
acid-base; no change in oxidation state.

    d. $Cu(s) + CuCl_2(aq) + 2Cl^-(aq) \rightarrow 2[CuCl_2]^-(s)$
redox; the copper metal is oxidized; the copper(II) is reduced.

> Sometimes referred to as a conproportionation reaction—the reverse of disproportionation.

    e. $HNO_3(aq) + KOH(aq) \rightarrow KNO_3(aq) + H_2O(l)$
acid-base; no change in oxidation state.

10.   a.   5.00 grams is 5.0/40 = 0.125 mol NaOH.
Molarity of the solution is 0.125 mol/0.600 liter = 0.208 M.

> Molar mass of NaOH = 40 g/mol.
> Molarity = moles/liter.
> Remember to convert mL to L.

    b.   Molarity × volume = #moles.
2.45 M × 2.0 liters = 4.90 moles.
4.90 moles × 74.55 g/mol = 365 grams.

    c.   24.63 grams of magnesium chloride = 24.63/95.21 = 0.259 mol.
The concentration of $MgCl_2$ = 0.259 mol/3 liters = 0.0862 mol/L.

> Molar mass of $MgCl_2$ = 95.21g/mol.

The concentration of Mg^{2+} ions must be the same, since there is one Mg^{2+} ion in every $MgCl_2$ formula unit.
However, the concentration of Cl^- ions must be twice this concentration, since each $MgCl_2$ formula unit produces two Cl^- ions.
The concentration of Cl^- ions = 0.172 mol/L.

11. a. In this dilution, 0.15 M × 25 mL must equal the unknown molarity × 500 mL.

So the unknown molarity is 0.0075 M (the solution is more dilute).

> Remember that in a dilution problem, the number of moles of solute does not change.

   b. This is the same kind of problem, in this case the unknown volume × 2.50 M hydrochloric acid must equal 2.0 liters × 0.30 M HCl.

So the unknown volume = 0.24 L or 240 mL.

12. 0.9256 gram of AgCl = 0.9256/143.32 = 0.006458 mol.

The number of moles of Cl^- ion is the same, since each AgCl formula unit contains one Cl^- ion.

However, one formula unit of calcium chloride $CaCl_2$ contains two Cl^- ions.

So the number of moles of calcium chloride $CaCl_2$ is one-half the number of moles of Cl^- ions = 0.003229 mol.

> The molar mass of AgCl = 143.32 g/mol.

This is the number of moles in 25 mL, or 0.025 L.

So the concentration of calcium chloride = 0.003229 mol/0.025 L = 0.129M (or 14.34 g/L).

> The molar mass of $CaCl_2$ = 110.98 g/mol.

13. pH = $-\log_{10}[H^+]$ = $-\log_{10}(5.6 \times 10^{-4})$ = 3.25.

14. This neutralization reaction has a 1:1 stoichiometry:

$$HCl(aq) \ + \ NaOH(aq) \ \rightarrow \ NaCl(aq) \ + \ H_2O(l)$$

The number of moles of NaOH must equal the number of moles of HCl at the equivalence point:

Volume of NaOH × 0.291 M NaOH = 25.0 mL HCl × 0.350 M HCl.

> Number of moles = volume × molarity.

So the volume of NaOH = (25.0 mL × 0.350 M)/0.291 M = 30.1 mL.

15. This neutralization reaction also has a 1:1 stoichiometry:

$$HC_8H_4O_4^-(aq) \ + \ OH^-(aq) \ \rightarrow \ C_8H_4O_4^{2-}(aq) \ + \ H_2O(l)$$

0.4856 gram of KHP = 0.4856 g/ 204.224 g/mol = 0.002378 mol.
This is the number of moles of KHP in 250 mL.

> The molar mass of KHP is 204.224 g/mol.

Therefore, the number of moles in 25 mL = 0.0002378 mol KHP.
This must also be the number of moles of sodium hydroxide in 18.76 mL (this is the result of the titration).
Therefore the concentration of NaOH = 0.0002378 mol/ 0.01876 liter.
Molarity of NaOH = 0.01268 M.

16. Each mole of acid requires two moles of base. The number of moles of base is therefore twice the number of moles of acid. Alternatively, if both solutions are of equal molarity, the volume of NaOH solution required is twice the volume of H_2SO_4 solution:

2 × number of moles of acid   =   number of moles of base
2 × molarity × volume of acid   =   molarity × volume of base

CHAPTER 6

Introduction

Why do some substances react whereas others do not? How can we predict if a reaction will happen? If it does happen, does it happen quickly? We begin to study these questions in this chapter.

Almost invariably, a chemical reaction either liberates or absorbs energy in the form of heat, light or electricity. In this chapter we will look at the energy liberated or absorbed in the form of heat. We will examine the relationship between heat and work as described by the first law of thermodynamics.

The relationship between temperature, heat, and specific heat capacity is explained.

Experimental methods for determining the heat released or absorbed in chemical reactions and physical processes—calorimetry—will be described.

Calculations of the energies involved in chemical reactions using Hess's Law and standard enthalpies of formation will be investigated.

Contents

Energy: Some Basic Principles
Specific Heat Capacity and Heat Transfer
Energy and Changes of State
The First Law of Thermodynamics
Enthalpy Changes for Chemical Reactions
Calorimetry
Hess's Law
Standard Enthalpies of Formation
Product- or Reactant-Favored Reactions and Thermochemistry
Energy Resources

Energy: Some Basic Principles

Energy is the capacity to do work; work requires energy, and work and energy have the same units. Energy can be classified as kinetic or potential energy.

Kinetic energy is the energy of movement; for example:

Thermal energy — random motion of molecules at the particulate level.
Mechanical energy — movement of a macroscopic object.
Electrical energy — movement of electrons through a conductor.
Sound energy — organized compression and expansion of the spaces between molecules.

Potential energy is the energy due to the position of an object. Potential energy is stored energy; it can be converted into kinetic energy. Examples of potential energy are:

Chemical energy — the energy of electrons and their positions relative to the nuclei.

Gravitational energy — due to position in a gravitational field.

Electrostatic energy — relative positions of positive & negative charges.

This is known as the First Law of Thermodynamics, or the Law of Conservation of Energy.

See study question #1.

Energy can neither be created nor destroyed; the energy of the universe is constant. Heat, work, and other forms of energy may be changed into one another but the total remains constant.

The entire **universe** can be divided into a system and its surroundings. The **system** is that part of the universe that is under examination; for example: a beaker on a hot plate, a balloon full of gas, an automobile engine, a house, or the planet earth. The **surroundings** are the rest of the universe—specifically that part of the universe that can exchange energy with the system.

An object may also possess kinetic energy by virtue of the macroscopic motion of the object as a whole. This energy can do work and the difference in the two kinetic energies is a way to distinguish between work and heat.

The kinetic energy of molecules (or other particulate matter) is called thermal energy. The thermal energy of a system is the sum of the kinetic energies of the individual particles (atoms or molecules) in the system.

Temperature is a measure of how hot an object (system) is. A knowledge of the temperatures of the system and surroundings allows a prediction of the direction of energy transfer between them—energy always transfers spontaneously from the hotter to the colder. Heat transfer will occur until both are at the same temperature and thermal equilibrium is reached.

Heating a system does not always increase the temperature of the system. An example is heating a block of ice, which remains at 0°C until the ice has all melted—the heat (energy) is used in breaking the bonds between the water molecules—an increase in the potential energy of the water molecules.

Two terms are used to describe the direction of heat transfer. In an **exothermic** process, heat is transferred from system to surroundings. In an **endothermic** process, heat is transferred from the surroundings to the system.

One calorie = 4.184 joules.
One dietary Calorie = 1000 cal.

See study question #2.

The unit of energy or work most commonly used by chemists is the **joule** J (or kilojoule kJ). This is the SI unit. An older unit is the **calorie** which is defined as the quantity of heat required to raise the temperature of 1 gram of water from 14.5 to 15.5°C.

Specific Heat Capacity and Heat Transfer

The heat transferred to or from an object when its temperature changes depends upon three things:

the quantity of material or mass of the object
the size of the temperature change
the identity or specific heat capacity of the material

The specific heat capacity is often called simply the specific heat.

This equation is often written:

$q = C \times m \times \Delta T$

Specific heat capacity refers to any homogeneous material — steel, wood, polystyrene, copper, etc.

See study questions #3, 4, & 5.

Heat (J) = specific heat capacity ($JK^{-1}g^{-1}$) × mass (g) × temp change (K)

The **specific heat capacity** is defined as the heat capacity per gram of material and has units of $JK^{-1}g^{-1}$. The specific heat capacity is therefore an intensive property.

The specific heat capacity can also be expressed per mole of material, in which case it is called the **molar heat capacity**.

The specific heat capacity of water is much larger than for most substances. The reason for this is related to the unusually strong bonds between water molecules in the liquid state which are gradually broken as more and more heat is added.

The temperature change, often represented as ΔT, is equal to $T_{final} - T_{initial}$. A positive ΔT means that the temperature of the system has increased and heat has been absorbed, i.e. q is also positive.

The bonds between water molecules are called hydrogen bonds. See page 172 in this study guide.

If a change takes place within an insulated system, then the sum of all heat changes within the system must equal zero. Another way of looking at this is to realize that any heat lost by one component within the insulated system must equal the heat gained by the other component within the system.

Both are statements of the first law of thermodynamics—energy is conserved.

See study question #6.

Energy and Changes of State

When a solid melts, the atoms, molecules, or ions that make up the solid have sufficient energy to loosen and break the bonds between themselves. A liquid is formed. When a liquid vaporizes, any attraction between the structural units becomes ineffective, the intermolecular bonds break completely, and a gas is formed. Both processes involve breaking bonds and both therefore require energy. The energy required to melt a substance is called the **heat of fusion**. The energy required to vaporize a liquid is called the **heat of vaporization**.

Fusion means melting.

See study questions #7, 8, & 9.

Note that these heats of fusion and vaporization can be expressed in units of Jg^{-1} or $Jmol^{-1}$ which are intensive quantities.

These **changes of state**, from solid to liquid, and from liquid to gas, occur at constant temperatures. For example, when ice melts at one atmosphere pressure, the temperature is 0°C and remains 0°C until all the ice has melted. Both heats of fusion and vaporization expressed in J are extensive properties.

Heat of fusion of ice
= 333J/g = 6.00 kJ/mol.

Heat of vaporization of water
= 2256 J/g = 40.65 kJ/mol.

The First Law of Thermodynamics

Thermodynamics is concerned with how **work** and **heat** are transferred between the system and its surroundings.

By definition, any work (w) done on, or heat (q) transferred into, the system (resulting in an increase in the energy of the system) is positive. Work done by the system or heat leaving the system is negative. The change in energy of the system is therefore:

This is one way to express the 1st law of thermodynamics.

See study question #10.

$$\Delta E = q + w$$

If there is no mechanical or electrical connection between the system and its surroundings, then no work can be exchanged between them. In this case, the change in the energy of the system equals the quantity of heat put into the system from the surroundings.

If the system does not change in volume and no work is done, w = zero and

$$\Delta E = q_v \text{ where the subscript v indicates constant volume.}$$

Mechanical work can be done, for example, if the system expands at constant pressure. In this case work is done by the system on the surroundings—ΔV is positive. The work is done by the system and is equal to the pressure multiplied by the change in volume. Because the system loses energy, the work is negative:

work = w = −PΔV

So ΔE = q + w = q − PΔV

or q_p = ΔE + PΔV, where the subscript p indicates constant pressure.

Most reactions occur under constant atmospheric pressure, so most heats of reaction measured in the laboratory are q_p rather than q_v. Because the quantity q_p (or ΔE + PΔV) is such a fundamental quantity (it is a state function), it is given its own name and symbol. It is called the **enthalpy change** ΔH.

Typically, a system is heated (and therefore gains energy q), and does some work on its surroundings (losing some energy w), resulting in an increase in energy of the system equal to q + w (where in this case q is positive and w is negative).

If a process requires energy (as heat) then the system will absorb heat as the process occurs. The enthalpy of the system will increase and ΔH will be positive. Such a process is called **endothermic**. If, on the other hand, a process releases energy, then ΔH is negative and the process is called **exothermic**.

A **state function** is a property of a system that does not depend upon how the state was arrived at. For example, temperature is a state function. If a system is at 25°C, it could have cooled down from 100°C or it could have warmed up from 0°C. Regardless of what the temperature has been, it is now 25°C.

Enthalpy is a state function. Because enthalpy is a state function, the enthalpy change in going from an initial state to a final state is always the same, regardless of the route taken.

Enthalpy Changes for Chemical Reactions

When reactants in a chemical reaction form products, the atoms rearrange, bonds are broken and new ones formed. The electrons are redistributed. The chemical potential energy of these electrons changes as the reactants form products. The difference in the energies of the reactants and products results in energy being absorbed (endothermic) or released (exothermic). For example, when hydrogen and oxygen combine to form water, a considerable amount of energy is released:

$$H_2(g) + 1/2 O_2(g) \rightarrow H_2O(l) + 241.8 \text{ kJ}$$

Energy is a product of the reaction. The amount of energy released is 241.8 kJ for every mole of water that is produced. The enthalpy change for the reaction is −241.8 kJ (exothermic) and the reaction is usually represented as:

$$H_2(g) + 1/2 O_2(g) \rightarrow H_2O(l) \qquad \Delta H = -241.8 \text{ kJ}$$

The negative sign for ΔH indicates that the heat is released. The reverse reaction, breaking up water to form hydrogen and oxygen, requires exactly the same quantity of energy. This process is endothermic:

$$H_2O(l) \rightarrow H_2(g) + 1/2 O_2(g) \qquad \Delta H = +241.8 \text{ kJ}$$

Where does the energy come from in an endothermic process? And where does it go? To answer the second question first, the process is endothermic because the potential energies of the electrons and nuclei of the product molecules are higher than their potential energies in the reactants. Energy is required to raise the potential

---

Using ΔH rather than ΔE avoids the necessity of figuring out what the change in volume is—which could be very difficult.

In processes involving little change in volume, ΔH and ΔE are very close in value.

Remember that if heat is transferred into the system, q is positive. If work is done on the system, w is positive.

See study question #11.

If ΔH is positive for a process in one direction, then ΔH is opposite in sign, but equal in magnitude, for the same process in the reverse direction.

Note that ΔH is an extensive property. The energy released or absorbed in a chemical reaction or physical process depends upon the quantities of matter involved.

See study question #12.

The positive sign is often omitted.

It's important to specify the states of the reactants and products.
More energy is released in this reaction when liquid water is produced than when water vapor is formed.

energies of these particles. There are two sources for this energy. The energy may come from the surroundings (the system could be heated for example). Or the energy could come from the system itself if the kinetic energy of the atoms and molecules in the system is reduced. In this case the temperature of the system decreases.

This is why water evaporating from your skin makes your skin feel cold. Evaporation is an endothermic process.

Calorimetry

The heat evolved or absorbed in a chemical reaction or physical process is determined by measuring a temperature change. The technique is called **calorimetry**, literally heat-measurement. The device in which the reaction takes place is called a calorimeter. If the heat capacity of the calorimeter and its contents is known, then the heat of reaction can be calculated from the temperature change:

$$\text{Heat (J)} = \text{heat capacity (JK}^{-1}) \times \text{temperature change (K)}$$

If the calorimeter is a constant volume calorimeter (a **bomb calorimeter**), then the heat equals ΔE, the change in the energy of the system. If the calorimeter and contents are under constant external pressure, then the heat equals ΔH, the change in enthalpy of the system.

The heat capacity depends upon the specific heats of all the substances involved. For a single substance, the heat capacity equals the specific heat × mass.

See study questions #13 & 14.

Hess's Law

If a reaction is the sum of two other reactions, then ΔH for the overall reaction is the sum of the two ΔH for the two constituent reactions. This is **Hess's law of constant heat summation**. In other words, ΔH is same regardless of the route from the starting point (the reactants) to the finishing point (the products).

Hess's law is useful because it allows you to calculate the enthalpy change for a reaction that might be difficult to determine experimentally.

Enthalpy is a state function.

There are two approaches to take in solving Hess's law problems. The first is the construction of an energy cycle, or energy level diagram, where two routes between the initial and final states are shown. The enthalpy change for each route must be the same, and setting them equal allows you to calculate the unknown enthalpy change. The second approach involves listing all the given equations so that when they are added together, the desired equation is produced. Adding the enthalpy changes therefore produces the desired ΔH.

See study questions #15 & 16.

It is important to remember that ΔH is an extensive property: If the stoichiometric coefficients are all doubled, the ΔH must also be doubled. If the reaction is reversed, the sign of ΔH must be reversed.

Standard Enthalpies of Formation

The **standard state** of a substance is the most stable state in which that substance exists at 25°C (usually) and a pressure of 1 bar. When a reaction occurs such that all reactants and products are in their standard states, the heat of reaction ΔH is called the **standard enthalpy change of reaction** $\Delta H°$, where the superscript ° indicates the standard conditions.

When one mole of a compound in its standard state is formed from its constituent elements all in their standard states, the heat of reaction is called the **standard**

1 bar is almost the same as 1 atm pressure.

1 bar = 0.98692 atm and 1 bar = 10^5 Pa exactly.

The enthalpy change for a reaction is commonly called the heat of reaction (at constant pressure).

$\Delta H_f°$ of an element = zero.

See www.nist.gov. for current values.

molar enthalpy of formation ΔH_f°. Since forming an element in its standard state from the same element in its standard state involves no change, the standard enthalpies of formation of all elements are zero.

Most ΔH_f° are negative; in other words, most compounds are formed in product-favored exothermic reactions. Some compounds however, such as acetylene C_2H_2 and hydrazine N_2H_2, have positive ΔH_f° values. Such compounds store considerable chemical potential energy, which is released when the compounds are broken down, and the compounds are therefore good fuels. Hydrazine, for example, is used as a rocket fuel.

Standard enthalpies of formation are known for many compounds. They are useful because the enthalpy change for any reaction can be calculated if the standard enthalpies of formation of the reactants and products are known.

$$\Delta H^\circ_{reaction} = \Sigma(\Delta H^\circ_f \text{ (products)} - \Delta H^\circ_f \text{ (reactants)})$$

This equation is simply another way of expressing the 1st law of thermodynamics. It can be derived using Hess's law.

Product- or Reactant-favored Reactions & Thermochemistry

When a reaction proceeds from reactants to products **spontaneously**, it is said to be **product-favored**. An example is the combination of hydrogen and oxygen to form water.

$$2H_2(g) + O_2(g) \rightarrow 2H_2O(l) \text{ Exothermic } \Delta H = -483.6 \text{ kJ}$$

The reverse reaction does not happen without some outside intervention. An example of such an intervention could be an electrical current passed through the water to break up the molecules to form hydrogen and oxygen—a process called electrolysis:

$$2H_2O(l) \rightarrow 2H_2(g) + O_2(g) \text{ This process is endothermic}$$

In many cases, product-favored reactions are exothermic, but by no means all. The fundamental reason why some reactions are product-favored and others are reactant-favored is the subject of the second law of thermodynamics.

Energy Resources

Thermodynamics is the science of the transfer of energy as heat and work. As such, it is relevant in the study of how energy is used in our economy.

Sources of energy include wood (biomass), fossil fuels (petroleum, coal, natural gas), hydroelectric, solar, geothermal, wind, ocean currents, and nuclear. Wood and fossil fuels contain chemical potential energy; a chemical reaction (combustion) releases this energy for use. This chemical potential energy derived originally from solar energy and was captured through photosynthesis. Wind, ocean currents, and hydroelectric sources all owe their potential and kinetic energies to the action of the sun. Solar energy can be transformed directly into electrical energy by photovoltaic cells.

Hydrogen gas is a clean fuel; the product of its combustion is water. A hydrogen economy, where the hydrogen is produced in artificial photosynthesis or electrolysis and used in a fuel cell, is very attractive. Combustion of hydrogen provides more

Energy is not used up (the energy of the universe is constant), but it is used. It is most useful when it does work.

Sources of energy in the US:

85% fossil fuels
    coal
    oil
    natural gas

8% nuclear fission

7% renewable
    hydroelectric
    biomass
    geothermal
    wind
    solar

energy per gram than any other fuel and the product, water, is benign.

Review Questions

1.   List and describe various forms of energy.

2.   What is the relation between power, energy, and time?

3.   Define the terms system and surroundings, and their relation to the entire universe.

4.   Which is the smaller unit, the calorie or the joule? How are they related?

5.   Define an exothermic and an endothermic process.

6.   Define specific heat capacity and molar heat capacity. What is heat capacity?

7.   Why does water have a high specific heat capacity? What does this mean?

8.   Define the heat of fusion and the heat of vaporization. What do these two quantities depend upon?

9.   Write different expressions for the 1st Law of Thermodynamics. How are they related?

10.   Define or describe heat and work.

11.   What is a state function?

12.   What is the enthalpy change for a process? How is it related to the change in the energy of a system? What is the purpose of using enthalpy rather than energy? When does the enthalpy change equal the energy change?

13.   Where does the energy come from in an endothermic process? And where does it go?

14.   What happens to ΔH for a reaction if the coefficients in the equation are all tripled.

15.   What does standard state mean?

16.   Define standard molar enthalpy of formation ΔH_f°. Why is the standard molar enthalpy of formation of an element equal to zero?

17.   Define the standard enthalpy change for a reaction ΔH°.

Key Terms:

thermodynamics
energy
kinetic energy
potential energy
chemical energy
system
surroundings
exothermic process
endothermic process
joule
calorie
specific heat capacity
molar heat capacity
heat of fusion
heat of vaporization
first law of thermodynamics
work
heat
internal energy
enthalpy
state function
calorimetry
Hess's law
standard state
enthalpy of formation
enthalpy of combustion
product-favored reaction
hydrogen economy

18. Derive diagrammatically, or by using Hess's law, the expression for the standard enthalpy change for a reaction in terms of the standard molar enthalpies of formation of the reactants and products.

19. Define a spontaneous reaction. How can you tell whether a reaction is spontaneous?

20. Which reactions studied in Chapter 5 of this study guide are "product-favored"?

Answers to Review Questions

1. Some examples of kinetic energy are: thermal, mechanical, electrical, and sound. Examples of potential energy include chemical, gravitational, and electrostatic.

2. Power is the rate at which energy is used (work is done). Power = work/time. The SI unit for power is the watt W which is defined as Js^{-1}.

3. The system is any part of the universe that is chosen for study. It could for example be a flask on a hot plate, a calorimeter, or the planet earth. The surroundings is the rest of the universe, specifically that part of the universe that can exchange energy with the system.

4. The joule is smaller than the calorie: one calorie = 4.184 joules.

5. An exothermic process is a process that liberates energy. An endothermic process is one which requires or absorbs energy.

6. The specific heat capacity is defined as the heat capacity per gram of any homogeneous matter. The units of specific heat capacity are $JK^{-1}g^{-1}$.
The molar heat capacity is defined as the heat capacity expressed per mole of substance. The units are $JK^{-1}mol^{-1}$.
The heat capacity is the relationship between the heat gained by an object and the temperature change that results. The higher the heat capacity, the more heat is required for a particular change in temperature. The units are JK^{-1}. The heat capacity of an object depends upon the masses and specific heat capacities of the materials from which it is made.

7. The specific heat capacity of water is much larger than for most substances because of the unusually strong bonds between the water molecules. These intermolecular bonds are progressively broken as more and more heat is added. What this means is that a considerable quantity of heat is required to heat water and a considerable amount of heat must be transferred out of the water before it cools down appreciably.

8. The heat of fusion is the quantity of heat required to melt a certain quantity of a substance. The heat of vaporization is similarly the heat required to vaporize a certain quantity of a substance. The heat required is extensive and therefore heats are normally expressed as quantities per gram or per mole. Both quantities depend upon the strength of the bonds between the structural units in the solid or liquid.

9. Some expressions for the 1st law are:

$$\Delta E = q + w \qquad \text{where } \Delta E \text{ refers to the system}$$

$$q_{in} = q_{out} \qquad \text{heat gained} = \text{heat lost}$$

$$\Delta E = zero \qquad \text{where } \Delta E \text{ refers in this case to the entire universe}$$

$$\Delta H^\circ_{reaction} = \Sigma(\Delta H^\circ_f \text{ (products)} - \Delta H^\circ_f \text{ (reactants)})$$

All these expressions represent an energy balance, reflecting the fact that energy can neither be created nor destroyed.

10. Heat, or thermal energy, is a chaotic or incoherent motion of particles at the atomic and molecular level. The hotter a substance, the more vigorous is the motion of the particles. Work is the result of a concerted or coherent movement of particles—for example, a wind blowing can do work by rotating a windmill regardless of the temperature (or thermal energy) of the air.

11. A state function is a property of a system whose value depends only upon the present state of the system and not upon how the system arrived at that state.

12. Enthalpy can be interpreted literally as the "heat within". If the enthalpy of a system decreases, then it loses heat. If the enthalpy increases, then it gains heat. In these instances, the heat refers to the heat released or absorbed at constant external pressure q_p. The energy of a system changes if either heat leaves or enters the system or work is done by or on the system.
Enthalpy is a useful concept because it incorporates any work done when the system changes volume at constant pressure. The relation between the energy change ΔE and the enthalpy change ΔH is $\Delta H = \Delta E + P\Delta V$. The enthalpy change equals the energy change when there is no change in volume.

13. In an endothermic process energy is required. There are two sources for this energy: the energy may come from the surroundings if the system is heated; or the energy could come from the system itself if the kinetic energy of the atoms and molecules in the system is reduced. In this case the temperature of the system decreases. In an exothermic process the reverse is true: the system invariably gets hot and/or the system may liberate energy. There will be movement of energy between the system and its surroundings unless the system is isolated (well-insulated).

14.   The enthalpy change for a reaction is a characteristic of that reaction, and as such, is constant under the prescribed conditions. The reaction is represented by an equation, and the ΔH is listed for the equation as it is written, where the stoichiometric coefficients represent moles of reactants and products. If these coefficients are tripled, then the value listed for ΔH must also be tripled.

15.   The standard state of a substance is the most stable form of that substance at a pressure of 1 bar and a specified temperature (usually 25°C).

16.   The standard molar enthalpy of formation of a substance is the enthalpy change for a reaction in which one mole of the substance in its standard state is made from its constituent elements in their standard states. For a substance that is an element, such a reaction represents no change, and therefore the enthalpy change must be zero.

17.   The standard molar enthalpy of reaction is the enthalpy change for the reaction in which all reactants and products are in their standard states.

18.   For the constituent elements of the reactants   →   the reactants
        $\Delta H° = \Delta H_f°$ (reactants), for the reverse reaction $\Delta H° = - \Delta H_f°$ (reactants)
        For the same set of constituent elements   →   the products
        $\Delta H° = \Delta H_f°$ (products)
        According to Hess's law, the $\Delta H°$ for the reaction is independent of the route:

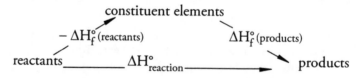

        Therefore, $\Delta H°_{reaction} = \Delta H°_f$ (products) $- \Delta H_f°$ (reactants)

19.   A spontaneous reaction is a reaction that happens by itself. It may happen quickly or slowly but it does happen. Calculations in thermodynamics can be done to determine whether or not a reaction is spontaneous. However, if a process or reaction does happen by itself, you can be sure that it is spontaneous.

20.   Reactions discussed in Chapter 5 of this study guide that are product-favored are:
                precipitate-forming reactions.
                gas-forming reactions.
                reactions in which a weak electrolyte is formed.
                reduction-oxidation reactions.

Study Questions and Problems

If you can measure that of which you speak, and you can express it by a number, you know something about your subject; but if you cannot measure it, your knowledge is meager and unsatisfactory.

*Lord Kelvin
(1824-1907)*

1.   What transfer of energy takes place when

     a.   A saucepan of water is heated to boiling
     b.   A tennis ball bounces to rest on the floor
     c.   Two automobiles collide head on
     d.   A flashlight is left on until the battery runs down
     e.   A fire burns
     f.   A wind turbine generates electricity
     g.   A chemical reaction liberates heat

2.   a.   Convert 800 kWh into J
     b.   Convert 377 kcal into J

3.   If the temperature of a 50.0 gram block of aluminum increases by 10.9 K when heated by 500 joules, calculate the
     a.   heat capacity of the aluminum block
     b.   molar heat capacity of aluminum
     c.   specific heat capacity of aluminum

4.   The specific heat capacity of gold is 0.128 $JK^{-1}g^{-1}$ and the specific heat capacity of iron is 0.451 $JK^{-1}g^{-1}$. Calculate the molar heat capacities of these two metals and compare to the value for aluminum calculated in question 3.

5.   Calculate the heat necessary to change the temperature of one kg of iron from 25°C to 1000°C. The specific heat capacity of iron is 0.451 $JK^{-1}g^{-1}$.

6.   If a 40 gram block of copper at 100°C is added to 100 grams of water at 25°C, calculate the final temperature assuming no heat is lost to the surroundings. The specific heat capacity of copper is 0.385 $JK^{-1}g^{-1}$ and the specific heat of water is 4.184 $JK^{-1}g^{-1}$.

7.   Calculate the amount of heat necessary to melt 27.0 grams of ice if the heat of fusion of ice is 6.009 kJ/mol.

8.   If 27.0 grams of ice at 0°C is added to 123 grams of water at 100°C in an insulated container, calculate the final temperature. Assume that the specific heat of water is 4.184 $JK^{-1}g^{-1}$.

9.   A 50 gram block of an unknown metal alloy at 100°C is dropped into an insulated flask containing approximately 200 grams of ice. It was determined that 10.5 grams of the ice melted. What is the specific heat capacity of the unknown alloy?

10. If a system absorbs 80 kJ of heat from the surroundings, and does 50 kJ of work as a result, what is the change in the internal energy of the system?

11. Which of the following properties of a system are state functions?

    enthalpy   volume
    temperature   heat
    internal energy   work
    time taken to increase the temperature of the system

12. If the enthalpy change for the combustion of propane is -2220 kJ/mol propane, what quantity of heat is released when 1.00 kg of propane is burned?

    $$C_3H_8(g) + 5O_2(g) \rightarrow 3CO_2(g) + 4H_2O(l) \qquad \Delta H = -2220 \text{ kJ}$$

    How much heat is released when 2.00 kg of propane is burned?

The enthalpy of solution is the heat released or absorbed when one mole of the solute dissolves in a great excess of water.

13. When 40 grams of ammonium nitrate is dissolved in 100 grams of water in a constant-pressure coffee-cup calorimeter, the temperature of the solution drops by 22.4°C. If the specific heat capacity of the solution is 4.18 $JK^{-1}g^{-1}$, calculate the enthalpy of solution of ammonium nitrate.

14. A 0.915 gram sample of sugar ($C_{12}H_{22}O_{11}$; molar mass 342 g/mol) was ignited in a bomb calorimeter in the presence of excess oxygen. Combustion was complete. The temperature of the calorimeter and its contents rose by 3.53°C. The heat capacity of the calorimeter and its contents is 4250 JK^{-1}. Calculate the heat released per mole of sugar.

15. Using the following thermochemical data, calculate the molar heat of combustion $\Delta H°$ of methane CH_4:

    $$CH_4(g) + 2O_2(g) \rightarrow CO_2(g) + 2H_2O(l) \qquad \Delta H° = ?$$
    $$2CH_4(g) + 3O_2(g) \rightarrow 2CO(g) + 4H_2O(l) \qquad \Delta H° = -1215 \text{ kJ}$$
    $$2C(s) + O_2(g) \rightarrow 2CO(g) \qquad \Delta H° = -221 \text{ kJ}$$
    $$C(s) + O_2(g) \rightarrow CO_2(g) \qquad \Delta H° = -394 \text{ kJ}$$

16. Calculate the standard molar enthalpy of formation of methane from the data given in question 15, your answer to question 15, and the following:

    $\Delta H_f°(H_2O(l)) = -286$ kJ/mol

17. When ammonia is oxidized to nitrogen dioxide and water, the quantity of heat released equals 349 kJ per mol of ammonia:

    $$2NH_3(g) + 7/2O_2(g) \rightarrow 2NO_2(g) + 3H_2O(l) \qquad \Delta H° = -698 \text{ kJ}$$

    Calculate the standard molar enthalpy of formation of ammonia if

    $\Delta H_f°(H_2O(l)) = -286$ kJ/mol

    $\Delta H_f°(NO_2(g)) = +33$ kJ/mol

Answers to Study Questions and Problems

If you can't stand the heat, get out of the kitchen.

Harry S. Truman
(1884–1972)
(but attr. by him to Harry Vaughan)

1. a. When a saucepan of water is heated, the heat derived from the burning gas or the electric hot plate causes the kinetic energy of the water molecules to increase. Therefore the temperature of the water increases. Some water molecules have sufficient energy to break the intermolecular bonds and enter the vapor phase—their potential energy increases. Eventually, the water exerts a pressure equal to that of the external atmospheric pressure and the water boils.

    b. The tennis ball starts with a high gravitational potential energy. When dropped, the potential energy is converted to kinetic energy. With each bounce on the floor some of the macroscopic kinetic energy of the ball is converted into microscopic thermal kinetic energy in the floor and the ball (both the floor and the ball get warmer).

    c. The kinetic energy of the two automobiles is converted into kinetic and thermal energy of the materials of which the cars are made. Some parts of the cars may temporarily gain some gravitational potential energy before returning to the ground.

    d. The chemical energy of the flashlight battery is converted to electrical energy. In the light bulb, the electrical energy is converted to light and heat. The light and heat energy is converted in turn to other forms of energy.

    e. The chemical potential energy of the fuel is converted to light and heat as the fire burns. Originally the fuel gained its chemical potential energy from the sun through photosynthesis.

    f. The macroscopic movement in the air is a concerted movement of all the molecules (not the random movement of thermal energy). This concerted movement can do work in driving a windmill or wind turbine. The mechanical energy of the windmill can then be converted into electricity or other forms of energy.

    g. Most chemical reactions liberate or absorb heat. Reactions that liberate heat are called exothermic; those that absorb heat are called endothermic. In exothermic reactions, the chemical potential energy of the system is converted into thermal energy of the system and its surroundings.

2. a. 800 kWh × 1000 W/kW × 60 min/1 h × 60 sec/1 min
          = 2.88×10^9 J

    b. 377 kcal × 1000 cal/1 kcal × 4.184J/1 cal
          = 1.58×10^6 J

Use dimensional analysis for problems like these.

3. a. heat capacity of the aluminum block = 500 J /10.9 K = 45.9 JK^{-1}

    b. molar heat capacity of aluminum
          = 45.9 JK^{-1} × 26.98 g mol^{-1}/50.0 g = 24.8 JK^{-1}mol^{-1}

    c. specific heat capacity of aluminum
          = 500 J/ (10.9K × 50.0 grams) = 0.917 JK^{-1}g^{-1}

4.   The molar heat capacity of gold = specific heat of gold × molar mass
                                        = 0.128 JK^{-1}g^{-1} × 196.97 g/mol
                                        = 25.2 JK^{-1}mol^{-1}
      The molar heat capacity of iron = specific heat of iron x molar mass
                                        = 0.451 JK^{-1}g^{-1} × 55.85 g/mol
                                        = 25.2 JK^{-1}mol^{-1}

The molar heat capacities of all metals at room temperature are approximately the same (theoretically = 3R = 24.9 JK^{-1}mol^{-1}).

This is known as the Law of Dulong and Petit. R is the gas constant = 8.314 JK^{-1}mol^{-1}.

Remember that for a temperature difference, K = °C.
1000 J = 1 kJ

Be very careful with the signs in problems like these!

If you state each heat as a positive quantity, then because the heat lost = heat gained, set the two equal and solve for T.

Alternatively, let the heat lost have its negative sign, the heat gained its positive sign, and then state that the sum of the two equals zero (energy must be conserved), and solve for T.

Notice that the temperature of the water does not increase very much; water has a very high specific heat capacity.

5.   Heat and temperature are related by:

Heat (J) = specific heat capacity (JK^{-1}g^{-1}) × mass (g) × temp change (K)

Heat (J) = 0.451 JK^{-1}g^{-1} × 1000 g × (1000-25) K = 440,000 J = 440 kJ

6.   Heat lost by the copper block:
Heat (J) = specific heat capacity (JK^{-1}g^{-1}) × mass (g) × temp change (K)

Heat (J) = 0.385 JK^{-1}g^{-1} × 40 g × (100–T) °C where T is the final temp.

Heat gained by the water:
Heat (J) = specific heat capacity (JK^{-1}g^{-1}) × mass (g) × temp change (K)

Heat (J) = 4.184 JK^{-1}g^{-1} × 100 g × (T–25) °C where T is the final temp.

The heat lost by the copper must be the same as the heat gained by the water:

1540 – 15.4 T = 418.4 T – 10460

433.8 T = 12000

T, the final temperature = 27.7°C.

7.   27.0 grams of ice = 27.0/18.016 moles of ice = 1.50 moles
      Heat required = 6.009 kJ mol^{-1} × 1.50 mol = 9.01 kJ.

8.   Heat is required to melt the ice at 0°C, *and* to heat the water produced from 0°C to the final temperature T.

The heat is provided by the 123 grams of water at 100°C which cools down to the same final temperature T.

The heat lost by the hot water must equal the heat needed to melt the ice and heat the water produced:

Heat required to melt the ice
        = 6.009 kJ mol^{-1} × 1.50 mol = 9014 J (*cf.* question 7)

Heat required to heat the water produced to the final temperature T
        = 4.184 JK^{-1}g^{-1} × 27.0 g × (T–0) °C.

Heat lost by the hot water
        = 4.184 JK^{-1}g^{-1} × 123 g × (100–T) °C

Therefore,

9014 + 113T = 51463 − 515T
T = 67.6°C

9. The quantity of heat required to melt 10.5 grams of ice
   = 10.5 g × 333 J g^{-1} = 3497 J

   For the metal alloy:

   Heat (J) = specific heat capacity (JK^{-1}g^{-1}) × mass (g) × temp change (K)

   3497 J = specific heat capacity (JK^{-1}g^{-1}) × 50 g × 100°C

   Therefore, specific heat capacity of the metal = 3497/(50 × 100) JK^{-1}g^{-1}

   = 0.70 JK^{-1}g^{-1}

   The metal block must be at a temperature of 0°C at the end of the experiment—not all the ice melted.

10. The system absorbs 80 kJ of heat from the surroundings, q = +80kJ
    The sytem does 50 kJ of work, w = −50 KJ
    Change in the internal energy of the system, ΔE = q + w = 80 − 50 = 30 kJ.

11. State functions are: enthalpy, volume, temperature, and internal energy. All these properties describe the current state of the system, regardless of how that state was reached. Heat, work, and the time taken for a temperature increase are not state functions. It is impossible to state that a system has so much work—it depends upon how the energy is used. Similarly, a system may be heated slowly or quickly to reach a particular temperature state—the time taken may vary and is therefore not a state function.

12. The enthalpy change for a chemical reaction is an extensive property—it depends upon the quantities of substances involved. A large fire generates more heat than a small fire. If the molar enthalpy of combustion of propane is −2220 kJ, this means that 2220 kJ of heat is generated for every mole (44 grams) of propane burned.

    The quantity of heat released when 1 kg propane is burned
    = 2220 kJ × 1000/44 = 50,000 kJ

    The quantity of heat released when 2 kg propane is burned is twice as much
    = 50,450 kJ × 2 = 101,000 kJ.

13. The mass of the solution = 100 g water + 40 grams ammonium nitrate.

    Heat (J) = specific heat capacity (JK^{-1}g^{-1}) × mass (g) × temp change (K)

    = 4.18 JK^{-1}g^{-1} × 140 g × 22.4°C = 13,108 J (for 40 grams)

    For one mole: Heat (J) = 13,108 × 80.04/40 = 26,230 J = 26 kJ/mol

    Molar mass of ammonium nitrate = 80.04 g/mol.

    ΔH°$_{solution}$ = +26 kJ/mol (an endothermic process)

14. Heat (J) = heat capacity (JK^{-1}) × temperature change (K)

    Heat (J) = 4250 JK^{-1} × 3.53°C = 15,000 J

    This is the heat released when 0.91 gram of sugar is burned. For one mole,

    Heat (J) = 15,000 J × (342 g/0.915 g) × (1 kJ/1000 J)= 5600 kJ.

ΔH° is extensive—whatever you do to the equation you must do to ΔH°.

Divide equation 1 by 2 since only one mole of CH₄ is required on the left side of the equation.

We need a CO on the left to cancel the CO on the right in the first equation, but only one, so reverse equation 2 and divide by 2.

We need a C on the left to cancel the C on the right in the second equation, equation 3.

15. Manipulate the data provided so that when the equations are added together, the desired equation is produced:

$$CH_4(g) + 3/2O_2(g) \rightarrow CO(g) + 2H_2O(l) \quad \Delta H° = -1215 \text{ kJ} /2$$
$$= -607.5 \text{ kJ}$$

$$CO(g) \rightarrow C(s) + 1/2 O_2(g) \quad \Delta H° = -221 \text{ kJ} \times -1 /2$$
$$= +110.5 \text{ kJ}$$

$$C(s) + O_2(g) \rightarrow CO_2(g) \quad \Delta H° = -394 \text{ kJ}$$

$$CH_4(g) + 2O_2(g) \rightarrow CO_2(g) + 2H_2O(l) \quad \Delta H° = -891 \text{ kJ}$$

16. The enthalpy of reaction can be calculated from the molar enthalpies of formation of the participants:

    $$\Delta H°_{reaction} = \Sigma(\Delta H°_f \text{(products)} - \Delta H°_f \text{(reactants)})$$

    $$CH_4(g) + 2O_2(g) \rightarrow CO_2(g) + 2H_2O(l) \quad \Delta H° = -891 \text{ kJ}$$

    $\Delta H°_f (H_2O(l))$ = −286 kJ/mol
    $\Delta H°_f (CO_2(g))$ = −394 kJ/mol (from the third equation in question 15)

Remember that "heat released" means that the process is exothermic, and that therefore ΔH is negative.

Oxygen is an element, and has a ΔH°f of zero.

Be careful with the signs!

$\Delta H°_{reaction}$ = $\Sigma(\Delta H°_f \text{(products)} - \Delta H°_f \text{(reactants)})$

−891 = $[(-394 + (2 \times -286)) - (\Delta H°_f \text{(methane)})]$

$\Delta H°_f$ (methane) = +891 −394 +(2 × −286)

= −75 kJ/mol

17. $$2NH_3(g) + 7/2O_2(g) \rightarrow 2NO_2(g) + 3H_2O(l) \quad \Delta H° = -698 \text{ kJ}$$

    $\Delta H°_f (H_2O(l))$ = −286 kJ/mol
    $\Delta H°_f (NO_2(g))$ = +33 kJ/mol

    $\Delta H°_{reaction}$ = $\Sigma(\Delta H°_f \text{(products)} - \Delta H°_f \text{(reactants)})$

    −698 = $[((2 \times +33) + (3 \times -286)) - (2 \times \Delta H°_f \text{(ammonia)})]$

    $\Delta H°_f$ (ammonia) = $[+698 +(2 \times +33) +(3 \times -286)]/2$

    = −47 kJ/mol

EXAMINATION 1

Introduction

This examination tests your knowledge and understanding of the chemistry in the first six chapters of this study guide. The questions are formatted as true–false questions and multiple choice questions—the sort you might encounter on your own examinations. Try the exam before looking at the answers provided at the end of this study guide.

True–false questions

1. All isotopes of an element have the same atomic number.

2. Iodine is a noble gas.

3. The number of atoms on both sides of a chemical equation is the same.

4. Heat capacity = specific heat capacity × mass.

5. A Celsius degree interval is equal in magnitude to a Kelvin degree interval.

6. The base SI unit for temperature is the °C.

7. If a reaction is exothermic in one direction, then it will be endothermic in the reverse direction.

8. The prefix milli– means $\times 10^{-3}$.

9. A compound must consist of two or more different elements.

10. Neon–22 has 12 neutrons in its nucleus.

11. An empirical formula for a compound indicates the simplest possible integer ratio of the elements in the compound.

12. Energy (in joules J) can be expressed as power (in watts W) × time (in seconds).

13. Volume, pressure, and temperature are all state functions.

14. Perchloric acid $HClO_4$ is a strong acid but chlorous acid $HClO_2$ is weak.

15. All molecules are compounds.

16. Solutions are always neutral at the end of a neutralization reaction.

17. $\Delta H_f^\circ (Br_2(g)) = \Delta H_{vaporization}^\circ (Br_2(l))$

18.   Molarity × volume = number of moles.

19.   Melting is always an endothermic process.

20.   The oxidizing agent in a redox reaction is always reduced.

21.   An exothermic reaction is always product-favored.

22.   When water boils, it decomposes into hydrogen and oxygen.

23.   Graphite and diamond are allotropes of carbon.

24.   Lead sulfate is an insoluble salt.

25.   Non-metal oxides produce acidic solutions when dissolved in water.

Multiple choice questions

1.   Which of the following processes represents a physical, not a chemical, change?

   a.   Sodium and chloride form sodium chloride
   b.   A balloon of hydrogen is ignited in air
   c.   Nitric acid acts upon copper to form a brown toxic gas
   d.   Gasoline is burned in an internal combustion engine
   e.   Steam condenses on a bathroom mirror
   f.   Baking soda reacts with vinegar to produce carbon dioxide

2.   If two atoms are atoms of the same element,

   a.   they must have the same mass numbers
   b.   they must contain the same number of neutrons
   c.   they must contain the same total number of subatomic particles
   d.   they must contain the same number of protons in the nucleus
   e.   the number of electrons must equal the number of protons
   f.   the mass number minus the atomic number must be the same for both

3.   Which one of the following formulas is *incorrect*?

   a. Li_2SO_3 lithium sulfite   d. NH_4NO_3 ammonium nitrate
   b. $BeBr_2$ beryllium bromide   e. Ca_3PO_4 calcium phosphate
   c. $NaOH$ sodium hydroxide   f. PF_5 phosphorus pentafluoride

4.   If there are exactly 2.54 cm in one inch, what is the area in cm^2 of a rectangle having sides of lengths 8.00 inches and 1.00 ft?

   a. $20.3 \ cm^2$ c. $244 \ cm^2$ e. $619 \ cm^2$
   b. $51.6 \ cm^2$ d. $77.4 \ cm^2$ f. $1570 \ cm^2$

5. Which of the following samples contains the same number of *atoms* as 40 grams of calcium?

    a. 40 g of anything   c. 38 g F_2 e. 18 g H_2O
    b. 2.0 g H_2 d. 19 g F_2 f. 48 g O_3

6. The molar mass of sodium sulfate is

    a. 119.06 g mol^{-1} c. 103.06 g mol^{-1} e. 215.13 g mol^{-1}
    b. 142.05 g mol^{-1} d. 126.05 g mol^{-1} f. 183.13 g mol^{-1}

7. Examples of a halogen, a transition metal, an alkaline earth metal, and a noble gas, are, in that order:

a. helium	copper	sodium	neon
b. nitrogen	chromium	magnesium	xenon
c. fluorine	magnesium	potassium	argon
d. neon	lithium	calcium	iodine
e. bromine	iron	beryllium	helium
f. chlorine	iron	lithium	neon

8. What is the average mass, in grams, of a single molecule of sulfur dioxide?

    a. 3.86×10^{25} c. 1.06×10^{-22} e. 1.66×10^{-24}
    b. 5.33×10^{-23} d. 6.02×10^{23} f. 3.76×10^{-25}

9. Which statement is correct?

    a. All atoms of an element are identical
    b. The base SI unit of mass is the gram
    c. A molecule always contains at least two different elements
    d. All molecules of the nonmetals are diatomic
    e. Mass divided by molar mass equals the number of moles
    f. Elements in the Periodic Table are arranged in order of increasing mass
    g. A mole of hydrogen molecules contains Avogadro's number of hydrogen atoms

10. Which one of the following is an extensive property?

    a. temperature   c. boiling point   e. color
    b. density   d. volume   f. molar mass

11. Copper exists in nature as a mixture of two isotopes. One isotope, with an abundance of 71%, has 34 neutrons. The atomic mass of copper (see the Periodic Table) is 63.55. What is the mass number of the other isotope of copper?

    a. 29   c. 34   e. 36   g. 65
    b. 31   d. 35   f. 63   h. 66

12. What is the percentage by mass of sulfur in the compound S_4N_4?

    a. 30.4%   c. 15.2%   e. 69.6%   g. 34.8%
    b. 41.6%   d. 57.8%   f. 72.3%   h. 81.8%

13. According to the equation: $COCl_2 + 4NaOH \rightarrow Na_2CO_3 + 2NaCl + 2H_2O$

    If 4.0 grams of sodium hydroxide is consumed in this reaction, what mass of water will be produced?

    a. 0.18 g   c. 0.45 g   e. 1.0 g   g. 9.0 g
    b. 0.36 g   d. 0.90 g   f. 2.0 g   h. 18 g

14. Ethanol has the molecular formula CH_3CH_2OH. What is the approximate mass of 6 moles of ethanol molecules?

    a. 7.7 grams   b. 46 grams   c. 276 grams   d. 23 grams   e. 138 grams

15. If 5 moles of boron atoms and 8 moles of hydrogen molecules are combined to form the maximum amount of diborane B_2H_6, how many moles of which reactant remain unused at the end?

    $$2\,B + 3\,H_2 \rightarrow B_2H_6$$

    a. 0.33 mol H_2 c. 0.5 mol B   e. 1 mol H_2
    b. 0.33 mol B   d. 0.5 mol H_2 f. 1 mol B

16. An oxide of phosphorus contains 56.36% oxygen, the remainder being phosphorus. Which of the following is a possible molecular formula for the compound?

    a. P_2O_4 c. P_2O_2 e. P_2O_3
    b. P_4O_{10} d. PO_3 f. P_3O_8

17. Acetic acid is ignited in the presence of oxygen and burns completely to produce carbon dioxide and water:

    $$\_\,CH_3CO_2H + \_\,O_2 \rightarrow \_\,CO_2 + \_\,H_2O$$

    When properly balanced, the equation indicates that _ moles of O_2 are required to burn 1 mole of acetic acid CH_3CO_2H.

    a. 1.0   c. 2.0   e. 3.0   g. 4.0   i. 5.0
    b. 1.5   d. 2.5   f. 3.5   h. 4.5   j. 6.0

18. Hydrazine and dinitrogen tetroxide can be used in combination as a rocket propellant. Products of the reaction are nitrogen and water. What coefficients are necessary to balance the equation for this reaction?

	$\_\,N_2H_4$	$\_\,N_2O_4$	$\_\,N_2$	$\_\,H_2O$
a.	1	1	1	2
b.	2	1	2	4
c.	2	2	4	2
d.	2	1	3	2
e.	2	1	3	4
f.	1	1	2	2

19. A sample of hydrated copper(II) sulfate, $CuSO_4 \cdot xH_2O$ weighs 5.29 g. When the water is driven off, the anhydrous $CuSO_4$ salt (molar mass 159.6) weighs 3.38 g. What is the value of x in the formula of the hydrated salt?

    a. 1   c. 2   e. 3
    b. 4   d. 5   f. 6

20. An unknown compound was analyzed and found to contain 26.7% carbon, 2.2% hydrogen, and 71.1% oxygen. In a separate experiment the molar mass was determined to be somewhere between 75 and 105 g/mol. What is a possible molecular formula of the unknown compound?

    a. $CH_3CH_2CH_2CO_2H$ c. $CH_2(CO_2H)_2$ e. C_6H_5OH
    b. C_4H_9CHO d. $(HO)CH_2CH_2CH_2CH_2(OH)$ f. $(CO_2H)_2$

The next three questions concern the following substances in aqueous solution:

    a. H_2SO_3 d. Na_3PO_4 g. KOH
    b. H_2CO_3 e. $FeCl_3$ h. HNO_3
    c. $NH_4CH_3CO_2$ f. $C_{12}H_{11}O_{22}$ (sugar)   i. $NaCl$

21. Which substance is a strong acid?

22. Which substance is a strong base?

23. Which substance is a nonelectrolyte?

For the next three questions, use the following key:

What are the oxidation numbers of the underlined elements in the following compounds?

    a. +1   c. +3   e. +5   g. +7   i. +14
    b. +2   d. +4   f. +6   h. +8   j. +16

24. $Al_2(\underline{S}O_4)_3$

25. $\underline{Kr}F_2$

26. $\underline{Cr}_2O_7{}^{2-}$

27. 1.5 moles of disodium hydrogen phosphate is dissolved in sufficient water to make 200 mL of solution. What is the molarity of the disodium hydrogen phosphate?

    a. 0.30 M   c. 1.50 M   e. 6.0 M   g. 9.0 M
    b. 0.50 M   d. 3.0 M   f. 7.5 M   h. 15.0 M

28. How many mL of the solution described in the previous question should be diluted to 1 liter to make a solution with a concentration of 0.15 M disodium hydrogen phosphate?

    a. 3.33 mL   c. 20.0 mL   e. 60 mL   g. 200 mL
    b. 16.7 mL   d. 33.3 mL   f. 167 mL   h. 333 mL

29.   A system absorbs 57 kJ of heat from its surroundings. As a result the system expands and does 32 kJ of
      work on the surroundings. What is the change in the internal energy ΔE of the system?

      a. +57 kJ   c. +32 kJ   e. +89 kJ   g. +25 kJ
      b. –57 kJ   d. –32 kJ   f. –89 kJ   h. –25 kJ

30.   Using the data given, calculate the enthalpy change for the reaction in which 56 grams of ethylene (C_2H_4)
      is hydrogenated to form ethane (C_2H_6).

$$C_2H_4(g) \; + \; H_2(g) \; \rightarrow \; C_2H_6(g)$$

      $2C(s) \; + \; 3H_2(g) \; \rightarrow \; C_2H_6(g)$ $\Delta H° \; = -84.7$ kJ
      $2C(s) \; + \; 2H_2(g) \; \rightarrow \; C_2H_4(g)$ $\Delta H° \; = +52.3$ kJ

      a. –137 kJ   c. –32.4 kJ   e. –274 kJ
      b. +137 kJ   d. +64.8 kJ   f. –64.8 kJ

31.   The molar heat of combustion ($\Delta H_{combustion}$) of methane (CH_4; natural gas) is 890 kJ mol^{-1}. Sufficient
      methane was burned to produce 9.0 grams of water. How much heat was released?

      a. 55.6 kJ   c. 222 kJ   e. 890 kJ   g. 3560 kJ
      b. 111 kJ   d. 445 kJ   f. 1780 kJ   h. 7120 kJ

32.   What is the net ionic equation representing the reaction between solutions of silver acetate and hydro-
      chloric acid to produce acetic acid and a precipitate of silver chloride?

      a. $AgCH_3CO_2(aq) \; + \; HCl(aq) \; \rightarrow \; AgCl(s) \; + \; CH_3CO_2H(aq)$

      b. $Ag^+(aq) \; + \; CH_3CO_2^-(aq) \; + \; H^+(aq) \; + \; Cl^-(aq) \; \rightarrow \; AgCl(s) \; + \; CH_3CO_2H(aq)$

      c. $Ag^+(aq) \; + \; CH_3CO_2^-(aq) \; + \; HCl(aq) \; \rightarrow \; AgCl(s) \; + \; CH_3CO_2H(aq)$

      d. $AgCH_3CO_2(aq) \; + \; Cl^-(aq) \; \rightarrow \; AgCl(s) \; + \; CH_3CO_2^-(aq)$

      e. $Ag^+(aq) \; + \; Cl^-(aq) \; \rightarrow \; AgCl(s)$

      f. $H^+(aq) \; + \; CH_3CO_2^-(aq) \; \rightarrow \; CH_3CO_2H(aq)$

33.   The specific heat of an unknown metal is 0.446 J K^{-1} g^{-1}. If the specific heat of all metals is 24.9 J K^{-1}
      mol^{-1}, what is the molar mass of the metal?

      a. 50.9   c. 52.0   e. 54.9   g. 55.8
      b. 10.8   d. 12.0   f. 101   h. 186

34.   If a 30 gram block of this unknown metal is heated from 20°C to 45°C, how much heat is required?

      a. 13.4 J   c. 602 J   e. 335 J   g. 3989 J
      b. 11.2 J   d. 268 J   f. 1682 J   h. 20 kJ

CHAPTER 7

Introduction

Chemical properties and reactions depend upon the arrangement and behavior of the electrons in atoms and molecules. In order to make some sense out of the thousands of reactions and structures of chemical compounds, it is essential to know something about the behavior of the electrons in atoms and molecules. In this chapter the electronic structure of atoms is examined.

Contents

Electromagnetic Radiation
Planck, Einstein, Energy, and Photons
Atomic Line Spectra and Niels Bohr
Wave Properties of the Electron
Wave Mechanical View of the Atom
Shapes of Atomic Orbitals
Atomic Orbitals and Chemistry

Electromagnetic Radiation

Radiation, such as microwaves, visible light, and x-rays, is called **electromagnetic radiation**. This radiation is composed of two mutually perpendicular oscillating electric and magnetic fields traveling through space. Waves are characterized by their frequency, wavelength, and velocity. The **frequency** is the rate at which complete waves pass a particular point. It has units of reciprocal time, s^{-1}, often referred to as hertz, Hz. The **wavelength**, as its name suggests, is the length of a complete wave—the distance between two closest corresponding points on the wave. It has units of length, m, cm, nm, etc. The frequency multiplied by the wavelength equals the **velocity** at which the wave is moving. The height of the wave above the axis of propagation is called the **amplitude**. A point of zero amplitude is called a **node**.

Electromagnetic waves are **traveling waves**. The speed of electromagnetic radiation depends upon the medium through which it passes; it is fastest through a vacuum.

Another type of wave motion is **stationary**. This is the type of wave motion seen in a vibrating violin string or on the surface of a drum. Only certain wavelengths are possible for stationary waves. The wavelength of a vibrating string, for example, has to satisfy the condition that a (the distance between the points at which the string is fastened) equals $n(\lambda/2)$, where n must be an integer (1, 2, 3, 4, 5...). A vibrating string is an example of a **quantized system**—only certain solutions, or energies, are allowed.

The symbols are:

frequency	ν	nu
wavelength	λ	lambda
velocity	v	

Do not confuse the greek ν and the v for velocity.

$$\nu \times \lambda = v$$
$$s^{-1} \quad m \quad ms^{-1}$$

The velocity of electromagnetic radiation in a vacuum is $2.998 \times 10^8\ ms^{-1}$.

Be able to calculate the frequency from the wavelength of electro-magnetic radiation and vice versa.

See study question #1.

A stationary wave is often referred to as a standing wave.

The two ends, where the string is fixed, are obvious points of zero motion. Sometimes these are included in the total number of nodes, sometimes not.

The electromagnetic spectrum is divided into different regions, some of which may be familiar to you. It is convenient to organize the regions by their wavelengths, each region differing by an approximate factor of 10^3:

These wavelengths are only approximate. For example, radio waves extend from 1 m all the way to 10^8 m. Microwaves from 10^{-3} m to 1 m and IR from 10^{-6} to 10^{-3} m.

Radiowaves	1 m
Microwaves	10^{-3} m
Visible	10^{-6} m
x-rays	10^{-9} m
γ-rays	10^{-12} m

You can remember these colors by their initials ROY G BIV.

The **visible spectrum** consists of the colors red, orange, yellow, green, blue, indigo, and violet, from low frequency to high frequency, or approximately 700 nm to 400 nm in wavelength. The infrared region is just beyond the long wavelength (low frequency) end of the visible region and the ultraviolet region is just beyond the short wavelength (high frequency) end of the visible region.

Planck, Einstein, Energy, and Photons

A white color indicates the presence of all visible wavelengths with intensities roughly symmetrical about the center.

Some atoms vibrate at high frequency and emit high frequency radiation; other vibrations are low frequency and emit low frequency radiation; most vibrations are somewhere in the middle.

The emission from a hot object depends upon the temperature of the object. As the temperature is increased, the color moves from the red end of the visible spectrum to the blue end. An object that is "white hot" is hotter than an object that is merely "red hot". A human body, at only 98.6°F, emits radiation only in the infrared region. Explanation of the radiation emitted by hot objects was a problem puzzling physicists at the end of the 19th century. The problem was solved by Max Planck in 1900. He knew that the atoms of the heated object vibrated and that it was this vibration that caused the emission. He suggested that the vibrations of the atoms were quantized—only specific frequencies of vibration were allowed. **Planck's equation**, one of the fundamental equations of **quantum mechanics**, relates the energy and frequency:

$$E = h\nu \qquad \text{where h is Planck's constant } 6.626 \times 10^{-34} \text{ J.s}$$

Planck suggested the idea that the vibrations of atoms in a heated object were quantized. Einstein suggested that the electromagnetic radiation itself was quantized.

When light strikes the surface of a metal, electrons may be emitted from the surface. These electrons are called photoelectrons and the phenomenon is called the **photoelectric effect**. The reason for this effect was not understood and could not be explained at all using classical physics. Einstein, in 1905, explained the effect using the idea that electromagnetic radiation was quantized.

Einstein suggested that light had particle-like properties. He said that these particles (light quanta, now called **photons**) possessed an energy proportional to the frequency of the light. The energy of the light is therefore proportional to the frequency and not the amplitude as classical physics would suggest. If light has a sufficiently high frequency, then the photons have a sufficiently high energy to cause the emission of an electron—one electron for each photon. Increasing the *frequency* of the light increases the kinetic energy of the photoelectrons. Increasing the *intensity* of the light increases the number of photons, and therefore increases the number of electrons (the current). This is how a photocell measures the intensity of light—by measuring the current.

Atomic Line Spectra and Niels Bohr

After atoms of an element in the gas state have been excited by a high voltage, the atoms return to their ground (lowest energy) state by emission of radiation. If the emission is in the visible region, the emission is colored. When the radiation is dispersed into individual wavelengths, it is seen to consist of lines at particular wavelengths, rather than a continuous (rainbow) spectrum. Every element has its own characteristic **line spectrum**.

Explanation of the existence of line spectra, rather than continuous spectra, puzzled physicists. An empirical mathematical expression was discovered by Balmer and Rydberg that could predict the wavelengths of the lines in the hydrogen spectrum, but why the lines existed was not understood.

Niels Bohr solved the problem by incorporating Planck and Einstein's ideas of the quantization of energy in the Rutherford model of the atom. Bohr suggested that the electron in the hydrogen atom could only occupy certain energy levels (or orbits)—the system was quantized. According to Bohr, the allowed energies of the electron in the hydrogen atom were restricted to $-Rhc/n^2$, where R is the Rydberg constant and n is a quantum number with integer values from 1 to infinity.

Dispersion can be accomplished through a prism or by diffraction.

The fact that each element has a unique spectrum is the basis for spectroscopic analysis.

The Rydberg equation is shown in the answer to review question #9.

$R = 1.097 \times 10^7 \text{ m}^{-1}$
$c = 2.998 \times 10^8 \text{ ms}^{-1}$
$h = 6.626 \times 10^{-34} \text{ Js.}$

Wave Properties of the Electron

Louis deBroglie, considering Einstein's assertion that light (electromagnetic radiation) could have particle-like properties, wondered whether particles could have wavelike properties. He derived his equation:

$$\text{wavelength } (\lambda) \times \text{ momentum } (mv) = h \text{ (Planck's constant)}$$

Wavelength (λ) is a wave property and momentum (mv) is a particle property. The equation relates the two and is another fundamental relationship of quantum mechanics—referred to as **wave-particle duality**. However, because h is so small, the wavelength is insignificant unless the particle (mass) is very small. In other words the wavelike properties of particles are unobservable unless the particle is as small as an electron or an atom.

Experimental proof of the wavelike properties of electrons was established by Davisson and Germer, and G. P. Thomson, through the diffraction of an electron beam by a thin metal sheet.

Wave Mechanical View of the Atom

A basic problem with Bohr's model for the behavior of an electron in an atom was a fundamental uncertainty in fixing both the position and momentum of the electron simultaneously. This is another principle determining the physics of small particles known as **Heisenberg's Uncertainty Principle**. In Bohr's model, the position (the orbit) and the momentum (angular momentum) of the electron are fixed and this is impossible. Electrons do not travel in fixed orbits.

The idea that small particles exhibited wavelike behavior prompted Schrödinger to write a **wave equation** to describe the behavior of the electron in a hydrogen atom. This wave equation was a 3-dimensional standing wave equation analogous to the equations for a vibrating violin string or a vibrating drum surface.

The solution of Schrödinger's wave equation yielded exactly the same energies as Bohr had obtained. The energy of the electron is quantized, just like the vibra-

This fundamental uncertainty comes about because in order to observe an object you have to use radiation with a wavelength comparable to the size of the object (that's why you cannot see objects smaller than about one μm using your eyes—no matter how good the microscope). So to observe an electron, the radiation wavelength would have to be very small, therefore the frequency would be very high, therefore the photon energy would be enormous, and the very act of observation would change the momentum of the electron. So you could use low frequency radiation and know the momentum but not the position, or use high frequency radiation and know the position but not the momentum. You cannot know both. The product of the two uncertainties is a function only of h.

What is a wavefunction?

It is a mathematical function that describes a wave. For example y = sin x is a wavefunction that describes a sine wave.

An orbit is a fixed path. An orbital is a region of space—an electron domain.

tions of a violin string are quantized. In addition, however, the solution yielded a **wavefunction** (φ) for each allowed energy level. The wavefunction is a description of the energy level. Although the wavefunction (φ) itself has no physical significance, the square of the wavefunction (φ^2) reflects the probability of finding the electron in any particular region of space around the nucleus—referred to as the **electron density**.

These patterns of electron density for each energy level are called **orbitals**. Just as the solutions to a one-dimensional standing wave equation for a violin string require one quantum number n, the solutions to Schrödinger's three dimensional wave equation require three quantum numbers n, ℓ, and m_ℓ.

The **principal quantum number** n indicates the energy of the orbital. As n increases, the electron is found on average further from the nucleus. The principal quantum n can have any integer value from 1, 2, 3, 4...to infinity. Electrons in an atom having the same value for n are said to be in the same **electron shell**.

The **secondary** (or **angular momentum**) **quantum number** ℓ indicates the shape of the orbital. It can have values from 0, 1, 2, 3, to a maximum of $n-1$. To avoid confusion, the value for ℓ is usually denoted by a letter, so that, if $\ell = 0$, the letter s is used, and the orbital is referred to as an s orbital. If $\ell = 1$, the letter p is used, and the orbital is referred to as a p orbital. If $\ell = 2$, the letter d is used, and the orbital is referred to as a d orbital. If $\ell = 3$, the letter f is used, and the orbital is referred to as an f orbital. Electrons in an atom having the same values for n and ℓ are said to be in the same **subshell**.

These letters have only historical significance. They are derived from descriptions of lines in emission spectra:

s   sharp
p   principal
d   diffuse
f   fundamental

The **magnetic quantum number** m_ℓ indicates a particular orbital within a subshell, it specifies the orientation of an orbital in the space around the nucleus. It can have integer values from $-\ell$ through 0 to $+\ell$. If $\ell = 0$, then the only possible value for m_ℓ is 0, and there is only one orientation. Therefore s orbitals come in sets of one only. If $\ell = 1$, then there are three possible values for m_ℓ: -1, 0, and $+1$. There are three possible orientations for p orbital (p_x, p_y, and p_z), and p orbitals always come in sets of three. Likewise d orbitals always come in sets of 5, f orbitals always in sets of 7, and so on.

If the three p orbitals are superimposed on each other, or the five d orbitals are superimposed on each other, a spherically symmetric electron density distribution (just like the single s orbital) results.

n = number of subshells in a shell.
2ℓ + 1 = number of orbitals in a subshell (orbital degeneracy).
n^2 = number of orbitals in a shell.

Shapes of Atomic Orbitals

The chemical properties of a substance are determined by its electrons—particularly those electrons on the outside of the atoms, highest in energy, or "at the frontier". These electrons in the highest shell (highest value of n) are called **valence electrons**. The orbitals containing the valence electrons are called **valence orbitals** and the shapes and orientations of these orbitals influence the properties.

All s orbitals are spherically symmetric. The electron density (the likelihood of finding the electron—as a particle—per unit volume) is a maximum at the nucleus and decreases further and further from the nucleus.

All p orbitals come in sets of three and all p orbitals have the same shape. The shape is like a sphere that has been cut into two. The plane running between the two halves is a plane on which the probability of finding the electron is zero; it is called a **nodal plane**. Because the nodal plane passes through the nucleus, the probability of an electron in a p orbital existing at the nucleus is zero.

All d orbitals come in sets of five, and all d orbitals in a set are energetically the same but differ in orientation. Each d orbital has two ($\ell = 2$) nodal surfaces. You will notice that one d orbital, the d_{z^2} orbital, is drawn with a different shape—the reason why is something to be left for a higher level chemistry course.

All f orbitals come in sets of seven and each has three ($\ell = 3$) nodal surfaces. The shapes of atomic orbitals get progressively more complicated as the values of n and ℓ increase.

You may one day, in a higher level chemistry course, solve Schrödinger's wave equation yourself. When you do, you will understand why the d_{z^2} orbital is drawn as it is.

Atomic Orbitals and Chemistry

Schrödinger's equation can only be solved for a single-electron system. However, the shapes of atomic orbitals for many-electron atoms are assumed to be similar. This permits an understanding of how atoms interact and bond together in molecules, and how the molecules react with one another. Chemistry is determined by the behavior of electrons.

Review Questions

Key terms:

electromagnetic radiation
frequency
wavelength
velocity
amplitude
node
stationary wave
visible spectrum
quantization
radiation from hot objects
photoelectric effect
photons
line spectrum
Rydberg equation
ground state
excited state
quantum mechanics
wave-particle duality
Heisenberg's uncertainty principle
Schrödinger's wave equation
wave function
atomic orbital
principal quantum number
secondary quantum number
magnetic quantum number
electron shell
subshell
nodal plane

1. Describe the electromagnetic spectrum. Describe the approximate wavelength range of the visible spectrum and list the colors of the spectrum in order of decreasing wavelength.

2. Define wavelength, frequency, velocity, and amplitude.

3. What is the relationship between frequency, wavelength, and velocity?

4. What is a node?

5. Two developments in physics took place in 1900 and 1905 that revolutionized our understanding of the interaction of matter and radiation. Describe these two developments.

6. When ν is the frequency of electromagnetic radiation, what is E in Planck's equation $E = h\nu$?

7. Why does an emission spectrum exist as lines rather than as a continuous rainbow?

8. Describe Niels Bohr's ideas about the behavior of electrons in atoms.

9. Derive the Rydberg-Balmer equation from Bohr's equation for the allowed energies for the electron in the hydrogen atom.

10. Why is Bohr's model for the behavior of an electron in an atom incorrect?

11. What information is derived from the solution of Schrödinger's wave equation in addition to the allowed energies of the electron?

12.   Describe the three quantum numbers that are used to characterize the solutions to Schrödinger's wave equation.

13.   What letters are used to signify the various values of the secondary (angular momentum) quantum number?

14.   Describe the physical significance of the three quantum numbers. In other words, what do the quantum numbers tell you about the orbitals?

15.   How do the values allowed for the three quantum numbers depend upon each other?

Answers to Review Questions

1.   The electromagnetic spectrum extends from 10^{-16} to 10^8 m in wavelength (corresponding to 10^{24} to 1 Hz in frequency). In decreasing wavelength the ranges are called: radio waves, microwaves, IR, visible, UV, X-rays, and γ rays. The wavelength range for the visible region is 700–400 nm (from red, orange, yellow, green, blue, indigo, to violet).

2.   The wavelength is the length of a complete wave—the distance between two closest identical points on the wave. The frequency is the rate at which complete waves pass a particular point. The frequency multiplied by the wavelength equals the velocity at which the wave is moving. The height of the wave above the axis of propagation is called the amplitude.

3.   Wavelength (λ) × frequency (ν) = velocity (ν).

4.   A node on a wave is a point at which the amplitude is zero. In the stationary vibration of a violin string it's where the string doesn't move up and down. In the wavefunction for an electron in a hydrogen atom, it's where the wavefunction changes sign and there is zero probability of finding the electron.

5.   The two developments involved black-body radiation and the photoelectric effect. The first describes the emission of radiation from a hot object. As the temperature is increased, the color changes from red to orange, to white, and then to bluish-white. Explanation of the emission was accomplished by Max Planck in 1900. He suggested that the vibrations of the atoms responsible for the emission were quantized—only vibrations of specific energies were allowed. Planck's equation relates the energy and frequency: $E = h\nu$.

When light strikes the surface of a metal, electrons may be emitted from the surface. This phenomenon is called the photoelectric effect. Einstein, in 1905, suggested that light had particle-like properties—in effect he said that electromagnetic radiation was quantized. He said that light quanta (photons) possessed an energy proportional to the frequency.

6. E, in Planck's equation E = hν, is the energy of one photon of electromagnetic radiation having a frequency ν. Multiply by Avogadro's number to obtain an energy in J/mol.

7. Only certain energies are allowed for an electron in an atom. As the electron moves from one energy level to another, it emits or absorbs radiation corresponding to the energy difference between the two levels: ΔE = hν. Each energy difference therefore has a characteristic frequency—a line in the spectrum.

8. Niels Bohr was the first person to incorporate the ideas of Planck and Einstein concerning the quantization of energy and radiation in a model for the behavior of electrons in atoms. He proposed that the electron could only exist in certain orbits at fixed energies which he established by imposing quantization on the angular momentum of the electron: mvr = $n(h/2\pi)$. He was able to derive Rydberg's empirical equation for the line spectrum of hydrogen.

9. The allowed energies for an electron in a hydrogen atom according to Niels Bohr were given by the equation: E = $-Rhc/n^2$ where R is the Rydberg constant equal to 1.097×10^7 m^{-1}. The difference between any two energy levels n_2 and n_1 is therefore:

$$\Delta E \ = \ h\nu \ = \ -Rhc/n_2^2 \ - \ Rhc/n_1^2 \ = \ Rhc(1/n_1{}^2 - \ 1/n_2^2)$$

10. According to Heisenberg's uncertainty principle, the position and momentum of a small particle like an electron cannot both be known at the same time. Although an electron in the lowest orbital of a hydrogen atom is most likely to be found at the radius calculated by Bohr, it can also be found nearer to, and farther from, the nucleus. The electron does not travel on a fixed path like a planet around the sun. All you can say is that there is a certain region of space somewhere around the nucleus in which it is probable you will find the electron. These regions of space are called orbitals.

11. The solution of Schrödinger's wave equation provides the allowed energies of the electron and wavefunctions which describe the behavior of the electrons in these energy levels. These wavefunctions are squared to obtain the probabilities of finding the electron at particular points or at certain distances from the nucleus.

12. The three quantum numbers that are used to characterize the solutions to Schrödinger's wave equation are the principal quantum number n, the secondary or angular momentum quantum number ℓ, and the magnetic quantum number m_ℓ.

13. If ℓ = 0, the letter s is used; if ℓ = 1, the letter p is used; if ℓ = 2, the letter d is used; and if ℓ = 3, the letter f is used.

14. The principal quantum number n indicates the energy of the orbital. As n increases, the electron is found on average further from the nucleus. The secondary (or angular momentum) quantum number ℓ indicates the shape of the orbital. The magnetic quantum number m_ℓ indicates the orientation of the orbital in the space around the nucleus.

The secondary quantum number ℓ can be related to the number of planar nodes (nodal surfaces) in the wavefunction.

15. The values allowed for the three quantum numbers depend upon each other. The principal quantum n can have any integer value from 1, 2, 3, 4...to infinity. The secondary (or angular momentum) quantum number ℓ can have values from 0, 1, 2, 3, to a maximum of $n-1$. The magnetic quantum number m_ℓ can have integer values from $-\ell$ through 0 to $+\ell$. The number of different values m_ℓ can have equals $2\ell+1$. This equals the number of orbitals within a set. For example, s orbitals come in sets of one only, p orbitals always come in sets of three, d orbitals always come in sets of five, and so on.

Study Questions and Problems

Natural science does not simply describe and explain nature, it is a part of the interplay between nature and ourselves.

Werner Heisenberg
(1901-1976)

1. a. Calculate the wavelength of electromagnetic radiation that has a frequency of 5.56 MHz.

    b. Calculate the frequency of electromagnetic radiation that has a wavelength equal to 667 nm.

2. Draw the first few stationary waves possible for a violin string fixed at ends 1 meter apart.

    a. What is the wavelength of the lowest frequency vibration?
    b. How many nodes (not including the ends) are there in the $n=5$ vibration?
    c. How many wavelengths fit within the boundaries in the $n=4$ vibration?
    d. At what points are the nodes in the $n=4$ vibration?
    e. What is the relationship between the frequency of the $n=2$ vibration and the $n=4$ vibration?

3. Electromagnetic radiation at the blue end of the visible spectrum has a wavelength of 400 nm.

    a. Calculate the frequency of the radiation.
    b. Calculate the energy of one photon of this radiation.
    c. Calculate the energy of one mole of photons of this radiation.

4. Examine the emission spectrum of hydrogen.

    a. How many lines appear in the visible region (Balmer series)?
    b. Why so few?

    The Lyman series occurs in the UV region.

c. How many lines would you expect in the Lyman series?

d. How many other series would you expect beyond the blue end of the visible spectrum?

e. How many different series would you expect beyond the red end of the visible spectrum?

5. Calculate the frequency of the line in the hydrogen spectrum corresponding to the electron transition from $n=9$ to $n=8$. Whereabouts in the electromagnetic spectrum does this line occur?

6. The first ionization energy of an element is the energy required to remove the most loosely held electron from atoms of the element in the gaseous state. It is usually expressed in units of kJ mol^{-1}.

   Given that R, the Rydberg constant, is 1.097×10^7 m^{-1}
   h, Planck's constant, is 6.626×10^{-34} J s
   c, the speed of light, is 2.998×10^8 m s^{-1}

   calculate from these data the ionization energy of hydrogen in kJ mol^{-1}. Compare the results of your calculation with the accepted value, 1312 kJ-mol^{-1}.

7. a. Calculate the wavelength of a neutron (mass 1.675×10^{-24} g) traveling at a speed equal to 1/1000th the speed of light.

   b. Calculate the wavelength of alpha (α) particles (emitted from a radioactive isotope) with a kinetic energy of 6.0×10^{11} J mol^{-1}.

8. Describe the electron density pattern for a
   a. 2s orbital
   b. 3p$_x$ orbital
   c. 3d$_{xy}$ orbital

9. Which statements are correct or incorrect? Explain why.

   a. If $m_\ell = 1$, the orbital must be a p orbital.
   b. If $n = 2$, only two orbitals are allowed, one s and one p.
   c. If $n = 3$, there are three different subshells.
   d. If $\ell = 3$, there are 3 possible values for the quantum number m_ℓ.
   e. If $m_\ell = 0$, the value of ℓ must equal 0.
   f. If $\ell = 2$, the subshell is referred to as a p subshell.
   g. If $n = 4$ and $\ell = 2$, only five orbitals are possible.

Answers to Study Questions and Problems

1. a. Wavelength (λ) × frequency (v) = velocity (v).
      The velocity of electromagnetic radiation is 2.998×10^8 m s^{-1}.
      So the wavelength (λ) is 2.998×10^8 m s^{-1} / 5.56×10^6 Hz = 53.9 m.

   b. Wavelength (λ) × frequency (v) = velocity (v).
      The frequency = 2.998×10^8 m s^{-1} / 6.67×10^{-7} m = 4.50×10^{14} Hz.

In effect, we have redefined the task of science to be the discovery of laws that will enable us to predict events up to the limits set by the Uncertainty Principle.

*Stephen W. Hawking
(1942-)
(A Brief History of Time 1988)*

2. a. Lowest frequency vibration; $n = 1$, where 1 meter = n(l/2). Wavelength = 2 meters
    b. Number of nodes = $n - 1 = 4$ (not including the fixed ends).
    c. Two complete wavelengths—three nodes.
    d. Equally spaced at 25 cm, 50 cm, and 75 cm.
    e. The frequency of the $n = 4$ vibration is twice the frequency of the $n = 2$ vibration (wavelength is inversely proportional to frequency).

3. Wavelength 400nm = 4.00×10^{-7} m
    a. frequency = 2.998×10^8 m s^{-1} / 4.00×10^{-7} m = 7.5×10^{14} s^{-1}
    b. energy = hv = 6.626×10^{-34} J s $\times$ 7.5×10^{14} s^{-1} = 5.0×10^{-19} J
    c. energy of one mole of photons
        = 5.0×10^{-19} J $\times$ 6.022×10^{23} photons/mol = 300 kJ/mol.

4. a. Four lines are visible in the Balmer series: red, green, blue, and violet.
    b. There are more lines—an infinite number in fact. The fifth line occurs at 397 nm which is just beyond the end of the visible region.
    c. An infinite number again, but the lines get closer and closer together toward the high energy end, becoming indistinguishable from one another.
    d. No others, only the Lyman series—corresponding to transitions down to the $n = 1$ energy level.
    e. An infinite number, but as the lines get closer, the series overlap and coalesce.

The five established series are: Lyman
(to n=1)   UV
Balmer (to n=2)   visible
Paschen (to n=3) IR
Brackett (to n=4) IR
Pfund (to n=5)   IR

5. Using the Rydberg equation:

    $\Delta E = hv = Rhc(1/n_1^2 - 1/n_2^2)$ where $n_1 = 8$ and $n_2 = 9$

    $\Delta E = hv = 2.179 \times 10^{-18} (1/64 - 1/81) = 7.146 \times 10^{-21}$

    Frequency $v = \Delta E/h = 1.08 \times 10^{13}$ s^{-1}
    This corresponds to a wavelength of 2.78×10^{-5} m; in the IR region.

6. The ionization energy of an element is the energy required to remove the most loosely held electron from atoms of the element in the gaseous state. Use the Rydberg equation, where $n_1 = 1$, but $n_2 = $ infinity (the electron is free).

    $\Delta E = Rhc(1/n_1^2 - 1/n_2^2)$ where $n_1 = 1$ and $n_2 = $ infinity.

    $\Delta E = Rhc(1 - 0) = Rhc = 2.179 \times 10^{-18}$ J/electron.

    $\Delta E = 2.179 \times 10^{-18}$ J/electron $\times$ 1kJ/1000J $\times$ 6.022×10^{23} mol^{-1}.

    $\Delta E = 1312$ kJ mol^{-1}.

1/infinity $\rightarrow$ zero.

R = 1.097×10^7 m^{-1}
c = 2.998×10^8 ms^{-1}
h = 6.626×10^{-34} Js.

Rhc = 2.179×10^{-18} J.

1/1000th speed of light
= 2.998×10^5 ms^{-1}

Mass of neutron
= 1.675×10^{-24} g
= 1.675×10^{-27} kg

7. a. $\lambda = h/mv$ = 6.626×10^{-34} Js/ 1.675×10^{-27} kg $\times$ 2.998×10^5 ms^{-1}
                = 1.32×10^{-12} m
                = 1.32 pm

b.   Mass of an α particle = 4.003 g/mol or $4.003/6.022 \times 10^{23}$ g/particle.

An α particle is a helium nucleus.

Kinetic energy is 1/2 mv², so the velocity
$$= [2 \times 6.0 \times 10^{11} \text{ J mol}^{-1}/ 4.003 \times 10^{-3} \text{ kg mol}^{-1}]^{1/2}$$
$$= 1.73 \times 10^7 \text{ ms}^{-1}$$

Using deBroglie's equation, $\lambda = h/mv =$

$$\frac{6.626 \times 10^{-34} \text{ Js}}{(4.003 \times 10^{-3} \text{ kg mol}^{-1}/ 6.022 \times 10^{23} \text{mol}^{-1}) \times 1.73 \times 10^7 \text{ ms}^{-1}}$$

J = kg m² s⁻²

Check that the units cancel correctly in this expression.

$$= 5.76 \times 10^{-15} \text{ m}$$
$$= 5.76 \text{ fm}$$

8. a. 2s orbital: spherically symmetric; no planar nodes

b. $3p_x$ orbital: an orbital with a planar node in the yz plane. Because n = 3, there is also a spherical node near the nucleus. The orbital lies along the x axis.

c. $3d_{xy}$ orbital: two planar nodes splitting the distribution into four lobes (a cloverleaf shape). The orbital lies in the xy plane.

9. a. Incorrect: if $m_\ell = 1$, the orbital could be a p orbital but it could also be a d or f orbital. It cannot be an s orbital. It is the value of ℓ that determines the type of orbital.

b. Incorrect: if $n = 2$, two types of orbitals are allowed, s and p. But p orbitals always come in sets of three ($2\ell + 1 = 3$), so for $n = 2$, there are 4 orbitals, one s and three p.

c. Correct: for $n = 3$, there are s, p, and d subshells.

d. Incorrect: if $\ell = 3$, there are 7 possible values for the quantum number m_ℓ. The number of values for m_ℓ is given by the expression $2\ell + 1$.

e. Incorrect: there is an $m_\ell = 0$ orbital in each set, s, p, d, f...

f. Incorrect: the letter d, not p, means that $\ell = 2$.

g. Correct, regardless of the value of n, if $\ell = 2$ then $2\ell + 1 = 5$ and there are 5 orbitals in the set (d orbitals).

People
—a crossword puzzle

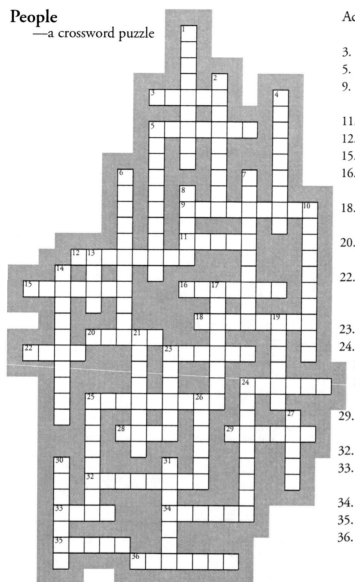

Across:

3. A man of energy, a student of *19 down*.
5. Wrote the laws of electrolysis in 1833.
9. Proposed the law of conservation of matter, then lost his head.
11. Discovered polonium, named after her native land.
12. Discovered the neutron in 1932.
15. Suggested the presence of electrons in all matter.
16. Developed an equation used to predict the lines in the emission spectrum of hydrogen.
18. An Italian whose ideas were a long time in being accepted—his is the number.
20. Incorporated Einstein's relativity into Schrödinger's equation.
22. Suggested that φ^2 should be interpreted as the probability of finding the electron at any point about the nucleus.
23. His burner was used to obtain emission spectra.
24. Proposed the law of constant composition.
25. His constant k is R/N_A.
28. Incorporated the quantization of energy into a model for the electronic structure of an H atom.
29. With *17 down*, he established the wave-particle duality of an electron beam.
32. He explained the photoelectric effect in 1905.
33. What was his name, the unit for power? A student of *14 down*.
34. He named the electron.
35. His series is in the UV region.
36. He determined that elements in the Periodic Table should be arranged by atomic number, not mass.

14. Made elliptical orbits from Bohr's circular ones.
17. With *28 across*, he established the wave-particle duality of an electron beam.
19. Forcefully revived the idea of atoms in 1803.
21. His unit is 100 pm in length.
23. His series is in the visible region.
24. He prepared and isolated oxygen—named by *9 across*.
25. The electrons fall to n=4 in his series.
26. The SI unit for force is named after him.
27. Proved the existence of electromagnetic radiation.
30. Described radiation in terms of electric and magnetic waves.
31. His was once called the centigrade temperature scale.

Down:

1. He discovered radioactivity.
2. Russian who discovered periodicity in the properties of elements and designed the first Periodic Table.
4. Proposed wave–particle duality.
5. His degree is smaller than that of Celsius.
6. Used the assertion of *4 down* to write a wave equation for the electron in a hydrogen atom.
7. A man of some uncertainty.
8. Distinguished heat, temperature, and heat capacity.
10. Proposed the nuclear model for the atom.
13. Developed the law of constant heat summation.

CHAPTER 8

Introduction

The atomic orbitals described in the last chapter are really only the orbitals for single electron systems like hydrogen. In this chapter, the idea of atomic orbitals is extended to the other elements in the Periodic Table—elements that have more than just one electron. Principles that determine how electrons are configured in these orbitals are examined.

The arrangement of elements in the Periodic Table according to their electron configurations is described and the dependence of the physical and chemical properties of atoms and ions on their electron configurations is discussed.

Contents

Electron Spin
The Pauli Exclusion Principle
Atomic Subshell Energies and Electron Assignments
Atomic Electron Configurations
Electron Configurations of Ions
Atomic Properties and Periodic Trends
Periodic Trends and Chemical Properties

Electron Spin

The three quantum numbers described in Chapter 7 of this study guide (n, ℓ, and m_ℓ) define an orbital in which an electron can exist. However, to characterize an electron in an atom completely, a fourth quantum number is required. This is the **electron spin magnetic quantum number, m_s.**

Electron spin is quantized. In a magnetic field, the electron can line up in only two ways characterized by two possible values for the spin quantum number $m_s = \pm \frac{1}{2}$. The electron spin is either aligned with the magnetic field or opposed to the magnetic field.

There are different types of magnetism: **Diamagnetic** substances are repelled by a magnetic field. **Paramagnetic** substances are drawn into a magnetic field. **Ferromagnetic** substances, such as iron, magnetite (Fe_3O_4), and alnico, possess a strong intrinsic magnetism. The different types of magnetism exhibited by different substances arises from their electron spins. A diamagnetic substance has no unpaired electrons; atoms of a paramagnetic substance have at least one unpaired electron; and a ferromagnetic substance has all its unpaired electron spins lined up in the same direction.

When the first electron is assigned to an orbital, it can take either value of m_s. However, if a second electron is assigned to the same orbital, it must take a value of m_s different from the first. The electrons become **paired**.

Two electrons can occupy the same orbital provided that their spin quantum numbers are different.

The Pauli Exclusion Principle

Orbitals are descriptions of electron behavior. If an electron is not present, then the orbital does not exist.

It is convenient however to represent an orbital as a small box or circle, and the electrons as arrows, pointing up for an electron spin = +½ and pointing down for an electron spin = –½.

For example, for n = 3:

There are three types of orbitals: s, p, and d, and there are 9 orbitals in total: one s, three p, and five d. The number of electrons that can be accommodated in the n=3 level is 18.

The filling in order of increasing energy is often referred to as the auf–bau principle.

In 1925 Wolfgang Pauli devised his **Exclusion Principle:** No two electrons in a single atom can have the same set of values for the four quantum numbers. Since one orbital has the same set of three quantum numbers n, ℓ, and m_ℓ and there are only two possible values for m_s, this means that one orbital can accommodate only two electrons.

The number of subshells (types of orbitals) in a principal quantum level n is equal to n. The number of orbitals in a principal quantum level n is equal to n^2. Therefore the number of electrons that can be accommodated in a principal quantum level n is equal to $2n^2$—two in each orbital. For example, in the $n = 1$ level, there is only an s orbital, so the $n = 1$ level can accommodate two electrons. In the $n = 2$ level, there are two subshells: s and p orbitals. But p orbitals always come in sets of 3, so the total number of orbitals in the $n = 2$ level equals 4 (= 2^2). The number of electrons that can be accommodated is 8 (equal to $2n^2$ where $n = 2$).

Atomic Subshell Energies and Electron Assignments

Electrons in a multi-electron atom are placed in orbitals in order of increasing energy. The electrons are assigned to **shells**, each shell characterized by the principal quantum number n. Within each shell there are **subshells** characterized by the secondary quantum number ℓ. The subshells are denoted by the letters: s, p, d, and f.

Experimental evidence for the existence of these shells and subshells can be obtained from the ionization energies for the elements. The ionization energy is the energy required to remove the most loosely held electron from an isolated atom or ion.

All subshells within a principal quantum level n for hydrogen have the same energy. However, for any atom with more than 1 electron, the subshells are no longer equal in energy. This is because an electron in a multi-electron atom repels other electrons and interferes with the attraction between the nucleus and other electrons. The subshells are filled in the sequence of increasing energy. Within a principal quantum level, the order of filling is always s, p, d, and then f.

The problem is that the principal quantum levels start to overlap, and therefore the s orbital of the nth level might be lower in energy than a d orbital of the $(n–1)^{th}$ level or an f orbital in the $(n–2)^{th}$ level. The rule is that electrons are assigned in order of increasing $n+\ell$, and if two orbitals have the same value for $n+\ell$, the one with the lower n is filled first.

For 4s, the value of n + ℓ is 4.
For 3d, the value of n + ℓ is 5.
So the 4s is filled before the 3d.

For 4p, the value of n + ℓ is 5.
For 3d, the value of n + ℓ is 5.
But 3 is lower than 4,
So the 3d is filled before the 4p.

The **effective nuclear charge** is the nuclear charge experienced by a particular electron in a multi-electron atom. This electron may be **shielded** from the full nuclear charge by intervening electrons. In general, s electrons are nearer to the nucleus than p electrons—the s electrons are said to **penetrate** nearer to the nucleus. Therefore s electrons shield p electrons from the full nuclear charge. The shielding capability, and the degree to which electrons penetrate toward the nucleus decreases in the order s > p > d > f.

Atomic Electron Configurations

Hydrogen, element number 1, has one electron in the lowest possible orbital (1s). Its configuration is written $1s^1$, where the superscript 1 indicates one electron in the 1s orbital. Helium, element number 2, has the configuration $1s^2$ which fills this orbital and completes the $n = 1$ level. The next element, lithium has the configuration $1s^2 2s^1$ and so on...

Be $1s^2 2s^2$
B $1s^2 2s^2 2p^1$
C $1s^2 2s^2 2p^2$
N $1s^2 2s^2 2p^3$
O $1s^2 2s^2 2p^4$
F $1s^2 2s^2 2p^5$
Ne $1s^2 2s^2 2p^6$ —Ne completes the $n=2$ level
Na $1s^2 2s^2 2p^6 \; 3s^1$ —or, more simply, [Ne] $3s^1$

You should be able to write the ground state electron configuration for any element in the Periodic Table—certainly the elements in the first 5 periods.

When electrons are assigned to a p, d, or f subshell, each successive electron is assigned to its own orbital until the set is half-full. Then the electrons are paired up in the orbitals. This minimizes the interelectronic repulsion leading to a lower energy configuration. For example, the lowest energy configuration for nitrogen is

This is known as Hund's rule of maximum spin multiplicity.

N $1s^2 2s^2 2p_x^1 2p_y^1 2p_z^1$ rather than $1s^2 2s^2 2p_x^2 2p_y^1$

1s   2s   2p   1s   2s   2p

| 1↓ | | 1↓ | | 1 | 1 | 1 | | 1↓ | | 1↓ | | 1↓ | 1 | |

Electrons in the outermost orbitals that are involved in chemical reactions are called **valence electrons**. The inner **core** electrons are not involved in chemical reactions and are often represented in brackets as above. [Ne], for example, represents the core electrons $1s^2 2s^2 2p^6$. For example, the configuration of sulfur is:

1s   2s   2p   3s   3p

Sulfur S | 1↓ | | 1↓ | | 1↓ | 1↓ | 1↓ | | 1↓ | | 1↓ | 1 | 1 |
These are the core electrons | These are valence electrons

Elements in the $n=4$ to $n=7$ shells also use d and f orbital subshells. The elements in which the d subshells are being filled are called the transition elements. These are the elements in the center block of 10 columns in the Periodic Table. The filling of the f orbital subshells occurs in the lanthanide and actinide series. These are the elements written in two rows of 14 at the bottom of the table.

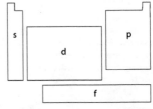

The blocks of elements in the Periodic Table are commonly referred to as the s-block, the p-block, the d-block, and the f-block.

There are a few anomalies in what you might expect the lowest energy electron configuration to be. A half-filled or completely filled d or f subshell is particularly stable. Atoms often adopt such a configuration at the expense of the expected order. For example chromium has the valence electron configuration $3d^5 4s^1$ rather than the expected $3d^4 4s^2$. Copper is $3d^{10} 4s^1$ rather than $3d^9 4s^2$. Gadolinium is $4f^7 5d^1 6s^2$ rather than $4f^8 6s^2$. Palladium is simply $4d^{10}$ rather than $3d^8 4s^2$. These exceptions are not particularly important.

Electron configurations can be written in order of increasing n or in the filling order, both are OK.

Electron Configurations of Ions

A cation is formed by the removal of electron(s) from an atom. The general rule is that the electron removed is the one with the highest n value. If there is more than one subshell available for the highest value of n, then the electron with the highest value of ℓ is removed. Some examples are:

Ni [Ar] $3d^8 4s^2$ $\rightarrow$ Ni^{2+} [Ar] $3d^8$ removal of two $4s^2$ electrons.

Fe [Ar] $3d^6 4s^2$ $\rightarrow$ Fe^{3+} [Ar] $3d^5$ removal of two $4s^2$ electrons and one d electron.

K [Ar] $4s^1$ $\rightarrow$ K$^+$ [Ar] removal of $4s^1$; note the remaining noble gas configuration.

For the formation of anions, add electrons to the next available orbitals.

Atomic Properties and Periodic Trends

The similarity in the chemical and physical properties of elements in the same group results from their similar valence shell electron configurations. For example, all the alkali metals have the valence electron configuration ns^1. Not only do elements in the same group have similar properties, but there are consistent and predictable variations in properties across a period.

Atomic size increases down a group as more shells of electrons are added. Atomic size decreases across a period as the nuclear charge increases and pulls the valence electrons closer to the nucleus.

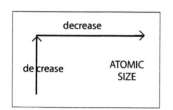

Atomic sizes can be obtained from bond lengths for atoms in molecules. For metals, atomic sizes can be derived from the metallic structure.

It's interesting that a fluorine atom (72 pm), with 9 electrons, is much smaller than a lithium atom (152 pm), with only 3 electrons. The electrons are much closer together in fluorine!

Gallium (below aluminum) with 31 electrons, is smaller than aluminum with only 13 electrons. The reason for this, and all the other anomalous properties of the elements gallium through to bromine, is the preceding block of 3d elements. For this 3d block, the nuclear charge increases by 10 from scandium to zinc without much compensating increase in the shielding—the electrons go into the poorly shielding d orbital subshell. The increase in the nuclear charge pulls in the valence s and p electrons and makes gallium smaller than it would otherwise have been.

Ionization energy is another property that varies systematically through the Periodic Table. The ionization energy is a measure of how strongly the outermost valence electron is held. It increases from left to right across a period, and decreases down a group, for exactly the same reasons as the atomic size changes. Small dips or peaks in the trends across a period are predictable. In general, the formation or breaking up of a completely filled or half-filled subshell of orbitals will influence the ionization energy. For example, removal of an electron to produce a half-filled p orbital subshell will be slightly favored, thus oxygen has a lower ionization energy than nitrogen for which the loss of an electron requires breaking up a half-filled p orbital set.

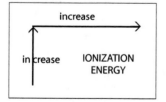

Electron affinity is related to ionization energy; it correponds to the energy released when an electron is added to an atom to form a negative ion. The process is exothermic and electron affinities are therefore negative. When an electron is added to a fluorine atom to form F$^-$, 328 kJ mol^{-1} of energy is released. The electron affinity is therefore –328 kJ mol^{-1}. The electron affinity can alternatively be defined as the energy required to remove an electron from the fluoride ion, which would be +328 kJ mol^{-1}—a measure of how much the fluorine wants the electron. In any event, the –328 kJ mol^{-1} (with the negative sign) is called the electron affinity. Trends in electron affinity parallel those in ionization energy (for the same reasons).

When an electron is added to an atom, there is always an increase in size. Similarly, if an electron is removed, there is always a decrease in size. Cations are always smaller than the atom; anions are always larger. The decrease in size is especially great when the last electron in a particular shell is removed. In a series of isoelectronic ions, there is a consistent decrease in size as the nuclear charge is increased.

Isoelectronic means having the same number of electrons.

Periodic Trends and Chemical Properties

Main group metals form cations with an electron configuration equivalent to the preceding noble gas. Likewise, nonmetals form anions with an electron configuration equivalent to the following noble gas. For example, all the alkali metals form 1+ ions, and all alkali metals have similar properties and form similar compounds. Periodicity is a function of electron configuration.

Transition metals, on the other hand, are characterized by variable oxidation states.

Products formed in chemical reactions, especially simple inorganic reactions, are generally the most (thermodynamically) stable products possible. Sodium and chlorine for example form NaCl, not Na_2Cl, or $NaCl_2$ because Na^+ is the stable sodium cation and Cl^- is the stable chlorine anion. Likewise, magnesium and oxygen form MgO where magnesium has lost 2 electrons and oxygen has gained 2 electrons.

Corresponding transition elements in the 2nd and 3rd series are very similar to each other. The reason for this is the block of 4f elements following lanthanum. For this 4f block, the nuclear charge increases by 14 across the series, without much compensating increase in the shielding—the electrons go into the very poorly shielding f orbital subshell. The increase in the nuclear charge pulls in the valence s and p electrons and makes the third series transition metal almost exactly the same size as the corresponding 2nd series metal. For example, platinum and palladium, tantalum and niobium, gold and silver. All pairs are difficult to separate chemically.

This is called the lanthanide contraction—a contraction exactly analogous to the reduction in the size of gallium described earlier.

Niobe (Z=41) was the daughter of Tantalus (Z=73).

Review Questions

1.   Describe the three types of magnetism. How is each related to the electron spins?

2.   What three principles govern the construction of the lowest energy (ground state) electron configuration for an element? Describe them.

3.   How does the ionization energy for an atom or an ion provide information about the existence of shells and subshells?

Key terms:

electron spin
4th quantum number
magnetism
diamagnetism
paramagnetism
ferromagnetism
auf-bau principle
Pauli exclusion principle
maximum multiplicity
shell
subshell
effective nuclear charge
electronic configuration
n+ℓ rule
ground state
core electrons
valence electrons
noble gas notation
s-block
p-block
d-block
f-block
lanthanides
actinides
periodic trend
atomic size
ionization energy
electron affinity
isoelectronic
lanthanide contraction

4. What are the expressions for:

The number of subshells (types of orbitals) in a principal quantum level.
The number of orbitals in a principal quantum level.
The number of electrons that can be accommodated in a principal quantum level.
The number of orbitals in a subshell (s, p, d, f, etc.)
The number of electrons that can be accommodated within a subshell.

5. Describe effective nuclear charge, the shielding effect, and the penetration effect.

6. What is the $n+\ell$ rule? How does it work?

7. Why does the 4s orbital lie lower in energy than the 3d orbital?

8. What is a core electron? How are the core electrons best represented in an electron configuration. What is a valence electron?

9. Why are the lanthanides and the actinides drawn in two rows at the bottom of the Periodic Table? Where do they really belong? If you draw a Periodic Table with the lanthanides and the actinides in their "proper" place, what pattern, if any, do you notice?

10. What are the general rules that determine which electron(s) to remove when a cation is formed from a neutral atom?

11. What are the general trends in atomic size, ionization energy, and electron affinity through the Periodic Table. Why are all three related?

12. Why are tantalum and niobium so difficult to separate from each other?

Answers to Review Questions

1. There are three types of magnetism: Diamagnetic substances are repelled by a magnetic field; they have no unpaired electrons. Paramagnetic substances are drawn into a magnetic field; they have at least one unpaired electron. Ferromagnetic substances possess a strong intrinsic magnetism; these substances have all the unpaired electron spins lined up in the same direction.

2. Auf-bau Principle: Place electrons into the lowest energy level available and build up the configuration from the bottom.
Pauli Exclusion Principle: No two electrons in a single atom can have the same set of values for the four quantum numbers n, ℓ, and m_ℓ and m_s. Since one orbital has the same set of three quantum numbers n, ℓ, and m_ℓ and there are only two possible values for m_s, this means that one orbital can accommodate only two electrons: each with a different value for m_s.

Hund's Rule of Maximum Spin Multiplicity: When electrons are assigned to a p, d, or f subshell, each successive electron is assigned to its own orbital until the set is half-full. Only then are the electrons paired up in the orbitals. This minimizes the interelectronic repulsion resulting in a lower energy configuration.

3. The ionization energy for an atom or an ion indicates directly the amount of energy required to remove an electron from a particular orbital. It indicates therefore the energy of that orbital. As the ionization energies vary in a systematic way through the Periodic Table, so therefore do the energies of the orbitals from which the electron is being removed.

4. The number of subshells in a principal quantum level = n
    The number of orbitals in a principal quantum level = n^2
    The number of electrons in a principal quantum level = $2n^2$
    The number of orbitals in a subshell = $2\ell + 1$
    The number of electrons in a subshell = $2(2\ell + 1)$

    It's not necessary to memorize all these expressions; especially if you know that each orbital can accommodate 2 electrons.

5. The effective nuclear charge is the nuclear charge experienced by a particular electron in a multi-electron atom. The shielding effect describes how an electron in one orbital shields an electron in another orbital from the nuclear charge. Electrons in s orbitals approach nearest to the nucleus and are the best shielders. In fact, the shielding capability decreases in the order s > p > d > f. The penetration effect describes how close to the nucleus a particular electron can get. The degree to which electrons penetrate toward the nucleus also decreases in the order s > p > d > f.

6. The $n + \ell$ rule is a rule that determines the order of the filling of orbitals in building up the electron configuration of a multi-electron atom. The orbitals are filled in the order of increasing $n + \ell$. For two equal values of $n + \ell$, the orbital with the lower value of n is filled first.
    The rule works because it takes into account (empirically) the splitting in energy of the subshells within a principal quantum level due to the shielding and penetration effects.

    Use the Periodic Table, left to right, row by row, to determine the order of the filling of the orbitals.

7. The 4s orbital lies lower in energy than the 3d orbital because the 4s orbital penetrates nearer to the nucleus than the 3d orbital. Electrons in a 4s orbital are pulled in more by the nucleus and are lower in energy than the 3d electrons.

8. A core electron is an electron in an orbital of the period in the Periodic Table above the period of the valence shell. A core electron is not involved in chemical reactions. The core electrons are best represented in an electron configuration by a noble gas in square brackets. A valence electron is an electron in the outermost subshells of an atom. These are the electrons that are involved in chemical reactions. For example, the electron configuration

of cobalt is written [Ar] $3d^7 4s^2$. The [Ar] represents the core electrons—the 18 electrons in the 1s, 2s, 2p, 3s, and 3p orbitals (Periods 1, 2, and 3). The $3d^7 4s^2$ is the valence shell configuration; these are the valence electrons.

9.   The lanthanides and the actinides are drawn in two rows at the bottom of the Periodic Table so that the table fits conveniently on one 8.5" × 11" page. They really belong in horizontal rows between La and Hf and between Ac and Rf. When placed in these positions, the steps in the table are more obvious: The principal quantum numbers of the d orbital subshells are off by 1 compared to the s and p subshells of the same period. The principal quantum numbers of the f orbital subshells are off by 2 compared to the s and p subshells of the same period. For example, Period 6 is composed of the 6s and 6p, but the 5d, and the 4f subshells.

10.   Electrons are removed from the highest energy orbitals—in other words, the electrons that are easiest to remove. The general rule is that the electron removed is the one with the highest n value. If there is more than one subshell available for the highest value of n, then the electron with the highest value of ℓ is removed.

11.   All general trends in atomic size, ionization energy, and electron affinity depend upon the effective nuclear charge experienced by the valence (outermost) s and p electrons. The greater this charge, the smaller the size, the higher the ionization energy, and the greater the electron affinity. All three trends are therefore related in a systematic way.

12.   Corresponding transition elements in the 2nd and 3rd series, such as niobium and tantalum, are very similar to each other. The reason for this is the block of 4f elements that occurs between the 2nd and 3rd series. Across the 4f block, the nuclear charge increases by 14+, without any compensating increase in the shielding—the electrons go into the poorly shielding f orbital subshell. The increase in the nuclear charge pulls in the valence s and p electrons and makes tantalum almost exactly the same size as niobium. The two metals behave similarly and are difficult to separate.

Tantalum, however is much denser than niobium:

tantalum d = 16.65 g cm^{-3}
niobium d = 8.57 g cm^{-3}

No human investigation can be called real science if it cannot be demonstrated mathematically.

*Leonardo da Vinci
(1452-1519)*

Study Questions and Problems

1.   Write the electron configurations of the following elements using the shorthand notation for the noble gas cores.

   a.   phosphorus
   b.   nickel
   c.   osmium
   d.   californium
   e.   titanium
   f.   europium
   g.   tellurium

2. Which orbital is filled following these orbitals?
    a. 3d   c. 5p   e. 6s
    b. 4s   d. 5f   f. 4d

3. How many electrons can be accommodated in
    a. a d subshell
    b. a set of f orbitals
    c. the $n = 4$ shell
    d. the 7s orbital
    e. a p_x orbital?

4. What is wrong with the following ground state electron configurations for neutral atoms?

5. How many unpaired electrons are there in
    a. a nitrogen atom   c. a nickel(II) cation
    b. an iodine atom   d. an oxide ion?

6. Which of the following sets of quantum numbers describe an impossible situation? Explain why.

    a. $n = 2$, $\ell = 1$, $m_\ell = 2$, $m_s = +\frac{1}{2}$
    b. $n = 5$, $\ell = 2$, $m_\ell = 1$, $m_s = -\frac{1}{2}$
    c. $n = 6$, $\ell = 5$, $m_\ell = 0$, $m_s = 0$
    d. $n = 3$, $\ell = 3$, $m_\ell = 1$, $m_s = -\frac{1}{2}$
    e. $n = 4$, $\ell = 2$, $m_\ell = 1$, $m_s = +\frac{1}{2}$

7. Arrange the elements S, Ge, P, and Si in order of increasing atomic size.

8. Arrange the ions Na^+, K^+, Cl^-, and Br^- in order of increasing size.

9. Arrange the elements Be, Ca, N, and P in order of increasing ionization energy.

10. Which one of each of the following pairs would you expect to have the highest electron affinity?
    a. Cl or Cl^-
    b. Na or K
    c. Br or I

11. Which ions would you expect to exist, and which wouldn't you expect to exist under normal conditions?

   a. K^{2+} e. P^{3-}
   b. Cl^- f. Mn^{7+}
   c. Al^{2+} g. Fe^{2+}
   d. Ar^+ h. Na^-

12. Which elements fit the following descriptions:

   a. the smallest alkaline earth metal
   b. has a valence shell configuration $4f^{14} 5d^{10} 6s^1$
   c. the halogen with the lowest ionization energy
   d. has 13 more electrons than argon
   e. the smallest non metal
   f. the Group 4A element with the largest ionization energy
   g. its 3+ ion has the electron configuration $[Kr] 4d^{10}$

13. Given the series of ionic radii:

   C^{4-} 260 pm; N^{3-} 171 pm; O^{2-} 126 pm; F^- 119 pm;
   Na^+ 116 pm; Mg^{2+} 86 pm; Al^{3+} 68 pm,

   Estimate the atomic radius of neon. Do you think the estimate is a fair one?

I ask you to look both ways. For the road to a knowledge of the stars leads through the atom; and important knowledge of the atom has been reached through the stars.

Sir Arthur Eddington
(1882-1944)

You may sometimes see the subshells of the valence shell listed in order of increasing n.

Answers to Study Questions and Problems

1.   a. phosphorus $[Ne] 3s^2 3p^3$
     b. nickel $[Ar] 4s^2 3d^8$
     c. osmium $[Xe] 6s^2 4f^{14} 5d^6$
     d. californium $[Rn] 7s^2 5f^{10}$
     e. titanium $[Ar] 4s^2 3d^2$
     f. europium $[Xe] 6s^2 4f^7$
     g. tellurium $[Kr] 5s^2 4d^{10} 5p^4$

2.   The easiest way to determine the order in which the orbitals are filled is to follow the Periodic Table row by row left to right.

   a. 3d is followed by 4p
   b. 4s is followed by 3d
   c. 5p is followed by 6s
   d. 5f is followed by 6d
   e. 6s is followed by $5d^1$ and then the 4f
   f. 4d is followed by 5p

3.   a. a d subshell   10 electrons; two in each of 5 orbitals
     b. a set of f orbitals   14 electrons; two in each of 7 orbitals
     c. the n = 4 shell $2n^2 = 32$ (or 2 in s; 6 in p; 10 in d, 14 in f)
     d. the 7s orbital   only 2
     e. a p_x orbital   only 2

4. a. | 3d | | | | | 4s | 4p | | |
    |---|---|---|---|---|---|---|---|---|
    | | | | | | ↑↓ | | | |

    OK, 4s is filled before 3d.

    b. | 3d | | | | | 4s | 4p | | |
    |---|---|---|---|---|---|---|---|---|
    | ↑↓ | ↑↓ | ↑↓ | ↑↓ | ↑↓ | ↑ | ↑ | ↑ | ↑ |

    4s should be filled before 4p subshell.

    c. | 3d | | | | | 4s | 4p | | |
    |---|---|---|---|---|---|---|---|---|
    | ↑↓ | ↑↓ | ↑↓ | ↑↓ | ↑↓ | ↑↑ | ↑ | ↑ | ↑ |

    4s cannot have 2 electrons with same spin.

    d. | 3d | | | | | 4s | 4p | | |
    |---|---|---|---|---|---|---|---|---|
    | ↑ | ↑ | ↑ | ↑ | ↑ | ↑ | | | |

    OK, stability of half-filled 3d subshell.

    e. | 3d | | | | | 4s | 4p | | |
    |---|---|---|---|---|---|---|---|---|
    | ↑↓ | ↑↓ | ↑↓ | ↑↓ | ↑↓ | ↑↓ | ↑↓ | | |

    4p should first fill one orbital at a time.

5. a. a nitrogen atom   3 unpaired electrons $(2s^2\ 2p^3)$

    b. an iodine atom   1 unpaired electron $(5s^2\ 5p^5)$

    c. a nickel(II) cation   2 unpaired electrons $(3d^8)$

    d. an oxide ion   no unpaired electrons   (closed shell [Ne])

6. a. $n = 2,\ \ell = 1,\ m_\ell = 2,\ m_s = +\frac{1}{2}$ maximum value for m_ℓ is $+\ell$

    b. $n = 5,\ \ell = 2,\ m_\ell = 1,\ m_s = -\frac{1}{2}$ OK

    c. $n = 6,\ \ell = 5,\ m_\ell = 0,\ m_s = 0$ m_s must be either $+\frac{1}{2}$ or $-\frac{1}{2}$

    d. $n = 3,\ \ell = 3,\ m_\ell = 1,\ m_s = -\frac{1}{2}$ maximum value for ℓ is $n - 1$

    e. $n = 4,\ \ell = 2,\ m_\ell = 1,\ m_s = +\frac{1}{2}$ OK

7. Increase from right to left and down from top to bottom:

    S < P < Si < Ge.

8. K^+ and Cl^- are isoelectronic; the negative ion is the larger of the two (the nuclear charge is greater for the positive ion). Br^- is larger than K^+ and Cl^- Na^+ is smaller than K^+ and Cl^-. So, in order of increasing size:

    $Na^+ < K^+ < Cl^- < Br^-$

9. Increase from left to right and up from bottom to top:

    Ca < Be < P < N.

    Elements lying close to a diagonal like Be and P are difficult to predict. Notice that Si, to the left of P, has an ionization energy less than Be.

10. a. Cl: the Cl^- ion has a complete shell and zero electron affinity. Cl is just one electron short and has a very high electron affinity.

    b. Na: you would expect the electron affinity to increase up a group.

    c. Br: you would expect the electron affinity to increase up a group; an exception is a decrease from Cl to F—attributed to electron-electron repulsion in the very small fluorine ion.

11. a. K^{2+} doesn't exist; the K^+ has the stable configuration [Ar].

   b. Cl^- this is the stable anion formed by chlorine.

   c. Al^{2+} doesn't exist; Al forms Al^{3+} —the same configuration as [Ne].

   d. Ar^+ Ar already has a stable configuration; never forms Ar^+.

   e. P^{3-} this is the phosphide ion; same configuration as [Ar].

   f. Mn^{7+} doesn't exist; charge is far too high.

   g. Fe^{2+} one of the stable ions formed by iron.

   h. Na^- sodide ion; can be made under certain conditions; $3s^2$.

12. a. the smallest alkaline earth metal — beryllium Be.

   b. has a valence shell configuration $4f^{14}\,5d^{10}\,6s^1$ — gold Au.

   c. the halogen with the lowest ionization energy — astatine At.

   d. has 13 more electrons than argon — gallium [Ar] $3d^{10}\,4s^1\,4p^2$.

   e. the smallest non metal — hydrogen H.

   f. Group 4A element with the largest ionization energy — carbon C.

   g. its 3+ ion has the electron configuration [Kr] $4d^{10}$ — indium In^{3+}.

13. C^{4-} 260 pm; N^{3-} 171 pm; O^{2-} 126 pm; F^- 119 pm;
    Na^+ 116 pm; Mg^{2+} 86 pm; Al^{3+} 68 pm.

   All these species are isoelectronic; all have the configuration [He]$2s^2\,2p^6$. However, the nuclear charge increases along the series and the result is a decrease in the radius as the electrons are pulled closer to the nucleus.

   Somewhere between 116 and 119 pm? This is where Ne fits in the isoelectronic series. Ne does not form compounds like the nonmetals in the preceding groups and measuring its atomic radius is therefore difficult. Some data could be obtained from the crystalline structure of solid neon but the bonding in such a solid is quite different from the bonding in elements like carbon or sulfur, or in compounds like sodium fluoride. There is wide variation in stated values for the atomic radius of neon—anywhere from 70 pm to 112 pm. Putting together a set of self-consistent data is not easy. For example, Na^+ itself is listed as having an atomic radius anywhere between 95 and 116 pm in different environments. You would expect Ne to be larger than Na^+. F is listed usually at about 72 pm — you might have expected Ne to be smaller. However, see the note in the margin.

In neon the interelectronic repulsion is high; the electrons are very crowded. As a result neon might well be larger than fluorine or oxygen. A value between 100 and 110 pm seems reasonable.

CHAPTER 9

Introduction

The goal of this chapter, and the two chapters that follow, is to explain how atoms are arranged in chemical compounds and how they are held together. The relationship between the structure of a compound and the properties of that compound are examined and explained. The bonding and structural characteristics of individual atoms are very similar from one compound to another—they depend upon the valence shell electron configuration of the atom. This consistency permits the development of the various principles of structure and bonding that will be examined in these chapters. A knowledge of a compound's structure and an understanding of the bonding between the atoms of the compound are necessary in order to explain its chemical properties.

Contents

Valence Electrons
Chemical Bond Formation
Bonding in Ionic Compounds
Covalent Bonding and Lewis Structures
Resonance
Exceptions to the Octet Rule
Charge Distribution in Covalent Bonds and Molecules
Bond Properties
Molecular Shapes
Molecular Polarity
The DNA Story—Revisited

Valence Electrons

Electrons in an atom can be divided into two groups: the **core** electrons and the **valence** electrons. The core electrons are not involved in chemical reactions and are often represented in an electronic configuration by the symbol of a noble gas in brackets. The valence electrons are in the outermost orbitals and these are the electrons that are involved in chemical reactions.

It is sometimes useful to draw symbols representing the valence electrons of an atom of a main group element. This symbol is called a **Lewis electron dot symbol** and is the symbol for the element surrounded by a number of dots equal to the number of valence electrons. Dots are placed singly up to 4, and then paired from 5 to 8—four orbitals are available in the valence shell of a main group element (one s and three p).

The valence shells of the main group elements, therefore, can accommodate an **octet** of electrons. An octet of electrons is regarded as a stable configuration.

This was described in Chapter 8 of this study guide. [Ne], for example, represents the core electrons $1s^2\,2s^2\,2p^6$.

The number of valence electrons for a main group element equals the group number. For transition metals, the valence electrons include the $(n-1)d$ subshell.

$\cdot\ddot{\underset{\cdot}{N}}\cdot$

The Lewis electron dot symbol for nitrogen.

Chemical Bond Formation

The driving force for the formation of any compound is the favorable energetics of the compound.

The structure of a compound is the one having the lowest potential energy, i.e. the greatest thermodynamic stability.

When two atoms combine, their valence electrons reorganize so that they decrease in energy. There is a net attractive force between the two atoms. This force is called a **chemical bond**. There are two general types of chemical bond—covalent and ionic.

An **ionic bond** forms when one or more valence electrons are transferred from one atom to another. Positive and negative ions are formed. The bond is the electrostatic attractive force between the ions.

A **covalent bond** is formed when the two atoms share one, two, or three pairs of electrons between them. The sharing, when the two atoms are different, is unequal.

Both processes usually involve the formation of complete octets around the atoms:

Each type of chemical bond describes a different way in which the electrons are redistributed:

covalent: electrons shared
ionic: electrons transferred
metallic: electrons delocalized

Sodium is a metal.
Chlorine is a covalent molecule. Between them, they produce an ionic compound: NaCl.

All three are different types of matter with quite different properties.

ionic bond Na^+ :$\ddot{\underset{\cdot\cdot}{Cl}}$:   covalent bond   :$\ddot{\underset{\cdot\cdot}{Cl}}$:$\ddot{\underset{\cdot\cdot}{Cl}}$:

Bonding in Ionic Compounds

Elements on the left side of the Periodic Table tend to form positive ions through the loss of electrons. Elements on the right side of the Periodic Table tend to form negative ions through the gain of electrons. For example:

$$Na(g) \rightarrow Na^+(g) + e^- \qquad \Delta H° = +502 \text{ kJ mol}^{-1} \quad \text{(ionization energy)}$$

$$Cl(g) + e^- \rightarrow Cl^-(g) \qquad \Delta H° = -349 \text{ kJ mol}^{-1} \quad \text{(electron affinity)}$$

These two processes together are endothermic (energy is required), but energy is released when the two ions form a pair:

$$Na^+(g) + Cl^-(g) \rightarrow NaCl(g) \quad \Delta H° = -498 \text{ kJ mol}^{-1} \quad \text{(ion-pair formation)}$$

The $\Delta H°_{ion-pair}$ is not measured directly but is calculated from Coulomb's law:

$E_{ion-pair} = (n^+e)(n^-e)/d$

n^+e = charge on cation
n^+e = charge on anion
d = internuclear distance

The overall process is exothermic. The attraction between the ions depends upon the magnitude of the charges and the sizes of the ions (the distance between them).

Lattice energy is a measure of the bonding in a crystalline solid. It is defined as the energy of formation of one mole of the crystalline lattice from the ions in the gas phase:

$$Na^+(g) + Cl^-(g) \rightarrow NaCl(s) \quad \Delta H° = -786 \text{ kJ mol}^{-1} \text{ (lattice energy)}$$

Lattice energy is usually expressed as an enthalpy change $\Delta H°$.

In the gas phase the ions are infinitely far apart.

There are no ion pairs in the crystalline lattice; each sodium ion is surrounded by six chloride ions and each chloride ion is surrounded by six sodium ions. The lattice energy is calculated from experimentally determined thermodynamic properties using Hess's law. Like the energy of ion–pair formation, the lattice energy depends upon the charges and sizes of the ions. For example, the lattice energy of magnesium oxide MgO is almost four times more than the lattice energy of sodium fluoride NaF; the charges on the magnesium and oxide ions are 2+ and 2–, compared to 1+ and 1– for sodium fluoride.

The lattice energy also depends upon the symmetry of the crystal—how well the ions pack together.

See study question #4.

9.4   Covalent Bonding and Lewis Structures

Covalent bonding involves the sharing of electrons between the atoms involved in the bond. Elements that bond covalently are commonly the nonmetals in the upper right hand corner of the Periodic Table.

In a simple description of covalent bonding, one or more electron pairs are shared between two atoms. These electron pairs, for example in the hydrogen molecule H_2, are represented by a line (H–H) or as a pair of dots (H:H). Pairs of electrons that are not involved in the bonding are called nonbonding or lone pairs and can also be represented as bars or as pairs of dots.

When two pairs of electrons are shared, the bond is called a **double bond** and is represented by two pairs of dots or by a double line. For example $H_2C::O$ or $H_2C=O$ for formaldehyde. Three pairs shared is a **triple bond**, as in the dinitrogen $N:::N$ or acetylene $HC:::CH$ molecules. This bond is represented by three pairs of dots, or by three lines.

There is a tendency for atoms in simple covalent molecules to achieve an octet of electrons (four pairs) around themselves. Although there are many instances where the central atom in a molecule does not follow the rule, it is almost always followed by the terminal or outside atoms in a molecule. The major exception is hydrogen which can accommodate only two electrons. The procedure for determining the best Lewis electron dot structure is:

single bond	:	
double bond	::	
triple bond	:::	

1. Determine the arrangement of atoms in the molecule.
2. Determine the total number of valence electrons.
3. Place one pair of electrons between each pair of bonded atoms.
4. Complete the octet of all terminal atoms (except hydrogen).
5. Place any electrons remaining on the central atom as lone pairs.
6. If the central atom has fewer than 8 electrons, consider moving nonbonding pairs of electrons from the terminal atoms into the bonds between the terminal atoms and the central atom.

The shapes of many molecules are related. Knowing the structure of one molecule will often allow you to predict the structure of another—when the pattern of bonding and nonbonding electrons is the same. For example, CCl_4 has the same structure as CH_4. The molecule NF_3 has the same structure as NH_3 or PCl_3. The nitrite ion NO_2^- has the same structure as sulfur dioxide SO_2.

In addition, in the formation of molecules with no charge, you will soon recognize that carbon always forms four bonds, nitrogen three bonds, oxygen two bonds, and fluorine just one bond. Because they follow the octet rule, this means that carbon has no lone pairs, nitrogen has one, oxygen has two, and fluorine has three pairs.

Isoelectronic molecules or ions have the same number of valence electrons. This is significant because it means the molecules will have the same structure.

Note that representative metals such as lithium, magnesium, beryllium, and aluminum can also form covalent bonds. There are also many covalent molecules or polyatomic ions of the transition metals.

See study question #5.

Patterns like these will become evident as you determine the structures of more and more simple molecules.

Note that there are some exceptions. For example, in a compound like CO, it is impossible for carbon to form 4 bonds; it forms three bonds and has a lone pair.

For example, the nitrate ion NO_3^- and the carbonate ion CO_3^{2-} are isoelectronic and have the same structure.

See study question #8.

Resonance

When the Lewis electron dot structure for a molecule like ozone, or an ion like the nitrate ion, is drawn, some bonds are drawn as double bonds and some bonds are drawn as single bonds. In reality, all the bonds are the same. Lewis structures are often poor representations of the actual electronic structure. Linus Pauling proposed the concept of **resonance** to reconcile Lewis structures with the actual structures. The idea is to draw all the possible Lewis structures and then to indicate that the true structure is a composite (or resonance hybrid) of all the contributing Lewis structures. For example, in the nitrate ion, the double bond could have been drawn between the nitrogen atom and any one of the three oxygen atoms. So all three structures are drawn and the true structure said to be a composite of all three.

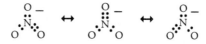

Exceptions to the Octet Rule

Although many covalent compounds can be drawn so that the octet rule is obeyed, there are exceptions. These include compounds with fewer than eight electrons around the central atom (example BCl_3), those with more than eight electrons around the central atom (examples SF_6, PF_5, ClF_3, and XeF_2), and those with an odd number of valence electrons.

In molecules with an odd number of valence electrons the electrons cannot be paired. Examples are nitric oxide NO and nitrogen dioxide NO_2. These molecules are called **radicals**. Most radicals are more reactive than ordinary molecules—they participate in reactions leading to the pairing of the odd electron. For example both NO and NO_2 react with each other and themselves (dimerize) to form N_2O_2, N_2O_3, and N_2O_4.

Charge Distribution in Covalent Molecules

In a Lewis structure, it appears that the bonding electrons are shared equally between the bonded atoms. Most often they are not. Usually the bonding electrons are nearer to one atom than the other. This results in a **charge distribution** that is uneven—some atoms are slightly negative, others slightly positive.

The **formal charge** of an atom in a molecule is the charge calculated on the basis of equal sharing. If an atom contributes more electrons to the bonding than it gets back by sharing, it acquires a positive formal charge. Similarly, if an atom gets back more electrons than it gives, it acquires a negative formal charge. The sum of all the formal charges equals the charge on the molecule or ion (i.e. zero for a molecule).

The formal charge is calculated by adding up all the valence electrons an atom has in the molecule and comparing the number to what the atom has in a neutral isolated state. Lone pairs belong to the atom on which they reside. Bonding pairs are assumed to be divided equally between the two atoms participating in the bond. For example, in the carbonate ion, the oxygen at the top has 2 lone pairs (4 elec-

One Lewis structure for the nitrate ion (lone pairs on the O omitted).

See study questions #7 & #12.

The double headed arrows indicate resonance—the fact that all three structures contribute to the real structure.

Note that the double bond does not move from one pair of atoms to another; the fourth pair of electrons is shared equally by all three bonds.

Elements in Period 3 down have d orbitals in their valence shells. The use of these d orbitals in expanding beyond the octet is the usual explanation of bonding in compounds like PCl_5 and SF_6.

See study question #3.

Bond character is a continuum from 100% covalent (equal sharing) to more and more ionic as the sharing becomes more and more unequal.

See study question #6.

trons) and a half–share in 2 bonding pairs (2 electrons) for a total of 6 electrons. Oxygen is in Group 6A and should have 6 valence electrons. Therefore this oxygen atom has a zero formal charge.

The other two oxygen atoms are both the same; they have 3 lone pairs (6 electrons) and a half–share in one bonding pair (1 electron) for a total of 7 electrons. Both these oxygen atoms have one too many electrons and therefore a formal charge of –1.

The carbon atom has no lone pairs and a half–share in 4 bonding pairs (4 electrons). Carbon is in Group 4A and should have 4 valence electrons. It therefore has a zero formal charge. The sum of the formal charges is –2, the charge on the ion.

In reality, all C–O bonds are the same in the carbonate ion, and the negative charge is delocalized over the entire ion, residing equally on each oxygen atom. Each oxygen atom has an average –2/3 negative formal charge.

The models used to represent covalent and ionic bonding are two extreme cases. Pure covalent bonding, with equal sharing of electrons, occurs only between identical atoms. A purely ionic bond assumes no sharing of electrons at all, and this is never the case. Between the two extremes, there is a wide range of bonds with increasing **polarity**. The sharing of electrons unequally in a bond results in one atom acquiring a slightly negative charge and the other a slightly positive charge—the bond is called a **polar covalent** bond.

A parameter called **electronegativity** (symbol χ) is a measure of the ability of an atom in a molecule to attract electrons to itself. If the two atoms participating in a bond have different electronegativities, then the bonding electrons are shared unequally, the electrons are pulled toward the more electronegative atom, and the bond is polar. In the extreme, an ionic bond results in which there is a complete transfer of the electrons to the more electronegative element. Thus, a bond between an element with a very low electronegativity (for example K) and an element with a very high electronegativity (for example F) is ionic—the sharing is very unequal. The closer the electronegativities of two nonmetals participating in a bond, the more equal the sharing of the electrons—the more covalent the bond.

There are some cases where the electronegativity seems at odds with the formal charge. For example, in the ion BF_4^-, the formal charge calculations would predict placement of the negative charge on the B. But, fluorine is more electronegative than boron, and the fluorine atoms should have the negative charge. The **electroneutrality principle** of Linus Pauling states that any negative charge should be on the more electronegative element, and that electrons should be distributed in a molecule to minimize formal charges. For example, in the cyanate ion OCN⁻ there are three possibilities. The first structure is best; it has the lowest formal charges and the negative charge is on the most electronegative element.

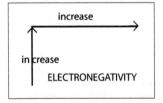

Bond polarities can be estimated from the electronegativity differences.

Bond Properties: Order, Length, Energy

See study question #11.

Bond order is the number of electron pairs shared between two atoms in a molecule. A single bond (one pair of electrons shared) has a bond order of 1. A double bond has a bond order of 2, and so on. Fractional bond orders are possible in molecules for which resonance is required. In the nitrate ion, for example, four pairs of electrons are shared by three pairs of atoms. Each bond has 1.33 pairs of electrons and therefore the bond order of each bond is 1.33.

Bond length is the distance between the nuclei of two atoms in a molecule. Bond lengths depend upon the sizes of the atoms and the number of electron pairs shared between the atoms (the bond order).

For example, the bond lengths increase H–F < H–Cl < H–Br < H–I because the size of the halogen increases. The bond lengths decrease C–O > C=O > C≡O because the bond order increases. A bond order between 1 and 2 results in a bond length between C–O and C=O. For example, the C–O bond in the carbonate ion, with a bond order of 1.33, has a bond length of 129 pm—between 143 pm for a single bond and 122 pm for a double bond.

Bond energy is the energy required to break the bond, or the energy released when the bond is made. The bond energy is related to the bond order; triple bonds are stronger than double bonds, and double bonds are stronger than single bonds. Although bond energies do vary from one compound to another, an estimate of the enthalpy of reaction $\Delta H°$ can be obtained from the difference between the bond energies of the bonds that need to be broken and the bond energies of the bonds that are formed in the reaction.

Bond breaking is always endothermic. Bond making is always exothermic.

See study question #9.

$$\Delta H°_{reaction} = \Sigma(\Delta H° \text{ (bonds broken)} - \Delta H° \text{(bonds made)})$$

Molecular Shapes

The **valence shell electron pair repulsion theory** (VSEPR) was devised by N. V. Sidgewick and H. M. Powell soon after Lewis proposed his ideas of chemical bonding based upon electron pairs. The theory was developed and expanded by R. J. Gillespie and R. S. Nyholm in the 1950's. VSEPR theory is remarkably successful in predicting the shapes of the compounds of the main group elements.

Because the two pairs of electrons in a double bond, or the three pairs of electrons in a triple bond, share the same space, a more recent name for this method of determining the shape of a molecule is called the electron domain (ED) theory.
This reinforces the idea that it is the number of bonds and lone pairs that determines the shape, not simply the number of electron pairs.

The idea is that lone pairs and bonding pairs of electrons around an atom repel each other and get as far apart as possible. The direction in which the bonding pairs point determines the direction of the bond and therefore the shape of the molecule. The basic arrangements of electron pairs are:

Be sure to distinguish between the arrangement of electron pairs around the central atom and the shape of the molecule (which is the arrangement of atoms).

2 electron pairs	linear arrangement
3 electron pairs	trigonal arrangement
4 electron pairs	tetrahedral arrangement
5 electron pairs	trigonal bipyramidal arrangement
6 electron pairs	octahedral arrangement

The actual shape of the molecule depends upon how many of the electron pairs are bonding and how many are nonbonding. The figure opposite is divided into 5 sections corresponding to the total number of electron pairs.

See study question #13.

	No lone pairs	1 lone pair	2 lone pairs	3 lone pairs
2 pairs	Linear			
3 pairs	Trigonal planar	Bent		
4 pairs	Tetrahedral	Trigonal pyramidal	Bent	
5 pairs	Trigonal Bipyramidal	Seesaw	T-shaped	Linear
6 pairs	Octahedral	Square pyramidal	Square planar	

The key to a successful use of the VSEPR theory is to determine the number electron pairs around the central atom in the molecule correctly. Note that when counting the number of electron pairs, double and triple bonds count the same as

The multiple bonds do take up more room and do distort the geometry.

See study question #14.

You can determine the number of electron pairs around the central atom without drawing the Lewis structure as follows:

Add up the total number of valence electrons in the molecule.

Divide this total by 8; the answer is the number of bonding electron pairs; the remainder is the number of non-bonding electrons on the central atom (divide by 2 to obtain the number of pairs).

This will work provided that H is not one of the terminal atoms—in which case draw the Lewis structure.

Try some of the molecules in the problems at the end of this chapter.

See study question #15.

single bonds. This is because the two pairs of electrons in a double bond, or the three pairs of electrons in a triple bond, share the same space.

The procedure to follow:

1. Draw the Lewis electron dot structure of the molecule, or determine by counting the number of electron pairs around the central atom.
2. Determine the arrangement of the electron pairs around the central atom (one of the five basic arrangements).
3. Determine the shape of the molecule.

Molecular Polarity

Many molecules are polar—there is an asymmetry in the electron distribution in the molecule. This polarity of a molecule means that the molecule has a dipole moment. The dipole moment μ is defined as the product of the magnitude of the partial negative $\delta-$ and positive $\delta+$ charges at the ends of the molecule and the distance between them.

To determine whether a molecule is polar, you have to determine if any of the bonds in the molecule are polar, and if so, what is their position relative to one another. Bonds are often polar, but when positioned symmetrically, the bond polarities will cancel one another. For example, in carbon dioxide CO_2 the C=O bonds are polar, but they point symmetrically to either side of the molecule. So carbon dioxide is a nonpolar molecule even though it contains polar bonds.

Nonpolar molecules have a balanced structure. In a polar molecule, one end or side of a molecule is different from the others.

Review Questions

1. What is a Lewis electron dot symbol?

2. Describe the two general types of chemical bond introduced in this chapter. How do they differ?

3. Why is the electron affinity expressed as a negative number, whereas the ionization energy is expressed as a positive number, in calculating the energy of ion–pair formation?

4. What is the difference between the energy of ion–pair formation and the lattice energy? Why is the lattice energy greater?

5. What is the difference between a bonding pair of electrons and a nonbonding pair of electrons?

6. What is the greatest number of valence electrons that can be shared between two main group atoms in the formation of a covalent bond?

7. Is there such a thing as a 100% covalent bond? Is a bond ever 100% ionic?

8. Summarize the procedure for drawing a Lewis electron dot structure and apply the procedure to the molecule BF_3.

9. What does it mean when two molecules are described as isoelectronic? What significance is there in the two molecules being isoelectronic?

10. What is resonance? How realistic is this concept?

11. What is a resonance hybrid?

12. Do all atoms in all molecules obey the octet rule? What are the common exceptions?

13. What is bond order?

14. How is bond length related to bond order?

15. How can you determine the enthalpy of reaction from the strengths of the bonds that are broken and the bonds that are formed in the reaction?

16. What is the formal charge on the atom in a molecule? Does it differ from the oxidation number? Why?

17. What is electronegativity? What is the difference between electronegativity and electron affinity?

18. Which is more significant, electronegativity or formal charge?

19. What is the basic idea behind VSEPR theory?

20. How is the shape of a molecule or polyatomic ion related to the number of electron pairs surrounding the central atom?

21. What is the difference between the "arrangement of electron pairs" and "the shape of the molecule"?

22. How can a molecule contain polar bonds and yet be a nonpolar molecule?

23. Is it correct to say that all polyatomic ions, with charges anywhere between +1 and −3, must be polar?

24. Are all trigonal pyramidal molecules polar? Are all tetrahedral molecules nonpolar?

Key terms:

Lewis electron dot symbol
octet of electrons
chemical bond
ionic bond
covalent bond
ion pair
lattice energy
Lewis structure
bonding pair
nonbonding pair
single bond
double bond
triple bond
isoelectronic
resonance
resonance hybrid
radical
charge distribution
formal charge
polarity
polar covalent bond
electronegativity
electroneutrality principle
bond order
bond length
bond energy
VSEPR theory
electron pair arrangement
molecular shape
linear
trigonal planar
tetrahedral
trigonal bipyramid
octahedral
dipole moment
DNA

25.   Are all molecules with an odd number of lone pairs around the central atom polar?

Answers to Review Questions

1.   A Lewis electron dot symbol is the symbol for the element surrounded by a number of dots equal to the number of valence electrons. Dots are placed singly up to 4, and then paired from 5 to 8. The symbol represents in a simple way the number of valence electrons of an atom and its potential for forming bonds.

2.   The attractive force between two atoms in a compound is called a chemical bond. There are two general types—covalent and ionic. An ionic bond forms when one or more valence electrons are transferred from one atom to another. A covalent bond is formed when the two atoms share one, two, or three pairs of electrons between them. The two types differ therefore in what happens to the valence electrons upon bond formation. The ionic bond involves a transfer of electrons; the covalent bond involves a sharing of electrons.

Electron affinity and ionization energy are described in Chapter 8 of this study guide.

3.   When an electron is added to a nonmetal to form the anion, energy is released and therefore $\Delta H°$ is negative (exothermic). The ionization energy is the energy required to remove an electron from the metal to form the cation. This is an endothermic process and $\Delta H°$ is positive.

4.   The energy of ion–pair formation is the energy released when an ion–pair is formed in the gas phase. The lattice energy is the energy released when the same gaseous ions form a solid crystal lattice. In the solid each cation is surrounded by several anions and vice versa; more bonds are formed and more energy is released. The lattice energy is always the greater of the two. The difference in energy equals the energy required to break up the solid lattice to form ion–pairs in the gaseous state.

5.   A bonding pair of electrons is a pair of electrons shared between two atoms in a molecule. A nonbonding pair of electrons is a pair of electrons that is not involved in the bonding; a nonbonding pair resides on just one atom in a molecule.

6.   The greatest number of electrons that can be shared in a covalent bond is 6 (3 pairs in a triple bond). For example acetylene or nitrogen. Quadruple bonds are known but these occur between transition metal atoms.

7.   A covalent bond is 100% covalent when the two atoms are identical (for example in O_2). When the two atoms differ in electronegativity, the bond is polar. However, a bond can never be 100% ionic—this would imply no sharing of electrons at all and an infinite distance between the two atoms.

8. 1. Determine the arrangement of atoms in the molecule.
    2. Determine the total number of valence electrons.
    3. Place one pair of electrons between each pair of bonded atoms.
    4. Complete the octet of all terminal atoms (except hydrogen).
    5. Place any electrons remaining on the central atom as lone pairs.
    6. If the central atom has fewer than 8 electrons, consider moving nonbonding pairs of electrons from the terminal atoms into the bonds between the terminal atoms and the central atom.

    Example BF_3

    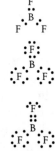

    1. B at the center of a triangle of F atoms.
    2. 24 valence electrons (3 from B and 7 each from F).
    3. One pair in each bond:
    4. Complete octets of terminal atoms:
    5. No lone pairs remaining for the B.
    6. Possible double bonding between B and F to relieve the deficiency of electrons on the boron. One resonance structure shown:

9. Isoelectronic molecules have the same number of valence electrons. This is significant because it means the molecules will have the same structure.

10. The concept of resonance reconciles a Lewis structure and the actual structure. The idea is to draw all the possible Lewis structures and then to indicate that the true structure is a composite (or resonance hybrid) of all these contributing Lewis structures. The Lewis structure is often unrealistic. For example a nitrate ion with the double bond fixed between the nitrogen and only one oxygen atom does not exist. Resonance indicates that the true structure is a composite that cannot be represented by dots for electrons.

11. A resonance hybrid is a composite of several Lewis dot structures. The resonance hybrid more accurately represents the actual distribution of electrons in the molecule.

12. There are exceptions to the octet rule:

    a. hydrogen (with a valence shell that can only accommodate 2 electrons).
    b. compounds with fewer than eight electrons around the central atom.
    c. compounds with more than eight electrons around the central atom.
    d. compounds with an odd number of valence electrons.

13. Bond order is the number of electron pairs shared between two atoms in a molecule. A single bond (one pair of electrons shared) has a bond order of 1. A double bond has a bond order of 2, and so on. Fractional bond orders occur when resonance is required.

14. Bond length is the distance between the nuclei of two atoms in a molecule. Bond lengths depend upon the bond order. For example, N–O (136 pm) > N=O (115 pm) > N≡O (108 pm). The bond length decreases as the bond order increases.

15. Although bond energies do vary from one compound to another, an estimate of the enthalpy of reaction ΔH° can be obtained from the difference between the bond energies of the bonds that need to be broken and the bond energies of the bonds that are formed in the reaction.

    ΔH°$_{reaction}$ = Σ(ΔH° (bonds broken) – ΔH°(bonds made))

16. The formal charge of an atom in a molecule is an indication of the electronic charge residing on the atom. It is, however, the charge calculated on the basis of equal sharing of bonding electrons. The formal charge is calculated by adding up all the valence electrons an atom has in the molecule and comparing the total to what the atom has in a neutral isolated state. If it has fewer electrons, then it has a formal positive charge; if it has more electrons, then it has a formal negative charge.

    Except for a monatomic ion, the oxidation number has little relation to the charge of the atom. The use of oxidation numbers is an electron accounting system used in redox reactions. For example, the formal charge on Mn in the permanganate ion MnO_4^- is anywhere between 0 and +3 depending upon the Lewis structure drawn; the oxidation number is +7.

17. Electronegativity (χ) is a measure of the ability of an atom in a molecule to attract electrons to itself. Electron affinity is the energy required to remove an electron from a negative ion. Electronegativity refers to an atom in a molecule. Electron affinity refers to an isolated (gaseous) atom.

18. Sometimes a negative formal charge appears to belong to an atom less electronegative than others. This is unrealistic. Negative charges in a moleule should reside on the more electronegative atoms. This is stated in Linus Pauling's electroneutrality principle.

19. The basic idea behind VSEPR theory is that lone pairs and bonding pairs of electrons around an atom repel each other and get as far apart as possible. The direction in which the bonding pairs point determines the direction of the bond and therefore the shape of the molecule.

20. There are 5 basic arrangements of electron pairs: linear, trigonal, tetrahedral, trigonal bipyramidal, and octahedral. Depending upon how many lone pairs there are, subsets of various molecular shapes result. These are shown on page 131 of this study guide.

21. The arrangement of electron pairs refers to the arrangement of both bonding and nonbonding pairs of electrons around the central atom. The shape

of the molecule refers to the arrangement of atoms in the molecule (i.e. just the bonding pairs).

22.   The polarities of the bonds must cancel each other. For example, in carbon dioxide CO_2 the C=O bonds are polar, but they point symmetrically to either side of the molecule. So carbon dioxide is a nonpolar molecule.

23.   No, it is not correct. For example, in NO_3^-, ClO_4^-, PO_4^{3-}, SO_4^{2-}, CO_3^{2-}, and NH_4^+, etc., the charges are symmetrically distributed over the entire ion and therefore these ions are nonpolar. Some ions are polar—it depends on their shape.

24.   All trigonal pyramidal molecules are polar—they all have a lone pair of electrons at one end of a tetrahedral arrangement. Some tetrahedral molecules are nonpolar—for example: CH_4, CCl_4, NH_4^+, BF_4^-, SO_4^{2-}. But many are not—for example: $CHCl_3$, CH_2Cl_2, $S_2O_3^{2-}$.

25.   No, not all. For example I_3^- and XeF_2 are not polar; they are linear.

Study Questions and Problems

1.   Classify the following substances as covalent molecules or ionic compounds:

a.	MgO	e.	$LiCl$
b.	NI_3	f.	SF_4
c.	CuS	g.	XeF_4
d.	NO_2	h.	CsF

2.   How many valence electrons do the following atoms or ions have? Write their Lewis symbols.

a.	Ca	e.	Mg^{2+}
b.	S	f.	C^{4-}
c.	P	g.	Li
d.	O^{2-}	h.	Ne

3.   Which of the following molecules do not obey the octet rule?

a.	$AlCl_3$	e.	SF_6
b.	PCl_3	f.	$BeCl_2$
c.	PCl_5	g.	NO_2
d.	$SiCl_4$	h.	XeF_4

4.   Order the following salts in increasing lattice energy:

CaS, MgO, KCl, CsI, NaF

In studies, whatsoever a man commandeth upon himself, let him set hours for it.

Francis Bacon (1561-1626)

5.   Draw Lewis electron dot structures for the following molecules:

    a. NCl_3 d. SF_4
    b. BCl_3 e. OCS
    c. ClO_2^- f. SO_2

6.   Assign formal charges to all the atoms in the following species:

    a. chlorite ion ClO_2^-
    b. hydroxylamine $HONH_2$
    c. phosphorous acid H_3PO_3
    d. ozone O_3
    e. nitrogen dioxide NO_2

7.   For which of the following molecules and polyatomic ions is the concept of resonance necessary to realistically represent the structure using Lewis dot structures?

    a. CH_4 e. SF_6
    b. SO_2 f. CO_2
    c. H_2CO g. NO_3^-
    d. C_6H_6 (benzene)   h. ClO_3^-

8.   Which of the following species are isoelectronic with CO_2; which are isoelectronic with SO_2?

    NO_2^+ NO_2^- CS_2 NCO^- O_3 NCS^- N_3^-

Bond Energies:

C-C   347 kJ/mol

C-O   351 kJ/mol

C-H   414 kJ/mol

O-H   464 kJ/mol

C=C   611 kJ/mol

O=O   498 kJ/mol

9.   Estimate, using the bond energies in the margin to the left, the enthalpy change $\Delta H°$ for the conversion of propene to isopropanol:

$$CH_3–CH=CH_2 \ + \ H_2O \ \rightarrow \ CH_3–CH(OH)–CH_3$$

10.   When ethanol burns in air, heat is released. Estimate the enthalpy of combustion of ethanol vapor $\Delta H°$ from the average bond energies listed in the margin to the left. Use thermochemical data in Chapter 6 of this study guide to calculate the same thing. Compare the two values obtained.

11.   What is the bond order of the listed bonds in the following molecules or ions?

    a. C–O in carbonate ion   e. O–O in oxygen O_2
    b. C–O in acetic acid   f. C–N in hydrogen cyanide
    c. N–O in nitrite ion   g. S–F in sulfur tetrafluoride
    d. C–C acetylene   h. C–O in carbon dioxide

12. Draw possible resonance structures for
    a. NO_2^-
    b. HCO_2^-
    c. NO_2Cl

13. What molecular shapes are associated with the following electron pairs around the central atom?

    a. 3 bonding pairs and 2 lone pairs
    b. 4 bonding pairs and 1 lone pair
    c. 3 bonding pairs and 1 lone pair
    d. 2 bonding pairs and 2 lone pairs
    e. 2 bonding pairs and 3 lone pairs
    f. 5 bonding pairs and 1 lone pair

14. What shapes are the following molecules or polyatomic ions?

    a. O_3 e. NO_2^+
    b. GaH_3 f. ClO_4^-
    c. SO_2Cl_2 g. IF_4^-
    d. XeO_4 h. ClF_2^-

15. Determine whether the following molecules are polar or nonpolar:

    a. CCl_4 e. BF_3
    b. XeF_4 f. $BeCl_2$
    c. PCl_5 g. SCl_2
    d. PCl_3 h. CS_2

Answers to Study Questions and Problems

*Whence is thy learning? Hath thy toil
o'er books consum'd the midnight oil?*

*John Gay
(1685-1732)*

1. Look first at the relative positions of the two elements in the Periodic Table and then, if necessary, examine the electronegativity difference between the two elements. Remember that some ionic bonds have considerable covalent character.

a.	MgO	ionic		e.	LiCl	ionic
b.	NI_3	covalent		f.	SF_4	covalent
c.	CuS	ionic		g.	XeF_4	covalent
d.	NO_2	covalent		h.	CsF	ionic

   An electronegativity difference of about 1.7 is often considered to be the dividing line between ionic and covalent bonding.

2.
a.	Ca	2 valence electrons	$\dot{Ca}\cdot$
b.	S	6 valence electrons	$\cdot\ddot{S}\cdot$
c.	P	5 valence electrons	$\cdot\dot{P}\cdot$
d.	O^{2-}	8 valence electrons	$:\ddot{O}:^{2-}$
e.	Mg^{2+}	0 valence electrons	
f.	C^{4-}	8 valence electrons	$:\ddot{C}:^{4-}$ Mg^{2+}
g.	Li	1 valence electron	
h.	Ne	8 valence electrons	$:\ddot{Ne}:$ $Li\cdot$

3. Terminal atoms almost always obey the octet rule; examine the number of electrons around the central atom:

Fewer than 8 electrons (an octet) usually results in dimerization or polymerization in a condensed phase. For example $AlCl_3$ exists in a nonpolar solvent as Al_2Cl_6 in which an octet is achieved. In the solid state there are 6 Cl around each Al.

a. $AlCl_3$ only 6 electrons   e. SF_6 12 electrons
b. PCl_3 OK   f. $BeCl_2$ only 4 electrons
c. PCl_5 10 electrons   g. NO_2 7 electrons (odd number)
d. $SiCl_4$ OK   h. XeF_4 12 electrons

4. Lattice energy depends upon the charge/size ratio:

$$MgO > CaS > NaF > KCl > CsI$$

5. a. NCl_3 d. SF_4

   b. BCl_3 e. OCS

   c. ClO_2^- f. SO_2

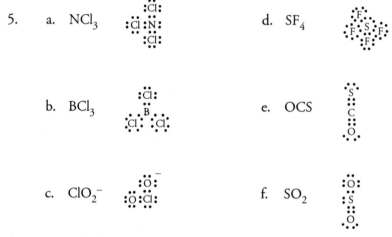

6. Formal charges:

   a. chlorite ion ClO_2^- Cl +1; both O −1
      (both single bonds)
   b. hydroxylamine $HONH_2$ all zero
   c. phosphorous acid H_3PO_3 all zero
   d. ozone O_3 central O +1; singly
      (one double bond; one single bond)   bonded oxygen −1
   e. nitrogen dioxide NO_2 nitrogen +1; singly
      (odd electron on N)   bonded oxygen −1

7. Resonance is necessary when there are alternative but equivalent positions for double or triple bonds in a molecule.

   a. CH_4 four single bonds only; no resonance
   b. SO_2 one single & one double S–O bond; resonance necessary
   c. H_2CO only one C=O double bond; no resonance
   d. C_6H_6 two equivalent structures; resonance necessary
   e. SF_6 six single bonds; no resonance
   f. CO_2 two identical double bonds; no resonance
   g. NO_3^- two single & one double N–O bond; resonance necessary
   h. ClO_3^- three single Cl–O bonds, no resonance

8. Isoelectronic with CO_2 (16 valence electrons):

    NO_2^+ CS_2 NCO^- NCS^- N_3^-

    Isoelectronic with SO_2 (18 valence electrons):

    NO_2^- O_3

9. $CH_3-CH=CH_2(g) + H_2O(g) \rightarrow CH_3-CH(OH)-CH_3(g)$

Bonds broken:		Bonds made:	
C=C	611 kJ	C–C	347 kJ
O–H	464 kJ	C–O	351 kJ
		C–H	414 kJ
Total	1075 kJ		1112 kJ

    Some broken remain unbroken. For example, one O–H bond and one C–C bond.

    Difference = $\Delta H° = 1075 - 1112$ kJ = -37 kJ mol^{-1}

10. $CH_3CH_2OH(g) + 3O_2(g) \rightarrow 2CO_2(g) + 3H_2O(g)$

Bonds broken:		Bonds made:	
C–C	347 kJ	4 C=O	4 × 803 kJ
C–O	351 kJ	5 O–H	5 × 464 kJ
5 C–H	5 × 414 kJ		
3 O=O	3 × 498 kJ		
Total	4262 kJ		5532 kJ

    Difference = $\Delta H° = 4262 - 5532$ kJ = -1270 kJ mol^{-1}

    From the heats of formation,
    $$\Delta H°_{reaction} = \Sigma(\Delta H°_f \text{ (products)} - \Delta H°_f \text{ (reactants)})$$
    $$= [(2 \times -393.5 + 3 \times -241.8) - (-235.1)] = -1277 \text{ kJ mol}^{-1}$$

    Often the agreement isn't quite so good as this.

11. Bond order:

a.	carbonate ion	1.33 (avg)		e.	oxygen O_2	2
b.	acetic acid	1.5 (avg)		f.	hydrogen cyanide	3
c.	nitrite ion	1.5 (avg)		g.	sulfur tetrafluoride	1
d.	acetylene	3		h.	carbon dioxide	2

12.

    a. nitrite ion   b. formate ion   c. nitryl chloride
        NO_2^- HCO_2^- NO_2Cl

13.   Determine the arrangement first; then the shape of the molecule:

		arrangement	*shape*
a.	3 bonding & 2 lone pairs	trigonal bipyramid	T–shape
b.	4 bonding & 1 lone pairs	trigonal bipyramid	seesaw
c.	3 bonding & 1 lone pairs	tetrahedral	trig. pyramid
d.	2 bonding & 2 lone pairs	tetrahedral	V–shape
e.	2 bonding & 3 lone pairs	trigonal bipyramid	linear
f.	5 bonding & 1 lone pairs	octahedral	square pyramid

14.

a.	O_3	V-shape	e.	NO_2^+	linear
b.	GaH_3	trigonal planar	f.	ClO_4^-	tetrahedral
c.	SO_2Cl_2	tetrahedral	g.	IF_4^-	square planar
d.	XeO_4	tetrahedral	h.	ClF_2^-	linear

Look for some asymmetry in the molecular structure—specifically some asymmetry in the electron distribution in the molecule.

15.

a.	CCl_4	nonpolar tetrahedral	e.	BF_3	nonpolar trigonal planar
b.	XeF_4	nonpolar square planar	f.	$BeCl_2$	nonpolar linear
c.	PCl_5	nonpolar trigonal bipyramid	g.	SCl_2	polar V-shape
d.	PCl_3	polar trigonal pyramid	h.	CS_2	nonpolar linear

CHAPTER 10

Introduction

In this chapter we take a closer look at just how atoms are held together in molecules. Electrons in molecules exist in orbitals, just as they do in individual atoms. There are two approaches to deriving these orbitals. The first is the valence bond approach of Linus Pauling and the second is the molecular orbital approach of Robert Mullikan and others.

Contents

Orbitals and Bonding Theories
Valence Bond Theory

Orbitals and Bonding Theories

Electrons are responsible for the bonds between atoms in a molecule. These electrons reside in orbitals belonging to more than just one atom. There are two common approaches used to derive these orbitals: valence bond (VB) theory and molecular orbital (MO) theory.

The **valence bond** approach is closely related to Lewis's idea of pairs of electrons shared between atoms in a molecule. The electron pairs are said to be in orbitals **localized** between adjacent atoms. In **molecular orbital theory**, on the other hand, orbitals are derived from *all* the atoms in the molecule and electrons in them are often **delocalized** (shared by more than just two atoms).

Valence bond theory is the simpler approach and gives an image of the bonding in a molecule in its ground state (lowest energy state) that's easy to picture. Molecular orbital theory is useful when excited states of a molecule need to be examined and for some molecules it is really the only theory to explain properties of the molecule satisfactorily.

Valence Bond Theory

When two atoms come together, the electrons of each come under the influence of the nuclei of both atoms and are pulled down in energy. The atoms do not approach too closely because the positive nuclei repel one another. The bond distance is the distance between the nuclei when the potential energy of the system is at a minimum.

The orbitals of the individual atoms overlap as the atoms approach. The basic principle of valence bond theory is that bonds form when the orbitals overlap. An electron in an orbital on one atom pairs up in the shared space with another electron in an orbital on the other atom; this constitutes the chemical bond. Sometimes both electrons in the bond originate from the same atom.

When an s orbital on one atom overlaps with an s orbital on another atom, the region of overlap lies along the internuclear axis. The pair of bonding electrons has a high probability of being found along the internuclear axis. This type of bond is called a σ bond. Similar σ bonds can be formed by any atomic orbital directed along the internuclear axis. This could be an s, p, d, or hybrid atomic orbital.

Many molecules have shapes based upon the five geometries discussed in the last chapter (linear, trigonal, tetrahedral, trigonal bipyramid, and octahedral). Which orbitals on the central atom can be used to create the bonds in these molecules? The atomic orbitals point in the wrong directions!

To solve this problem, Pauling proposed the concept of **hybridization** as an integral part of valence bond theory. He proposed that a new set of **hybrid atomic orbitals** could be created that would accommodate the shape of the molecule. These orbitals are created by mixing together an appropriate set of atomic orbitals:

atomic orbitals	number of orbitals	hybrid orbitals	direction in which they point
s and p	2	sp	linear
s and two p	3	sp^2	trigonal
s and three p	4	sp^3	tetrahedral
s, three p, one d	5	dsp^3	trigonal bipyramid
s, three p, two d	6	d^2sp^3	octahedral

Hybridization creates a set of valence orbitals pointing in the correct direction for the formation of valence bonds. For example, in methane CH_4, the 2s and three 2p orbitals mix to form the four orbitals of the sp^3 hybrid set. These orbitals in the hybrid set are identical in everything but direction. Each points to one corner of a tetrahedron. The four valence electrons are distributed evenly among them. The hybrid orbitals then form σ bonds with the 1s orbitals on the four hydrogen atoms.

Hybrid orbitals have to accommodate the nonbonding pairs of electrons on the central atom as well. For example, in ammonia NH_3, a tetrahedral sp^3 set is still required. Three sp^3 hybrid orbitals are used for bonding, the fourth sp^3 hybrid orbital is used for the lone pair. Similarly, in the water molecule, two sp^3 hybrid orbitals are used for bonding and two sp^3 hybrid orbitals are used for the two lone pairs. The key to a successful use of VB theory is to make use of VSEPR theory:

1. Determine the number of electron pairs around the central atom in the molecule. Include any lone pairs.
2. Use VSEPR theory to determine the arrangement of those electron pairs.
3. Select the hybrid orbital set necessary to accommodate that arrangement according to the table above.
4. Superimpose any π bonding on the σ framework.

Bonds are named according to their symmetry about the internuclear axis. A σ bond, when viewed down the internuclear axis, looks circular, just like an s orbital. A π bond looks just like a p orbital, and so on. The Greek letters used correspond directly to the letters for the atomic orbitals:

Atomic	Molecular
s	σ
p	π
d	δ

See study question #1.

Note that the number of hydrid orbitals created equals the number of atomic orbitals used.

It is usually unnecessary to hybridize the orbitals of the terminal atoms—just the central atom.

The participation of d orbitals in the bonding of main-group elements is now considered to be minimal (i.e hybrid sets like dsp^3 and d^2sp^3 are unrealistic).
[See J.Chem.Educ 75 910 (1998)]

In a situation like this the contribution of each atomic orbital to a particular hybrid orbital is not equal. The lone pair hybrid orbital has more s character than the bonding hybrids. This reconciles the slightly smaller than tetra-hedral angles in the ammonia and water molecules.

Remember that a molecule is not tetrahedral because the hybridization is sp^3. The hybridization is sp^3 because the molecule is tetrahedral.

A **multiple bond** is a bond in which more than one pair of electrons is shared. Although a single bond requires just one orbital in the region of overlap between the two atoms (for the single pair of bonding electrons), a double bond requires two orbitals, and a triple bond requires three orbitals (for the additional shared pairs of electrons).

When an atom like the carbon in ethylene, or the nitrogen in the nitrate ion, is sp^2 hybridized, there is a p orbital left over that is perpendicular to the plane of the molecule. This leftover p orbital can overlap sideways on with a similar p orbital on an adjacent atom. This overlap results in a π bond. Note that in a π bond the electron density lies to either side of the internuclear axis. Note also that the two p orbitals must be lined up in the same way in order to combine to form a π bond. The σ bond and the π bond together make up the double bond.

When atoms are sp hybridized, like carbon in acetylene, then two p orbitals are left over on each carbon atom, and these two p orbitals can form two π bonds with similar orbitals on an adjacent atom. A triple bond results.

A important feature of multiple bonds is that they restrict movement about the bond. Rotation about a single bond requires little energy; the bond can remain intact, with constant overlap of the atomic orbitals, throughout the rotation. When rotation of a double bond or a triple bond is attempted however, the π overlap of the p_π orbitals is destroyed in the process. Breaking the π bond requires energy and the rotation is impossible at normal temperatures.

A consequence of **restricted rotation** about multiple bonds is the existence of **structural isomers** called **stereoisomers**. An example is cis– and trans– 1,2–dichloro-ethylene. In the cis– isomer the chlorine atoms are on the same side of the molecule and in the trans– isomer the two chlorine atoms are on opposite sides.

The bonding in the six–membered **benzene ring** is particularly interesting. The σ bonding involves sp^2 hybridization at each carbon atom in the ring: two of the three sp^2 hybrid orbitals are used for bonding to the adjacent carbon atoms and the third sp^2 hybrid is used for bonding to the hydrogen atom. This leaves a p_π orbital on each carbon atom perpendicular to the molecular plane. The interesting aspect of the bonding is the interaction of the six p_π orbitals. Each p_π orbital overlaps with the p_π orbitals on its adjacent carbon atoms—the π interaction is unbroken around the six–membered ring. The π bond in benzene extends over all six carbon atoms. Two electrons in such a bond are delocalized over the entire benzene ring. In order to obtain this picture of the bonding in benzene using valence bond theory, resonance is required. Picturing the π bonding in terms of localized electron pairs between adjacent atoms is unsatisfactory.

For many commonly encountered molecules and polyatomic ions—those for which resonance was necessary in drawing a Lewis electron dot structure—the σ bonding is most easily described in terms of valence bond theory and the localized sharing of electron pairs. For the π bonding, however, a different approach is desirable—one which describes the **delocalization of electrons**.

single bond   :

double bond   ::

triple bond   :::

one σ bond = single bond

one σ bond and one π bond
= double bond

one σ bond and two π bonds
= triple bond

p orbitals can be designated p_σ or p_π:
A p_σ orbital is a p orbital lying along the internuclear axis able to form a σ bond.
A p_π orbital is an orbital perpendicular to the bond axis table to form a π bond.

Key terms:

valence bond theory
molecular orbital theory
orbital overlap
σ bond
π bond
orbital hybridization
restricted rotation
cis-trans isomerism
molecular orbital
delocalization

Review Questions

1. Explain the concept of hybridization. Why is it a necessary component of valence bond theory?

2. Describe a procedure for determining the hybridization of atomic orbitals around the central atom in a molecule.

3. What is a multiple bond? How is a multiple bond viewed in valence bond theory?

4. What is the difference between a σ bond and a π bond?

5. Is a single bond always a σ bond, or can it be a π bond?

6. Can an s orbital form a π bond or is a p orbital the only orbital that can form a π bond? Can a p orbital form a σ bond?

7. Explain how restricted rotation about a multiple bond leads to stereoisomerism.

8. Describe the bonding in an aromatic compound like benzene.

9. Describe the bonding in a molecule like sulfur dioxide.

Answers to Review Questions

1. Linus Pauling proposed the concept of hybridization as an integral part of valence bond theory. He proposed that an appropriate set of atomic orbitals could be mixed together to create a set of hybrid atomic orbitals that would accommodate the shape of any molecule. The hybrid orbitals point in the correct direction for the formation of valence bonds with the terminal atoms. Hybridization is necessary because the s and p atomic orbitals do not point in the right direction and because they cannot generate the equivalent valence bonds observed in molecules like CH_4 or H_2O.

2. Make use of the VSEPR theory! Determine the number of electron pairs around the central atom in the molecule and remember to include the lone pairs. Use VSEPR theory to determine the arrangement of those electron pairs. Then select the hybrid orbital set necessary to accommodate that arrangement.

3. A multiple bond is a bond in which more than one pair of electrons is shared between the two atoms. A single bond requires one orbital in the region of overlap between the two atoms for the single pair of bonding electrons. A double bond requires two orbitals for the two pairs of electrons. A triple bond requires three orbitals for the three pairs of electrons. In valence bond

theory, all electron pairs in a multiple bond are localized between the adjacent atoms—the first pair in a σ bond on the internuclear axis and the next two pairs in π bonds off the internuclear axis.

4.   The electron density (the probability of finding the electron) in a σ bond is concentrated along the internuclear axis. When viewed down the internuclear axis a σ bond has a circular shape just like an s orbital. The electron density in a π bond is concentrated on either side of the internuclear axis. When viewed down the internuclear axis a π bond has a shape just like an p orbital.

5.   A single bond is always a σ bond.

6.   No, an s orbital cannot form a π bond, it has the incorrect symmetry. There is no way to view an s orbital that will make it look like a p orbital! A p orbital can certainly form a π bond, but so can a d orbital. If a d orbital is viewed sideways on, it looks like a p orbital. And yes, a p orbital can form a σ bond; when it lies along the internuclear axis it has the correct symmetry to form a σ bond. In other words, when viewed lengthways on, it has the circular shape required for a σ bond.

Assuming the internuclear axis is the z axis:

s orbital — only σ

p_z orbital — σ
p_x orbital — π
p_y orbital — π

and, to complete the pattern, although you don't need to know these until later in your studies of chemistry :

d_{z^2} orbital — σ
d_{xz} orbital — π
d_{yz} orbital — π
d_{xy} orbital — δ
$d_{x^2-y^2}$ orbital — δ

7.   Multiple bonds restrict movement about the bond. When rotation of a double bond or a triple bond is attempted, the π overlap of the p_π orbitals and any π bonding is destroyed in the process. Breaking the π bond requires energy and the rotation is impossible at normal temperatures. A consequence of this restricted rotation is the existence of stereoisomers. An example is cis– and trans– 1,2–dichloroethylene. These two isomers cannot interconvert at normal temperatures:

cis–   trans–

8.   The σ bonding in the six–membered benzene ring involves sp² hybridization at each carbon atom in the ring: two sp² hybrid orbitals are used for bonding to the adjacent carbon atoms and the third sp² hybrid is used for bonding to the hydrogen atom. This leaves a p_π orbital on each carbon atom perpendicular to the molecular plane.

9.   In sulfur dioxide, as with most simple molecules, the σ bonding framework is best described using valence bond theory. The sulfur is sp² hybridized with two bonding pairs and one nonbonding pair. This leaves a p_π orbital on the sulfur that can bond with an appropriate orbital on either oxygen—leading to resonance in valence bond theory.

*Nature has some sort of arithmetical-
geometrical coordinate system, because
nature has all kinds of models. What
we experience of nature is in models,
and all of nature's models are so
beautiful.*

R. Buckminster Fuller
(1895-1983)

Study Questions and Problems

1. What hybridization is required at the central atom of the following molecules or ions? (Most are the same molecules examined in questions 3, 5, 14, and 15 in Chapter 9 of this study guide.)

    a. $AlCl_3$
    b. PCl_3
    c. PCl_5
    d. $SiCl_4$
    e. NCl_3
    f. BCl_3
    g. ClO_2^-
    h. O_3
    i. GaH_3
    j. SO_2Cl_2
    k. XeO_4
    l. CCl_4
    m. SCl_2

    n. SF_6
    o. $BeCl_2$
    p. NO_2
    q. XeF_4
    r. SF_4
    s. OCS
    t. SO_2
    u. NO_2^+
    v. ClO_4^-
    w. IF_4^-
    x. ClF_2^-
    y. BF_3
    z. CO_2

2. In the organic chemistry of carbon, three hybridizations are common. What are they, and why are they limited to three?

3. Examine the bonding in the following molecules using valence bond theory. Describe each bond in terms of the orbitals on adjacent atoms that overlap to create the bond:

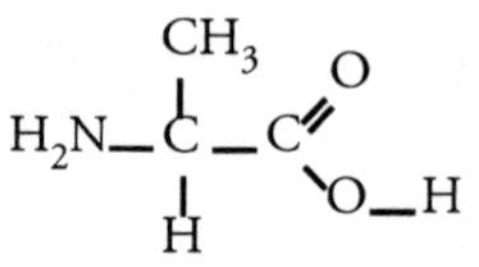

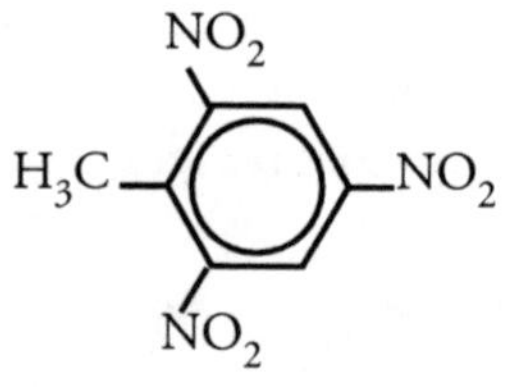

4. Draw the Lewis electron dot structure of the nitrite ion. Describe the bonding in terms of valence bond theory.

5. Describe the hybridization at each atom (other than H) in the following molecule (the anesthetic novocaine).

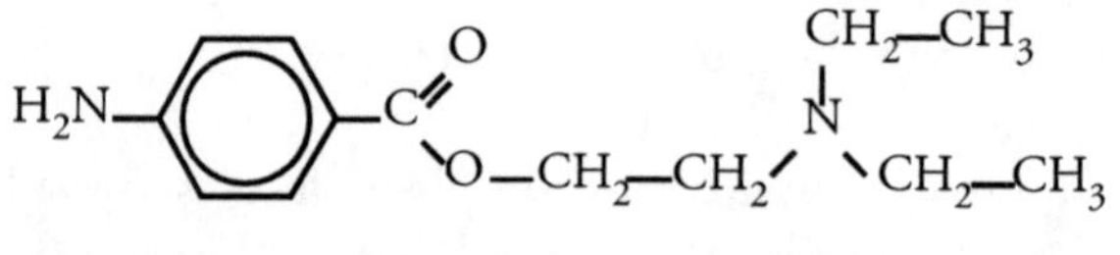

6. Using valence bond theory describe the σ bonding and the π bonding in the molecule allene $CH_2=C=CH_2$.

7. Use valence bond theory to describe the bonding in the molecule carbon dioxide CO_2.

Answers to Study Questions and Problems

1. First determine the arrangement of the electron pairs around the central atom; the hybridization must accommodate *all* electron pairs (not just the bonding pairs). So look at the arrangement of electron pairs, not the shape of the molecule. There are five arrangements and five corresponding hybridizations. The arrangements are listed on page 130 of this study guide).

a.	$AlCl_3$	sp^2	n.	SF_6	d^2sp^3
b.	PCl_3	sp^3	o.	$BeCl_2$	sp
c.	PCl_5	dsp^3	p.	NO_2	sp^2
d.	$SiCl_4$	sp^3	q.	XeF_4	d^2sp^3
e.	NCl_3	sp^3	r.	SF_4	dsp^3
f.	BCl_3	sp^2	s.	OCS	sp
g.	ClO_2^-	sp^3	t.	SO_2	sp^2
h.	O_3	sp^2	u.	NO_2^+	sp
i.	GaH_3	sp^2	v.	ClO_4^-	sp^3
j.	SO_2Cl_2	sp^3	w.	IF_4^-	d^2sp^3
k.	XeO_4	sp^3	x.	ClF_2^-	dsp^3
l.	CCl_4	sp^3	y.	BF_3	sp^2
m.	SCl_2	sp^3	z.	CO_2	sp

linear	sp
trigonal	sp^2
tetrahedral	sp^3
trigonal bipyramid	dsp^3
octahedral	d^2sp^3

2. The three hybridizations common in the organic chemistry of carbon are:

sp	linear arrangement of two σ bonds	two π bonds
sp2	trigonal arrangement of three σ bonds	one π bond
sp3	tetrahedral arrangement of four σ bonds	no π bonds

   They are limited to these three because carbon only has s and p orbitals available; no d orbitals. Carbon forms 4 bonds.

3.

   $-NO_2 = -N\overset{O}{\underset{O}{\lessgtr}}$

$N(sp^3)–H(1s)$	$C(sp^3)–H(1s)$
$C(sp^3)–H(1s)$	$C(sp^2)–C(sp^2)$ in the ring
$C(sp^2)–O(2p)$	$C(sp^3)–C(sp^2)$
$C(sp^3)–N(sp^3)$	$C(sp^2)–N(sp^2)$
$C(sp^3)–C(sp^3)$	$N(sp^2)–O(2p)$
$C(sp^3)–C(sp^2)$	$C(sp^2)–H(1s)$ on the ring
$O(sp^3)–H(1s)$	

   It is usually unnecessary to hybridize the orbitals of the terminal atoms—just the central atoms.

4.   Lewis electron dot structure of the nitrite ion NO_2^-:

In the valence bond picture, the nitrogen valence orbitals are sp^2 hybridized. The arrangement of electron pairs (including the lone pair) is trigonal planar. In the Lewis diagram, one N–O bond is drawn as a double bond and the other as a single bond. Resonance between the two possibilities leads to a bond order of 1.5 for each.

5.   Count up the number of σ bonds and lone pairs around an atom. Establish the arrangement; then the corresponding hybridization.

You may notice that the hybridization is related to the number of double bonds around the atom. How?

Note that all the carbon atoms in the benzene ring are sp^2 hybridized. Note also that the lone pairs on oxygen and nitrogen atoms are often omitted!

6.   In allene $CH_2=C=CH_2$, the hybridization at each end carbon atom is sp^2 (trigonal). This leaves a p_π orbital perpendicular to the trigonal plane of the carbon atom and the two hydrogen atoms. The hybridization at the central carbon atom is sp (linear); the entire 3–carbon chain is linear. There are two p_π orbitals on the central carbon atom—at right angles to one another and the axis of the molecule. One p_π orbital forms a π bond with the carbon at one end of the molecule and the other p_π orbital forms a π bond with the carbon at the other end. Therefore the two π bonds are not in the same plane; they too are at right angles to each other. This means, of course, that the four hydrogen atoms are not in the same plane either.

7.   Superficially, the carbon dioxide molecule has a structure similar to allene in the last question. And, according to valence bond theory the π bonding is the same. The hybridization at the central carbon atom is sp (linear) and the entire molecule is linear. There are two p_π orbitals on the central carbon atom—at right angles to one another and the axis of the molecule. One p_π orbital forms a π bond in one direction and the other p_π orbital forms a π bond in the other direction.

However, unlike in allene, there are two orbitals on each terminal oxygen atom in carbon dioxide that have the correct orientation to π bond, and they do. So the π bonds in carbon dioxide are still at right angles to one another, but they extend the entire length of the molecule. Electrons in them are delocalized over all three atoms.

EXAMINATION 2

Introduction

This examination tests your knowledge and understanding of the chemistry in Chapters 7 through 10 of this study guide. The questions are again formatted as true–false questions and multiple choice questions. Try the exam before looking at the answers provided at the end of this book.

True–false questions

1. Red light has a lower frequency than blue light.

2. The maximum allowed value for m_ℓ is $+\ell$.

3. Diamagnetic materials are drawn into a magnetic field.

4. A fluorine atom is larger than a boron atom.

5. The number of electrons that can be placed in a subshell of orbitals = $2(2\ell+1)$.

6. The most stable ion of sodium is the Na^- ion.

7. A lone pair of electrons is a nonbonding pair of electrons.

8. The bond order can be determined from the number of pairs of electrons shared in the bond.

9. Electronegativity is a measure of the ability of an atom in a compound to attract electrons to itself.

10. An ionic bond is the result when the both participating elements have low electronegativity.

11. The see-saw molecular geometry is derived from the trigonal bipyramidal arrangement of electron pairs.

12. Bonding pairs of electrons repel each other more than nonbonding pairs of electrons.

13. A triple bond indicates that three atoms are involved in the bond.

14. There's no such thing as a 100% ionic bond.

15. If an ion has a charge it must be polar.

16. The geometry of a set of sp hybrid orbitals is linear.

17. The number of hybrid orbitals always equals the number of atomic orbitals used to make the set.

18.   Cis-trans isomerism is possible about any multiple bond.

19.   p orbitals can form σ bonds and π bonds.

20.   Because there are 3 π bonding pairs of electrons in a benzene molecule, the bond order is 3.

21.   Resonance is required in valence bond theory when π electrons are delocalized.

22.   A single bond is a σ bond.

Multiple choice questions

The following 2 questions refer to the electromagnetic spectrum:

a.	radio waves	c.	visible radiation	e.	x-radiation
b.	γ-radiation	d.	ultraviolet	f.	microwaves

1.   Which part of the spectrum listed above has the longest wavelength?

2.   Which part of the spectrum listed above has the highest energy per photon?

3.   If the length of a vibrating string (the distance between the fixed ends) is equal to 3 wavelengths, how many nodes are present between the ends?

   a. 1   b. 2   c. 3   d. 4   e. 5   f. 6   g. 7

4.   The significance of the three orbital quantum numbers can be described as energy, shape, and orientation. Which description belongs to which quantum number?

	n	l	m_l
a.	shape	orientation	energy
b.	orientation	shape	energy
c.	energy	orientation	shape
d.	energy	shape	orientation
e.	shape	energy	orientation
f.	orientation	energy	shape

5.   What orbital is designated by n = 4, l = 1, and m_l = 0?

   a. 4s   b. 4p   c. 3d   d. 5p   e. 5d

6.   For any one atom, what is the total number of electrons that can have a principal quantum number of 5 and an secondary (angular momentum) quantum number of zero?

a.	2	c.	5	e.	7	g.	14
b.	4	d.	6	f.	10	h.	18

7. According to the auf-bau principle, which set of orbitals is filled after the 6p set?

   a. 8s   c. 4d   e. 5d   g. 6d
   b. 4f   d. 5f   f. 6s   h. 7s

8. The following diagram represents the ground state electron configuration of an element in the Periodic Table. Which element is it?

1s	2s	2p	3s	3p	4s	3d	4p
↑↓	↑↓	↑↓ ↑↓ ↑↓	↑↓	↑↓ ↑↓ ↑↓	↑↓	↑↓ ↑↓ ↑↓ ↑↓ ↑↓	↑ ↑

   a. Al   c. Si   e. Cu   g. Sn
   b. Zn   d. Ga   f. Ge   h. In

9. Which of the following electron configurations is impossible?

   a. $1s^2\, 2s^2\, 2p^6\, 3s^2\, 3p^4$

   b. $1s^2\, 2s^2\, 2p^6\, 3s^1$

   c. $1s^2\, 2s^2\, 2p^6\, 3s^2\, 3p^6\, 4s^2\, 3d^{10}\, 4p^6$

   d. $1s^2\, 2s^2\, 2p^6\, 3s^2\, 3p^8\, 4s^2$

   e. $1s^1$

   f. $1s^2\, 2s^2\, 2p^6\, 3s^2\, 3p^6\, 4s^1\, 3d^{10}$

10. According to Hund's Rule, how many singly occupied orbitals are there in the valence shell of a iron atom in its lowest energy state?

    a. none   b. 1   c. 2   d. 3   e. 4

11. An electronic transition in a hydrogen atom emits radiation with a wavelength of 450 nm. What is the energy of a photon of this radiation?

    a. 4.42×10^{-19} J   c. 4.42×10^{-35} J   e. 2.26×10^{34} J
    b. 4.91×10^{-22} J   d. 1.47×10^{-27} J   f. 2.66×10^{5} J

The following four questions refer to the block of nine elements in the Periodic Table shown on the right:

   a. Al   d. Si   g. P
   b. Ga   e. Ge   h. As
   c. In   f. Sn   i. Sb

12. Which element is the smallest in atomic size?

13. Which element has the highest electronegativity?

14. Which element has the highest first ionization energy?

15. Which element is most metallic in character?

16. If two elements combine to form a compound, and both elements have relatively high (greater than 2.0) but different electronegativities, what kind of bond is formed between the two elements?

    a. covalent   c. ionic
    b. polar covalent   d. metallic

17.   How many valence shell electron pairs are there around the phosphorus atom in the phosphite ion, PO_3^{3-}?

       a. 2   b. 3   c. 4   d. 5   e. 6

18.   What is the arrangement of electron pairs around the central atom in the molecule $XeOF_2$?

       a. linear   c. trigonal planar   e. tetrahedral
       b. trigonal bipyramidal   d. octahedral

19.   What is the shape of the ion BrF_4^+?

       a. linear   d. trigonal planar   g. tetrahedral
       b. trigonal pyramidal   e. square planar   h. octahedral
       c. T-shaped   f. see-saw   i. V-shaped (bent)

20.   What hybridization of atomic orbitals on the central atom of the sulfate ion is necessary to accommodate the arrangement of electron pairs on the sulfur atom?

       a. sp   b. sp^2 c. sp^3 d. sp^3d e. sp^3d^2

21.   What is the average bond order of the C–O bond in the carbonate ion CO_3^{2-}?

       a. 1.0   c. 1.25   e. 1.33   g. 2.0
       b. 2.5   d. 3.0   f. 1.67

22.   Which of the following polyatomic ions is polar?

       a. SO_4^{2-} c. NH_4^+ e. PF_6^- g. PO_4^{3-}
       b. CO_3^{2-} d. ClO_3^- f. IF_2^- h. XeO_6^{4-}

23.   Imagine a double bond between two carbon atoms in a molecule. The internuclear axis (the bond axis) is the z axis. Which two orbitals, one on each of the two carbon atoms, can combine to form the π bond?

       a. s and p_x c. p_x and p_y e. p_z and p_z g. d_{xy} and p_y
       b. p_y and s   d. s and s   f. p_y and p_y h. p_y and p_z

24.   How many electrons are shared between two atoms participating in a triple bond?

       a. 1   c. 3   e. 5   g. 7
       b. 2   d. 4   f. 6   h. 8

25.   Draw a Lewis dot structure for the cyanate ion, NCO^- with a triple bond between the C and the O. What is the formal charge on the nitrogen atom if the structure is drawn this way?

       a. –3   b. –2   c. –1   d. 0   e. +1   f. +2   g. +3

26. Resonance is

    a. a way to ensure that each atom has a complete octet of electrons
    b. a way to avoid problems with odd numbers of electrons in molecules
    c. the delocalization of π electrons in a molecule
    d. a method used to predict the hybridization of atomic orbitals on a central atom
    e. the minimization of repulsion between different electron domains in a molecule
    f. a way to reconcile Lewis electron dot structures with the actual or real structure

27. Estimate the heat of formation ΔH_f° of methane in kJ/mol if

    the bond energy of the H–H bond = 436 kJ/mol
    the bond energy of the C–H bond = 413 kJ/mol
    the sublimation energy of graphite = 716 kJ/mol

    a. +1565   c. +1652   e. +652   g. −64
    b. +739   d. −780   f. +808   h. −500

28. Orbital hybridization is the

    a. creation of bonding and antibonding orbitals from atomic orbitals
    b. combination of atomic orbitals to form a new set of orbitals with directional properties more appropriate for bonding
    c. formulation of many Lewis dot resonance structures for a molecule
    d. filling of molecular orbitals with electrons according to the aufbau principle
    e. creation of a set of molecular orbitals in which the electrons can be delocalized over the entire molecule

29. What is the hybridization of the carbon valence orbitals in benzene, C_6H_6?
    a. sp   b. sp^2 d. sp^3 d. dsp^2 e. dsp^3

CHAPTER 11

Introduction

Of the three states of matter, the gas state is perhaps the simplest to understand from a molecular point of view. It is possible to describe the behavior of molecules in the gas state under ordinary conditions in terms of relatively simple mathematical equations. In this chapter we will examine the properties of gases and how they are characterized and described. The kinetic molecular theory is reintroduced.

Contents

The Properties of Gases
Gas Laws: The Experimental Basis
The Ideal Gas Law
Gas Laws and Chemical Reactions
Gas Mixtures and Partial Pressures
The Kinetic–Molecular Theory of Gases
Diffusion and Effusion
Some Applications of Gas Laws
Nonideal Behavior: Real Gases

The Properties of Gases

A sample of gas can be described using only four quantities: pressure, volume, temperature, and amount.

Pressure is exerted by a gas when molecules of the gas strike a surface. The force exerted per unit area is the pressure of the gas. A **barometer** is a device used to measure atmospheric pressure. At sea level, the pressure exerted by the atmosphere—the result of the collisions of the molecules in the atmosphere with the surface of the liquid—can support a column of mercury 76 cm high or a column of water about 1025 cm high.

Pressure = force per unit area
$Pa = Nm^{-2}$

Force = mass × acceleration
$N = kg\ ms^{-2}$

So $Pa = kg\ m^{-1}s^{-2}$

The Pa is a small unit and ordinary pressures are expressed in kPa.

1 atm pressure = 101.325 kPa
1 bar = 100 kPa exactly
1 atm pressure = 14.7 psi
1 atm pressure = 760 torr

A torr is another name for mm Hg.

Be able to convert between the common units of pressure.

See study question #1.

Gas Laws: The Experimental Basis

Gases are compressible; if you increase the pressure, the volume occupied by the gas decreases. In 1660, Robert Boyle discovered that for a fixed quantity of gas at a constant temperature, the pressure and volume are inversely proportional. This is known as **Boyle's law**. Mathematically, the law is written as PV = constant (at constant temperature).

In 1787, Jacques Charles discovered that the volume of a fixed quantity of gas increased if the temperature was increased at constant pressure. If plots of volume *vs.* temperature are extrapolated to zero volume, then all the lines meet at a common temperature: –273.15°C. **Kelvin** proposed a new temperature scale—now known

$K = °C + 273.15$

Another relationship was discovered by a Frenchman Guillaume Amontons in the late 1600s that stated that the pressure of a gas is directly proportional to its temperature:

$P = kT$

Amonton's data led to the first suggestion of an absolute zero temperature.

n = the number of moles of gas.

as the Kelvin scale—with a value of zero at this common temperature. **Charles' law** can now be expressed as: the volume of a given quantity of gas at constant pressure is proportional to its temperature in K. Mathematically, this is written as V = constant $\times$ T (or $V = kT$ where k is a constant).

A general gas law combines both Boyle's law and Charles' law: $PV = kT$ where the temperature is in K and the quantity of gas is constant.

Joseph Gay-Lussac discovered that the ratio of the volumes of gases involved in a chemical reaction was always a small whole number—provided that the gas volumes were measured at the same temperature and pressure. This is now known as **Gay-Lussac's law** of combining volumes. For example, the volume of hydrogen in the reaction of hydrogen and oxygen to produce water is always twice the volume of oxygen. Amedeo Avogadro explained this law with his hypothesis that at the same temperature, volume, and pressure, a gas always contains the same number of molecules. **Avogadro's law** is expressed as V is proportional to n at constant pressure and temperature.

The Ideal Gas Law

You should be able to do calculations involving the ideal gas law; be able to solve for any one of the four variables, pressure, volume, temperature, and quantity, if you are given the other three.

The laws discussed in the previous section can be combined into a single law called the **ideal gas law**. If

Boyle: PV = constant, at constant T and n
Charles: V = constant $\times$ T, at constant P and n   then $PV = nRT$
Avogadro: V = constant $\times$ n, at constant T and P

Be sure to use the correct value of R in your problems—it depends upon the units of pressure and volume that you are using.

The other common mistake when doing gas law problems is to forget to use the Kelvin temperature.

See study questions #2, 3, & 4.

The combined proportionality constant R is called the gas constant. It has a value equal to 0.08206 L atm K^{-1} mol^{-1} or 8.314 J K^{-1} mol^{-1}.

The density of a gas decreases if the temperature is increased. Jacques Charles, a balloonist of some renown, knew this. The relationship of the density to the temperature, pressure, and molar mass of the gas can be derived from the ideal gas law:

$$\text{density} = \frac{PM}{RT} \quad \text{where M is the molar mass of the gas.}$$

There's no such thing as an ideal gas; all gases are real. However, under ordinary conditions, most gases behave almost ideally. Some are more ideal than others.

Standard temperature and pressure (STP) describes the conditions of 1.00 atm pressure and 273.15K temperature ($0°C$). The volume of an ideal gas at STP is 22.414 liters.

Gas Laws and Chemical Reactions

Problems involving the ideal gas law, and problems in calculating density or molar mass, are provided in the section at the end of this study guide. Solutions are provided but try the problems before looking at the solutions!

See study questions #5 & 6.

The stoichiometry of a chemical reaction (the coefficients in the equation) provides information about the relative numbers of moles of reactants required and moles of products produced. The ideal gas law relates the number of moles of a gas to the pressure, temperature, and volume of the gas. Therefore stoichiometric calculations for reactions involving gases can be done.

The determination of the limiting reactant, the calculation of theoretical and percent yields, and the calculation of how much excess reactant remains at the end of the reaction, all apply in exactly the same way as they did earlier.

Gas Mixtures and Partial Pressures

The pressure exerted by a gas is due to the millions of collisions that the gas molecules have with the surface of the container every second. If the gas is a mixture of different gas molecules, then the different gases in the mixture will all contribute to the total pressure because they will all collide with the surface of the container. The contribution that each gas makes to the total pressure will depend upon how much of that gas is present. John Dalton observed that the pressure of a mixture of gases is the sum of the partial pressures of the different gases in the mixture. This is known as **Dalton's law of partial pressures.**

An ideal gas is one in which the individual molecules behave quite independently of one another. They collide without interaction; they have zero attraction for one another. The identity of the gas is therefore immaterial; a mixture of ideal gases behaves just like a single ideal gas. Therefore, each gas in an ideal mixture can be considered separately:

For gas a, for example, $P_aV = n_aRT$ and likewise for gas b, or c, etc.

For the total mixture, $P_{total}V = n_{total}RT.$

Dividing the first expression by the second:

$$\frac{P_a}{P_{total}} = \frac{n_a}{n_{total}}$$

or $P_a = (n_a/n_{total})P_{total}$

or $P_a = X_aP_{total}$ where X_a is called the **mole fraction** n_a/n_{total} of a in the mixture.

An application of the use of Dalton's law occurs when gases are collected or prepared in the presence of water. Water vapor is just like any other gas; it contributes to the total pressure exerted by a gas mixture. Therefore the total pressure is the sum of the partial pressure of water vapor at that particular temperature and the partial pressure of the gas being collected.

> The partial pressure of a gas in a mixture is the contribution that gas makes to the total pressure.

> The sum of the mole fractions of all components in the mixture must equal 1.

> If the mole fraction equals one, then there must be only one gas present, and the partial pressure is equal to the total pressure. In other words, the partial pressure of a gas equals the pressure it would exert if it were the only gas present. This is a particularly useful thing to know in calculations involving partial pressures.

> See study questions #7, 8, 9, & 10.

The Kinetic-Molecular Theory of Gases

At a particulate level, molecules in the gas state are in constant motion, travelling at high velocities and in constant collision with each other and the container. This picture of the gaseous state is described by the **kinetic-molecular theory.** The average kinetic energy of the gas molecules depends only upon the temperature—the higher the temperature, the higher the average kinetic energy, and the faster the molecules move.

Because kinetic energy is $\frac{1}{2}mu^2$, the average kinetic energy of many molecules is related to the average of the squares of the speeds of all the molecules. This average is referred to as the **mean square speed** and is written $\overline{u^2}$.

- The principal features of the kinetic-molecular theory are:

- Gases consist of molecules with intermolecular distances much greater than their size.
- Molecular motion is continual, random, and rapid.
- The average KE is proportional only to the temperature of the gas. All gases have the same KE at the same temperature.
- No energy is "lost" during the collisions with each other and the container.

> At room temperature, the average speed of molecules of oxygen and nitrogen in the air is 1000 mph.

> The square root of the mean square speed is called, logically enough, the root mean square speed. The significance of the rms speed is that it is the speed of a molecule possessing average kinetic energy.

> Maxwell's equation relates the root mean square speed to the temperature and the molar mass:

$$\sqrt{\overline{u^2}} = \sqrt{\frac{3RT}{M}}$$

> See study questions # 11 & 12.

All the experimental gas laws can be derived from the kinetic molecular theory. Pressure is caused by molecules colliding with the container walls. If the temperature is increased, the kinetic energy of the molecules is increased, and the molecules hit the container with greater force. Therefore pressure is proportional to temperature. Increasing the number of molecules, without changing the temperature or pressure, means that the molecules need more room, so volume is proportional to n. The other laws can be explained in the same way.

Not all molecules in a gas sample move at the same speed; some have low speeds (and low KE), whereas others are moving very fast (with high KE). The distribution of molecular speeds is called a **Boltzmann distribution**. The distribution shifts to higher speeds as the temperature is increased.

Diffusion and Effusion

Effusion is the movement of a gas through a small opening or a porous barrier.

Diffusion is the mixing of gases.

See study question #13.

Thomas Graham (1805–1869) studied the effusion of gases. He found that the rate at which a gas effused was inversely proportional to the square root of its molar mass. This law, called **Graham's law of effusion**, can be derived directly from the kinetic molecular theory. If the average kinetic energies of all gases are the same at the same temperature, then a gas with a greater molar mass must have a lower speed (so that $\frac{1}{2}mu^2$ is the same).

$$\frac{\text{Rate of effusion of A}}{\text{Rate of effusion of B}} = \frac{\sqrt{\overline{u_A^2}}}{\sqrt{\overline{u_B^2}}} = \sqrt{\frac{M_B}{M_A}}$$

Some Applications of Gas Laws

Rubber balloons leak because the molecules inside the balloon can escape through small holes in the rubber latex. They will escape until the pressures on both sides of the balloon are equal. Hydrogen and helium escape more easily because their molar masses are low, they are smaller particles, and their molecular speeds are higher.

Oxygen is mixed with helium for deep sea diving.

When deep sea diving, the pressure of air in your lungs is higher the deeper you go. At 33 feet, the pressure is 2 atm. When using compressed air, the higher partial pressure of nitrogen at depths below 33 feet can cause nitrogen narcosis. High partial pressures of oxygen can cause oxygen toxicity (the partial pressure of oxygen in air at 150 feet is equivalent to breathing pure oxygen).

Nonideal Behavior

At ordinary temperatures and pressures the ideal gas law works well. However, at low temperatures, where the molecules are moving much more slowly and attract one another, and at high pressures, where the molecules are squeezed together, deviation from ideal behavior is observed.

Two assumptions made in the derivation of the ideal gas law from the kinetic molecular theory do not hold at low temperatures and high pressures. The first, the more important, is that molecules do attract one another; because of this attraction a gas will eventually liquefy as the temperature is lowered. The effect of the attraction is to reduce the observed pressure exerted by the gas; the molecules, because of their attraction for one another, are held back in their collisions with the surface of the container, thus reducing the pressure.

The second, the less important, is that the actual volume of the molecules is not zero. Although the volume is very small, it becomes more and more significant the higher the pressure and the lower the temperature.

Johannes van der Waals developed a modification of the ideal gas law to accommodate the facts that there is attraction between molecules and that molecules do have a finite volume. This modified gas law is called the **van der Waals equation (of state)**:

$$[P + a(\tfrac{n}{V})^2][V - nb] = nRT$$

The correction factor for the pressure term contains $\tfrac{n}{V}$, which is the concentration in moles/liter. Squared, and multiplied by a, it is a measure of what proportion of the molecules stick together. The van der Waals constant a is a measure of the strength of the intermolecular attraction. The correction factor for the volume term is nb, where the van der Waals constant b is a measure of the volume of one mole of molecules. The two constants, a and b, are determined experimentally. Notice that the two correction terms have opposite signs; they do to some extent compensate for one another.

Review Questions

1. What is the difference between a gas and a vapor?

2. Write an expression for Boyle's law. If the pressure on a gas is tripled at constant temperature, what happens to the volume?

3. Write an expression for Charles' law. Explain why the temperature must be in K.

4. What is the combined gas law? Write a mathematical expression for the law.

5. Write statements of Gay-Lussac's law and Avogadro's law.

6. To what does the 'ideal' refer in the ideal gas law? Is there such a thing as an ideal gas?

7. Derive the expression for the density of a gas $d = \dfrac{PM}{RT}$ from the ideal gas equation.

8. One property that distinguishes the gas state from the other two states is its compressibility. Why can gases be compressed whereas liquids and solids cannot?

9. Derive the expression $P_a = X_a P_{total}$ for the partial pressure of component a in a mixture of gases. What is X_a in this expression?

One mole of water vapor occupies 22.4 L at 25°C and 1 atm pressure. One mole of water liquid occupies 18 mL — very small in comparison.

The equation is often referred to as an equation of state because it describes the behavior of the gaseous state.

See study question #14.

Key terms:

pressure
torr
atm
pascal
bar
psi
Boyle's law
Charles' law
Kelvin
law of combining volumes
Avogadro's law
ideal gas law
R, gas constant
gas density
standard temperature & pressure
parial pressure
mole fraction
Dalton's law
kinetic molecular theory
rms speed
Boltzmann distribution
diffusion
effusion
Graham's law
van der Waals' equation of state
real gases

10.   Is air containing a high proportion of water vapor (high humidity) less dense or more dense than dry air?

11.   How is the speed of a molecule in the gaseous state related to the temperature and the molar mass of the gas?

12.   Does a single molecule have a temperature?

13.   Describe the principal features of the kinetic-molecular theory.

14.   Derive Graham's law from the result you obtained in question 11.

15.   Why does a helium-filled mylar balloon last longer if you put it in the freezer?

16.   Describe the conditions under which a gas might start to deviate from ideal behavior. Explain why the deviation occurs.

Answers to Review Questions

1.   There is no significant difference between a gas and a vapor. A gas is a substance that is normally a gas at ordinary temperatures and pressures (for example, oxygen, carbon dioxide). A vapor is a substance that is normally a liquid or solid at ordinary temperatures and pressures (for example, water, naphthalene).

2.   Boyle's law can be expressed in several ways; one is PV = constant at constant temperature; another is $P_1V_1 = P_2V_2$ for two states 1 and 2 at the same temperature. If the pressure exerted on a gas is tripled, then the volume must decrease to one third of its initial volume to keep the product PV constant (at constant temperature).

3.   Charles' law can be expressed as $V = kT$ at constant pressure. Alternatively, it can be written as $V_1/T_1 = V_2/T_2$ for two states 1 and 2 at the same pressure. The temperature must be in K for the volume to be directly proportional (i.e. a slope with an origin = zero). You could write the law using °C but you would have to include the intercept −273.15°C.

k is a constant.

4.   The combined gas law is a combination of Boyle's law and Charles' law. It can be written as $PV = kT$ where the temperature is in K and the quantity of gas is constant. Or it can be written as $P_1V_1/T_1 = P_2V_2/T_2$ for two states 1 and 2 where the temperature is again in K and the quantity of gas is constant.

5.   Gay-Lussac's law states that the volumes of gases involved in a chemical reaction is always a small whole number ratio—provided that the volumes are measured at the same temperature and pressure.

Avogadro's law states that the volume occupied by a gas at constant pressure and temperature is directly proportional to the number of molecules of gas in the sample.

6. The 'ideal' in the ideal gas law means the attraction between the molecules is zero and the actual volume of the molecules is zero. There is no such thing as a molecule with zero volume! However, most gases at ordinary temperatures and pressures behave ideally because the attraction is essentially zero and the volume of the molecules is infinitesimal.

7. The number of moles n equals the mass of the gas divided by its molar mass:

$$n = \frac{m}{M} \quad \text{therefore } PV = \frac{m}{M}RT \quad \text{or} \quad PM = \frac{m}{V}RT$$

$\frac{m}{V}$ is density, so density $= \frac{PM}{RT}$

8. Liquids and solids are called the condensed states. Molecules in these states are next to one another, held together by intermolecular forces of attraction. As a result, both liquids and solids have surfaces. A gas, on the other hand, will always fill whatever volume is available. Molecules in the gas state behave independently and are on average far apart from one another. So the volume occupied by a certain quantity of gas can change quite dramatically whereas the same quantity of liquid or solid occupies a comparatively small volume which changes little.

Gases on earth are held by gravitational attraction, they don't, fortunately, expand to fill the entire space of the universe. Gases released from space craft will however expand for ever until individual molecules are trapped by the gravitational fields of various stars, planets, etc.

9. The ideal gas law can be written for any component in a mixture of gases, or it can be written for the entire mixture.

For gas a, for example: $\quad P_a V = n_a RT$
For the total mixture $\quad P_{total} V = n_{total} RT$

Dividing the first expression by the second: $\quad \dfrac{P_a}{P_{total}} = \dfrac{n_a}{n_{total}}$

or $P_a = (n_a/n_{total})P_{total}$

or $P_a = X_a P_{total}$ where X_a is the mole fraction of a in the mixture.

10. The molar mass of water (18 g mol^{-1}) is lower than the molar masses of nitrogen and oxygen (28 and 32 g mol^{-1}). Air containing water vapor (high humidity) is therefore less dense than dry air—even though it may feel more oppressive.

11. The average kinetic energy of the molecules of any gas at the same temperature is always the same. If the molar mass of one gas is greater than the molar mass of another gas, then it must have a proportionately lower mean square speed. The average kinetic energy is proportional to the temperature:

$$\tfrac{1}{2}m\overline{u^2} = \text{constant} \times T$$

12.   The temperature of a gas is proportional to the average kinetic energy of the molecules of the gas. It is a macroscopic property that refers to the entire sample. However, in a gas, there are molecules travelling fast with high speeds and high kinetic energies and there are molecules travelling at slow speeds with low kinetic energies. The distribution of molecular speeds is illustrated by a Boltzmann distribution curve; this curve shows that most molecules have speeds somewhere in the center. In the sense that kinetic energy and temperature are related, the molecules in a sample that have high kinetic energies can be described as "hot"; those with low kinetic energies as "cold".

13.   The principal features of the kinetic-molecular theory are:

Gases consist of molecules with intermolecular distances much greater than the size of the molecules.
Molecular motion is continual, random, and rapid.
The average kinetic energy of the molecules in a gas is proportional only to the temperature of the gas. All gases have the same average kinetic energy at the same temperature.
No energy is lost during the collision of one molecule with another or in a collision of a molecule and its container.

14.   The result from question 11 was: $\frac{1}{2}m\overline{u^2} = \text{constant} \times T$ for all gases.
In other words, if T is the same, then

for two gases A and B: $\frac{1}{2}m_A\overline{u_A^2} = \frac{1}{2}m_B\overline{u_B^2}$

Multiplying through by 2, collecting the m's and u's on either side:

$$\frac{\overline{u_A^2}}{\overline{u_B^2}} = \frac{m_B}{m_A}$$

The rate at which molecules effuse is proportional to their rms speeds and the masses of the individual molecules can be multiplied by Avogadro's number to obtain the ratio of molar masses:

$$\frac{\text{Rate of effusion of A}}{\text{Rate of effusion of B}} = \frac{\sqrt{\overline{u_A^2}}}{\sqrt{\overline{u_B^2}}} = \sqrt{\frac{M_B}{M_A}}$$

15.   If the temperature is lowered, the rate at which a gas effuses or diffuses must decrease, so a helium filled mylar balloon will stay inflated longer in the freezer.

16.   The ideal gas law does not hold well at low temperatures and high pressures. Molecules do attract one another and molecules do have a finite volume. The effect of the attraction is that molecules are held back in their collisions with the surface of the container. The observed pressure is less than the ideal pressure. And although the volume of molecules is very small, it becomes more and more significant the higher the pressure and the lower the temperature. The observed volume is greater than the ideal volume. Johannes van der

Waals developed an alternative gas law to accommodate the intermolecular attraction and the finite volume of molecules—a real gas law.

Study Questions and Problems

The formulation of a problem is far more often essential than its solution, which may be merely a matter of mathematical or experimental skill.

*Albert Einstein
(1879-1955)*

1. Convert the following pressures to atm.

    a. 726 torr   b. 2.31 bar   c. 98 kPa   d. 16.33 psi

2. Consider the following changes imposed upon a sample of gas, assuming the variables not mentioned remain constant:

    a. What happens to the pressure if the temperature in K is doubled?

    b. What happens to the volume if the pressure is tripled?

    c. What happens to the volume if the temperature decreases from 300K to 200K?

    d. What happens to the temperature if one-half of the gas is removed?

    e. What happens to the pressure if volume increases from 2 liters to 4 liters and the temperature increases from 25°C to 323°C?

3. An ideal gas occupies a volume of 10 liters at 27°C. If the pressure on the gas is tripled at this temperature, the volume changes. To what value must the temperature be changed to restore the volume to the initial 10 liters at the new pressure?

4. What is the volume of 6 moles of helium gas at 0.34 atm pressure and 33°C? What is the density of the helium gas under these conditions?

5. Methane burns in air to produce carbon dioxide and water:

    $$CH_4(g) \; + \; 2O_2(g) \; \rightarrow \; CO_2(g) \; + \; H_2O(l)$$

    What volume of carbon dioxide, at 1 atm pressure and 112°C, will be produced when 80.0 grams of methane is burned?

6.   Jacques Charles used the reaction of hydrochloric acid on iron to produce the hydrogen for one of his balloons. For one flight in 1783 he used 1000 lbs of iron and excess acid. What volume of hydrogen gas (in cubic meters) did he produce for this flight? Assume the pressure is 1 atm and the temperature is 22°C.

$$Fe(s) \ + \ 2HCl(aq) \ \rightarrow \ FeCl_2(aq) \ + \ H_2(g)$$

7.   If 1.0 liter of oxygen at 2.0 atm pressure, 2.0 liters of nitrogen at 1.0 atm pressure, and 2.0 liters of helium at 2.0 atm pressure, are all mixed in a 3.0 liter vessel with no change in temperature, what is the final pressure of the mixture in the 3.0 liter vessel?

8.   What is the partial pressure of oxygen in the atmosphere at the top of Mt Everest? Atmospheric pressure at the summit of Mt Everest is 253 torr. The partial pressure of oxygen in air at 1 atm pressure is 0.20946 atm.

9.   A vessel contains 0.10 mol N_2, 0.20 mol O_2, and 0.30 mol Ne at a total pressure of 2.0 atm. At constant temperature and volume, what is the partial pressure of oxygen O_2
   a.   under the described conditions?
   b.   if another 0.30 mol of Ne is added?
   c.   if, in addition, another 0.10 mol of O_2 is added?

10.   The apparatus shown consists of two glass bulbs connected by a tap which is closed. In the first bulb, volume 3 liters, there is a sample of pure nitrous oxide at 3 atm pressure. In the second bulb, volume 2 liters, there is a sample of pure oxygen at 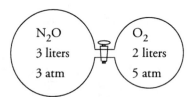 a pressure of 5 atm. Maintaining a constant temperature throughout, the tap is opened, the gases are allowed to mix, and they react to produce nitrogen dioxide according to the equation written below. Assume that the reaction goes as far as possible to completion:

$$2N_2O(g) \ + \ 3O_2(g) \ \rightarrow \ 4NO_2(g)$$

   a.   What is the partial pressure of the nitrogen dioxide in the apparatus at the end of the reaction?
   b.   What is the partial pressure of the excess (nonlimiting) reactant at the end of the reaction?
   c.   What is the total pressure in the apparatus at the end of the reaction?

11.   Using the Maxwell equation, calculate the root mean square speed of nitrogen gas at 25°C. What happens to the rms speed if the temperature is doubled to 50°C?

12.   Imagine three automobiles travelling down the road at 20 mph, 32 mph, and 68 mph. Calculate the average speed and the rms speed. What is the significance of the rms speed?

13.   A gas diffuses 5/3 times faster than carbon dioxide. Which gas might it be?
       a. O_2 b. N_2 c. CO   d. He   e. CH_4

14.   For nitrogen, the van der Waals constants a and b have values 1.39 and 0.0391 respectively. Calculate the pressure of 5 moles of nitrogen gas confined to a 1.0 liter vessel at a temperature of 300K using the ideal gas equation and the van der Waals equation of state. Comment on the difference.

Answers to Study Questions and Problems

1.   a.   726 torr × (1 atm / 760 torr) = 0.955 atm
       b.   2.31 bar × (1 atm / 1.01325 bar) = 2.28 atm
       c.   98 kPa × (1 atm / 101.325 kPa) = 0.97 atm
       d.   16.33 psi × (1 atm / 14.696 psi) = 1.111 atm

2.   Use the ideal gas law to establish the relationships between the four variables pressure, volume, temperature, and number of moles. Variables not mentioned are constant. It's useful to write the equation, or draw a set of boxes as illustrated in the margin, to see the relationship between the variables.

       a.   Pressure is proportional to temperature in K, so if the temperature in K is doubled, the pressure must also double.

       b.   Volume and pressure are inversely proportional (Boyle's law), so if the pressure is tripled, the volume must decrease to one-third of the initial volume.

       c.   A decrease from 300K to 200K is a decrease to two-thirds of the initial temperature. Volume is proportional to temperature, so the volume too must decrease to two-thirds of its initial value.

       d.   Temperature and the number of moles are inversely proportional. If one-half of the gas is removed, the temperature must double—if the remaining gas is to occupy the same volume at the same pressure.

       e.   Remember to convert the temperature to K: 25°C is 298K and 323°C is equal to 596K (double the initial temperature). Pressure is inversely proportional to the volume but proportional to the temperature, so if the volume is doubled and the temperature is also doubled, the pressure does not change.

3.   Use the ideal gas law to establish the relationship between the variables. In this problem, the volume is restored to its original value by adjusting the temperature. So, in effect, the volume doesn't change. The initial temperature

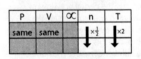

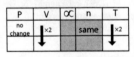

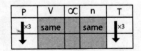

is 27°C or 300K. If the pressure is to be tripled, then so must the temperature, to 900K, or 627°C.

4.   PV = nRT so

     0.34 atm × volume in L
         = 6.0 mol × 0.08206 L atm $K^{-1}mol^{-1}$ × (33+273.15)K.
     Volume = 443 liters.

     Using the expression: density = PM/RT, the density = 0.0542 g/L, or, having already calculated the volume, density = mass/volume, so the density = 24.018g /443 L = 0.0542 g/L again.

Molar mass = 4.003 g mol^{-1}
Mass of 6.0 moles = 24.018 g

5. $CH_4(g)$ + $2O_2(g)$ → $CO_2(g)$ + $H_2O(l)$

     80.0 grams of methane is 80.0 g × (1 mol / 16 g mol^{-1}) = 5.0 mol. According to the 1:1 stoichiometry of the equation, 5.0 mol of CO_2 will be produced. The ideal gas law can be used to calculate the volume:

     PV = nRT so
     1atm × volume in L
         = 5.0 mol × 0.08206 L atm $K^{-1}mol^{-1}$ × (112+273.15)K.
     Volume = 158 liters.

Remember to use the correct value for R.

6.   1000 lbs of iron = 453.6 kg = 8122 moles of iron.

     Fe(s) + 2HCl(aq) → $FeCl_2(aq)$ + $H_2(g)$

     According to the equation, 8122 moles of hydrogen were produced.
     PV = nRT so
     1 atm × volume in L
         = 8122 mol × 0.08206 L atm $K^{-1}mol^{-1}$× (22+273.15)K.
     Volume = 200,000 liters   = 200 m^3.

The partial pressure of a gas in a mixture is the pressure it would exert if it were the only gas present.

Notice that the partial pressures of both oxygen and nitrogen are the same. This is because P×V is the same for both, and P×V is proportional to n, the number of moles. The number of moles of oxygen = the number of moles of nitrogen and their partial pressures must therefore be the same.

7.   The 1.0 liter of oxygen at 2.0 atm pressure is expanded to occupy 3.0 liters, so its pressure decreases by a factor of 1/3 to 2/3 atm.
     Likewise, the pressure of nitrogen is 1.0 atm × 2.0/3.0 = 2/3 atm.
     And the pressure of helium is 2.0 atm × 2.0/3.0 = 4/3 atm.
     The total pressure is the sum of these partial pressures:
     Total pressure   = P_O + P_N + P_{He}

                 =   2/3 + 2/3 + 4/3 atm = 8/3 atm = 2.67 atm.

8.   The partial pressure of oxygen in the atmosphere at the top of Mt Everest is equal to 253 torr × 0.20946 atm / 1atm = 53 torr.
     In atmospheres, this is 0.070 atm, not very much!

9.   Total number of moles of gas = 0.10 mol N_2 + 0.20 mol O_2 + 0.30 mol Ne
     Mole fraction of O_2 = 0.20/(0.10 + 0.20 + 0.30) = 0.33
     a.   Initial partial pressure of O_2 = 0.33 × 2 atm = 0.67 atm

b. No change in the amount of O_2, therefore the partial pressure remains unchanged regardless of what else is added to the vessel, 0.67 atm.

c. Moles of O_2 multiplied by 1.5 (0.10 moles added to the 0.20 mol already present), so the partial pressure increased by a factor of 1.50 to 1.0 atm.

10. When the tap is opened, the gases mix and both occupy the total space available. Assuming that no reaction occurs (yet):

Initial partial pressure of nitrous oxide = 3 atm × (3/5) = 9/5 atm.
Initial partial pressure of oxygen = 5 atm × (2/5) = 10/5 atm.

The volume and temperature are the same for both gases, so the partial pressure is directly proportional to n, the number of moles, and the partial pressures can be used in stoichiometric calculations just as n would be used.
The mole ratio required by the equation is 2 N_2O to 3 O_2, so oxygen is the limiting reactant.

The amount of N_2O used = 10/5 × (2/3) atm = 4/3 atm.
The amount of N_2O remaining at the end = 9/5 – 4/3 atm = 7/15 atm.
The amount of oxygen remaining at the end = zero (it's all used up).
The amount of NO_2 produced = 10/5 × (4/3) atm = 8/3 atm.

Total pressure = partial pressure of N_2O + partial pressure of NO_2
= 7/15 + 8/3 atm = 3.13 atm

11. The Maxwell equation relates rms speed to the molar mass and the temperature of the gas.

The root mean square speed
= $(3 × 8.314\ JK^{-1}mol^{-1} × 298.15\ K\ /\ 28.02\ g\ mol^{-1} × 1kg/1000g)^{\frac{1}{2}}$
= 515 ms^{-1}

If the temperature is <u>doubled</u> to 50°C, then the rms speed will increase proportionately—by $\sqrt{(323/298)}$—to 536 ms^{-1}. Use degrees K!

$$\sqrt{\overline{u^2}} = \sqrt{\frac{3RT}{M}}$$

You must have the correct units —use SI units!
So use the SI value for the gas constant R and use the correct base units, for example kg for mass. Then you know that the units of the answer must be SI also, i.e. ms^{-1}. Check to see if they cancel correctly.
One J = kg m^{2}s^{-2}

12. The average speed is (20 + 32 + 68)/3 = 120/3 = 40 mph.

To calculate the rms speed, square the speeds, take the average, then take the square root of the average:

Rms speed = $[(20^2 + 32^2 + 68^2)/3]^{\frac{1}{2}}$
= $[(400 + 1024 + 4624)/3]^{\frac{1}{2}}$ = $[2016]^{\frac{1}{2}}$ = 45 mph

The rms speed is higher than the average speed. The rms speed is the speed at which an automobile would have to travel if it were to have a kinetic energy equal to the average kinetic energy of the other three cars.

13. According to Graham's law, the rate of diffusion is inversely proportional to the square root of the molar mass. The unknown gas diffuses faster and therefore must have a lower molar mass than carbon dioxide. The ratio of the molar masses must be $(3/5)^2$.

44 g mol^{-1} × (3/5)^2 = 15.8 g mol^{-1}, the gas is methane, CH_4.

14. Using the ideal gas equation PV = nRT:
P = 5.0 mol × 0.08206 L atm K^{-1} mol^{-1} × 300 K / 1.0 L = 123 atm.

Using the van der Waals equation of state [P + a$(\frac{n}{V})^2$][V – nb] = nRT:

[P + 1.39×(5.0/1.0)^2] × [1–(5.0×0.0391)] = 5.0 × 0.08206 × 300

[P + 34.75] × [0.8045] = 123.1 atm

P = 118 atm

The two pressures agree tolerably well, but the temperature is still quite high, and the pressure is not very high. An increase in pressure by a factor

People of this chapter and their States

—*a crossword puzzle*

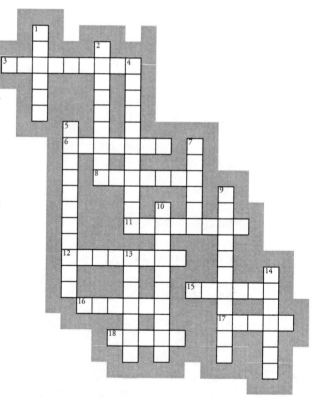

Across:

3. He was concerned with probabilities and distributions...
6. ...and his country.
8. Jacques, the hydrogen-balloonist.
11. Country of *1 down*.
12. He is remembered by his number.
15. His law states that the total pressure is the sum of the partial pressures.
16. Country of *8 across* and *2 down*, amongst others.
17. Country of *12 across* and *10 down*.
18. A sceptical chemist, his was the first gas law.

Down:

1. His was the absolute temperature scale.
2. He formulated the law of combining volumes.
4. Country of the scientist ...
5. ...who developed a gas law for real gases.
7. Mathematician for whom the SI unit of pressure is named.
9. Joseph and Etienne, who designed the first balloon.
10. He invented the mercury barometer in 1643.
13. Another Frenchman, he discovered the relationship between pressure and temperature.
14. Country of *15 across*.

CHAPTER 12

Introduction

The liquid and solid states of matter are condensed states—the molecules, atoms, or ions that make up the matter are close together, held together by strong interparticle forces of attraction. In this chapter we will examine these forces of attraction and investigate the properties of different kinds of liquids and solids. The energies involved in changing from one state to another will be examined.

Contents

States of Matter and the Kinetic Molecular Theory
Intermolecular Forces
Hydrogen bonding
Summary of Intermolecular Forces
Properties of Liquids
Solid State Chemistry: Metals
Solid State Chemistry: Structures and Formulas of Ionic Salts
Other Kinds of Solid Materials
The Physical Properties of Solids
Phase Diagrams

States of Matter and the Kinetic Molecular Theory

Although molecules behave independently in the gas state, their behavior in the liquid and solid states is more complicated. Molecules do attract one another—without such attraction all substances would be gases. In both liquids and solids, molecules are held together to a finite volume by their attraction for one another. This volume is approximately the same for the liquid and solid states, much smaller than for the gas state. For example, 18 mL of liquid water, or 18 g of ice, produces 22.4 liters of water vapor—a dramatic change in volume.

Intermolecular Forces

Intermolecular forces are the electrostatic forces of attraction between molecules or between ions and molecules. There are a variety of different types. For example, there is the attraction between ions and polar molecules, between polar molecules themselves, and between nonpolar molecules. Those forces not involving ions are generally referred to as **van der Waals forces**.

Intermolecular forces are considerably weaker than intramolecular bonds. A single covalent bond has an energy between 100 and 400 kJ mol^{-1}. Multiple bonds are stronger. Typical ionic forces in an ionic compound vary between 700 and 1100 kJ mol^{-1}. Intermolecular forces are in general much weaker.

A N_2 triple bond has a bond energy of 946 kJ/mol.

When two molecules have dipole moments, they attract one another. The positive end of one molecule attracts the negative end of another molecule and *vice versa*. This attraction is called **dipole-dipole attraction**. The greater the forces of attraction between molecules, the greater the energy required to separate them. Polar compounds therefore have a higher boiling point, melting point, heat of vaporization, and viscosity, etc. than nonpolar molecules of comparable size.

Intermolecular forces influence solubility. Polar molecules tend to dissolve in polar solvents. Nonpolar molecules tend to dissolve in nonpolar solvents.

Some molecules are nonpolar, and yet at sufficiently low temperatures they will liquefy and solidify. What holds nonpolar molecules together? All molecules are held together by **dispersion forces**. Even the attraction between polar molecules like HCl involves more dispersion force than dipole–dipole attraction. A dispersion force is the attraction between **induced dipoles**—these induced dipoles are temporary displacements in the electron cloud surrounding the atoms in a molecule. The inducement of such temporary dipoles explains how a nonpolar molecule like oxygen can dissolve in polar solvent like water: As the water molecule approaches an oxygen molecule, the dipole of the water molecule distorts the electron distribution in the oxygen molecule. The result is an attraction between the dipole of the water molecule and the induced dipole of the oxygen molecule.

The larger the electron cloud, the more easily **polarized** it is—the easier it is to induce a dipole. Thus, nonpolar iodine is a solid, bromine is a liquid, and chlorine is a gas. But in these halogens there are no polar molecules to induce the dipole, so how does the induced dipole attraction work? As the temperature is decreased, molecules slow down; the molecules approach one another long enough to allow the electron clouds and nuclei of different molecules to interact; this leads to a mutual distortion of the electron clouds on adjacent molecules; a temporary induced dipole attraction is the result.

Hydrogen Bonding

Many molecules with the groups O–H, N–H, and F–H have properties indicating an exceptionally strong intermolecular force of attraction. This force is called **hydrogen bonding** and involves a partial sharing of a hydrogen atom attached to O, N, or F, with another N, O, or F. It is the high electronegativity and small size of oxygen, nitrogen, and fluoride that is responsible for the strength of the hydrogen bond. Consider the hydrogen compounds of all the elements in Groups 3, 4, 5, 6, and 7; compounds like SiH_4, PH_3, HBr, B_2H_6, CH_4, H_2S—all are gases except for water which is a liquid. Water is a liquid because of the strong intermolecular hydrogen bonds. The open-cage structure of ice is dictated by the hydrogen bonding between the water molecules, and ice is less dense than water at 0°C.

Hydrogen bonding has important implications for any property of a compound that is related to the intermolecular forces of attraction. Examples of such properties are melting and boiling points, heats of fusion, vaporization and sublimation, viscosity, and structure in the liquid and solid states. Examples of some substances in which hydrogen bonding plays an important role in the structure and properties of the substance are water, proteins, synthetic polymers such as kevlar (a polyamide), and DNA.

Breaking bonds always requires energy.

"Like" dissolves "like."

Three possibilities:

dipole-dipole
dipole-induced dipole
induced dipole-induced dipole

Induced dipole-induced dipole forces are often referred to as London dispersion forces.

You may ask why ammonia NH_3 and hydrogen fluoride HF are not liquids like water. The structure of water, with two H atoms and two lone pairs on the oxygen, is perfect for the formation of four hydrogen bonds from each molecule. Ammonia has too many H, and HF has too many lone pairs, and so they form half as many hydrogen bonds as water and are gases.

Remember:
The hydrogen bond is a bond between two water molecules not a bond in a water molecule. Generally hydrogen bonding is an intermolecular attraction although there are many examples of hydrogen bonding between two functional groups of the same molecule.

Hydrogen bonding involving
N–H...N–
N–H...O–
O–H...O–
O–H...N–
is extraordinarily important in biological and biochemical structures and reactions.

Summary of Intermolecular Forces

In general, for molecules of comparable size, the strength of intermolecular forces decreases in the order hydrogen bonding > dipole-dipole > dipole-induced dipole > induced dipole-induced dipole.

See study questions #1-4.

Properties of Liquids

Molecules in the liquid state are in constant motion, just like they are in the gas state, but, unlike in the gas state, they are not independent of one another. The molecules are held together by intermolecular forces of attraction. The speeds and energies of the molecules range from low to high; the distribution is similar to that described for the gas state. Some molecules have sufficient energy to break free of the intermolecular attraction and enter the gas phase. The ability of a molecule to break free depends upon the strength of the intermolecular force and its kinetic energy. The latter depends upon the temperature. The **boiling point** and the **heat of vaporization** are indications of the strength of the intermolecular bonding.

Vaporization requires breaking bonds and is an endothermic process. The stronger the bonding, the higher the boiling point and the greater the heat of vaporization.

A liquid left in an open container will eventually evaporate; molecules escape from the liquid and diffuse away through the atmosphere. If the container is closed, the escaping molecules cannot diffuse away and may eventually collide with the surface of the liquid and reenter the liquid phase. After some time, the rate at which molecules leave the liquid will equal the rate at which molecules reenter the liquid. At this point the concentration of the molecules in the vapor phase will be constant. The system is said to be in **dynamic equilibrium**. The partial pressure of the molecules in the gas above the liquid at equilibrium is called the **equilibrium vapor pressure**. This vapor pressure is a measure of how easy it is for the molecules in the liquid to escape—often referred to as the **volatility**.

The movement of molecules between the liquid and vapor phases does not stop at equilibrium—it's just that the two rates are equal so there is no macroscopic change in the system. The two processes continue unabated.

The vapor pressure increases with temperature—the molecules have greater energy at higher temperatures and therefore find it easier to escape. A mathematical relationship between vapor pressure (P) and temperature (T) was determined by Clausius and Clapeyron:

$$\ln P = -(\frac{\Delta H_{vap}}{RT}) + C \qquad \text{(where C is a constant)}$$

If the temperature is increased to the point at which the vapor pressure equals the atmospheric pressure, then the liquid will boil. The pressure exerted by the molecules in the atmosphere colliding with the surface of the liquid is balanced by the force of the molecules escaping from the surface, and bubbles form in the liquid.

The increase in vapor pressure with temperature does not continue upward without limit. The curve stops at the **critical point**. At this point it is no longer possible to distinguish between liquid and vapor. The combination of high pressure and high temperature means that the molecules are still close to one another but have sufficient kinetic energy to overcome the intermolecular forces. The substance is said to be in a supercritical state—it's like a liquid in which the intermolecular forces are ineffective—just like a gas.

A plot of the vapor pressure vs. the temperature is called the vapor pressure curve.

Supercritical fluids have interesting properties and commercial uses.

Supercritical CO_2, for example, is used to extract caffeine from coffee beans.

Molecules at the surface of a liquid experience an unbalanced attraction. There are molecules within the liquid pulling the surface molecules, but no molecules beyond the surface to balance the pull. As a result there is a net inward force referred to as **surface tension**. This surface tension tends to minimize the surface area—so that drops of water are spherical for example. **Capillary action** is related to surface tension. Water will rise in a small diameter glass tube because of the adhesive forces between the water molecules and the glass surface and the cohesive forces between the water molecules. The water will be pulled up the tube until the cohesive and adhesive forces are balanced by the downward gravitational forces.

Viscosity is the resistance of a liquid to flow. Stronger intermolecular forces will increase the viscosity of a liquid. Physical entangling of long chain molecules will also inhibit flow and increase viscosity.

Solid State Chemistry: Metals

In a solid, the structural units—molecules, atoms, or ions—do not move as they do in liquids and gases. They vibrate and sometimes rotate, but they cannot move. A regular repetitive pattern of structural units is characteristic of the solid state. Identical points (lattice points) in the crystal define what is called a **crystal lattice**.

A **unit cell** is the smallest repeating unit of a crystalline material. The unit cell has all the symmetry characteristics of macroscopic crystal and is drawn so that, as far as possible, the structural units are at the corners of the cell. The shape of the unit cell is defined by the **crystal system**. There are seven crystal systems—seven different shapes for the unit cells. They vary in the angles at the corners and the lengths of the sides—the simplest is the cubic crystal system. For this system the unit cell is a cube.

How the structural units are placed in the unit cell is defined by the **crystal lattice**. There are 14 crystal lattices (sometimes referred to as Bravais lattices). The cubic system has three lattices associated with it—the simple cubic lattice (sc), the body-centered cubic lattice (bcc), and the face-centered cubic lattice (fcc). Many metals adopt a fcc lattice (for example: copper, aluminum, gold), some adopt a bcc lattice (for example: sodium, potassium, iron), and one (polonium) adopts a sc lattice.

When the unit cells pack together to form the crystal lattice, the atoms on the edge of one unit cell are shared with the adjacent unit cell(s). Corner atoms are shared by the 8 unit cells sharing that corner, so that only 1/8 of the atom belongs to one of the cells. Likewise, an atom on an edge is shared by 4 unit cells and an atom on a face is shared by 2 unit cells.

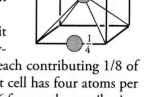

A simple cubic unit cell therefore has one atom per unit cell: 8 corners each contributing 1/8 of an atom. A body-centered unit cell has two atoms per unit cell: 8 corners each contributing 1/8 of an atom plus one atom at the center. A face-centered unit cell has four atoms per unit cell: 8 corners each contributing 1/8 of an atom plus 6 faces each contributing 1/2 of an atom.

Margin notes:

Cohesive forces are the forces within the substance, holding the substance together.
Adhesive forces are the forces between one substance and another.

See study questions #6, 7, & 8.

Crystal system—
the shape of the unit cell.

Crystal lattice—
the arrangement of structural units within the unit cell.

Contribution to a unit cell:

inside:	contribution 1
on a face:	contribution 1/2
on an edge:	contribution 1/4
on a corner:	contribution 1/8

Cubic system:

simple cubic lattice
(1 structural unit per cell)

body-centered cubic lattice
(2 structural units per cell)

face-centered cubic lattice
(4 structural units per cell)

Solid State Chemistry: Structures & Formulas of Ionic Salts

See study questions #9 & 10.

Ionic salts are composed of at least two different particles, one positive and the other negative. The lattices of many ionic compounds are built up by creating a lattice (often face-centered cubic) of the larger of the two ions (usually the anion) and then filling the holes in this lattice with the smaller ion (usually the cation). The type of hole (tetrahedral, octahedral, or cubic) is determined by the relative sizes of the ions. The fraction of holes filled is determined by the stoichiometry of the salt. If the unit cell of the ionic compound is determined, then the stoichiometry of the compound can be calculated from the composition of the unit cell.

For example, in cesium chloride, the chloride ions form a simple cubic lattice. There is one chloride ion per unit cell (8 corners × 1/8). The cesium ion occupies a position at the center of the cube and has the eight chloride ions as nearest neighbors (the coordination number is 8). There is therefore one cesium ion per unit cell and the formula of cesium chloride must be 1:1 or CsCl.

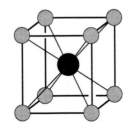

Other Kinds of Solid Materials

The structural units in a crystal can be molecules; for example, the water molecules that make up ice. How the molecules are arranged in the lattice depends upon the shape of the molecules and their intermolecular forces. The molecules tend to pack together as densely as possible and are aligned to maximize their attraction for one another.

Network solids are crystalline lattices in which the structural units are atoms covalently bonded together—a really giant molecule. These solids are typically high-melting, hard, rigid materials. This reflects the large amount of energy required to break the covalent bonds in the lattice. Examples are diamond, graphite, silicon, carborundum, silica, boron nitride, boron carbide, etc.

True solids are crystalline. However, there are some materials that appear to be solid that are not crystalline. The order within the material is random—just as in a liquid. Such materials are called **amorphous**. Window glass is an example. In glass the molecular order is random but the intermolecular forces are sufficiently strong to prohibit much movement of the molecules. The glass, although apparently solid, is just a very viscous liquid. Many plastics (polymers) are similar in structure.

If you ever come across a very old (>200 years) glass window, examine it to see if the thickness of the glass is greater at the bottom than at the top.

The Physical Properties of Solids.

See study question #11.

Solids are characterized by their regular crystalline lattice structure. The melting point and heat of fusion depend upon the strength of the intermolecular forces in the lattice. The energy required to break up the lattice is often referred to as the lattice energy. Metals vary considerably in their melting points and lattice energies. Mercury is a liquid at room temperature; tungsten has a melting point of 3422°C. Most representative group metals have relatively low melting points. Most transition metals have relatively high melting points, reaching a maximum at the middle of the series.

Fusion means melting in this context.

The melting points of ionic compounds depend upon the lattice energies—which in turn depend upon the charges and sizes of the ions. Covalent network materials

Be able to do calculations involving the heats of fusion and vaporization. These have been encountered before in Chapter 6 of this study guide.

Solids made up of small molecules have low melting points. An example is ice. Indeed, most small molecules are liquids or gases.

This is why it is called a phase diagram rather than a state diagram.

For the mathematicians amongst you: Can you derive a mathematical relationship between the number of phases that exist or coexist in equilibrium and how the conditions of temperature and pressure can vary?

(e.g. diamond) generally have very high melting points.

Molecular solids have a range of melting points and heats of fusion. Again, both depend upon the strength of the intermolecular force. Dispersion forces increase as the size of the molecule increases, so within any series, the melting point will increase as the molar mass increases.

Molecules can escape directly from the solid state to the vapor state in a process called **sublimation**. The process, like vaporization, requires breaking bonds and is endothermic.

Phase Diagrams.

A **phase diagram** is a summary of the conditions of temperature and pressure under which each of the three states of matter exists. The diagram also describes the conditions under which two, or even three, phases can coexist in equilibrium. And it often includes information about the particular phases that can exist within the solid state. On the phase diagram:

· the areas represent conditions under which only one phase will exist,
· the lines represent conditions under which two phases will coexist, and
· the point where the lines meet represents conditions under which three phases will coexist in equilibrium—the **triple point**.

Review Questions

1.   Summarize the differences in the behavior of molecules in the three states of matter.

2.   Describe the different types of interparticle forces that can occur between atoms, molecules, and ions. Distinguish the forces called intermolecular forces. What forces are referred to as van der Waals forces? Draw a flow chart or diagram to summarize these intermolecular forces.

3.   What is a hydrogen bond? Describe the requirements for hydrogen bonding.

4.   Why do larger molecules (higher molar mass) melt at higher temperatures?

5.   Describe the process of dynamic equilibrium that exists between a liquid and its vapor in a closed container. Why does a system in an open container never reach equilibrium?

6.   What is the critical point?

7.   Describe what you understand by surface tension.

8.   What is the difference between a crystal system and a crystal lattice?

9. Describe or draw the three lattices of the cubic system.

10. Describe how you would calculate the number of ions in the unit cell of an ionic crystal lattice.

11. Is an amorphous solid really a liquid? Explain.

12. Draw a generic phase diagram and indicate the areas in which the various states are stable. What is the significance of the lines on the diagram and the point at which the lines meet? Name the processes involved in crossing each line.

13. On the diagram you drew for question 12, draw a horizontal line at a pressure of 1 atm. The line crosses the solid-liquid line and the liquid-vapor line (the vapor pressure curve). What is the significance of these points?

14. What is significant about the direction in which the solid–liquid line on the phase diagram slopes?

Answers to Review Questions

1. **Solid:** very regular array or lattice of molecules; very effective attraction between molecules; molecules close together; no translational motion.

   Liquid: random order of molecules, some close-range order; intermolecular forces of attraction intermediate in effectiveness; molecules close together; molecules move with respect to one another but are held together.

   Gas: totally random order of molecules; intermolecular forces of attraction totally ineffective; molecules far apart; molecules move independently of one another.

2. There are three major classes of bonds. These are characterized by the behavior of the valence electrons in the bond which, in turn, depends upon the electronegativity difference between the elements involved: covalent: sharing of electrons (need not be equal sharing), ionic: transfer of electrons, and metallic: delocalization of electrons.

   The bonding between molecules, or between molecules and ions can be classified as follows:

   Intermolecular forces: ion–molecule forces (e.g. solvation)
   van der Waals forces of attraction
   van der Waals forces can
   be subdivided into: hydrogen–bonding
   dipole–dipole attraction
   dipole–induced dipole attraction
   dispersion forces (induced dipole-induced dipole)

Key terms:

intermolecular forces
van der Waals forces
ion-dipole attraction
dipole-dipole attraction
dipole-induced dipole attraction
induced dipole-induced dipole attraction
London dispersion forces
polarizability
hydrogen bond
evaporation
enthalpy of vaporization
dynamic equilibrium
vapor pressure
volatility
vapor pressure curve
Clausius-Clapeyron equation
critical temperature
critical point
supercritical fluid
surface tension
capillary action
adhesive and cohesive forces
viscosity
lattice points
crystal lattice
unit cell
crystal system
simple cubic lattice
body-centered cubic lattice
face-centered cubic lattice
network solid
amorphous material
sublimation
phase diagram
triple point

3.   A hydrogen bond involves a partial sharing of a hydrogen atom attached to O, N, or F, with another N, O, or F. The N, O, or F must have a lone pair of electrons. The high electronegativity and small size of oxygen, nitrogen, and fluoride is responsible for the strength of the hydrogen bond because this polarizes the O–H, N–H, or F–H bond. Strong intermolecular hydrogen bonding has important implications for any property that is related to the intermolecular forces of attraction.

4.   All molecules are held together by dispersion forces. A dispersion force is the attraction between induced dipoles—these induced dipoles are temporary polarizations in the electron cloud surrounding the atoms in a molecule. The larger the electron cloud, the more easily polarized it is—the easier it is to induce a dipole. Larger molecules also move more slowly than smaller molecules, and therefore the interaction between the molecules is more effective.

5.   In a closed container, the molecules escaping from the surface of the liquid cannot diffuse away and eventually collide with the surface of the liquid and reenter the liquid phase. After some time, the rate at which molecules leave the liquid will equal the rate at which molecules reenter the liquid. The system is then said to be in dynamic equilibrium; at this point the concentration of the molecules in the vapor phase is constant. A liquid left in an open container will eventually evaporate; molecules escape from the liquid and diffuse away through the atmosphere—the system can never reach equilibrium.

6.   At the critical point it is no longer possible to distinguish between the liquid and vapor states. The combination of high pressure and high temperature means that the molecules are still close to one another but have sufficient kinetic energy to overcome the intermolecular forces.

7.   Molecules at the surface of a liquid experience an attraction by the molecules within the liquid. This pulls the surface molecules inward; this inward force is referred to as surface tension. The surface tension tends to minimize the surface area because the smaller the area the lower the energy. Drops of water are spherical for example. It appears as if the surface of the water has a skin; an insect walking on the surface causes a slight indentation in the surface that is resisted by the cohesive forces within the liquid water.

8.   The crystal system defines the shape of the unit cell. There are seven crystal systems—seven different shapes for the unit cells. The unit cells of the seven systems vary in the angles at the corners and the lengths of the sides.
        The crystal lattice describes how the structural units are placed in the unit cell. There are 14 crystal lattices (sometimes referred to as Bravais lattices). For example, the cubic system has three associated lattices—simple, body-centered, and face-centered.

9. The three lattices of the cubic system are: simple cubic (sc), body-centered cubic (bcc), and face-centered cubic (fcc). These are illustrated on the right.

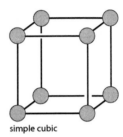

simple cubic

10. The key to determining the number of ions in the unit cell of an ionic crystal lattice is to remember that ions (or any structural unit) on the edge of one unit cell are shared with all adjacent unit cells. Thus, the contributions to a particular unit cell are:

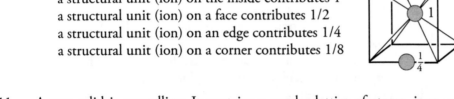

a structural unit (ion) on the inside contributes 1
a structural unit (ion) on a face contributes 1/2
a structural unit (ion) on an edge contributes 1/4
a structural unit (ion) on a corner contributes 1/8

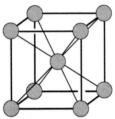

body centered cubic

11. A true solid is crystalline. It contains a regular lattice of atoms, ions, or molecules. In an amorphous material the array of structural units is random or disordered. By this definition, amorphous materials are not solids. Many modern materials, including polymers, plastics, and composites are amorphous. Some would prefer to define a solid as something hard, as something with sufficiently strong intermolecular bonding to prevent movement of the molecules, or as something that hurts if you kick it.

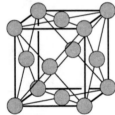

face-centered cubic

12. The areas on a phase diagram illustrate the conditions under which only a single phase is the stable state of the substance. The lines on a phase diagram represent the conditions under which two states are in equilibrium together. The triple point, where the lines meet, represents the only condition of temperature and pressure at which three phases can coexist in equilibrium together.

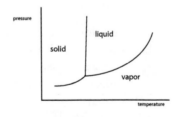

There is a rule, called Gibbs' Phase Rule, that relates the number of phases P, the number of components in the mixture C, and how the pressure and temperature can vary F:

$F = C - P + 2$

For a pure substance, C = 1:

$F = 3 - P$

For one phase (an area), P = 1 and therefore F = 2 and P and T can vary independently.

For two phases (on a line), P = 2 and therefore F = 1 and P can change only if T does and vice versa.

For three phases (at the triple point), P = 3, and F = 0 and neither P nor T can change.

13. The temperatures at which the line at 1 atm crosses the solid-liquid line and the liquid-vapor line (the vapor pressure curve) correspond to the normal melting point and the normal boiling point of the substance. The word normal signifies 1 atm pressure.

14. If the line slopes to the right (as it does for almost all substances), then it means that at a particular temperature, the solid state is more dense than the liquid state. This means that an increase in pressure will cause the liquid to solidify. If the line slopes to the left (as it does for water, bismuth, and antimony), then at a particular temperature, the solid is less dense than the liquid. The solid will float on the liquid. In this case, an increase in pressure at a melting point will cause the solid to melt.

*Our ideas must be as broad as Nature
if they are to interpret Nature.*

Sir Arthur Conan Doyle
(1859-1930)

Study Questions and Problems

1. Describe the interparticle forces at work in the following:

    a. within a water molecule H_2O
    b. between water molecules in ice
    c. in a solution of potassium nitrate KNO_3
    d. in diamond
    e. in a fiber of nylon
    f. in liquid butane
    g. in a crystal of the salt NaCl
    h. between the two strands in the double helix of DNA
    i. in paraffin wax
    j. between the molecules of carbon dioxide CO_2 in dry ice.
    k. between the molecules of HCl in liquid HCl.
    l. in tungsten metal
    m. in a solution of perchloric acid

2. Which one of the following pairs of molecules would you expect to have the higher melting point?

    a. Cl_2 or Br_2 d. Na or Mg
    b. C_4H_{10} or C_5H_{12} e. BeO or KCl
    c. NH_3 or PH_3 f. ICl or Br_2

3. Which states or types of matter would be characterized by each of the following statements?

    a. High individual molecular speeds.
    b. A melting point spread over a wide temperature range.
    c. A regular repeating array of structural units.
    d. Molecules move with respect to one another but are held together in a condensed state.
    e. Molecules close together but having sufficiently high kinetic energies to overcome the intermolecular forces.
    f. Valence electrons delocalized over huge arrays of atoms.
    g. Totally random molecular order with comparatively great distances between individual molecules.
    h. A three-dimensional network of covalent bonds.

4. Acetone and chloroform form an unusually strong intermolecular bond. Why is this? Draw a picture of how the molecules attract each other.

5. a. How much heat is required to melt 15 grams of ice at 0°C?

    b. How much heat is released when 100 grams of steam condenses at 100°C?

    c. If a system of ice and water has a mass of 12 grams, and it is converted completely to water at 0.0°C by supplying 1.33 kJ of heat, how much water was initially present?

Heat of fusion of ice
= 333 J/g

Heat of vaporization of water
= 2250 J/g

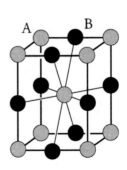

6. Silver crystallizes in a face-centered cubic lattice. If the edge of the cube is 407 pm in length, what is the radius of a silver metal atom?

7. From the data provided in question 6, calculate the density of silver metal.

8. Draw a unit cell of a body-centered cubic lattice of atoms. Show that the number of atoms within the unit cell equals 2.

9. The unit cells of five salts are illustrated in the margin on the right. Determine the stoichiometry (empirical formula) of each salt.

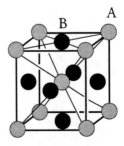

10. Assuming atoms of equal size, how would you expect the sizes of the sc, bcc, and fcc unit cells to be related? Which lattice has the highest density? Is the density of the fcc lattice four times the density of the simple lattice?

11. Examine the unit cell of the ionic crystalline solid $A_aB_bC_c$ illustrated below. The AB_6 unit is a polyatomic ion.

    a. How many A ions are there in the unit cell?
    b. How many B ions are in the unit cell?
    c. How many C ions are in the unit cell?
    d. How is the lattice structure of the AB_6 ions described?
    e. How is the lattice structure of the C ions described?
    f. What is the stoichiometry of the salt?

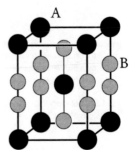

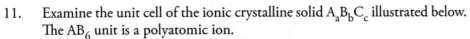

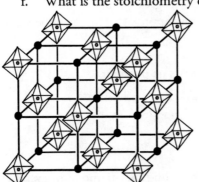

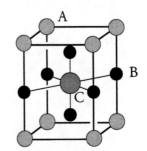

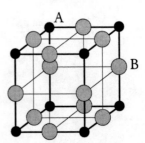

Answers to Study Questions and Problems

1. a. in a water molecule   covalent bonding (between H and O atoms)
    b. in ice   hydrogen bonding (between H_2O molecules)
    c. in a solution of KNO_3 ion–molecule interparticle bonding (solvation)
    d. in diamond   covalent bonding (covalent network)
    e. in a fiber of nylon   covalent bonding within the polymer; intermolecular hydrogen bonding and dispersion forces between the polymer chains
    f. in liquid butane   dispersion forces
    g. in a crystal of NaCl   ionic bonding
    h. between DNA strands   hydrogen bonding
    i. in paraffin wax   dispersion forces
    j. in dry ice   dispersion forces
    k. in liquid HCl   dipole–dipole attraction and dispersion forces
    l. in tungsten metal   metallic bonding
    m. in perchloric acid   strong ion–molecule interaction (solvation of the hydrogen and perchlorate ions by water)

2. a. Br_2 greater molar mass; greater dispersion forces
    b. C_5H_{12} greater molar mass; greater dispersion forces
    c. NH_3 hydrogen bonding
    d. Mg   stronger metallic bonding (2 valence electrons *vs.* 1)
    e. BeO   charges on the ions greater, higher lattice energy
    f. ICl   polar; molar mass approximately the same as Br_2

3. a. a gas
    b. an amorphous material (a glass or polymer)
    c. a crystalline solid
    d. a liquid
    e. a supercritical fluid
    f. a metallic solid
    g. a gas
    h. a crystalline covalent network solid like diamond or graphite

4. As a rule, the hydrogen atoms attached to carbon do not participate in hydrogen bonding. However, the chlorine atoms on the carbon of the chloroform $CHCl_3$ are electronegative—they pull the electrons away from the carbon atom, and from the hydrogen attached to the carbon. Effectively, the electronegativity of the carbon is increased. As a result, hydrogen bonding is possible between the H of the $CHCl_3$ and the O of the $(CH_3)_2C=O$.

It is interesting that ICl was discovered before Br_2. As a result, the first samples of the red-brown Br_2 were mistaken for ICl. The molar masses are almost the same:

Br_2 159.82 g/mol   mpt –7°C
ICl   162.35 g/mol   mpt 27°C

5. a. Heat required to melt 15 grams of ice
        = 333 J/g × 15 g = 5 kJ
    b. Heat released when 100 grams of steam condenses
        = 2250 J/g × 100 g = 225 kJ
    c. Since 4 g × 333 J/g = 1.33 kJ, this heat is sufficient to melt 4 grams
        of ice. So the quantity of water originally present = 8 grams.

This is why steam can cause severe burns.

6. If the lattice is face-centered cubic, then the distance across the diagonal of
    one face is equal to four times the radius of one silver atom. If the edge of
    the cube is 407 pm in length, the diagonal = $\sqrt{(407^2+407^2)}$ = 575.6 pm.
    The radius of one atom, therefore is 144 pm.

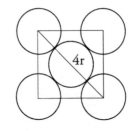

7. The volume of one unit cell = 407^3 = 6.742×10^7 pm^3.
    This equals 6.742×10^{-23} cm^3.
    There are four atoms in a fcc unit cell, each having a mass equal to
    107.8682 g mol^{-1}/ 6.02214×10^{23} mol^{-1} = 1.791×10^{-22} grams.
    The density is therefore 4 × 1.791×10^{-22} / 6.742×10^{-23} g cm^{-3}.
        = 10.6 g cm^{-3}.

One pm = 10^{-10} cm

One pm^3 = 10^{-30} cm^3

The actual density of silver is 10.49 g cm^{-3} at 20°C.

8. There is an atom at the center of the cube and one at each corner. The atoms
    on the corners contribute only 1/8 each to the total, the remainder belongs
    to adjacent unit cells in the lattice.. So the number of atoms in the unit cell
    = 1 + (8×1/8) = 2 atoms.

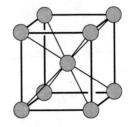

9. A: 8 corners and 1 center = (8×1/8)+1 = 2
    B: 8 edges = (8×1/4) = 2   so AB

    A: 8 corners and 1 center = (8×1/8)+1 = 2
    B: 6 faces = (6×1/2) = 3   so A$_2$B$_3$

    A: 8 corners and 1 center = (8×1/8)+1 = 2
    B: 8 edges and 2 inside = (8×1/4)+2 = 4   so AB$_2$

    A: 8 corners = 1
    B: 4 edges and 2 inside = (4×1/4)+2 = 3
    C: 1 center = 1   so AB$_3$C

    A: 8 corners = (8×1/8) = 1
    B: 12 edges = (12×1/4) = 3   so AB$_3$

If r = radius of the atom:

volume of a simple cubic cell
= $8r^3$

volume of a body-centered cell
= $12.32 \, r^3$

volume of a face-centered cell
= $22.63 \, r^3$

ratio of densities
= $1.00 : 1.30 : 1.41$

You can count the B individually and get the same answer:

At each of 8 corners, there is
1 on a face = $8 \times 1/2 = 4$
1 on an edge = $8 \times 1/4 = 2$ total = 4
+ 2 = 6.

On each of 6 faces, there is
1 inside the cell = $6 \times 1 = 6$
4 on the face = $4 \times 6 \times 1/2 = 12$
total = 18.

Total number of B = 24.

10.   Assuming atoms of equal size, the sizes of the unit cells should increase sc < bcc < fcc. The atoms are packed most closely together in the fcc lattice and therefore this lattice has the highest density. However, the density of the fcc lattice is not four times the density of the simple lattice, there are four times as many atoms in the unit cell, but the cell is larger.

11.   a.   The lattice array of the AB_6 octahedral ions is face-centered cubic. There are ions on each corner (contribution $8 \times 1/8$) and one in the center of each face (contribution $6 \times 1/2$). The total number of AB_6 octahedra is therefore 4. So there are 4 A in one unit cell.

      b.   There must be 6 times as many B as there are A, so there are 24 B per unit cell.

      c.   There are C ions halfway along each edge, and there are twelve edges. Each C ion on an edge contributes 1/4 to that unit cell, so the total contribution form the C ions on the edges is 3. There is also an C ion in the center of the unit cell—contribution 1. So the total number of C ions in the unit cell = 4.

      d.   The lattice structure of the AB_6 ions is face-centered cubic.

      e.   The lattice structure of the C ions is also face-centered cubic.

      f.   The stoichiometry is CAB_6.

CHAPTER 13

Introduction

Solutions are homogeneous mixtures of two or more substances; they are everywhere. The air we breathe, the water we drink, and all sorts of materials encountered every day, are solutions. Chemists perform many reactions in solution because, in the solution state, molecules are free to move about and react. So in this chapter we will look further into the solution state, investigate the solution process itself, and examine the properties of solutions called colligative properties. At the end of the chapter we will look at colloids and surfactants.

Contents

    Units of Concentration
Factors Affecting Solubility: Pressure and Temperature
    The Solution Process
    Factors Affecting Solubility: Pressure and Temperature
    Colligative Properties
    Colloids

Units of Concentration

In a **solution** there are at least two components: the **solute** dissolved in the **solvent**. The solvent is that component that determines the state of the solution. For example, when sugar dissolves in water, water is the solvent because the solution is a liquid. Otherwise, the solvent is that component present in the greater amount.

The word "component" refers to a solute or the solvent in the solution. Very often there is more than one solute. Note that components are (pure) substances.

There are many ways to express the concentration of the various components in a solution. Each has its own merits. **Molarity** is a concentration expressed as the number of moles of solute per liter of solution and is particularly useful in stoichiometric calculations for reactions occurring in solution.

Recall that molarity is defined as the number of moles per liter of solution.

Other concentrations units are **molality**, **mole fraction**, **mass percent**, and parts per million or billion (**ppm** or **ppb**):

$$\text{Molality} = \frac{\text{moles of solute}}{\text{kg of solvent}}$$

$$\text{Mole fraction} = \frac{\text{moles of one component}}{\text{total moles of the solution}}$$

$$\text{Mass percent} = \frac{\text{mass of one component}}{\text{total mass of all components in the solution}} \times 100$$

$$\text{Parts per million} = \frac{\text{mass of one component in mg}}{\text{total mass of the solution in kg}}$$

Do not confuse molality with molarity. The advantage of the molality concentration unit over molarity is that it is temperature independent. Mass doesn't change when the temperature changes but volume does.

Mass percent is often called weight percent.

Be able to calculate concentrations using these units and be able to convert between them.

See study questions #1, 2, 3, &4.

The concentration ppm is often expressed as mg/L (approximately the same as mg/kg). The concentration ppb is expressed as μg/kg or μg/L. Although solutions are often thought of as being liquids, remember that solutions can be homogeneous mixtures in any one of the three states (solid, liquid, or gas).

The Solution Process

When one substance dissolves in another, any intermolecular bonds in the two substances have to be at least partially broken, and new intermolecular bonds between the two substances are made. For example, when sodium chloride salt dissolves in water, the salt crystal is broken up, the intermolecular bonds in the water are partially broken, and the ions are hydrated (solvated) by the water (ion–dipole attraction).

There is a limit to the amount of sodium chloride that will dissolve. Before the limit is reached, the solution is said to be **unsaturated**. At the limit, it is **saturated**, and beyond the limit(!) it is **supersaturated**.

When the two components of a solution are both liquids, and they can be mixed in any proportion, they are said to be **miscible**. If they do not dissolve in each other, they are called **immiscible**. Often two liquids are partially miscible. A common rule that indicates the likely solubility of one substance in another is "like dissolves like". A polar molecule is likely to be soluble in a polar solvent, a nonpolar molecule in a nonpolar solvent. The reason for this is that the character of the bonds in each of the components and those between the components should be similar if the solution process is going to be product–favored.

Whether energy is liberated or absorbed during the solution process depends upon the relative strengths of the bonds broken and formed in the process. The bonds broken are those in the solute (for example, the lattice energy of a NaCl crystal) and in the solvent (for example, some hydrogen bonds in water). The bonds made are those between the solute and the solvent (for example, in the hydration of the sodium and chloride ions). There is a direct correlation between the enthalpy of solution and the water solubility of ionic compounds. The more exothermic the solution process, the higher the solubility. If the disparity in the bond strengths is sufficiently large, the salt may not dissolve. For example, silver chloride is very sparingly soluble.

Heats of solution can be measured in a calorimeter just like the other heats of reaction described in Chapter 6 of this study guide. They can also be calculated from the difference between the standard heat of formation of a substance and the heat of formation of the same substance in the solution state.

Factors Affecting Solubility: Pressure and Temperature

Temperature affects the solubility of most substances. If the solute is a gas, its solubility is also affected by pressure.

The effect of pressure on the solubility of a gas is described by **Henry's law.** This law states that the solubility of a gas is directly proportional to the partial pressure of the gas above the solution. The higher the pressure of a gas above a liquid, the more gas will dissolve in the liquid.

Unsaturated:
concentration < solubility

Saturated:
concentration = solubility

Supersaturated:
concentration > solubility

The supersaturated state is thermodynamically unstable, and given half a chance, a supersaturated solution will precipitate the excess solute with the evolution of considerable energy.

There two driving forces for any process:
The first is a decrease in the enthalpy of the system—an exothermic process.
The second is an increase in the disorder of the system.
Both lead to an increase in the entropy of the universe.

See study question #5.

Silver chloride:
Heat of solution = +61 kJ/mol
Solubility = 0.000089 g/mL

Lithium fluoride:
Heat of solution = +32 kJ/mol
Solubility = 0.3 g/mL

Rubidium fluoride:
Heat of solution = –3 kJ/mol
Solubility = 130.6 g/mL

Henry's law is valid providing that the solvent and solute do not react.

See study questions #6 & 7.

$$S_g = k_H P_g$$

The constant k_H is a characteristic of both gas and solvent. The reason why helium–oxygen mixtures are used in preference to nitrogen–oxygen mixtures for deep water diving is the lower solubility of helium in blood.

The solubility of a gas in water decreases as the temperature is raised. The solution process is a dynamic process—gas molecules are leaving and reentering the solution all the time. If allowed, the process will reach equilibrium when the two rates are equal and the concentration reaches a steady value. Because no intermolecular bonds between the gas molecules need to be broken in a solution process, and solute–solvent bonds are made, processes involving the solution of a gas in water are exothermic:

There are no intermolecular bonds in a gas.

Gas + liquid solvent ⇌ saturated solution of the gas + HEAT

According to LeChatelier's Principle, addition of heat (on the product side), drives the reaction to the left so that the heat is absorbed by the system. In other words, if a solution of a gas (e.g. a carbonated drink) is heated, the gas will bubble out of the solution. The effect of temperature on the solubility of solids is less easy to predict. If the solution process is endothermic, an increase in temperature will increase the solubility.

LeChatelier's Principle will be discussed again in the chapter on chemical equilibria (Chapter 15 of this study guide).

The principle states that: A system in equilibrium will adjust so as to reduce or accommodate any stress placed on the system.

For example, in this case, the system will adjust to absorb the heat added to the system; the equilibrium will shift to the left.

Colligative Properties

Solutions have properties different from those of the pure solvent. The freezing point, boiling point, vapor pressure, osmotic pressure are all different. These properties of the solution, called **colligative properties**, depend upon the relative numbers of solute and solvent particles in the solution.

The equilibrium vapor pressure is the partial pressure of the vapor above a liquid (solvent) when the system is in equilibrium. Addition of a solute to the solvent results in fewer solvent molecules being able to escape; there is a lower probability of the solvent molecules being at the surface. The disorder in the solution state is increased and the rate at which solvent molecules escape into the vapor is reduced. As a result the equilibrium vapor pressure is less for the solution.

Recall that at equilibrium, the rate at which molecules leave the liquid phase equals the rate at which molecules re-enter the liquid phase; it is a dynamic equilibrium. At equilibrium the partial pressure of the vapor is constant.

Raoult's law states that the equilibrium vapor pressure of the solvent in a solution depends upon two factors: one is the volatility of the solvent (usually expressed as the vapor pressure of the pure solvent $P^\circ_{solvent}$), and the second is the concentration of solvent molecules in the solution (usually expressed as the mole fraction $X_{solvent}$):

See study question #8.

$$P_{solvent} = X_{solvent} P^\circ_{solvent}$$

Raoult's law assumes that the solution is an **ideal solution**. An ideal solution is one in which the forces of intermolecular attraction in the two components (solute and solvent) are very similar to one another and to the forces of attraction in the solution. Ideal solutions are therefore ones for which the enthalpy of solution is zero. They occur when solute and solvent are very similar—for example, hexane and heptane.

If the forces of attraction differ in the two components and the solution, the solution is said to deviate from ideal behavior, or to deviate from Raoult's law.

An ideal solution is often said to be a solution that obeys Raoult's law. Dilute solutions generally obey Raoult's law reasonably well.

Positive deviation, when the vapor pressure is higher than Raoult's law would predict, occurs when $\Delta H_{solution}$ is positive. Negative deviation occurs when $\Delta H_{solution}$ is negative.

All colligative properties are the result of the increased entropy (disorder) of the liquid phase. There is no solute in the solid and vapor phases (assuming the solute is nonvolatile). This increase in disorder means that (compared to the pure solvent) the change in entropy during vaporization is less and the change in entropy during freezing is greater.

A lowering of the vapor pressure causes an increase in the boiling point. A higher temperature is required to compensate for the lower vapor pressure caused by the presence of the solute particles. The **elevation of the boiling point** ΔT_b is given by the relationship:

$$\Delta T_b = k_b \times m$$

where m is the molality of the solute and k_b is a constant characteristic of the solvent.

The freezing point of a solvent is depressed when a solute is added. This is why salt is spread on an icy road, or ethylene glycol is added to radiator fluid. The solid–liquid interface is altered just as it was for the vaporization process. A lower temperature is required to compensate for the increased disorder in the liquid phase. The **depression of the freezing point** ΔT_f is given by a similar relationship:

The values of k_f and k_b are now known for most common solvents.

See study questions #9 & 10.

$$\Delta T_f = k_f \times m$$

where m is the molality of the solute and k_f is a constant characteristic of the solvent.

It is possible to determine the molar mass of an unknown solute by measuring the depression in the freezing point of its solution. The constant k_f is established using a known solute and then the experiment is repeated using the unknown solute.

A colligative property depends upon the relative number of solute particles in the solution. It doesn't matter whether the particles are molecules or ions. If a solute breaks up to form ions, it has a greater effect on the freezing point depression or boiling point elevation than a solute that doesn't break up. This effect was discovered by Raoult, studied by van't Hoff and explained by Arrhenius. Arrhenius proposed that salts like sodium chloride dissociate in solution to form two solutes, one sodium ions and the other chloride ions. Thus the effect is twice as great. It is not the identity, but the relative number, of solute particles that matters.

Recall that the depression of the freezing point when a solute is added is a result of the increased disorder in the solution. A solute that breaks up to form two particles in solution creates twice as much disorder as one that doesn't.

The **van't Hoff factor**, i, represents the extent to which solutes break up to form ions. In dilute solution, NaCl, for example, breaks up to form two ions per formula unit, and therefore $i = 2$. The value of i, which can be determined by experiment, indicates the extent to which ionization occurs. In all but very dilute solution, there is always association between ions, and i is less than the ideal integer. The earlier equations can be modified to include the van't Hoff factor:

For a 0.50M solution:

i for NaCl = 1.87 not 2.00
i for Na_2SO_4 = 2.51 not 3.00

See study question #11.

k_f is usually given as a negative number because the freezing point decreases.
The units of k_f and k_b are Km^{-1}.

$$\Delta T_b = k_b \times m \times i$$
$$\Delta T_f = k_f \times m \times i$$

Osmosis is the movement of solvent molecules through what is called a semi-permeable membrane. A semipermeable membrane allows solvent molecules to pass through but not the solute particles. The water molecules move from the side of low solute concentration to the side of high solute concentration in attempt to equalize the concentrations and reach equilibrium. The interface at the membrane is just the same as the solid–liquid and liquid–vapor interfaces already described.

The osmosis continues until the concentrations are equal, or until pressure is applied to the high concentration side to equalize the rates of movement of solvent molecules through the membrane. The pressure required to equalize the rates from one side to the other is called the **osmotic pressure** Π. The osmotic pressure is related to the concentration of solute by a equation similar to the ideal gas law:

$$\Pi V = nRT \qquad \text{or} \qquad \Pi = cRT \quad \text{where } c = \frac{n}{V}$$

Large osmotic pressures result from relatively small molar concentrations and measurement of the osmotic pressure of a solution is an effective method of determining the molar mass of an unknown solute—particularly for solutes having high molar masses and low solubilities (for example, proteins and polymers).

Solutions having the same osmotic pressure are said to be isotonic.

Intravenous drips are made isotonic with the patient's blood to prevent rupture of cells.

See study question #13.

Colloids

A solution is a homogeneous mixture; the mixing of solute and solvent particles occurs at the molecular or particulate level. If the solute particle is large in size (about 1 μm) or large in mass (molar mass in the thousands), but not so large that the particles settle out or precipitate, a **colloidal dispersion** forms.

A colloidal dispersion is not a solution, nor is it a suspension; it is somewhere between. The interesting properties of colloids are due to the relatively large surface areas of the particles. A **hydrophobic** colloid is one in which there are weak forces of attraction between the colloid particle and water. Hydrophobic colloidal particles carry charges due to ions absorbed on the surface. The repulsion between the like charges prevents the coagulation of the particles and the formation of a suspension and precipitation. A **hydrophilic** colloid exhibits a strong attraction for water molecules. This is often due to hydrogen bonding. Examples are colloids of proteins and starch.

Emulsions are colloidal dispersions of one liquid in another—for example, milk and mayonnaise. Mayonnaise is a dispersion of oil in water. Lecithin (a protein in egg yolk) is added to stabilize the emulsion, or the oil and water would separate. Lecithin is a **surfactant** or emulsifying agent.

A surfactant is a surface active agent. **Soaps** and **detergents** are examples. A soap is the sodium or potassium salt of a long chain fatty acid. This salt has a polar hydrophilic end and a long chain nonpolar hydrophobic end. It is able to bridge the interface between oil and water. It therefore facilitates the emulsion of the oil and water, enabling the removal of the oil stain. Magnesium and calcium salts of the fatty acids are insoluble and create soap scum. To avoid the problem, synthetic detergents use sulfonate instead of carboxylate salts (the calcium and magnesium sulfonate salts are more soluble). An example of a detergent is sodium lauryl benzenesulfonate (which is biodegradable):

As the size of the solute particle increases:

solution

↓

colloid

↓

suspension

Colloids have the ability to scatter light (like dust in a sunbeam). This is called the Tyndall effect.

A colloid, like a solution, has two components:
the dispersing medium (the "solvent") and the
dispersed phase (the "solute").

sol: a colloidal dispersion of a solid in a liquid.
gel: a colloidal dispersion of a liquid in a solid.
aerosol: a colloidal dispersion of a liquid or solid in a gas.
foam: a colloidal dispersion of a gas in a liquid or solid.
emulsion: a colloidal dispersion of one liquid in another liquid.

See study question #14.

$$CH_3-CH_2-CH_2-CH_2-CH_2-CH_2-CH_2-CH_2-CH_2-CH_2-CH_2-CH_2$$ 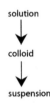 $$-SO_3^-$$

$$Na^+$$

Review Questions

1. Define solute, solvent, and solution.

2. Define unsaturated, saturated, and supersaturated. How would you make a supersaturated solution?

3. Define the concentration units molarity, molality, mole fraction, mass percent, and ppm.

Key terms:

solution
solvent
solute
molarity
molality
mass percent
mole fraction
ppm
ppb
unsaturated
saturated
supersaturated
miscibility
immiscibility
lattice energy
solvation energy
heat of solution
Henry's law
LeChatelier's principle
Raoult's law
colligative property
vapor pressure lowering
elevation of boiling point
depression of freezing point
van't Hoff factor i
osmotic pressure
isotonic
colloid
colloidal dispersion
dispersing phase
dispersed phase
Tyndall effect
hydrophobic
hydrophilic
sol
gel
emulsion
aerosol
foam
surfactant

4.   Define the terms miscible and immiscible.

5.   What two factors are largely responsible for determining the magnitude and sign of the enthalpy of solution?

6.   Given that a decrease in energy favors a reaction, how is it that some solution processes are endothermic? Why does the solution process happen in these cases?

7.   Describe how temperature and pressure affect the solubility of a gas.

8.   What is Henry's law?

9.   Why is ammonia much more soluble than oxygen in water ?

10.   Describe Henri LeChatelier's principle.

11.   What is Raoult's law?

12.   What is an ideal solution?

13.   What is a colligative property?

14.   Describe how the solid–liquid and liquid–vapor phase interfaces are affected in the same way by the addition of a solute. How do these interfaces compare with the interface across a semipermeable membrane in osmosis?

15.   Why does the freezing point *decrease*, and the boiling point *increase*, upon addition of a solute?

16.   Explain what the van't Hoff factor *i* is. What does it mean if *i* is less than the ideal integer value for a salt?

17.   Describe the terms isotonic, hypotonic, and hypertonic.

18.   What is a colloidal dispersion?

19.   Summarize the different types of colloids and give eamples of each.

20.   Soaps and detergents are both surfactants; what is the difference between them?

Answers to Review Questions

1.   Solute: the substance dissolved in the solvent.
        Solvent: the component that determines the state of the solution.
        Solution: the homogeneous mixture of solute and solvent.

2. Unsaturated: concentration less than the solubility, more solute can be dissolved.

    Saturated: concentration = solubility at that temperature.

    Supersaturated: concentration exceeds the solubility; this solution is thermodynamically unstable.

    A saturated solution is made at a high temperature where the solubility is higher. The solution is then allowed to cool slowly to a temperature where the solubility is lower. If the excess solute does not precipitate out, the solution becomes supersaturated.

    The fact that the excess solute does not precipitate out is a kinetic, not a thermodynamic, effect.

3. Molarity (M) = moles of solute / liter of solution

    Molality (m) = moles of solute / kg of solvent

    Mole fraction (X) = moles of solute / total moles in solution

    Mass percent (%) = (mass of solute / mass of solution) × 100

    ppm = mass of solute in mg / mass of solution in kg

    Because volume changes with temperature, molarity is temperature dependent also.
    Molality is temperature independent.

4. Miscible means that the two liquids making up the solution can mix (usually in all proportions).

    Immiscible means that two liquids do not dissolve in one another (for example, oil and water are immiscible).

5. As in any reaction, the energy released or absorbed is a measure of the strength of the bonds that have to be broken, and the strength of the bonds that are made. In the solution process, there are bonds in the solute and bonds in the solvent that need to be broken. Bonds are formed between the two components. For example, when sodium chloride dissolves in water, the lattice energy of the NaCl crystal must be supplied. In addition, some hydrogen bonds in the water are broken. The ions are solvated by the water; strong ion–molecule bonds are formed. Therefore the two factors largely responsible are: the lattice energy of the solute and the solvation energy. The energy required or released is the difference between these two.

6. The predominant driving force for many solution processes is the increase in the disorder (entropy) of the system. This often overcomes any unfavorable enthalpy change.

    There two driving forces for any process:
    The first is a decrease in the enthalpy of the system.
    The second is an increase in the disorder of the system.

7. The solubility of a gas in water decreases as the temperature is raised. Because no intermolecular bonds between the gas molecules need to be broken in a solution process, and solute–solvent bonds are made, processes involving the solution of a gas in water are exothermic. According to LeChatelier's Principle, addition of heat drives the reaction from the product (solution) side to the reactant side to absorb the heat. In other words, if a solution of a gas is heated, gas will bubble out of the solution.

    The effect of pressure on the solubility of a gas is described by Henry's law. This law states that the solubility of a gas is directly proportional to the partial pressure of the gas above the solution: $S_g = k_H P_g$. The constant k_H is a characteristic of both gas and solvent.

Carbon dioxide and sulfur dioxide are two other gases that are very soluble in water because of the interaction between these molecules and the water molecules. Carbon dioxide forms carbonic acid H_2CO_3 to some extent and sulfur dioxide forms sulfurous acid H_2SO_3 to some extent.

8. Henry's law describes how the solubility of a gas depends upon the partial pressure of the gas above the liquid: $S_g = k_H P_g$.

9. Ammonia interacts with the water to a much greater extent than oxygen does. Hydrogen bonding between the ammonia molecules and the water molecules leads to an exceptionally high solubility. A solution of ammonia in water is sometimes referred to as ammonium hydroxide although the ammonia is present predominantly as ammonia molecules. The interaction between oxygen and water is only a dipole–induced dipole attraction and its solubility is much less.

All systems move toward equilibrium. A system moved away from equilibrium will adjust in order to return to equilibrium.

10. Henri LeChatelier's principle states that any system in equilibrium will adjust so as to reduce or accommodate any stress placed on the system.

11. Raoult's law states that the equilibrium vapor pressure of a solution depends upon two factors: one is the volatility of the solvent (expressed as the vapor pressure of the pure solvent $P^\circ_{solvent}$), and the second is the concentration of solvent molecules in the solution (expressed as the mole fraction $X_{solvent}$):

$$P_{solvent} = X_{solvent} P^\circ_{solvent}$$

Raoult's law assumes that the solution is an ideal solution.

12. An ideal solution is a solution that obeys Raoult's law! It is a solution in which the forces of intermolecular attraction in the two components (solute and solvent) are very similar to one another and to the forces of attraction in the solution. Ideal solutions are therefore ones for which the enthalpy of solution is zero. They occur when solute and solvent are very similar—for example, hexane and heptane, benzene and toluene, or pentanol and hexanol. If the forces of attraction differ in the two components and the solution, the solution is said to deviate from ideal behavior, or to deviate from Raoult's law.

13. A colligative property is a property that depends only upon the relative numbers of solute and solvent particles in the solution and not their identity.

There are of course many instances where the solute is volatile.

14. When a solute is dissolved in a solvent to make a solution, in most cases the solute exists only in solution. The solute is nonvolatile. The vapor state and the solid state contain only solvent molecules. It is the increase in the disorder of the liquid state that affects the colligative properties of the solution. In both the vaporization process and the freezing process, the movement of solvent molecules from the liquid phase to the solid or vapor phases is inhibited by the disorder created by the solute particles in solution. In terms of probability, there is a lower probability of the solvent particles being at the surface. The situation is the same across the semipermeable membrane in osmosis.

15. Freezing is a process in the direction of increased order; vaporization (boiling) is a process in the direction of increased disorder. The directions are opposite. A lower temperature is required to create order from a more disordered solution (compared to the pure solvent). A higher temperature is required to create the disordered vapor from a more disordered solution. From a molecular point of view, the solute particles in the solution interfere with the freezing or boiling process. At equilibrium, at the phase interface, the numbers of solvent molecules travelling in both directions must be equal. Because of the presence of the solute particles in the liquid phase, the temperature must be lower at the freezing point, and must be higher at the boiling point, to achieve the equal rates.

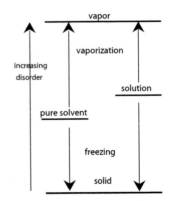

If $T\Delta S$ is constant, and ΔS is greater, then T (freezing point) must be lower. If $T\Delta S$ is constant and ΔS is larger, then T (boiling point) must be higher.

16. The van't Hoff factor i is an indication of how many particles are produced when a solute is dissolved. If the solute breaks up to form individual ions, then the van't Hoff factor i is greater than 1. For example, sodium chloride $NaCl$ produces two ions (Na^+ and Cl^-) in solution and therefore i might be expected to be 2. In a very dilute solutions it is. In more concentrated solutions, the oppositely charged Na^+ and Cl^- ions associate to form ion-pairs so that i is less than 2. In very concentrated solutions, the degree of association between ions is high and i is correspondingly lower.

Values of i are, for example:

Concentration	NaCl	MgSO$_4$
0.10 m	1.87	1.21
0.01 m	1.94	1.53
0.001 m	1.97	1.82
infinitely dilute	2.00	2.00

Notice the greater attraction between the doubly charged ions.

17. Isotonic: equal osmotic pressures (equal solute concentrations).
Hypotonic: the osmotic pressure is less (than a standard).
Hypertonic: the osmotic pressure is greater (than a standard).

18. A colloidal dispersion is not a solution, nor is it a suspension; it is somewhere between. If the solute particle is large in size (about 1 μm or larger) or large in mass (molar mass in the thousands), but not so large that the particles settle out, a colloidal dispersion is produced.

19. sol: a colloidal dispersion of a solid in a liquid.
         e.g. milk of magnesia
gel: a colloidal dispersion of a liquid in a solid.
         e.g. jello
aerosol: a colloidal dispersion of a liquid or solid in a gas.
         e.g. fog and smoke
foam: a colloidal dispersion of a gas in a liquid or solid.
         e.g. whipped cream
emulsion: a colloidal dispersion of one liquid in another liquid.
         e.g. mayonnaise

20. A soap is a sodium or potassium salt of a long chain carboxylic acid (a fatty acid). A detergent is a sodium or potassium salt of a long chain sulfonic acid. The magnesium and calcium salts of the sulfonic acids are more soluble than those of the carboxylic acids and so the detergents do not form insoluble soap scums like the soaps do.

Study Questions and Problems

1. A solution of a salt (molar mass 90 g mol^{-1}) in water has a density of 1.29 g/mL. The concentration of the salt is 35% by mass.

    a. Calculate the molality of the solution.
    b. Calculate the molarity of the solution.
    c. Calculate the total number of moles in the solution.
    d. Calculate the mole fraction of the salt in the solution.

2. Ethylene glycol ($C_2H_4(OH)_2$; 150 grams) is added to ethanol (C_2H_5OH; 250 grams).

    a. Calculate the mass % of ethylene glycol in the solution.
    b. Calculate the molality of ethylene glycol in the solution.
    c. Calculate the mole fraction of ethylene glycol in the solution.

3. For a dilute aqueous solution, the molality is moreorless the same as the molarity. Explain why. Is this true for all solvents?

4. Concentrated sulfuric acid contains very little water, only 5.0% by mass. It has a density of 1.84 g/mL. What is the molarity of this acid?

5. The lattice energy of a salt is 350 kJ/mol and the solvation energies of its ions add up to 320 kJ/mol for the preparation of a 0.50 M solution. In the preparation of this solution would the solution get colder or warmer? What is the driving force for this solution process?

6. Addition of excess sodium nitrate to water to form a saturated solution results in the following equilibrium. The solution process is endothermic.

    $$NaNO_3(s) \quad \rightleftharpoons \quad Na^+(aq) \quad + \quad NO_3^-(aq)$$

    How could the concentration of sodium nitrate in the solution be increased?

    a. add more $NaNO_3(s)$
    b. increase the pressure on the solution
    c. increase the temperature
    d. stir the solution more vigorously

7. The value of Henry's law constant k_H for oxygen in water at 25°C is 1.66×10^{-6} M/torr.

    a. Calculate the solubility of oxygen in water at 25°C when the total external pressure is 1 atm and the mole fraction of oxygen in the air is 0.20.

    b. Calculate the solubility at the same temperature with the same atmospheric composition but at an increased pressure of 2 atm.

    c. What would happen to the solubility of the oxygen gas if the temperature was increased?

8. Ethanol and methanol form an almost ideal solution. If 64 g of methanol is mixed with 69 g of ethanol, what is the total vapor pressure above the solution?

   The vapor pressure of pure methanol at this temperature = 90 torr.

   The vapor pressure of pure ethanol at the same temperature = 45 torr.

9. A 3.0 molal solution of naphthalene in cyclohexane boils at 89.4°C. What is the boiling point of pure cyclohexane? Although solid naphthalene is slightly volatile, assume its volatility is zero in this calculation. The constant k_b for cyclohexane is +2.80 Km^{-1}.

10. Which of the following solutions would you expect to have the lowest freezing point? Assume that the values of i are ideal.

    a. 0.010m NaCl
    b. 0.100m sugar
    c. 0.070m KNO$_3$

    d. 0.050m glycerol
    e. 0.060m Ca(NO$_3$)$_2$
    f. 0.075m KCl

11. In order to depress the freezing point of water to −12°C, how much magnesium nitrate would you have to add to 500 grams of water? Assume that the van't Hoff factor i is the ideal value.

    k_f for water = −1.86 Km^{-1}.

12. Suppose that you have 10 grams of ice and 100 grams of water at 0°C in a well-insulated container. You add to the container 40 grams of ammonium nitrate at 0°C and stir gently to dissolve. What happens? Does ice melt due to the depression of the freezing point? Or does water freeze due to the endothermic solution process?

    $\Delta H_{solution}$ (NH$_4$NO$_3$) = +25.7 kJ mol^{-1}

    heat of fusion of ice = +333 J g^{-1}

    k_f for water = −1.86 Km^{-1}

    molar mass of ammonium nitrate = 80.04 g mol^{-1}

    specific heat capacity of water = 4.184 JK^{-1}g^{-1}; assume that the specific heat of the solution is the same.

    specific heat of ice = 2.06 JK^{-1}g^{-1}

    Assume that i, the van't Hoff factor, for the concentrated solution of ammonium nitrate is 1.6.

13. An unknown protein (350 mg) was dissolved in water to produce 10 ml of solution. The osmotic pressure of the solution at 25°C was determined to be 10.8 torr. What is the molar mass of the unknown protein?

14.   Classify the following materials as foam, aerosol, emulsion, gel, or sol.

   a.   homogenized milk   f.   atmospheric dust
   b.   red jelly   g.   oil & vinegar dressing
   c.   cheese   h.   pumice stone
   d.   shaving cream   i.   clouds
   e.   wet modelling clay   j.   meringue

Answers to Study Questions and Problems

To me education is a leading out of what is already there in a pupil's soul. To Miss Mackay, it is a putting in of something that is not there, and that is not what I call education, I call it intrusion.

The Prime of Miss Jean Brodie
Muriel Spark
(1918-)

1.   The concentration of the salt is 35% by mass; this means that in 100 g of solution there is 35 g of salt. So there must be 65 g of water.

   a.   Number of moles of salt = 35 g / 90 g mol^{-1} = 0.389 mol
        Molality = moles of solute / kg of solvent = 0.389 mol / 0.065 kg water
        The solution is 6.0 m.

   b.   100 g of solution = 100 g /1.29 g mL^{-1} = 77.52 mL solution
        Molarity = moles of solute / liter of solution = 0.389 mol / 0.07752 L
        The solution is 5.0 M.

   c.   Number of moles of solute in 100 g of solution = 0.389 mol
        Number of moles of water = 65 g / 18 g mol^{-1} = 3.61 mol
        Total number of moles = 4.0 mol.

   d.   Mole fraction of the salt = 0.389 / 4.0 = 0.10.

2.   Mass of ethylene glycol = 150 grams
        Mass of ethanol = 250 grams
   a.   Mass % of ethylene glycol = 150/400 × 100% = 37.5%

   b.   Number of moles of ethylene glycol = 150 g / 62 g mol^{-1} = 2.42 mol.
        Molality = 2.42 mol / 0.250 kg solvent = 9.68 m.

Moles of ethanol
   = 250 g / 46 g mol^{-1}
   = 5.43 mol

   c.   Mole fraction = 2.42 / (2.42 + 5.43) = 0.31.

3.   If the solution is dilute, the mass of solute compared to the mass of the solvent is negligible, and since the density of the solution is 1.00 g/mL, the mass of the solution in kg is numerically equal to the volume in L. The same is not true for other solvents where the density is not 1.00 g/mL.

4.   In 100 g there are 95 g of sulfuric acid.
        The volume is 100 g / 1.84 g mL^{-1} = 54.35 mL.
        The number of moles is 95 g / 98 g mol^{-1}= 0.969 mol.
        Molarity = 0.969 mol / 0.05435 L = 17.8 M.

This is LeChatelier's principle; the system will adjust to accommodate any stress placed upon the system. Heat is a reactant in this solution process; it is an endothermic process.

5.   More energy is required (lattice energy 350 kJ/mol) than is released (solvation energies 320 kJ/mol). So the process is endothermic; energy is absorbed and the solution will get cold. The process is not driven by a decrease in enthalpy! As in many cases, the solution process is driven by the increase in disorder.

6. $$NaNO_3(s) \rightleftharpoons Na^+(aq) + NO_3^-(aq)$$

    a. adding more solid $NaNO_3$ has no effect, the solution is already saturated.

    b. changing the pressure on a solution of a solid in a liquid has virtually no effect on the position of equilibrium.

    c. increasing the temperature will shift the equilibrium to the right; the concentration of the sodium and nitrate ions will increase.

    d. stirring the solution more vigorously may allow the equilibrium state to be reached more quickly (a kinetic effect) but the position reached will be the same.

7.   The value of Henry's law constant k_H for oxygen in water at 25°C is 1.66×10^{-6} M/torr.

    a. $S_g = k_H P_g = 1.66 \times 10^{-6}$ M/torr $\times (0.20 \times 760)$ torr $= 2.52 \times 10^{-4}$ M.   1 atm = 760 torr.

    b. The solubility will be twice as high $= 5.05 \times 10^{-4}$ M.

    c. At a higher temperature the solubility of the oxygen gas will be less.

8.   64 g of methanol = 2.0 moles
    69 g of ethanol = 1.5 moles

    The total vapor pressure above the solution is the sum of the partial vapor pressures, and the partial vapor pressures depend upon the mole fractions of the components in the solution.   This is Raoult's law.

    The vapor pressure due to methanol = $(2.0/3.5) \times 90$ torr = 51.4 torr
    The vapor pressure due to ethanol = $(1.5/3.5) \times 45$ torr = 19.3 torr
    Total vapor pressure = 51.4 + 19.3 torr = 70.7 torr.

9.   The elevation of the boiling point = $k_f \times m \times i$.   ($i = 1$ in this case)
    $\Delta T = 2.80 \times 3.0 \times 1 = 8.40$°C.
    The boiling point of pure cyclohexane = 89.4 − 8.40°C = 81.0°C.

10.   The solution with the lowest freezing point is the solution with the greatest concentration of solute particles. Calculate $m \times i$ for each solution:

    a. 0.010m NaCl $m \times i = 0.010 \times 2 = 0.020$ molar

    b. 0.100m sugar $m \times i = 0.100 \times 1 = 0.100$ molar

    c. 0.070m KNO_3 $m \times i = 0.070 \times 2 = 0.140$ molar

    d. 0.050m glycerol $m \times i = 0.050 \times 1 = 0.050$ molar

    e. 0.060m $Ca(NO_3)_2$ $m \times i = 0.060 \times 3 = 0.180$ molar — lowest f.pt.

    f. 0.075m KCl $m \times i = 0.075 \times 2 = 0.150$ molar

11. $\Delta T = k_f \times m \times i$ where $\Delta T = -12$°C, $k_f = -1.86$, and $i = 3$ (ideally).

    Molality $m = 12 / 1.86 \times 3 = 2.15$ moles / 1000 g water.

    In 500 grams of water, you would dissolve 1.075 moles $Mg(NO_3)_2$.
    = 159 grams $Mg(NO_3)_2$.

This solution is very concentrated and the value of i will be considerably less than 3 in reality. In other words, this concentration of magnesium nitrate would lead to less of a depression in the freezing point.

12. 40 grams of NH_4NO_3 = 0.50 mol in 100 g water so molality = 5.0 m
If i, the van't Hoff factor, is assumed to be 1.6, the depression in the freezing point of the water = 1.86 × 5.0 × 1.6 = 15°C.

In fact, if you do the experiment, you will find that the lowest temperature you can reach is about –14.5°C.

Adding 40 grams of NH_4NO_3 to 100 g water at room temperature causes a temperature drop of about 22°C. This is in good agreement with the stated heat of solution of ammonium nitrate:

This assumes that the specific heat of the solution is the same as the specific heat of water.

heat   = specific heat × mass × temperature change
         = 4.184 $JK^{-1}g^{-1}$ × 140 g × 22K   = 12.9 kJ for 0.5 mol
         compared to $\Delta H_{solution}$ (NH_4NO_3) = 25.7 kJ mol^{-1}

However, starting from 0°C, the freezing point will be reached before the temperature has fallen 22°C; it can only fall 15°C before the water starts to freeze. Which, if you do the experiment, you will see that it does.

The amount of ice that forms is the amount necessary to supply the additional heat for the solution process (approx. 4000J).
Heat of fusion of ice = +333 J g^{-1} so 4000J / 333J g^{-1} = 12 grams of ice.

13. $\Pi = cRT$ where c is the concentration of the solute in moles per liter.

The osmotic pressure = 10.8 / 760 atm = 0.0142 atm.
The temperature = 25 + 273.15 K = 298.15 K.
R = 0.082057 L atm K^{-1} mol^{-1}.
Therefore c = 0.0142 / (0.082057 × 298.15) = 5.808 × 10^{-4} M.

The number of moles in 10 mL = 5.808 × 10^{-6} moles.
The mass was 350 mg or 0.350 grams, so the molar mass is
0.350g / 5.808 × 10^{-6} moles = 60,300 g mol^{-1}.

A large molar mass can be determined by measurement of the osmotic pressure.

14.

a.	homogenized milk	liquid in liquid	emulsion
b.	red jelly	liquid in solid	gel
c.	cheese	liquid in solid	gel
d.	shaving cream	gas in liquid	foam
e.	wet modelling clay	solid in liquid	sol
f.	atmospheric dust	solid in gas	aerosol
g.	oil & vinegar dressing	liquid in liquid	emulsion
h.	pumice stone	gas in solid	foam
i.	clouds	liquid in gas	aerosol
j.	meringue	gas in solid	foam

EXAMINATION 3

Introduction

This examination tests your knowledge and understanding of the chemistry in Chapters 11 through 13 of this study guide. The questions are again formatted as true–false questions and multiple choice questions. It is essential to try the exam before looking at the answers provided at the end of this study guide.

True–false questions

1. There's no such thing as an ideal gas.

2. The only way to increase the pressure of a fixed volume of an ideal gas, without changing the amount of gas present, is to increase the temperature.

3. The partial pressure of a gas in a mixture of gases is the pressure the gas would exert under the same conditions if it were the only gas present.

4. The larger a molecule in the gas phase, the faster its speed at the same temperature.

5. There are exactly 100 kPa in one atmosphere.

6. The stronger the intermolecular forces, the more a gas deviates from ideal behavior.

7. If nitrogen gas and hydrogen gas react to form ammonia gas in a constant volume vessel, and the initial and final temperatures are the same, the pressure inside the vessel would increase.

8. The rms speed of a gas is the speed of a molecule possessing average kinetic energy.

9. It's possible to see the color of a gas only if it condenses to form a liquid.

10. The liquid and solid states are condensed states of matter.

11. The strongest van der Waals intermolecular force is the hydrogen bond.

12. Dispersion forces are not important if the molecules are polar.

13. Doubly–charged metal ions are more strongly solvated than singly–charged metal ions.

14. Hydrogen bonding cannot occur between ethanol molecules.

15. HF has the lowest boiling point of HF, HCl, HBr, and HI.

16. Most substances are less dense in the solid state than the liquid state.

17.   If the heat of vaporization for a compound is higher than for another compound, its boiling point will also be higher.

18.   The vapor pressure curve for a liquid starts at the triple point and ends at the critical point.

19.   Surface tension is due to the accumulation of impurities at the surface of the liquid.

20.   There are only seven crystal systems.

21.   There are 14 crystal lattices because there are 2 lattices for each system.

22.   There are 9 structural units within a body–centered unit cell; and 14 within a face–centered unit cell.

23.   Molality is a temperature-independent concentration unit.

24.   It is impossible for a solute concentration to exceed its solubility at that temperature.

25.   When gases dissolve in a solvent, heat is usually released.

26.   If a solution process has a positive ΔH, then the process does not occur, the solute does not dissolve.

27.   According to Raoult's law, the vapor pressure of the solvent over a solution must be lower than over the pure solvent.

28.   The freezing point of a solution is depressed, compared to that of the pure solvent, because the vapor pressure of the solution is reduced.

29.   The van't Hoff factor i is an integer only in extremely-dilute solutions.

30.   Immiscible liquids will mix in any proportion with one another to form a homogeneous solution.

Multiple choice questions

1.   The SI derived unit for pressure is the

    a. bar   c. torr   e. Pa
    b. psi   d. atm   f. kg m^{-2}

2.   A sample of ammonia gas at 10°C and 380 torr is contained in a 2.50 L vessel. How many moles of the ammonia gas are there in the vessel? Assume that the gas behaves ideally.

    a. 5.6   c. 0.24   e. 0.12
    b. 0.054   d. 38   f. 1.52

3.   If an ideal gas in a balloon has a volume of 3.00 liters at 1.00 atm pressure, and the pressure is increased to 1013 torr at constant temperature, what does the volume become?

    a. 1.33 L   c. 2.33 L   e. 2.67 L
    b. 2.25 L   d. 2.50 L   f. 4.0 L

4. Propane burns in air to produce carbon dioxide and water. How many liters of oxygen at standard temperature and pressure are required to oxidize 2.2 grams of propane?

$$C_3H_8(g) + 5O_2(g) \rightarrow 3CO_2(g) + 4H_2O(l)$$

a. 1.12 L	c. 5.60 L	e. 22.4 L
b. 2.24 L	d. 11.20 L	f. 44.8 L

5. A 2.0 L vessel of hydrogen gas at 1 atm pressure and a 4.0 L vessel of nitrogen gas at 1.5 atm pressure are connected and the gases allowed to mix at constant temperature. What is the final pressure?

a. 1.0 atm	c. 1.67 atm	e. 2.33 atm
b. 1.33 atm	d. 2.0 atm	f. 2.5 atm

The next five questions concern the following problem:

Suppose that there are two vessels connected by a tap that is closed. The first vessel is 2.0 liters in volume and contains hydrogen sulfide gas at a pressure of 2.0 atm. The second vessel is 3.0 liters in volume and contains fluorine gas at 3.0 atm pressure. The tap is opened, the two gases mix, and react to form as much product (hydrogen fluoride gas and sulfur tetrafluoride gas) as possible. Assume the gases are ideal and the temperature is the same at the end of the experiment as it was at the beginning.

$$H_2S(g) \quad + \quad 3\,F_2(g) \quad \rightarrow \quad 2\,HF(g) \quad + \quad SF_4(g)$$

Use the following key for questions 6 through 10:

a. 0 atm	c. 3/10 atm	e. 1/2 atm	g. 6/5 atm	i. 9/5 atm
b. 1/5 atm	d. 2/5 atm	f. 1.0 atm	h. 7/5 atm	j. 2.0 atm

6. After the tap is opened, but before any reaction has taken place, what is the initial partial pressure of fluorine gas?

7. What is the partial pressure of the limiting reactant after the reaction has gone to completion and has formed as much product as possible?

8. What is the partial pressure of the non-limiting reactant after the reaction has gone to completion and has formed as much product as possible?

9. What is the partial pressure of the hydrogen fluoride gas at the end of the reaction?

10. What is the total pressure in the apparatus at the end of the reaction?

11. If argon diffuses through a porous barrier at a rate of 2.0 mol/min, at what rate would nitrogen gas diffuse through the same barrier?

a. 0.70 mol/min	c. 1.4 mol/min	e. 2.4 mol/min
b. 1.2 mol/min	d. 1.67 mol/min	f. 3.4 mol/min

12. Common forces between structural units in a crystalline solid are metallic, ionic, covalent, and intermolecular. In which sequence are these forces correctly assigned?

	Metallic	*Covalent*	*Ionic*	*Intermolecular*
a.	iron	graphite	titanium	diamond
b.	nickel	diamond	iodine	paraffin
c.	sodium chloride	silica	copper	ice
d.	sulfur	methane	sodium iodide	boron nitride
e.	copper	graphite	lithium fluoride	methane
f.	calcium	quartz	barium nitrate	diamond

13. In a cubic lattice, what fraction of a structural unit at the corner of a unit cell belongs to that unit cell?

    a. 1/2   c. 1/4   e. 1/8   g. all
    b. 1/3   d. 1/6   f. 1/12

14. Copper crystallizes in a cubic lattice. If the side dimension of the unit cell is 362 pm and the density of copper is 8.93 g cm^{-3}, how many copper atoms are there in each unit cell?

    a. 1   c. 4   e. 8
    b. 2   d. 6   f. 12

15. In the unit cell of calcium carbide shown on the right below, the black spheres represent calcium atoms, and the shaded spheres represent carbon atoms. The carbon atoms along the central axis lie completely within the unit cell. The remaining carbon atoms lie on the edges of the cell. What is the stoichiometry of calcium carbide?

    a. CaC
    b. Ca$_2$C
    c. CaC$_2$
    d. CaC$_3$
    e. Ca$_3$C
    f. Ca$_2$C$_3$
    g. Ca$_9$C$_{10}$

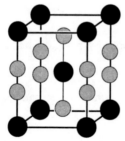

16. In which substance would you expect hydrogen bonding to play a significant role?

    a. butane C$_4$H$_{10}$
    b. methylamine CH$_3$NH$_2$
    c. carbon dioxide CO$_2$
    d. sodium chloride NaCl
    e. nickel hydride NiH$_2$
    f. hydrogen H$_2$

17. What property of a liquid explains that liquids have an associated vapor pressure?

    a. liquids exhibit surface tension
    b. liquids have a low compressibility
    c. gases are soluble only to a slight extent in liquids and escape with little difficulty
    d. some molecules in a liquid have sufficient energy to escape intermolecular attraction
    e. molecules attract one another
    f. a liquid adopts the shape of its container

18. Which of the following phase changes are endothermic (mark all that apply)?

a. melting
b. vaporization

c. sublimation
d. condensation

e. freezing
f. deposition

19. On a phase diagram for a substance, the lines represent the conditions under which

a. only one phase is stable
b. only the solid state can exist; liquids being the stable state between the lines.
c. any or all three phases can coexist in equilibrium
d. two phases coexist in equilibrium
e. the substance is at its normal boiling point

20. Within a group of metal ions, the one most strongly solvated is the one with

a. the smallest charge and the smallest size
b. the largest charge and the smallest size

c. the smallest charge and the largest size
d. the largest charge and the largest size

21. What happens to the concentration of oxygen in water if the partial pressure of oxygen above the water is tripled at the same temperature, without changing the total pressure?

a. it triples
b. it stays the same

c. it decreases to one-third
d. it increases by 1.5

22. At room temperature, the vapor pressure of acetone is 176 torr, and the vapor pressure of ethanol is 50 torr. What is the mole fraction of ethanol in the solvent vapor above an equimolar solution?

a. 0.11
b. 0.22

c. 0.28
d. 0.50

e. 0.72
f. 0.78

23. How many grams of sodium hydroxide must be dissolved in 200 grams of water to make a 0.15 m solution?

a. 0.03 g
b. 0.15 g

c. 0.75 g
d. 1.20 g

e. 6.0 g
f. 30 g

24. What is the molality of a 20% solution of methanol in ethanol?

a. 0.78 m
b. 2.5 m

c. 6.25 m
d. 7.8 m

e. 25 m
f. 32 m

25. A 2.0 m solution of sugar in pure acetic acid has a boiling point of 124°C. What is the boiling point of pure acetic acid? k_b for acetic acid = -3.0 Km^{-1}.

a. 118°C
b. 119°C

c. 121°C
d. 122°C

e. 126°C
f. 130°C

26. What is the molar mass of a substance if a 50 mg sample dissolved in 25 mL of water has an osmotic pressure of 9.8 torr at 20°C?

a. 920
b. 1850

c. 3730
d. 4290

e. 5730
f. 14900

27. An aerosol is a colloidal dispersion of

   a. a liquid in a gas
   b. a liquid in another liquid
   c. a gas in a liquid
   d. a gas in a solid
   e. a solid in a liquid

28. Which one of the following solutions has the lowest vapor pressure?

   a. 0.010m NaCl   c. 0.050m sugar   e. 0.020 $Mg(NO_3)_2$
   b. 0.100 glycerol   d. 0.075 KCl   f. 0.040 Na_2SO_4

29. The enthalpy of vaporization ΔH_v of methanol is 38 kJ mol^{-1} at its boiling point. The entropy change for this process ΔS_v is 113 JK^{-1} mol^{-1}. What is the boiling point of methanol?

   a   23°C   c. 53°C   e. 83°C
   b. 33°C   d. 63°C   f. 336°C

30. The *rate* of evaporation of a liquid increases dramatically at the boiling point of the liquid. The reason for this increase is

   a. an increase in the average kinetic energy of the molecules in the liquid phase
   b. a weakening of the intermolecular forces holding the molecules together
   c. an increase in the surface area of the interface between liquid and vapor
   d. that the dissolved gases are released from the solution
   e. a positive value for the entropy change in going from liquid to vapor

31. An mixture of two ideal gases A and B contains three times as many molecules of A as B. The partial pressure of A will be

   a. equal to 25% of the total pressure
   b. equal to 33% of the total pressure
   c. equal to 50% of the total pressure
   d. equal to 67% of the total pressure
   e. 3 times higher than the partial pressure of B

32. An ideal solution of two substances A and B contains three times as many molecules of A as B. The vapor pressure above the solution due to the component A will be

   a. equal to 25% of the vapor pressure of pure A at the same temperature
   b. equal to 33% of the vapor pressure of pure A at the same temperature
   c. equal to 67% of the vapor pressure of pure A at the same temperature
   d. equal to 75% of the vapor pressure of pure A at the same temperature
   e. 3 times higher than the vapor pressure due to component B

CHAPTER 14

Introduction

Chemical thermodynamics provides information about whether or not a reaction will go, and if so, how far it will go. What thermodynamics doesn't say anything about is how fast the reaction will happen. Indeed, many spontaneous reactions occur extremely slowly.

It is the chemical kinetics of a reaction that provides information about how fast the reaction goes (the rate of the reaction) and how the rearrangement of atoms actually takes place (the mechanism of the reaction).

The spontaneity of a reaction is a thermodynamic property of the system—a spontaneous reaction is one that happens on its own.

Do not confuse the word spontaneous with the word instantaneous. Spontaneous does not mean fast.

Contents

Rates of Chemical Reactions
Reaction Conditions and Rate
Effect of Concentration on Reaction Rate
A Microscopic View of Reaction Rates

Rates of Chemical Reactions

The rate of a chemical reaction is the rate at which the concentration of a substance changes per unit time. It may be the rate at which reactants are used up, or the rate at which a product appears. Consider the decomposition of N_2O_5 in solution:

$$2\,N_2O_5 \;\rightarrow\; 4\,NO_2 \;+\; O_2$$

The progress of the reaction can be followed by monitoring the change in concentration of any one of the three components. The relative rates of appearance of products and disappearance of reactants depend upon the stoichiometry of the reaction. In this case NO_2 appears at twice the rate that N_2O_5 disappears —the stoichiometric ratio is 1:2. However, oxygen appears at a rate one-quarter of the rate of production of NO_2.

See study questions #1 & 2.

The reaction rate can be expressed by an equation:

$$\text{Rate of reaction} = \frac{\text{change in } [N_2O_5]}{\text{change in time}} = \frac{-\Delta[N_2O_5]}{\Delta t}$$

The square brackets represent the concentration of the species inside the brackets.
The negative sign indicates that the concentration of N_2O_5 decreases as the reaction proceeds.

The rate of a reaction decreases as the reaction proceeds because the reactants are used up and their concentrations decrease. A plot of rate *vs.* time is a curve. The instantaneous rate at a particular time is the slope of the curve at that point.

Reaction Conditions and Rate

A chemical reaction is a rearrangement of atoms. For the rearrangement to take place, the reactant molecules must get together. For this reason, reactions are often carried out in the gas phase or in solution where the molecules are free to move about. Several factors influence the rate of the reaction:

- the concentrations of reactants
- the temperature
- the presence of a catalyst
- the nature of the reactant (state, surface area, particle size)

Effect of Concentration on Reaction Rate

Changing the concentration of a reactant often changes the rate of the reaction. In the earlier example of the decomposition of dinitrogen pentoxide, doubling the concentration doubles the rate. Data are, for example:

Concentration $[N_2O_5]$	Rate: $-\Delta[N_2O_5]/\Delta t$
0.34 mol L^{-1}	0.0014 mol L^{-1} min^{-1}
0.68 mol L^{-1}	0.0028 mol L^{-1} min^{-1}

Most often, increasing the concentration increases the rate, but this doesn't always happen.

In this reaction, the rate is directly proportional to the concentration of dinitrogen pentoxide. The rate equation is:

Rate of reaction = $k[N_2O_5]$ where k is a proportionality constant called the rate constant

The rate equation is sometimes referred to as the rate law.

For a general reaction:

aA + bB $\rightarrow$ xX   the rate equation is:

Rate = $k[A]^m[B]^n$

The rate of the reaction may depend upon the concentration of any of the reactants and upon the concentration of any homogeneous catalyst. It is important to note that the exponents in the rate equation are not necessarily the stoichiometric coefficients in the chemical equation. The **rate constant** k relates the rate and the concentrations at a specific temperature.

The exponents in the rate equation are called the **orders** of the reaction with respect to the corresponding reactants. For example, in the above rate equation the order with respect to the reactant A is m. The order m describes how the reaction rate depends upon the concentration of A. The order may be zero, it may be an integer, it may be a fraction, and it may be positive or negative.

The sum of the orders of all the components in the rate equation is called the **overall order** of the reaction. The overall order in the example above = m + n.

If the order with respect to a reactant is 2, for example, it means that doubling the reactant concentration leads to a quadrupling of the rate, because $2^2 = 4$; the order is an exponent, the power to which the concentration term is raised. An order of zero means that the rate is independent of that reactant.

Any number raised to the power zero equals 1.

The relation between rate and concentration must be determined experimentally. One method is the **method of initial rates** in which the rate is determined before very much of the reactants have been consumed. Different experiments, with different initial concentrations of reactants, are run and the rates determined. Comparison of the rates allows the determination of the orders of reaction for the various reactants.

See study question #3.

It is impossible to write the rate equation just by looking at the chemical equation.

Once the orders are known, the rate equation can be written, and the value of k, the rate constant, can be determined.

A Microscopic View of Reaction Rates

A rate equation describes how the rate depends on the concentrations of the reactants. It does not explain why the rate depends upon, for example, the square of one concentration but is directly proportional to another, or why it does not depend at all upon the concentration of another reactant; it doesn't explain why temperature affects the rate, and how a catalyst participates in a reaction but is not included in the chemical equation. In order to understand these things, it is necessary to examine the reaction at the particulate level—to examine what actually happens in the reaction.

The **collision theory** of reaction rates states three conditions that must be met for a reaction to occur:

• The molecules must collide.
• They must collide with sufficient energy.
• They must collide with the correct orientation with respect to each other.

The frequency of collisions depends in part upon the concentrations of the reactants; the higher the concentrations the higher the rate of reaction. If the temperature is increased, the kinetic energies of the molecules are higher and the more likely the collision is to result in a successful reaction.

The increase in temperature also leads to an increase in the collision frequency but by far the more important result is the increased energy involved in the collision.

All reactions require some minimum initial energy. In the collision between molecules, if a successful reaction is to take place, bonds need to be broken, the atoms must rearrange. The minimum energy required in a successful collision is called the **activation energy**. This energy can be represented as a barrier between reactants and products. At low temperatures there are few collisions that result in enough energy to get over the top of the barrier; at higher temperatures more collisions have sufficient energy.

The reason why reaction rates vary so much is that the reactions have widely different activation energies.

In a collision, the molecules must be oriented correctly, so that the correct bonds are broken and the desired rearrangement takes place. This steric requirement is sometimes quite critical. And the lower the probability of attaining the correct orientation, the slower the reaction.

One of the main reasons why enzymes are so efficient in increasing the rate of biochemical processes is that they orient the reacting molecules precisely.

A summary of the effects of temperature, activation energy, and orientation is provided by the **Arrhenius equation** for the rate constant k:

See study question #5.

R in the Arrhenius equation is 8.314 $JK^{-1}mol^{-1}$.

$$k \text{ (reaction rate constant)} = A\, e^{-\frac{E_a}{RT}}$$

The factor A is often referred to as the frequency factor.

The pre-exponential factor A is a parameter that is related to the collision frequency and the orientation requirements. The exponential term is interpreted as that fraction of molecules having the minimum energy required for reaction. The Arrhenius equation is useful in determining the activation energy E_a.

A homogeneous catalyst is a catalyst in the same phase as the reactants. A heterogeneous catalyst is a catalyst in a different phase than the reactants.

Catalysts speed up reactions; sometimes by many orders of magnitude. Reactions that are painfully slow can occur with explosive speed in the presence of a catalyst. A catalyst is involved in the reaction but does not appear in the chemical equation; it is not used up. The function of a catalyst is to provide an alternative path for the reaction, one with a much lower activation energy. The use of catalysts allow reactions to be run at lower temperatures, with greater yields, with fewer side reactions, and much more efficiently and cheaply.

Key terms:

kinetics
thermodynamics
reaction rate
instantaneous rate
rate equation
rate constant
order
overall order
method of initial rates
collision theory
activation energy
Arrhenius equation
reaction intermediate
catalyst
homogeneous catalyst
heterogeneous catalyst

Review Questions

1. How would you define the rate of a chemical reaction?

2. How is the rate at which a reactant is used up related to the rate at which a product is formed in a reaction?

3. Summarize the ways in which the rate of a chemical reaction can be changed.

4. How does the reaction order describe the dependence of the reaction rate upon the concentrations of the reactants?

5. Explain the method of initial rates for determining the order of reaction with respect to the reactants.

6. List the three requirements for a successful collision between molecules.

7. Describe what the activation energy is.

8. What is the Arrhenius equation and what does it describe?

9. Describe three ways to speed up a reaction and why the reaction does speed up when these three things are done.

10. What does a catalyst actually do? What is the difference between a homogeneous catalyst and a heterogeneous catalyst?

Answers to Review Questions

1.   The rate of a chemical reaction is the rate at which the concentration of a substance changes per unit time. It may be the rate at which reactants are used up, or the rate at which the product appears.

2.   The relative rates of appearance of products and disappearance of reactants depend upon the stoichiometry of the reaction. If two reactant molecules yield three product molecules—a stoichiometric ratio of 2:3— the rate of appearance of the product is 1.5 times faster than the rate of disappearance of the reactant.

3.   Several factors influence the rate of the reaction: the concentrations of re-actants, the temperature, the presence of a catalyst, and the nature of the reactants. A reaction is a rearrangement of atoms, molecules must be in contact for this rearrangement to take place, and anything that facilitates this will increase the rate of the reaction.

4.   The rate equation includes concentration terms for the reactants, each raised to some power. An exponent of a concentration term is called the order of reaction with respect to that particular reactant. If the order is one, then the rate is directly proportional to that concentration. If the order is 2, then the rate is proportional to the square of the concentration, and so on. Orders can be fractions and may even be negative.

The order may be 0, in which case the rate does not depend upon the concentration of that reactant.

5.   In the method of initial rates the rate of the reaction is determined as soon as the reaction has started and has not progressed very far. The advantage of this method is that the initial concentrations are known, and they can be varied easily to determine the rate equation.

It is only necessary to monitor the change in one reactant or product; the other concentrations are related by the stoichiometry of the reaction.

6.   The molecules must first collide so the rearrangement of atoms is possible; they must collide with sufficient energy to overcome the activation energy; and they must collide with the correct orientation with respect to each other.

7.   All reactions require some minimum initial energy. If a successful reaction is to take place between molecules, bonds need to be broken so that the atoms can rearrange. This takes energy. The minimum energy required in a success-ful collision is called the activation energy. This energy can be represented as a barrier between reactants and products. At low temperatures there are few collisions that result in enough energy to get over the top; at higher temperatures more collisions have sufficient energy.

8.   The Arrhenius equation is an expression for k (the rate constant) that includes all the factors that affect a reaction other than concentration.

$$k \text{ (reaction rate constant)} = A\,e^{-\frac{E_a}{RT}}$$

A is a parameter that is related to the collision frequency and the orientation requirements. The exponential term is interpreted as that fraction of molecules having the minimum energy required for reaction.

9.   a.   Increase the concentrations of the reactants. Usually this increases the rate because collisions between the molecules increase in frequency. The exact influence the concentration has is described by the rate equation.

      b.   Increase the temperature. Although this also increases the collision frequency, the predominant effect is to increase the effectiveness of those collisions that do occur. More energy is available at the higher temperature and the fraction of molecules possessing sufficient energy to overcome the activation energy barrier is higher.

      c.   Add a catalyst. This usually has the most profound effect. The catalyst provides a different mechanism by which the reaction can happen.

10.   A homogeneous catalyst is a catalyst in the same phase as the reactants. A heterogeneous catalyst is a catalyst in a different phase than the reactants. The catalyst provides a different route for the reaction.

Science is a way of thinking much more than it is a body of knowledge.

Carl Sagan (1934–1996)

Study Questions and Problems

1.   In the following reaction, what is the relationship between the rate at which the nitrous oxide is used up, the rate at which the oxygen is used, and the rate at which the nitrogen dioxide is produced?

$$2N_2O(g) \;+\; 3O_2(g) \;\rightarrow\; 4NO_2(g)$$

2.   Ammonia can be oxidized by oxygen to produce nitrogen dioxide according to the equation:

$$4NH_3(g) \;+\; 7O_2(g) \;\rightarrow\; 4NO_2(g) \;+\; 6H_2O(g)$$

If, in this reaction, water is formed at a rate of 36 mol L^{-1} min^{-1},

      a.   at what rate is the ammonia used?
      b.   at what rate is the oxygen used?
      c.   at what rate is the nitrogen dioxide formed?

3. For each of the following rate equations, describe what would happen to the rate if the concentration of reactant A was tripled and the concentration of reactant B is halved.

   a. Rate = k [A][B]
   b. Rate = k $[A]^2[B]^2$
   c. Rate = k $[A]^2[B]$
   d. Rate = k $[A][B]^3$

4. Describe some industrial uses of catalysts.

5. If the rate of a reaction increases by a factor of 10 when the temperature is increased by 35°C from 300K to 335K, what is the activation energy E_a for the reaction?

Answers to Study Questions and Problems

The eventual goal of science is to provide a single theory that describes the whole universe.

Stephen W. Hawking (1942-) (A Brief History of Time 1988)

1. The relative rates at which reactants are used up and products are formed is provided by the stoichiometry of the balanced equation. In this reaction, the relative rates are 2:3:4; the oxygen is used at a rate 1.5 times faster than the rate at which the nitrous oxide is used, and the nitrogen dioxide is formed at a rate 2 times faster than the rate at which the nitrous oxide is used.

$$2N_2O(g) \;+\; 3O_2(g) \;\rightarrow\; 4NO_2(g)$$

2. Water is formed at a rate of 36 mol L^{-1} min^{-1}:

$$4NH_3(g) \;+\; 7O_2(g) \;\rightarrow\; 4NO_2(g) \;+\; 6H_2O(g)$$

   a. the rate that ammonia is used = 36 × 4/6 = 24 mol L^{-1} min^{-1}
   b. the rate that oxygen is used = 36 × 7/6 = 42 mol L^{-1} min^{-1}
   c. the rate that NO_2 is formed = 36 × 4/6 = 24 mol L^{-1} min^{-1}

The factors 4/6 and 7/6 are the mole ratios in the equation—the stoichiometric factors.

3. [A] is tripled and [B] is halved:

   a. Rate = k [A][B], rate is multiplied by 3, divided by 2; × 1.5
   b. Rate = k $[A]^2[B]^2$, rate is multiplied by 3^2, divided by 2^2; × 2.25
   c. Rate = k $[A]^2[B]$, rate is multiplied by 3^2, divided by 2; × 4.5
   d. Rate = k $[A][B]^3$, rate is multiplied by 3, divided by 2^3; × 0.375

4.   Catalysts are used in most industrial chemical manufacture. Thirteen of the top twenty synthetic chemicals produced in this country are made by catalytic processes. Some examples are:

Ostwald Pt-Rh in oxidation of ammonia.
Ziegler-Natta catalyst in the manufacture of polyethylene.
Wilkinson's $RhCl(PPh_3)_3$ catalyst for the hydrogenation of alkenes.
Monsanto $RhI_2(CO)_2^-$ catalyst for oxidation of methanol to acetic acid.

Notice how much rhodium is used! Other metals often used are palladium and platinum.

5.   A useful alternative form of the Arrhenius equation is:

$$\ln\left(\frac{k_2}{k_1}\right) = -\frac{E_a}{R}\left(\frac{1}{T_2} - \frac{1}{T_1}\right)$$

$\ln(10) = -E_a/8.314 \times (1/335 - 1/300)$

$\quad\quad = -E_a/8.314 \times (-35/(335 \times 300))$

$2.303 = -E_a/8.314 \times (-3.483 \times 10^{-4})$

$E_a = 55.0 \text{ kJ/mol}$

CHAPTER 15

Introduction

All chemical reactions are reversible, at least in principle. Hydrogen and oxygen combine to form water. Water can be decomposed to form hydrogen and oxygen. Most reactions continue until they reach an equilibrium—a balance between the forward and reverse reactions.

Contents

The Nature of the Equilibrium State
The Reaction Quotient and Equilibrium Constant
Determining an Equilibrium Constant
Using Equilibrium Constants in Calculations
More about Balanced Equations and Equilibrium Constants
Disturbing a Chemical Equilibrium
Applying the Concepts of Chemical Equilibrium

The Nature of the Equilibrium State

A system in equilibrium is a **dynamic system**, reactants are combining together to form products and the products are combining to reform the reactants. The two reactions, the forward one and the reverse one, occur at the same rate so that there is no net change in the concentrations.

It takes a finite amount of time to reach the equilibrium state, and the state can be reached from either direction, from the reactant side or from the product side. Consider the ionization of acetic acid in water:

$$CH_3CO_2H(aq) \quad + \quad H_2O(l) \quad \rightleftharpoons \quad H_3O^+(aq) \quad + \quad CH_3CO_2^-(aq)$$

The system reaches equilibrium from the reactant side when pure acetic acid is added to water as indicated in the equation above. However, exactly the same equilibrium is established when a strong acid is added to an acetate salt (for example hydrochloric acid and sodium acetate) but in this case the equilibrium is approached from the product side:

$$H_3O^+(aq) \quad + \quad CH_3CO_2^-(aq) \quad \rightleftharpoons \quad CH_3CO_2H(aq) \quad + \quad H_2O(l)$$

If the number of moles of acetic acid used in the first experiment is equal to the number of moles of sodium acetate and hydrochloric acid used in the second experiment, and the volume of solution is the same for both experiments, then the two systems are identical—the position of equilibrium is exactly the same.

The Reaction Quotient and Equilibrium Constant

Any system can be characterized by the relative concentrations of products and reactants present. The ratio of the concentrations of the products to the concentrations of the reactants is represented by the **reaction quotient**, Q.

Always $\dfrac{products}{reactants}$ —over—

$$Q = \frac{[Products]}{[Reactants]}$$

For example, consider the system:

$$H_2(g) \; + \; I_2(g) \quad \rightleftharpoons \quad 2HI(g)$$

The reaction quotient Q is:

Each concentration term is raised to a power equal to its stoichiometric coefficient in the balanced equation.

$$Q = \frac{[HI]^2}{[H_2][I_2]}$$

K is temperature dependent—otherwise for any particular reaction it is constant.

Experiments have shown that when this system reaches equilibrium, at the same temperature, the ratio of the square of the HI concentration to the product of the H_2 and I_2 concentrations is always the same—at 425°C it is always 56. This constant is called the **equilibrium constant**, K. At the same temperature the value is always the same regardless of the quantities of HI, H_2, and I_2 initially present.

$$K = \frac{[HI]^2}{[H_2][I_2]} = 56$$

This expression is called the **equilibrium constant expression**. Only at equilibrium does Q = K.

See study question #1.

Equilibrium expressions do not contain concentration terms for species in a phase different from that in which the equilibrium exists. For example, equilibria in solution do not include solids or gases in the expression; equilibria in the gas state do not include liquids or solids. Also, a solution equilibrium expression does not include the solvent.

The two are related by the expression:

$K_p = K_c(RT)^{\Delta n}$

where Δn = moles of gaseous products – moles of gaseous reactants.

See study question #3.

The equilibrium constant can be written in terms of the component concentrations as K_c, or it can be expressed in terms of the partial pressures of the components as K_p.

A large value for K means a proportionately large concentration of product at equilibrium, i.e. a product-favored process. On the other hand, a smaller value for K means less product at equilibrium. For example:

See study question #4.

product favored	$S(s) + O_2(g) \rightleftharpoons SO_2(g)$	$K = 4.2 \times 10^{52}$
reactant favored	$AgCl(s) \rightleftharpoons Ag^+(aq) + Cl^-(aq)$	$K = 1.8 \times 10^{-10}$

At a particular temperature, the value of K for a particular reaction is constant. In other words, the ratio of products to reactants must be constant. Suppose, as an example, an equilibrium system has a value of K = 3:

$$\text{Reactants} \; \rightleftharpoons \; \text{Products} \qquad K = \frac{[Products]}{[Reactants]} = 3$$

The constant K indicates that the ratio of the concentration of product to the concentration of reactant at equilibrium must be 3; the concentrations can vary infinitely as long as the ratio (the reaction quotient) is 3:1; the system will still be in equilibrium. This condition can be represented by a line, slope K, on a graph of [Product] *vs.* [Reactant].

If the reaction quotient is not 3, the system lies off the line, and it is not in equilibrium! If the value for the reaction quotient Q is equal to K, then the system is on the line and is in equilibrium. If the reaction quotient Q is larger than K, the system contains too much product and in order to get into equilibrium, some product must reform reactant. If the reaction quotient Q is less that K, then there is not enough product and the reaction must proceed further to the product side.

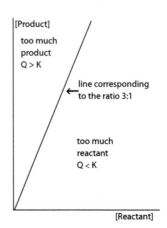

If Q = K, equilibrium!
if Q > K, there is too much product, and the system must move left to get into equilibrium.
if Q < K, there is too much reactant, and the system must move right to get into equilibrium.

Determining an Equilibrium Constant

If the equilibrium concentrations are known, the equilibrium constant can be calculated by simply substituting these concentrations in the equilibrium constant expression. More often, however, the initial concentrations are known, one of the equilibrium concentrations is measured, and the other equilibrium concentrations must be calculated. The general procedure is to set up what is called an ICE box, where I stands for initial, C for change, and E for equilibrium. Consider, for example, the system:

$$2SO_2(g) \ + \ O_2(g) \ \rightleftharpoons \ 2SO_3(g)$$

Suppose initially 2 moles of sulfur dioxide and 2 moles of oxygen gas are placed in a 1 liter vessel. After reaching equilibrium, the concentration of sulfur trioxide was found to be 1.84 moles. What is the equilibrium constant for this system at this temperature? Set up the box and figure out the unknown equilibrium concentrations:

Don't forget always to use concentrations, not just the number of moles. (In this case the volume is 1 liter.)

		$2SO_2(g)$ +	$O_2(g)$ $\rightleftharpoons$	$2SO_3(g)$
I	Initial	2.00	2.00	0.00
C	Change	−1.84	−1.84 × 1/2	+1.84
E	Equilibrium	0.16	1.08	1.84

The change in the concentrations is always in the same ratio as the stoichiometry: if the change in SO_3 is +1.84, then the change in SO_2 has to be −1.84, and the change in O_2 must be −1.84 × 1/2.

Now the equilibrium constant can be calculated:

$$K = \frac{[SO_3]^2}{[SO_2]^2[O_2]} = \frac{(1.84)^2}{(0.16)^2(1.08)} = 122$$

Usually K is given without units.

See study question #2.

Using Equilibrium Constants in Calculations

Quite often the equilibrium constant is already known. In this case, the initial concentrations might be known, and you might be required to calculate the equilibrium concentrations. There are two things to keep in mind:

The quantities of reactants and products in these calculations must be expressed as concentrations or pressures (not as amounts).

It is sometimes possible to assume that a change in a concentration of a reactant is so small that it can be ignored. If it can be ignored, it makes the calculation much easier. A sensible procedure is to assume the simplification is valid, and then

There are a variety of problems involving chemical equilibria—they are all basically the same! Do not try to memorize a set procedure—think about the question and then set about solving it in a logical way. Often a little algebra is required. Using a table to organize your data is highly recommended!

See study questions #5, 8-14, &17.

once the calculation is done, check to see if it was. A general guideline is that the change in the concentration of a reactant can be ignored if the initial concentration of reactant is greater than $100 \times$ the value of K. Consider this example:

The ionization of acetic acid is represented by the equation:

$$CH_3CO_2H(aq) \quad + \quad H_2O(l) \quad \rightleftharpoons \quad H_3O^+(aq) \quad + \quad CH_3CO_2^-(aq)$$

Suppose that a 1.0 M solution of acetic acid is prepared, what is the $[H_3O^+]$, the hydronium ion concentration, in the solution? $K = 1.8 \times 10^{-5}$.

Ignore x in the denominator if [Reactant]$_0$ > 100K.

		$CH_3CO_2H(aq)$ $\rightleftharpoons$	$H_3O^+(aq)$ +	$CH_3CO_2^-(aq)$
I	Initial	1.00	0.0	0.0
C	Change	−x	+x	+x
E	Equilibrium	1.00 − x	x	x

Assume that 1−x is near enough to 1 that the x can be ignored. Substituting in the expression for the equilibrium constant:

In this case 1 is > 100 ×1.8 ×10^{-5}, so ignore x in the denominator.

Notice the absence of [H$_2$O] from the equilibrium constant expression, it is the solvent.

$$K = \frac{[H_3O^+][CH_3CO_2^-]}{[CH_3CO_2H]} \quad = \quad \frac{(x)^2}{(1-x)} \quad = \quad x^2 \quad = 1.8 \times 10^{-5}$$

$$x = 4.24 \times 10^{-3} \text{ M}$$ — this is the hydronium ion concentration (it is also the acetate ion concentration).

Always remember what the unknown x is. Just because you calculate x, don't assume this is the answer required. It is however in this case.

Does this assumption make much difference?—it certainly makes the calculation easier. If the quadratic is solved in this case, x = 4.234 × 10^{-3} (as opposed to 4.243 × 10^{-3} with the simplification), not much difference.

More about Balanced Equations and Equilibrium Constants

Chemical equations can be balanced using different sets of coefficients. For example:

$$C(s) \quad + \quad \tfrac{1}{2} O_2(g) \quad \rightleftharpoons \quad CO(g) \qquad K_1$$

and $$2\,C(s) \quad + \quad O_2(g) \quad \rightleftharpoons \quad 2\,CO(g) \qquad K_2$$

Both are equally good, but do they have the same equilibrium constant? If the two equilibrium constant expressions are compared, you will see that $K_2 = (K_1)^2$. Similarly, what happens to K if the reaction is reversed?

$$CO(g) \quad \rightleftharpoons \quad C(s) \quad + \quad \tfrac{1}{2} O_2(g) \qquad K_3$$

See study questions #6 & 7.

In this case K_3 is the reciprocal of K_1, in other words: $K_3 = 1/K_1$. Finally, if two equations are added to yield a net equation, the K for the net equation is the product of the values of K for the two added equations.

Disturbing a Chemical Equilibrium

See study questions #15 &16.

There are three common ways to disturb a chemical equilibrium:

Change the temperature.
Change the concentration of a reactant or product.
Change the volume (or pressure).

LeChatelier's Principle states that if a system in equilibrium is subjected to a stress by altering the conditions that determine the state of equilibrium, the system will tend to adjust itself to accommodate the stress placed upon it.

If a reaction is exothermic, like the combination of two nitrogen dioxide molecules to form dinitrogen tetroxide, then heat can be regarded as a product of the reaction:

$$2NO_2(g) \quad \rightleftharpoons \quad N_2O_4(g) \qquad \Delta H = -57.2 \text{ kJ}$$

Addition of heat will drive the system to the left, breaking the N_2O_4 molecule to form two NO_2 molecules. The movement of the system to the left is a way to accommodate the applied stress; as the system moves to the left the added heat is absorbed. Addition of heat—an increase in temperature—will always move an exothermic reaction back toward the reactants and an endothermic reaction forward toward the products.

Addition or removal of a reactant or product can be predicted in the same way. Think of an equilibrium system as a system in balance; disturb the balance and the system has to regain balance by moving one way or the other. Addition of a product moves the system toward the left; addition of a reactant moves the system toward the product side. Removal of product drives the system to form more product; removal of reactant drives the system back toward the reactant side. The movement will occur until the value of the reaction quotient again becomes equal to the equilibrium constant.

Volume and pressure changes affect equilibria in which the number of moles of gas on the two sides is different. The system will shift to the side occupying the smaller volume to accommodate an increase in pressure or a reduction in volume.

Applying the Concepts of Chemical Equilibrium

Ammonia is manufactured on a huge scale by the Haber-Bosch process:

$$N_2(g) \quad + \quad 3 H_2(g) \quad \rightleftharpoons \quad 2 NH_3(g)$$

The conditions used in the manufacture are a balance between the kinetics and the thermodynamics of the process.

The reaction is exothermic and would be product-favored at low temperatures (thermodynamics). However, the reaction is run a higher temperatures to increase the rate of the reaction (kinetics).

To increase the equilibrium concentration of ammonia, the reaction is run at high pressure (thermodynamics—LeChatelier's principle).

To increase the rate of the reaction, a catalyst is used (Fe_3O_4 with KOH, SiO_2, and Al_2O_3). In fact, without a catalyst, the reaction would be prohibitively slow (kinetics). The catalyst however is ineffective below 400°C, and so the reaction is run at 450°C.

Key terms:

equilibrium
reaction quotient
equilibrium constant
equilibrium constant expression
product-favored reaction
reactant-favored reaction
ICE box
LeChatelier's principle

Review Questions

1. What is a chemical equilibrium?

2. What sort of process never reaches equilibrium?

3. What is the reaction quotient? How is its expression derived?

4. What does a comparison of Q and K tell you about the state of the system?

5. What sorts of reactants or products are not included in a equilibrium constant expression?

6. What is the difference between K_c and K_p?

7. What does the numerical value of K tell you about the state of the system at equilibrium?

8. When is it reasonable to neglect the change in concentration in the denominator of an equilibrium constant expression. When does $(1-x) \cdot 1$?

9. What happens to the equilibrium constant when the stoichiometric coefficients in the chemical equation are all doubled? What is the general relationship between what happens to K and what is done to the coefficients?

10. What happens to the value of K when the reaction is reversed?

11. What disturbances are possible for a system in equilibrium?

12. Is K always constant regardless of the disturbance of the system?

13. Describe in your own words the meaning of LeChatelier's principle.

14. Does addition of a catalyst change the position of a system in equilibrium?

Answers to Review Questions

1. A chemical equilibrium is a dynamic system; reactants are combining to form products and the products are combining to form reactants. The two reactions, the forward one and the reverse one, occur at the same rate so that there is no net change in the concentrations.

2. There are many nonequilibrium systems, systems which never reach equilibrium. An example is water evaporating from an open beaker, the water will eventually all evaporate as the water vapor diffuses away from the open system. In order to reach equilibrium, the system must be closed—a lid must be put on the beaker.

3. Any system can be characterized by the relative concentrations of products and reactants present. These relative concentrations of reactant and product are represented by the reaction quotient, Q.

    $$Q = \frac{[\text{Products}]}{[\text{Reactants}]}$$

    The expression is derived by dividing the concentrations of the products, raised to powers equal to their stoichiometric coefficients, by the concentrations of the reactants, with exponents equal to their stoichiometric ceoefficients.

4. If the concentrations [Products] and [Reactants] are equilibrium concentrations then Q = K and the system is at equilibrium. If the reaction quotient Q is larger than K, the system contains too much product and in order to get into equilibrium, some product must form reactant. If the reaction quotient Q is less that K, then there is not enough product and the reaction must proceed further to the product side. The comparison of Q and K tells you which way the system will move in order to get into equilibrium.

5. Expressions for the equilibrium constant K do not contain concentration terms for species in a phase different from that in which the equilibrium exists. For example, equilibria in solution do not include solids or gases in the expression; equilibria in the gas state do not include liquids or solids. Also, a solution equilibrium expression does not include the solvent—its concentration is considered constant.

6. K_c is the equilibrium constant written in terms of the component concentrations (in mol liter^{-1}). K_p is the equilibrium constant written in terms of the partial pressures of the components. There are related by the expression $K_p = K_c(RT)^{\Delta n}$, where Δn is the change in the number of moles of gas in going from reactants to products.

7. A large value for K means a proportionately large concentration of product, i.e. a product-favored process. A value greater than 1, in fact, means that the concentration of product is higher than the concentration of reactant at equilibrium. On the other hand, a smaller value for K means less product at equilibrium.

8. It's reasonable to assume that the change in a concentration x is negligible compared to the original concentration (i.e. (1–x) = 1), when 100K is less than the original concentration of the reactant.

9. The equilibrium constant is squared when the stoichiometric coefficients in the chemical equation are all doubled. In general the value of the new K equals the value for the original K raised to a power equal to the factor by which the coefficients were changed.

10. The value of K when the reaction is reversed is the reciprocal of the original value.

11. There are three common ways to disturb a chemical system in equilibrium:

    • Change the temperature.
    • Change the concentration or partial pressure of reactant or product.
    • Change the volume (or pressure) for a system involving gases.

12. No, K will change if the temperature changes. Note that K will remain unchanged if the temperature stays the same (regardless of concentration, volume, or pressure changes).

13. LeChatelier's Principle states that if a system in equilibrium is subjected to a stress by altering the conditions that characterize that state of equilibrium, the system will tend to adjust itself to accommodate the stress placed upon it and will be driven to regain equilibrium.

14. No, the position of equilibrium will not change if a catalyst is added. The equilibrium will undoubtedly be reached more quickly, but the final composition of the system will be the same.

Study Questions and Problems

Ce que je rêve, c'est un art d'équilibre, de pureté, de tranquillité, sans sujet inquiétant ou préoccupant, que soit...

What I dream of is an art of balance, of purity and tranquility, without troubling or depressing subject matter...

Henri Matisse
(1869-1954)

1. Write the expressions for the equilibrium constant K_c for the following reactions:

   a. $4NH_3(g) + 7O_2(g) \rightleftharpoons 4NO_2(g) + 6H_2O(l)$

   b. $HCN(aq) + H_2O(l) \rightleftharpoons H_3O^+(aq) + CN^-(aq)$

   c. $PCl_5(g) \rightleftharpoons PCl_3(g) + Cl_2(g)$

   d. $CaCO_3(s) \rightleftharpoons CaO(s) + CO_2(g)$

   e. $3O_2(g) \rightleftharpoons 2O_3(g)$

   f. $2H_2O(l) \rightleftharpoons H_3O^+(aq) + OH^-(aq)$

   g. $3Zn(s) + 2Fe^{3+}(aq) \rightleftharpoons 2Fe(s) + 3Zn^{2+}(aq)$

2. Calculate the value of the equilibrium constant for the following system, given the data shown:

   $$H_2(g) + CO_2(g) \rightleftharpoons H_2O(g) + CO(g)$$

   Concentrations at equilibrium:
   $[H_2]$ = 1.5 mol liter^{-1}
   $[CO_2]$ = 2.5 mol liter^{-1}
   $[H_2O]$ = 0.5 mol liter^{-1}
   $[CO]$ = 3.0 mol liter^{-1}

3. Chlorine molecules will dissociate at high temperatures into chlorine atoms. At 3000°C, for example, K_c for the equilibrium shown is 0.55. If the partial pressure of chlorine molecules is 1.5 atm, calculate the partial pressure of the chlorine atoms:

$$Cl_2(g) \quad \rightleftharpoons \quad 2Cl(g)$$

4. Consider the two equilibria shown: What are the predominant species present in each case? Classify the systems as product-favored or reactant-favored.

   a. $NH_3(aq) + H_2O(l) \rightleftharpoons NH_4^+(aq) + OH^-(aq)$ $K = 1.8 \times 10^{-5}$

   b. $NH_3(aq) + HF(aq) \rightleftharpoons NH_4^+(aq) + F^-(aq)$ $K = 6.3 \times 10^5$

5. Suppose that 0.50 moles of hydrogen gas, 0.50 moles of iodine gas, and 0.75 moles of hydrogen iodide gas are introduced into a 2.0 liter vessel and the system is allowed to reach equilibrium.

$$H_2(g) + I_2(g) \rightleftharpoons 2HI(g)$$

Calculate the concentrations of all three substances at equilibrium. At the temperature of the experiment K_c equals 2.0×10^{-2}.

6. If the mechanism of a chemical equilibrium consists of two reversible elementary steps, each with its own equilibrium constant K_{c1} and K_{c2}, what expression relates the equilibrium constant K_c for the overall equilibrium to the two constants K_{c1} and K_{c2}?

7. Write the equilibrium constant expressions for the following reactions. How are they related to one another?

   a. $2N_2O(g) + 3O_2(g) \rightleftharpoons 4NO_2(g)$

   b. $N_2O(g) + 3/2\, O_2(g) \rightleftharpoons 2NO_2(g)$

   c. $4NO_2(g) \rightleftharpoons 2N_2O(g) + 3O_2(g)$

8. When 2.0 mol of carbon disulfide and 4.0 mol of chlorine are placed in a 1.0 liter flask, the following equilibrium system results. At equilibrium, the flask is found to contain 0.30 mol of carbon tetrachloride. What quantities of the other components are present in this equilibrium mixture?

$$CS_2(g) + 3Cl_2(g) \rightleftharpoons S_2Cl_2(g) + CCl_4(g)$$

9. 3.0 moles each of carbon monoxide, hydrogen, and carbon are placed in a 2.0 liter vessel and allowed to come to equilibrium according to the equation:

$$CO(g) + H_2(g) \rightleftharpoons C(s) + H_2O(g)$$

If the equilibrium constant at the temperature of the experiment is 4.0, what is the equilibrium concentration of water? What happens to the other particpants in this equilibrium?

10.   Nitrosyl chloride NOCl decomposes to nitric oxide and chlorine when heated:

$$2NOCl(g) \quad \rightleftharpoons \quad 2NO(g) \quad + \quad Cl_2(g)$$

At 600K, the equilibrium constant K_p is 0.060. In a vessel at 600K, there is a mixture of all three gases. The partial pressure of NOCl is 675 torr, the partial pressure of NO is 43 torr and the partial pressure of chlorine is 23 torr.

a.   What is the value of the reaction quotient?
b.   Is the mixture at equilibrium?
c.   In which direction will the system move to reach equilibrium?
d.   When the system reaches equilibrium, what will be the partial pressures of the components in the system?

11.   Sulfuryl chloride decomposes at high temperatures to produce sulfur dioxide and chlorine gases:

$$SO_2Cl_2(g) \quad \rightleftharpoons \quad SO_2(g) \quad + \quad Cl_2(g)$$

At 375°C, the equilibrium constant K_c is 0.045. If there are 2.0 grams of sulfuryl chloride, 0.17 gram of sulfur dioxide, and 0.19 gram of chlorine present in a 1.0 liter flask,

a.   what is the value of the reaction quotient?
b.   is the system at equilibrium?
c.   in which direction will the system move to reach equilibrium?

12.   Ammonium chloride is placed inside a closed vessel where it comes into equilibrium at 400°C according to the equation shown. Only these three substances are present inside the vessel. If K_p for the system at 400°C is 0.640, what is the pressure inside the vessel?

$$NH_4Cl(s) \quad \rightleftharpoons \quad NH_3(g) \quad + \quad HCl(g)$$

13.   Bromine and chlorine react to produce bromine monochloride according to the equation. K_c = 36.0 under the conditions of the experiment.

$$Br_2(g) \quad + \quad Cl_2(g) \quad \rightleftharpoons \quad 2BrCl(g)$$

If 0.180 moles of bromine gas and 0.180 moles of chlorine gas are introduced into a 3.0 liter flask and allowed to come to equilibrium, what is the equilibrium concentration of the bromine monochloride? How much BrCl is produced?

14. When ammonia is dissolved in water, the following equilibrium is established. If the equilibrium constant is 1.8×10^{-5}, calculate the hydroxide ion concentration in the solution if 0.100 mol of ammonia is dissolved in sufficient water to make 500 mL of solution.

$$NH_3(aq) \; + \; H_2O(l) \; \rightleftharpoons \; NH_4^+(aq) \; + \; OH^-(aq)$$

15. The following reaction is exothermic:

$$Ti(s) \; + \; 2Cl_2(g) \; \rightleftharpoons \; TiCl_4(g)$$

List all the ways the yield of the product $TiCl_4$ could be increased.

16. Consider the equilibrium: $2N_2O(g) \; + \; 3O_2(g) \; \rightleftharpoons 4NO_2(g) \; + \;$ heat

What would happen to this system if

a. the volume is increased
b. oxygen gas is added
c. the product, nitrogen dioxide, is removed
d. the temperature is increased

17. The apparatus shown consists of two glass bulbs connected by a tap which is closed. In the first bulb, volume 4 liters, there is a sample of pure oxygen at 2 atm pressure. In the second bulb, volume 3 liters, there is a sample of pure sulfur dioxide at a pressure of 3 atm.

These calculations involve solving high order equations and iteration using a spreadsheet or an advan-ced calculator is recommended.

x cannot be neglected in these calculations.

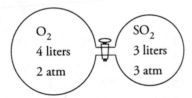

Maintaining a constant temperature of 1000K throughout, the tap is opened, the gases are allowed to mix, and they react to produce sulfur trioxide according to the equation written below. Assume that the reaction reaches equilibrium, where $K_p = 3.00$.

$$2SO_2(g) \; + \; O_2(g) \; \rightleftharpoons \; 2SO_3(g)$$

a. What is the partial pressure of the sulfur dioxide in the apparatus at the end of the reaction?

b. What is the partial pressure of the oxygen in the apparatus at the end of the reaction?

c. What is the partial pressure of the sulfur trioxide in the apparatus at the end of the reaction?

d. What is the total pressure in the apparatus at the end of the reaction?

Answers to Study Questions and Problems

I go...where no disturbance can be, no disturbance in the world.

Charles I
(1600–1649)

1. a. $K = \dfrac{[NO_2]^4}{[NH_3]^4[O_2]^7}$ $H_2O(l)$ is a liquid and therefore not included.

 b. $K = \dfrac{[H_3O^+][CN^-]}{[HCN]}$ $H_2O(l)$ is the solvent and is not included.

 c. $K = \dfrac{[PCl_3][Cl_2]}{[PCl_5]}$

 d. $K = [CO_2]$ $CaCO_3(s)$ and $CaO(s)$ are not included.

 e. $K = \dfrac{[O_3]^2}{[O_2]^3}$

 f. $K = [H_3O^+][OH^-]$ $H_2O(l)$ is the solvent and is not included.

 g. $K = \dfrac{[Zn^{2+}]^3}{[Fe^{3+}]^2}$ $Zn(s)$ and $Fe(s)$ are not included.

2. $K = \dfrac{[H_2O][CO]}{[H_2][CO_2]}$ $= (0.5 \times 3.0)/(1.5 \times 2.5) = 0.40$

3. $Cl_2(g) \rightleftharpoons 2Cl(g)$ $K_c = \dfrac{[Cl]^2}{[Cl_2]}$ and $K_p = \dfrac{P_{Cl}^2}{P_{Cl_2}}$

$\Delta n = 1$
an increase of one mole of gas

$K_p = K_c(RT)^{\Delta n} = 0.55 \times 0.08206 \times 3273K = 1.48 \times 10^2 = \dfrac{P_{Cl}^2}{P_{Cl_2}}$

$P_{Cl_2} = 1.5$ atm and therefore $P_{Cl} = \sqrt{1.48 \times 10^2 \times 1.5} = 14.9$ atm

4. a. $NH_3(aq) + H_2O(l) \rightleftharpoons NH_4^+(aq) + OH^-(aq)$ $K = 1.8 \times 10^{-5}$

K is very small, the system is reactant-favored. Most of the ammonia exists in solution as ammonia molecules. Very few ions are present in solution.

 b. $NH_3(aq) + HF(aq) \rightleftharpoons NH_4^+(aq) + F^-(aq)$ $K = 6.3 \times 10^5$

K is large, the system is product-favored. The ammonia and HF react almost completely. There is very little NH_3 and HF present in the solution.

Remember always to use concentrations (or partial pressures). Convert amounts given in moles to concentrations by dividing by the volume.

Remember that the change is always in the stoichiometric ratio.

If you don't know which way the system will move, just choose a direction arbitrarily, then see if x turns out to be negative or positive.

5.

		$H_2(g)$ +	$I_2(g)$ $\rightleftharpoons$	$2HI(g)$
I	Initial	0.25	0.25	0.375
C	Change	+x	+x	−2x
E	Equilibrium	0.25+x	0.25+x	0.375−2x

$$K = \frac{[HI]^2}{[H_2][I_2]} = \frac{(0.375-2x)^2}{(0.25+x)(0.25+x)} = 2.0 \times 10^{-2}$$

Take the square root of both sides: $= \dfrac{(0.375-2x)}{(0.25+x)} = 0.1414$ so $x = 0.159$

and the equilibrium concentrations are:

Look for the opportunity to take the square root of both sides, it avoids having to solve the quadratic equation.

$[H_2] = 0.41$ moles liter^{-1}

$[I_2] = 0.41$ moles liter^{-1}

$[HI] = 0.058$ moles liter^{-1}

6. The equilibrium constant for the combination of two successive equilibria is the product of the equilibrium constants for the two steps.

$$K_c = K_{c1} \times K_{c2}$$

7. a. $2N_2O(g) + 3O_2(g) \rightleftharpoons 4NO_2(g)$ $K_1 = \dfrac{[NO_2]^4}{[N_2O]^2[O_2]^3}$

    b. $N_2O(g) + 3/2\, O_2(g) \rightleftharpoons 2NO_2(g)$ $K_2 = \dfrac{[NO_2]^2}{[N_2O][O_2]^{3/2}}$

    c. $4NO_2(g) \rightleftharpoons 2N_2O(g) + 3O_2(g)$ $K_3 = \dfrac{[N_2O]^2[O_2]^3}{[NO_2]^4}$

$K_1 = (K_2)^2$ and $K_1 = (K_3)^{-1}$ and $K_2 = (K_3)^{-1/2}$

8.

		$CS_2(g)$ +	$3Cl_2(g)$	$\rightleftharpoons$ $S_2Cl_2(g)$ +	$CCl_4(g)$
I	Initial	2.0	4.0	0.0	0.0
C	Change	−0.30	−0.90	+0.30	+0.30
E	Equilibrium	1.7	3.1	0.30	0.30

Don't make problems like these more complicated than they have to be; there's no need for any algebra in this problem.

If 0.30 moles of CCl_4 are formed, then the changes in the other concentrations can be calculated directly from the stoichiometry.

9.

		$CO(g)$ +	$H_2(g)$	$\rightleftharpoons$ $C(s)$ +	$H_2O(g)$
I	Initial	1.5	1.5	3.0	0.0
C	Change	−x	−x	+x	+x
E	Equilibrium	1.5−x	1.5−x	3.0+x	x

Note that C(s) is not included in the equilibrium expression! However, it is sometimes useful to include the quantities in the table—just in case there's any likelihood of all the solid being used up.

Remember always to use concentrations (or partial pressures). Convert amounts given in moles to concentrations by dividing by the volume.

$$K = \frac{[H_2O]}{[CO][H_2]} = \frac{(x)}{(1.5-x)(1.5-x)} = 4.0$$

Therefore $x = 1.0$ which is the equilibrium concentration of water.
The concentrations of CO and H_2 are both 0.5 moles/liter.
The amount of carbon present has been reduced to 2.0 moles.

10. $$2NOCl(g) \quad \rightleftharpoons \quad 2NO(g) \quad + \quad Cl_2(g)$$

a. $Q_p = \dfrac{P_{NO}^2 \times P_{Cl2}}{P_{NOCl}^2} = (43^2 \times 23)/675^2 = 0.093$

b. No, Q_p is greater than K_p; ie. there is too much product present.

c. The system will move to the left.

Solving higher order equations like this for x using algebra is not especially easy. An iterative method using a good calculator or a spreadsheet is highly recommended. Using a spreadsheet for example, enter the expression for K in a cell, referencing another cell for x. Then put values for x in that cell until the expression yields a value of 0.060. You should be able to narrow the value for x to a sufficient number of sig. fig. in 5 or 6 tries.

		2NOCl(g) $\rightleftharpoons$	2NO(g) +	Cl$_2$(g)
I	Initial	675	43	23
C	Change	+2x	−2x	−x
E	Equilibrium	675+2x	43−2x	23−x

d. $K_p = \dfrac{P_{NO}^2 \times P_{Cl2}}{P_{NOCl}^2} = (43-2x)^2(23-x)/(675+2x)^2 = 0.060$

x = 2.90 so the partial pressure of NOCl at equilibrium = 681 torr
and the partial pressure of NO = 37 torr
and the partial pressure of Cl$_2$ = 20 torr

11. $$SO_2Cl_2(g) \quad \rightleftharpoons \quad SO_2(g) \quad + \quad Cl_2(g)$$

Must convert to moles and then to moles/liter.

SO$_2$Cl$_2$	2.0 grams	MM = 134.97 g mol^{-1}	Moles = 0.0148/L
SO$_2$	0.17 gram	MM = 64.064 g mol^{-1}	Moles = 0.0027/L
Cl$_2$	0.19 gram	MM = 70.91 g mol^{-1}	Moles = 0.0027/L

a. $Q_p = (0.0027)^2/0.0148 = 4.93 \times 10^{-4}$.

b. No, the system is not at equilibrium. Q_p does not equal K_p.

c. Q_p is too small, the reaction will move toward product.

12. $$NH_4Cl(s) \quad \rightleftharpoons \quad NH_3(g) \quad + \quad HCl(g)$$

The expression for K_p is:

The amount of NH$_3$ present must equal the amount of HCl present since one cannot be made without the other. Therefore their partial pressures are equal.

$K_p = P_{NH} \times P_{HCl} = 0.640$

Since the partial pressures of ammonia and hydrogen chloride must be equal to one another, each must equal 0.80 atm.

The total pressure is the sum of the partial pressures, so the total pressure = 1.60 atm.

13.

Take the square root of both sides.

Don't assume x is the desired answer to the problem! In this case the required quantity is the concentration of BrCl (which is 2x) and the total amount of BrCl (which is the volume of 3 liters × this concentration).

		Br$_2$(g) +	Cl$_2$(g) $\rightleftharpoons$	2BrCl(g)
I	Initial	0.060	0.060	0.0
C	Change	−x	−x	+2x
E	Equilibrium	0.060−x	0.060−x	+2x

$K = \dfrac{[BrCl]^2}{[Br_2][Cl_2]} = \dfrac{(2x)^2}{(0.060-x)(0.060-x)} = 36.0$

x = 0.045

So the concentration of BrCl produced = 2x = 0.090 mol L^{-1}.

Quantity produced = 0.090 mol L^{-1} × 3 L = 0.27 mol = 31 grams.

14.

		NH_3 + H_2O $\rightleftharpoons$ NH_4^+ + OH^-		
I	Initial	0.200	0.0	0.0
C	Change	−x	+x	+x
E	Equilibrium	0.200−x	+x	+x

Remember to convert amounts into concentrations—it's easy to forget.

Can assume that 0.200−x is near enough to 0.200.

$$K = \frac{[NH_4^+][OH^-]}{[NH_3]} = \frac{x^2}{(0.200-x)} = 1.8 \times 10^{-5}$$

x = 1.90×10^{-3} M   —this is the concentration of hydroxide ion.

15.   Ti(s) + 2Cl$_2$(g) $\rightleftharpoons$ TiCl$_4$(g) + heat

The yield of the product TiCl$_4$ is increased by moving the system to the right:

a.   remove heat; cool the system down.

b.   remove TiCl$_4$(g).

c.   add chlorine gas Cl$_2$(g).

d.   increase the pressure (or decrease the volume).

Note that:

adding more Ti(s) has no effect.
adding a catalyst has no effect.

16.   2N$_2$O(g) + 3O$_2$(g) $\rightleftharpoons$ 4NO$_2$(g) + heat

a.   increase volume: system moves to the side with the larger volume, left; there are 5 moles of gas on the left, four on the right.

b.   add oxygen gas: system moves to the product side to restore the required product/reactant ratio K.

c.   remove nitrogen dioxide: the system moves to the right

d.   increase temperature (add heat): the system moves to the left

17.

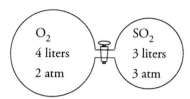

Using partial pressures:

		$2SO_2(g)$	$+$	$O_2(g)$	$\rightleftharpoons$	$2SO_3(g)$	
	initial volume	3		4			liters
	initial pressure	3		2			atm
I	initial partial pressure	$3 \times 3/7$		$2 \times 4/7$			atm
C	change	$-2x$		$-x$		$+2x$	atm
E	equilibrium	$(9/7 - 2x)$		$(8/7 - x)$		$2x$	atm
	after solving for x	0.513		0.756		0.773	atm
	total pressure = sum of the partial pressures = 0.513 + 0.756 + 0.773 = 2.04 atm						

This is another high order equation that is difficult to solve using conventional algebra. An iterative method is highly recommended.

Using a spreadsheet for example, enter the expression for K in a cell, referencing another cell for x. Then put some sensibles values for x in that cell, for example 0.2 or 0.4, until the expression yields a value of 3.0. You should be able to narrow the value for x to a sufficient number of sig. fig. in 5 or 6 tries.

It is possible to satisfy the requirement that the expression = 3.0 using unrealistic values for x (e.g. negative concentrations)!

Try it.

Solving the equilibrium constant expression for x requires solution of the equation:

$$K_p = \frac{P_{SO3}^2}{P_{SO2}^2 P_{O2}} = \frac{(2x)^2}{(9/7 - 2x)^2 (8/7 - x)} = 3.00$$

$$x = 0.3864$$

Alternatively, if you really want to use concentrations instead of partial pressures:

		$2SO_2(g)$	$+$	$O_2(g)$	$\rightleftharpoons$	$2SO_3(g)$	
	initial volume	3		4			liters
	initial pressure	3		2			atm
	temperature	1000		1000			K
	no of moles	0.1097		0.0975		0	mol
I	initial concentration	0.01567		0.01393		0	mol L^{-1}
C	change	$-2x$		$-x$		$+2x$	
E	equilibrium	$0.01567 - 2x$		$0.01393 - x$		$2x$	
	after solving for x	0.00625		0.00922		0.00942	mol L^{-1}
	total no of moles in 1 L = 0.00625 + 0.00922 + 0.00942 = 0.0249 mol						
	pressure = (n/V) RT = 0.0249 × 0.08206 × 1000 = 2.04 atm (same answer)						

$K_c = K_p(RT)^{\Delta n} = 246.18$

CHAPTER 16

Introduction

Earlier in this study guide, you learned to classify chemical reactions in terms of acid-base, redox, and precipitate or gas forming reactions. Because they are among the most common substances in nature, we will look at acids and bases and their reactions more closely in this chapter and the next. Many of the acid-base reactions that you will encounter occur in aqueous solution. Like the reactions described in Chapter 15 of this study guide, a reaction between an acid and a base will continue until the system reaches equilibrium. We will examine various definitions of what an acid is and what a base is, and investigate how they behave in solution.

Contents

Acids, Bases, and the Equilibrium Concept
The Brønsted Concept of Acids and Bases
Water and the pH Scale
Equilibrium Constants for Acids and Bases
Equilibrium Constants for Acid-Base Reactions
Types of Acid-Base Reactions
Calculations with Equilibrium Constants
Polyprotic Acids and Bases
The Lewis Concept of Acids and Bases
Molecular Structure, Bonding, and Acid-Base Behavior

Acids, Bases, and the Equilibrium Concept

An **acid** was described in Chapter 5 of this study guide as a substance that increases the concentration of hydrogen ions $[H^+]$ in solution. A **base** is a substance that increases the concentration of hydroxide ions $[OH^-]$. Acids and bases can be divided into those that are **strong** and those that are **weak**. For example, hydrochloric acid is strong and is completely ionized in solution. Acetic acid is weak and is only slightly ionized in solution:

$$HCl(aq) \ + \ H_2O(l) \ \rightleftharpoons \ H_3O^+(aq) \ + \ Cl^-(aq)$$

$$CH_3CO_2H(aq) \ + \ H_2O(l) \ \rightleftharpoons \ H_3O^+(aq) \ + \ CH_3CO_2^-(aq)$$

The equilibrium constants for acids and bases are called ionization constants and are a measure of how much of the acid or base is ionized in solution. For acetic acid the constant is:

$$K_a = \frac{[H_3O^+][CH_3CO_2^-]}{[CH_3CO_2H]} \ = 1.8 \times 10^{-5}$$

Always $\dfrac{\text{products}}{\text{reactants}}$ over

Note that water, the solvent, is not included in the equilibrium constant expression.

The Brønsted Concept of Acids and Bases

In 1923 Johannes Brønsted and Thomas Lowry proposed a new set of definitions for acids and bases. They proposed that an acid is a substance that donates a hydrogen ion (proton) to another substance. And they proposed that a base is the substance that accepts the hydrogen ion (proton) from the acid. Consider the ionization of acetic acid:

$$CH_3CO_2H(aq) \; + \; H_2O(l) \; \rightleftharpoons \; H_3O^+(aq) \; + \; CH_3CO_2^-(aq)$$

The acetic acid molecule donates a hydrogen ion and becomes an acetate ion. Acetic acid is an acid! The water molecule accepts the hydrogen ion and becomes the hydronium ion; in this reaction water is acting as a base. In the reverse direction, the hydronium ion donates a hydrogen ion to the acetate ion, forming acetic acid and water. So the hydronium ion is an acid, and the acetate ion is a base.

Acids can be molecules like HNO_3, they can be cations like NH_4^+, or they can be anions like $H_2PO_4^-$.

Some acids are capable of donating one proton only, and are known as **monoprotic** acids. Other acids can donate more than one proton and are called **polyprotic** acids. Some bases can accept more than one proton and are called polyprotic bases. Anions of the polyprotic acids, such as SO_4^{2-} and CO_3^{2-}, are examples.

Amphiprotic substances can act as either acids or bases depending upon the conditions. Water is an example; it acts as a base when it accepts a proton from acetic acid (see reaction above), but it acts as an acid when it donates a proton to ammonia:

$$NH_3(aq) \; + \; H_2O(l) \; \rightleftharpoons \; NH_4^+(aq) \; + \; OH^-(aq)$$

In a Brønsted-Lowry acid-base equilibrium, an acid donates a proton and a base accepts it. The reaction is a proton transfer. The reaction can go in the reverse direction; again an acid donates a proton and a base accepts it. So, on both sides of the equilibrium, there is an acid and a base. When an acid gives up its proton it forms a base; this base is called its conjugate base; together the acid and base make a **conjugate pair**. The two always differ by one proton:

$$HCN(aq) \; + \; H_2O(l) \; \rightleftharpoons \; H_3O^+(aq) \; + \; CN^-(aq)$$
acid   base   acid   base

HCN is the conjugate acid of CN^-.
CN^- is the conjugate base of HCN.
Together HCN and CN^- make a conjugate acid-base pair.
H_2O and its conjugate acid H_3O^+ make the second conjugate acid-base pair.
The two partners differ by one H^+.
Of the two partners, the acid has the H^+, the base does not.

Sidebar notes:

Brønsted-Lowry acid: hydrogen ion donor.

Brønsted-Lowry base: hydrogen ion acceptor.

Hydrated metal cations like $[Cu(H_2O)_6]^{2+}$ are often acidic. The metal withdraws electrons from the water molecule making loss of a proton easier.

Strong acids:

Monoprotic:
nitric acid HNO_3
perchloric acid $HClO_4$
hydrochloric acid HCl
hydrobromic acid HBr
hydroiodic acid HI

Diprotic:
sulfuric acid H_2SO_4

Weak acids:

Monoprotic:
acetic acid CH_3CO_2H
hydrocyanic acid HCN
hypochlorous acid $HOCl$
hydrofluoric acid HF
nitrous acid HNO_2

Polyprotic:
phosphoric acid H_3PO_4
carbonic acid H_2CO_3
oxalic acid $H_2C_2O_4$
sulfurous acid H_2SO_3

Movement from one side of the equilibrium system to the other involves the transfer of the proton.

Be able to identify the acids and bases in a Brønsted-Lowry acid-base equilibrium.

Be able to pair the acids and bases in conjugate pairs.

Water and the pH Scale

Water is often called the universal solvent; it has many unusual properties. Most of the acid-base reactions we will examine will be in water solution so let's first examine water itself. Ions are hydrated in water—there is a strong attraction between the ion and the dipole of the water molecule. The *(aq)* notation indicates this hydration. The hydroxide ion and the hydrogen ion are hydrated just like any other ion. The hydrated hydrogen ion is often represented as the hydronium ion H_3O^+ to indicate that the H^+ ion does not exist alone in aqueous solution.

Even in pure water, H_3O^+ and OH^- ions exist. The water is said to **autoionize**. When two water molecules are hydrogen bonded together, there is sometimes enough energy to break the bond in a molecule instead of the bond between the molecules. Hydronium and hydroxide ions are the result:

$$K = \frac{[H_3O^+][OH^-]}{[H_2O]^2}$$

$$K_w = [H_3O^+][OH^-]$$

$$H_2O(l) + H_2O(l) \rightleftharpoons H_3O^+(aq) + OH^-(aq)$$

In pure water at 25°C the hydronium ion concentration and the hydroxide ion concentration are both equal to 1.0×10^{-7} M and the **ion-product** K_w equals 1.0×10^{-14}; the solution is **neutral**. If acid is added, the hydronium ion concentration increases and the hydroxide ion concentration falls until the quotient Q_w again equals 1.0×10^{-14} and the system is back into equilibrium. Likewise, if base is added, the $[OH^-]$ increases and the $[H_3O^+]$ decreases, but the product K_w is constant.

An alternative way of expressing the hydronium ion concentration is by using the pH scale. The pH of a solution is defined as the negative logarithm to the base 10 of the hydronium ion concentration:

$$pH = -\log_{10}[H_3O^+]$$

Similarly the pOH is defined as:

$$pOH = -\log_{10}[OH^-] \qquad \text{and therefore } pH + pOH = pK_w = 14$$

The pH of a solution can be determined using a pH meter or by using indicator solutions. These indicators have different colors at different pHs.

Equilibrium Constants for Acids and Bases

One way to define the relative strengths of acids and bases would be to measure the pHs of solutions of equal concentrations. A strong acid ionizes completely and produces a hydronium ion concentration equal to the original acid concentration. Within a series of weak acids, the weaker the acid the less it ionizes, and the lower the concentration of hydronium ion $[H_3O^+]$. As the $[H_3O^+]$ decreases, the pH increases.

The relative strengths of acids and bases can be expressed quantitatively by an equilibrium constant K_a or K_b for the ionization process, where the larger the constant, the more extensive the ionization, and the stronger the acid or base.

The properties perhaps do not appear unusual because they are so familiar, but compared to most other solvents, water is unusual.

H_2O is the solvent and $[H_2O]$ is considered constant and is not included in the equilbrium constant expression.

K_w is constant in aqueous solution provided that the temperature remains constant.

At 25°C, $K_w = 1.0 \times 10^{-14}$

At 50°C, $K_w = 5.5 \times 10^{-14}$

This is Henri LeChatelier's principle again.

In fact:
p(anything) = $-\log_{10}$[anything]

For example,
$pK_w = -\log_{10}[K_w] = 14$ at 25°C

Most acids and bases are weak; they ionize relatively little in aqueous solution and remain predominantly in the molecular form.

Recall that the solvent (water) is not included in the equilibrium constant expression.

The higher K_a, the stronger the acid:

$K_a > 1$:   strong acid
                               v. weak conjugate base

$K_a = 1$ to 10^{-16}:   weak acid
                               weak conjugate base

$K_a < 10^{-16}$:   very weak acid
                               strong conjugate base

For a weak acid HA:

$$HA(aq) \; + \; H_2O(l) \; \rightleftharpoons \; H_3O^+(aq) \; + \; A^-(aq)$$

$$K_a = \frac{[H_3O^+][A^-]}{[HA]}$$

For a weak base B, a similar equilibrium equation and expression for the equilibrium constant K_b can be written:

$$B(aq) \; + \; H_2O(l) \; \rightleftharpoons \; BH^+(aq) \; + \; OH^-(aq)$$

$$K_b = \frac{[BH^+][OH^-]}{[B]}$$

In a Brønsted-Lowry acid-base equilibrium, the stronger the acid, the weaker its conjugate base, and *vice versa*. This is because the more the acid wants to donate its proton, the less its conjugate base wants it back. Compare, for example, the two bases ammonia and methylamine:

$$NH_3(aq) \; + \; H_2O(l) \; \rightleftharpoons \; NH_4^+(aq) \; + \; OH^-(aq) \qquad K_b = 1.8 \times 10^{-5}$$

$$CH_3NH_2(aq) \; + \; H_2O(l) \; \rightleftharpoons \; CH_3NH_3^+(aq) \; + \; OH^-(aq) \quad K_b = 5.0 \times 10^{-4}$$

The K_b for a weak base is related to the K_a for its conjugate acid by the expression (at 25°C):

$K_w = K_a \times K_b = 1.0 \times 10^{-14}$

Methylamine is a slightly stronger base than ammonia (the K_b is slightly higher). The conjugate acid of methylamine, $CH_3NH_3^+$, is therefore a weaker acid that the conjugate acid of ammonia, the ammonium ion, NH_4^+ (the K_a is slightly lower, 2.0×10^{-11} for $CH_3NH_3^+$ *vs.* 5.6×10^{-10} for NH_4^+).

The conjugate bases (salts) of weak acids are basic. When the anions of these salts dissolve in water, they produce hydroxide ions through **hydrolysis**:

Hydrolysis literally means the splitting of a water molecule; an anion of a weak acid (the conjugate base) removes a hydrogen ion from the water molecule leaving a hydroxide ion which causes the solution to be basic.

$$A^-(aq) \; + \; H_2O(l) \; \rightleftharpoons \; HA(aq) \; + \; OH^-(aq)$$

The weaker the acid HA, the stronger the conjugate base A^-. The anions of very weak acids produce solutions that are quite basic. On the other hand, the anions of strong acids (for example nitrates, chlorides, and perchlorates) are such weak bases that these anions have no effect upon the pH of the solution.

Similarly, the cations of strong bases (for example Na^+ and K^+) have no effect upon the pH of a solution. They are extremely weak acids. The cations of weak bases (for example, the $CH_3NH_3^+$ and NH_4^+ mentioned above) produce slightly acidic solutions.

See examples on page 706 of the text.

Qualitatively, the pH of a salt solution can be determined by establishing the strengths of the acid and base used to make the salt:

Be careful with the anions of polyprotic acids. For example, $NaHSO_4$ is acidic not neutral. It ionizes to lose a second hydrogen ion; it does not hydrolyze.

Cation	Anion	pH of the salt solution
from a strong base	from a strong acid	neutral, pH = 7
from a strong base	from a weak acid	basic, pH > 7
from a weak base	from a strong acid	acidic, pH < 7
from a weak base	from a weak acid	depends upon relative strengths of acid & base

The K_a for an acid, or K_b for a base, are often reported as a pK_a or pK_b, which are the negative logarithms of K_a and K_b respectively. As the acid strength increases, the K_a increases and the pK_a decreases.

The K_a for an acid and K_b for its conjugate base are related. For example, consider the weak acid HF:

$$HF(aq) \ + \ H_2O(l) \ \rightleftharpoons \ H_3O^+(aq) \ + \ F^-(aq) \qquad K_a = \frac{[H_3O^+][F^-]}{[HF]}$$

$$F^-(aq) \ + \ H_2O(l) \ \rightleftharpoons \ HF(aq) \ + \ OH^-(aq) \qquad K_b = \frac{[HF][OH^-]}{[F^-]}$$

Adding the two equations yields the equation for the autoionization of water. The HF and the F^- cancel from each side. Multiplying K_a and K_b together yields K_w.

If you know either K_a or K_b at 25°C, you can always calculate the other.

Or $pK_a + pK_b = pK_w$

Equilibrium Constants and Acid-Base Reactions

All acid-base aqueous equilibria can be characterized as the reaction of an acid and a base on the reactant side to produce an acid and a base (their conjugate partners) on the product side. For example, consider again the weak acid HF:

HF*(aq)* + H₂O*(l)* ⇌ H₃O⁺*(aq)* + F⁻*(aq)*
weaker acid   weaker base   stronger acid   stronger base
equilibrium lies on this side ⟵

Think of a Brønsted-Lowry acid base equilibrium as a competition for the hydrogen ion. The stronger acid doesn't want it, and the stronger base gets it, so the system lies on the side of the conjugate base of the stronger acid (the weaker base) and the conjugate acid of the stronger base (the weaker acid)—i.e on the weaker side.

There are two acids, HF and H_3O^+, and there are two bases, H_2O and F^-. Of the two bases, the fluoride ion is the stronger, and it is the base that gets the hydrogen ion. In other words, it exists as HF. Likewise, the hydronium ion is a stronger acid than HF, and it gets to give away its H^+, it exists as H_2O. Equilibria always lie predominantly on the weaker side. Note that the stronger acid and the stronger base lie on one side of the equilibrium, and the weaker acid and the weaker base lie on the other side.

Types of Acid-Base Reactions

Acids react with bases, and the acid or base may be strong or weak. The reaction of any **strong acid** and any **strong base** has the net ionic equation:

$$H_3O^+(aq) \ + \ OH^-(aq) \ \rightleftharpoons \ 2H_2O(l) \qquad K = 1.0 \times 10^{14}$$

The reaction is driven virtually to completion because K is so large. And K is large because K_w is so small. It is the formation of the weak electrolyte H_2O that drives the reaction.

Consider next the reaction between the **weak acid** acetic acid and a **strong base**:

$$CH_3CO_2H(aq) \ + \ OH^-(aq) \ \rightleftharpoons \ CH_3CO_2^-(aq) \ + \ H_2O(l)$$

The equilibrium lies on the right. The value of the equilibrium constant can be derived from the following information:

The cation of the base and the anion of the acid are spectator ions.

When equal molar quantities of acid and base are used, the equivalence point is reached, the acid and base are said to be neutralized.

The reaction between an acid and a base is generally called a neutralization reaction, even though the solution at the equivalence point is only neutral if both acid and base are equally strong.

$$CH_3CO_2H + H_2O \rightleftharpoons H_3O^+ + CH_3CO_2^- \qquad K_a = 1.8 \times 10^{-5}$$

$$H_3O^+ + OH^- \rightleftharpoons 2H_2O \qquad\qquad K = 1/K_w = 1.0 \times 10^{14}$$

Adding these equations produces the equation on the previous page, so the equilibrium constant for the neutralization reaction is the product of the two equilibrium constants:

$$K_{neut} = K_a \times 1/K_w = (1.8 \times 10^{-5})(1.0 \times 10^{14}) = 1.8 \times 10^9$$

Unless both the acid and base involved in the neutralization reaction are strong, the pH of the solution that results will not be neutral. The salt that results from this reaction is an acetate, the conjugate base of a weak acid. Therefore the solution will be basic at the **equivalence point**.

Consider now the reaction of any **strong acid** with a **weak base** like ammonia. The net ionic equation is:

$$H_3O^+(aq) + NH_3(aq) \rightleftharpoons NH_4^+(aq) + H_2O(l) \qquad K = 1.8 \times 10^9$$

The value of the equilibrium constant can again be derived from:

$$NH_3 + H_2O \rightleftharpoons NH_4^+ + OH^- \qquad K_b = 1.8 \times 10^{-5}$$

$$H_3O^+ + OH^- \rightleftharpoons 2H_2O \qquad\qquad K = 1/K_w = 1.0 \times 10^{14}$$

Adding these equations produces the desired equation. Again the driving force for the reaction is the formation of the weak electrolyte water. In this case the solution at the equivalence point contains the ammonium ion, the conjugate acid of a weak base, and the solution is acidic.

When a weak acid reacts with a weak base, the pH of the solution at the equivalence point depends upon which is the stronger, the acid or the base.

Calculations with Equilibrium Constants

The principles of the equilibria encountered in Chapter 15 of this study guide can be applied to aqueous solutions of weak acids and bases. The equilibrium constants K_a and K_b can be determined if the concentrations of the various species present in the solution are known. Most often these are determined by measuring the pH of the solution. If the acid or base is weak, and the initial concentration of acid (or base) is at least $100 \times K_a$ (or K_b), then the approximation that $[acid]_{initial} = [acid]_{equilibrium}$ is valid. Otherwise a quadratic equation must be solved.

For a weak acid:

$$HA(aq) + H_2O(l) \rightleftharpoons H_3O^+(aq) + A^-(aq)$$

$$K_a = \frac{[H_3O^+][A^-]}{[HA]} \quad \text{and because } [H_3O^+] = [A^-],$$

$$= \frac{[H_3O^+]^2}{[HA]} \quad \text{or } [H_3O^+] = \sqrt{K_a[HA]_{equil}}$$

The assumption that $[HA]_{equil} = [HA]_{initial}$ is valid if $[HA]_{initial} > 100 \times K_a$

The equilibrium constant is referred to here as K_{neut} just to distinguish it from the other equilibrium constants.

The reaction is product-favored.

The fact that both acetic acid and ammonia have the same value for K_a and K_b is pure coincidence.

For a weak acid - weak base titration,

$$K_{neut} = \frac{K_a \times K_b}{K_w}$$

These equilibrium problems are exactly the same as those described in Chapter 15 of this study guide.

See study questions #16, 22, & 23.

Keep the data organized in an ICE table.

Because K_a and K_b are typically quite small, the approximation that $[HA]_{eq} = [HA]_{init}$ is very often valid.

Polyprotic Acids and Bases

Some acids are capable of donating more than one proton; they are called **polyprotic**. Examples are the diprotic strong acid H_2SO_4, the diprotic acid oxalic acid $H_2C_2O_4$, and the triprotic phosphoric acid H_3PO_4:

$$H_3PO_4(aq) + H_2O(l) \rightleftharpoons H_3O^+(aq) + H_2PO_4^-(aq) \quad K_{a1} = 7.5 \times 10^{-3}$$

Successive K_a values for polyprotic acids usually differ by about 10^{-5}.

$$H_2PO_4^-(aq) + H_2O(l) \rightleftharpoons H_3O^+(aq) + HPO_4^{2-}(aq) \quad K_{a2} = 6.2 \times 10^{-8}$$

It gets harder and harder to remove successive hydrogen ions from a polyprotic acid.

$$HPO_4^{2-}(aq) + H_2O(l) \rightleftharpoons H_3O^+(aq) + PO_4^{3-}(aq) \quad K_{a3} = 3.6 \times 10^{-13}$$

Because the difference in the successive ionization constants is so large (about 10^5), it is always reasonable to assume that there is only one conjugate acid base pair present in the solution to any appreciable extent at one time. This makes the calculation of the pH of the solution easier.

The Lewis Concept of Acids and Bases

A more general theory of acids and bases was developed by G. N. Lewis in the 1930s. He defined an acid as a substance that would accept an electron pair to form a new bond and a base as a substance that would donate the pair of electrons. An acid is therefore a substance that has an empty orbital available or can make one available. A base is a substance that has a pair of electrons available for donation. Some examples are:

A still more generalized approach than Lewis's concept is referred to as donor-acceptor theory.

H^+	+	H_2O	$\rightarrow$	H_3O^+
empty 1s		lone pair on O:		
BF_3	+	NH_3	$\rightarrow$	$F_3B–NH_3$ acid-base adduct
empty sp^3		lone pair on N:		
$Cu^{2+}(aq)$	+	$4NH_3(aq)$	$\rightarrow$	$[Cu(NH_3)_4]^{2+}(aq)$ complex ion
empty sp^3		lone pair on N:		

The bond that is formed is called a coordinate covalent bond. The product of the Lewis acid base reaction is often called an adduct or complex.

The third Lewis acid-base reaction is an example of the coordination chemistry of transition metal ions. The hydroxide ion, as well as being the Arrhenius base, is also an excellent Lewis base. It readily donates electron pairs to metal cations to produce metal hydroxides. An important feature of some metal hydroxides is that they are **amphoteric**. This is a species that acts as an acid in the presence of a base, and as a base in the presence of an acid. A good example is $Al(OH)_3$.

Nonmetal oxides such as carbon dioxide are Lewis acids. In CO_2 the carbon is slightly positive because of the electronegative oxygen atoms; it attracts the hydroxide base to yield, ultimately, the carbonate ion.

Molecular Structure, Bonding, and Acid-Base Behavior

Some insight into the relative strengths of acids can be obtained from the molecular structures of the acids and the strengths of the H–A bonds in the acid molecules.

The inductive effect is seen in the series:

CH_3CO_2H	pK_a	4.74
$ClCH_2CO_2H$		2.85
Cl_2CHCO_2H		1.49
Cl_3CCO_2H		0.7

As more and more Cl atoms are substituted for H, the electrons are pulled more and more away from the O-H bond. Therefore the H^+ is lost more easily and the acid is stronger.

Key terms:

acid
base
strong
weak
Brønsted-Lowry acid
Brønsted-Lowry base
monoprotic
polyprotic
amphiprotic
conjugate acid-base pair
autoionization
water ionization constant K_w
pH
pOH
PK_w
K_a and K_b
pK_a and pK_b
Lewis acid
Lewis base
acid-base adduct
coordination compound
amphoteric
inductive effect

For example, in the series HF, HCl, HBr, HI, the bond strengths decrease and the acid strength increases. In the series HOCl, HOClO, $HOClO_2$, $HOClO_3$, the acid strength increases as the electrons in the HO bonds are more and more strongly withdrawn from the H. The extent to which adjacent atoms, or groups of atoms, attract electrons from other parts of the molecule is called the **inductive effect**.

Review Questions

1. Write a common definition of an acid in aqueous solution. What is a base?

2. What is the difference between a strong acid and a weak acid?

3. What are the definitions of a Brønsted-Lowry acid and base.

4. What is the difference between a monoprotic acid and a polyprotic acid? Is there such a thing as a polyprotic base?

5. Define, and give an example of, an amphiprotic substance.

6. What is a conjugate acid-base pair? By what do the two components of a pair differ? How many conjugate acid-base pairs make up a simple Brønsted-Lowry acid-base equilibrium?

7. What is autoionization?

8. Write an equation and an expression for K_w, the water ionization constant.

9. How is the strength of an acid related to the strength of its conjugate base and *vice versa*?

10. How can you determine on what side of an equilibrium a system predominantly lies?

11. How can you tell whether an acid or base is weak or strong?

12. Write examples of anions acting as acids in aqueous solution.

13. What does the numerical value of K_a or K_b tell you about the state of the aqueous system at equilibrium?

14. What is the relationship between K_a for a weak acid and K_b for its conjugate base? Prove the relationship for the weak acid acetic acid.

15. When is it reasonable to assume that change in the concentration x of a weak acid or base is negligible compared to the original concentration. In other words, when can you assume that $[acid]_{initial} = [acid]_{equilibrium}$ or $[base]_{initial} = [base]_{equilibrium}$?

16. How do you calculate the equilibrium constant for a neutralization reaction between a weak acid HA and a weak base B?

17. What is the net ionic equation for all strong acid–strong base neutralizations?

18. How can you predict whether the solution resulting from a neutralization reaction will be acidic, basic, or neutral?

19. For a generic weak acid, HA, write an expression for the equilibrium constant K_a. Then write an expression for the equilibrium constant K_b for the hydrolysis of its conjugate base, A^-. Then write an expression for the equilibrium constant K for the neutralization reaction of HA by a strong base OH^-. How are these equilibrium constants related to one another?

20. Prove that the concentration of sulfite ion $[SO_3^{2-}]$ in a solution of sulfurous acid is independent of the concentration of sulfurous acid. What is the concentration of sulfite ion?
$K_{a1} = 1.7 \times 10^{-2}$
$K_{a2} = 6.4 \times 10^{-8}$

21. Define the Lewis concept of an acid and a base. How do these definitions differ from the Arrhenius and Brønsted-Lowry definitions?

Answers to Review Questions

1. The common definition for aqueous systems is that an acid is a substance that increases the concentration of hydrogen ions H^+ in solution. A base is a substance that increases the concentration of hydroxide ions OH^-. These definitions are attributed to Arrhenius.

2. Strong acids are virtually 100% ionized; weak acids are only partially ionized. For example, nitric acid is a strong acid; one mole of nitric acid yields one mole of H^+ ions in solution. Nitrous acid, on the other hand, is a weak acid, one mole of nitrous acid in solution yields only 0.01 mole of H^+ ions; most of the nitrous acid remains as un-ionized molecules.

   Acids stronger than H_3O^+ are called strong acids.
   Acids weaker than H_3O^+ are called weak acids.

   H_3O^+ is the dividing line.

3. Brønsted and Lowry proposed that an acid be defined as a substance that donates a hydrogen ion (proton) to another substance. And they proposed that a base be defined as the substance that accepts the hydrogen ion (proton) from the acid. The acid-base reaction is a proton transfer reaction.

4. Monoprotic acids can donate only one proton (for example HCl). Polyprotic acids can donate more than one proton (for example H_2SO_4). Polyprotic bases exist—they are bases that accept more than one proton. The carbonate ion (CO_3^{2-}) is an example; it accepts one proton to produce the bicarbonate ion (HCO_3^-) and then another to become carbonic acid (H_2CO_3).

5. Amphiprotic substances can act as acids or bases depending upon the conditions. The bicarbonate ion (HCO_3^-) is an example; it acts as a base when it accepts a proton to produce carbonic acid (H_2CO_3), but it acts as an acid when it donates a proton to produce the carbonate ion (CO_3^{2-}).

6. In a Brønsted-Lowry acid-base equilibrium, an acid donates a proton and a base accepts it. A proton is transferred. The reaction can go in the reverse direction; again an acid donates a proton and a base accepts it. So, on both sides of the equilibrium, there is an acid and a base. Two conjugate acid-base pairs make up a simple Brønsted-Lowry acid-base equilibrium. When an acid gives up its proton it forms a base; this base is called its conjugate base; and together the acid and base make a conjugate pair. The two always differ by one proton.

$$HA(aq) \quad + \quad H_2O(l) \quad \rightleftharpoons \quad H_3O^+(aq) \quad + \quad A^-(aq)$$
$$\text{acid} \qquad\qquad \text{base} \qquad\qquad\qquad \text{acid} \qquad\qquad \text{base}$$

7. An autoionization reaction is one in which the same substance acts as both acid and base. One molecule donates a hydrogen ion and another molecule of the same substance accepts it.

8. An example of autoionization occurs in water:

$$H_2O(l) \quad + \quad H_2O(l) \quad \rightleftharpoons \quad H_3O^+(aq) \quad + \quad OH^-(aq)$$

The autoionization constant for water is $K_w = [H_3O^+][OH^-]$

9. In a Brønsted-Lowry acid-base equilibrium, the stronger the acid, the weaker its conjugate base, and *vice versa*. This is because the more the acid wants to donate its proton, the less its conjugate base wants it back. For example consider the strong acid HCl; the conjugate base of HCl is the chloride ion. The chloride ion is very willing to give up its proton; that's what makes the acid strong. It does not want the proton back; that's what makes the base weak.

10. In a Brønsted-Lowry acid-base equilibrium, the stronger acid and the stronger base lie on one side of the equilibrium, and the weaker acid and the weaker base lie on the other side. The system exists predominantly on the weak side.

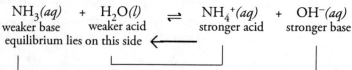

$$NH_3(aq) \quad + \quad H_2O(l) \quad \rightleftharpoons \quad NH_4^+(aq) \quad + \quad OH^-(aq)$$
weaker base   weaker acid   stronger acid   stronger base
equilibrium lies on this side ⟵

There are other strong acids, but these are the six common ones.

11. Remember the six common strong acids: perchloric $HClO_4$, nitric HNO_3, hydrochloric HCl, hydrobromic HBr, hydroiodic HI, and sulfuric H_2SO_4. Any other acid you encounter is probably weak. And remember the weak base ammonia NH_3; other common weak bases are derivatives of ammonia called

amines. For example, methylamine CH_3NH_2, aniline $C_6H_5NH_2$, pyridine C_5H_5N, and amphetamine $C_6H_5CH_2CH(CH_3)NH_2$. The other bases you commonly encounter are the hydroxides of Group 1 and Group 2 metals, and these are all strong.

12.　Any anion still possessing a hydrogen, in other words an anion of a polyprotic acid, can act as an acid in aqueous solution. Examples are the bisulfate ion HSO_4^- and the dihydrogen phosphate ion $H_2PO_4^-$:

The hydrogens have to be acidic hydrogens. For example the hydrogens of the CH_3 group in acetic CH_3CO_2H acid are not acidic and acetic acid is only monoprotic. Likewise, the third H in H_3PO_3 is not acidic and phosphorous acid is only diprotic.

$$HSO_4^-(aq) \ + \ H_2O(l) \ \rightleftharpoons \ H_3O^+(aq) \ + \ SO_4^{2-}(aq)$$

$$H_2PO_4^-(aq) \ + \ H_2O(l) \ \rightleftharpoons \ H_3O^+(aq) \ + \ HPO_4^{2-}(aq)$$

13.　A large value for K_a or K_b means a proportionately large concentration of product, i.e. a high concentration of hydronium ions or hydroxide ions respectively. The higher the value of K_a, for example, the stronger the acid. On the other hand, a smaller value for K_a means less product at equilibrium and a weaker acid.

14.　The product of the K_a for a weak acid and K_b for its conjugate base is equal to K_w, the water ionization constant.

$K_w = K_a \times K_b = 1.0 \times 10^{-14}$ at 25°C.

$$CH_3CO_2H(aq) \ + \ H_2O(l) \ \rightleftharpoons \ H_3O^+(aq) \ + \ CH_3CO_2^-(aq)$$

$$K_a = \frac{[H_3O^+][CH_3CO_2^-]}{[CH_3CO_2H]}$$

$$CH_3CO_2^-(aq) \ + \ H_2O(l) \ \rightleftharpoons \ OH^-(aq) \ + \ CH_3CO_2H(aq)$$

$$K_b = \frac{[OH^-][CH_3CO_2H]}{[CH_3CO_2^-]}$$

$$K_a \times K_b = \frac{[H_3O^+][CH_3CO_2^-]}{[CH_3CO_2H]} \times \frac{[OH^-][CH_3CO_2H]}{[CH_3CO_2^-]} = [H_3O^+][OH^-] = K_w$$

15.　The assumption that $[HA]_{equil} = [HA]_{initial}$ is valid if $[HA]_{initial} > 100 \times K_a$.

16.　The reaction between the weak acid HA and the weak base B:

$$HA(aq) \ + \ B(aq) \ \rightleftharpoons \ BH^+(aq) \ + \ A^-(aq)$$

The ionization equilibria for the weak acid and the weak base are:

K_a is the acid ionization constant, and K_b is the base ionization constant, for the acid and base involved in the neutralization reaction.

$$HA(aq) \ + \ H_2O(l) \ \rightleftharpoons \ H_3O^+(aq) + A^-(aq) \qquad \text{equil. const.} = K_a$$

$$B(aq) \ + \ H_2O(l) \ \rightleftharpoons \ BH^+(aq) + OH^-(aq) \qquad \text{equil. const.} = K_b$$

$$H_3O^+(aq) \ + \ OH^-(aq) \ \rightleftharpoons \ 2H_2O(l) \qquad \text{equil. const.} = 1/K_w$$

Notice that the stronger the base, and the stronger the acid, the more the neutralization reaction is product-favored (the higher the value of K_{neut}).

Adding these equations produces the desired equation above so the equilibrium constant for the reaction is:
$$\frac{K_a \times K_b}{K_w}$$

For example, for the weak acid acetic acid and the weak base ammonia:

	K_{neut}
weak acid – weak base	10^4
weak acid – strong base	10^9
strong acid – weak base	10^9
strong acid – strong base	10^{14}

where the strong acid is a typical strong acid like HCl and the strong base is a typical strong base like NaOH.

Be aware of anions such as HSO_4^- and $H_2PO_4^-$ that ionize to produce acidic solutions.

17. Strong acids, strong bases, and salts are all completely ionized in solution. As a result the anion of the acid, and the cation of the base are merely spectator ions and do not appear in the net ionic equation:

$$H_3O^+(aq) + OH^-(aq) \rightleftharpoons 2H_2O(l)$$

18. The pH of a salt solution can be estimated by establishing the strengths of the acid and base used to make the salt:

Cation	Anion	pH of the salt solution
from a strong base	from a strong acid	neutral, pH = 7
from a strong base	from a weak acid	basic, pH > 7
from a weak base	from a strong acid	acidic, pH < 7
from a weak base	from a weak acid	depends upon relative strengths of acid & base

19. For a generic weak acid HA:

$$HA(aq) + H_2O(l) \rightleftharpoons H_3O^+(aq) + A^-(aq) \quad \text{equil. const.} = K_a$$

For the hydrolysis of the conjugate base of the weak acid:

$$A^-(aq) + H_2O(l) \rightleftharpoons HA(aq) + OH^-(aq) \quad \text{equil. const.} = K_b$$

For the neutralization of the weak acid by a strong base:

$$HA(aq) + OH^-(aq) \rightleftharpoons A^-(aq) + H_2O(l) \quad \text{equil. const.} = K_{neut}$$

The K_a of an acid and the K_b for its conjugate base are related by the expression:

$$K_a = \frac{K_w}{K_b} \quad \text{or} \quad K_a \times K_b = K_w$$

The K_{neut} for the acid and the K_b for its conjugate base are the reciprocal of one another:

$$K_{neut} = \frac{1}{K_b} \quad \text{or} \quad K_{neut} \times K_b = 1$$

20.
$$H_2SO_3(aq) + H_2O(l) \rightleftharpoons H_3O^+(aq) + HSO_3^-(aq) \quad K_{a1} = 1.7 \times 10^{-2}$$
$$HSO_3^-(aq) + H_2O(l) \rightleftharpoons H_3O^+(aq) + SO_3^{2-}(aq) \quad K_{a2} = 6.4 \times 10^{-8}$$

$$K_{a2} = \frac{[H_3O^+][SO_3^{2-}]}{[HSO_3^-]} \quad \text{but } [H_3O^+] = [HSO_3^-] \quad \text{so } K_{a2} = [SO_3^{2-}]$$

21. Lewis defined an acid as a substance that would accept an electron pair to form a new bond and a base as a substance that would donate the pair of electrons. The Lewis definitions are more general than the Arrhenius and Brønsted-Lowry definitions—acid-base reactions are no longer restricted to those involving a hydrogen ion transfer.

Study Questions and Problems

A good teacher is one who explains a concept; a better teacher is one who asks questions about the concept; the best teacher is one who demonstrates the concept then solicits questions from the students.

Hubert N. Alyea
(1903-1996)

the last graduate student of Svante Arrhenius
(1859-1927)

1. Write examples of acids that are molecular, cationic, and anionic. Write an example of an anionic base and a molecular base.

2. Write an example of a monoprotic acid, a diprotic acid, and a triprotic acid.

3. For the following aqueous equilibria, designate the Brønsted-Lowry conjugate acid-base pairs and establish the weaker side:

   a. $NH_3(aq)$ + $H_2O(l)$ $\rightleftharpoons$ $NH_4^+(aq)$ + $OH^-(aq)$

   b. $HCN(aq)$ + $H_2O(l)$ $\rightleftharpoons$ $H_3O^+(aq)$ + $CN^-(aq)$

   c. $NH_4^+(aq)$ + $CO_3^-(aq)$ $\rightleftharpoons$ $NH_3(aq)$ + $HCO_3^-(aq)$

4. Write the name and formula for the conjugate bases of the following acids:

   a. HNO_2
   b. H_2SO_4
   c. $H_2PO_4^-$
   d. HF
   e. CH_3CO_2H
   f. $HOCl$
   g. NH_4^+

5. Complete the Brønsted-Lowry equilibria, label the components acid or base, and pair up the conjugate acid-base pairs:

   a. HSO_4^- + H_2O $\rightleftharpoons$

   b. NH_3 + H_2O $\rightleftharpoons$

   c. CN^- + H_2O $\rightleftharpoons$

   d. H^- + H_2O $\rightleftharpoons$

   e. $HClO_4$ + H_2O $\rightleftharpoons$

6. Is the monohydrogenphosphate ion HPO_4^{2-} amphiprotic? If so, write the formulas of its conjugate acid and its conjugate base.

7. Write net ionic acid-base reactions for:

   a. the reaction of acetic acid with aqueous ammonia solution
   b. the reaction of hydrofluoric acid with sodium hydroxide
   c. the reaction of ammonium chloride with potassium hydroxide
   d. the reaction of sodium bicarbonate with sulfuric acid
   e. the reaction of chlorous acid with aqueous ammonia solution
   f. the reaction of disodium hydrogen phosphate with acetic acid

8.   Of the following acids, determine

   a. the strongest acid.
   b. the acid that produces the lowest concentration of hydronium ions per mole of acid.
   c. the acid with the strongest conjugate base.
   d. the diprotic acid.
   e. the strong acid.
   f. the acid with the weakest conjugate base.

$$HNO_3(aq) + H_2O(l) \rightleftharpoons H_3O^+(aq) + NO_3^-(aq) \quad K_a = \text{very large}$$

$$HSO_4^-(aq) + H_2O(l) \rightleftharpoons H_3O^+(aq) + SO_4^-(aq) \quad K_a = 1.2 \times 10^{-2}$$

$$HCN(aq) + H_2O(l) \rightleftharpoons H_3O^+(aq) + CN^-(aq) \quad K_a = 4.0 \times 10^{-10}$$

$$H_2CO_3(aq) + H_2O(l) \rightleftharpoons H_3O^+(aq) + CO_3^-(aq) \quad K_a = 4.2 \times 10^{-7}$$

$$NH_4^+(aq) + H_2O(l) \rightleftharpoons H_3O^+(aq) + NH_3(aq) \quad K_a = 5.6 \times 10^{-10}$$

$$HF(aq) + H_2O(l) \rightleftharpoons H_3O^+(aq) + F^-(aq) \quad K_a = 7.2 \times 10^{-4}$$

9.   What is the pH of

   a. 0.0010 M HCl solution?
   b. 0.15 M KOH solution?
   c. 10^{-8} M HNO_3 solution?

10.   List the following substances in order of increasing acid strength:

   H_2O, H_2SO_3, HCN, $H_2PO_4^-$, NH_4^+, $[Cu(H_2O)_6]^{2+}$, NH_3, H_3O^+, HCO_2H, HCl.

11.   Complete the table for each aqueous solution at 25°C. State whether the solutions are acidic or basic:

$[H_3O^+]$	$[OH^-]$	pH	pOH	acidic or basic
2.0×10^{-5}				
		6.25		
	5.6×10^{-2}			
			9.20	
8.7×10^{-10}				

12.   What is the pH of a solution that contains 2.60 grams of NaOH in 250 mL of aqueous solution?

13.   If the pH of a sample of rainwater is 4.62, what is the hydronium ion concentration $[H_3O^+]$ and the hydroxide ion concentration $[OH^-]$ in the rainwater?

14. A 0.12M solution of an unknown weak acid has a pH of 4.26 at 25°C. What is the hydronium ion concentration in the solution and what is the value of its K_a? What is the pK_a?

15. Hydroxylamine is a weak base with a $K_b = 6.6 \times 10^{-9}$. What is the pH of a 0.36 M solution of hydroxylamine in water at 25°C?

16. Suppose you dissolved benzoic acid in water to make a 0.15 M solution. What is

    a. the concentration of benzoic acid?
    b. the concentration of hydronium ion?
    c. the concentration of benzoate anion?
    d. the pH of the solution?

    K_a for benzoic acid = 6.3×10^{-5} at 25°C

17. Which of the following salts, when dissolved in water to produce 0.10 M solutions, would have the lowest pH?

    a. sodium acetate
    b. potassium chloride
    c. sodium bisulfate
    d. magnesium nitrate
    e. potassium cyanide

18. For each of the following salts, predict whether an aqueous solution would be acidic, basic, or neutral.

    a. sodium nitrate $NaNO_3$
    b. ammonium iodide NH_4I
    c. sodium bicarbonate $NaHCO_3$
    d. ammonium cyanide NH_4CN
    e. sodium hypochlorite $NaOCl$
    f. potassium acetate KCH_3CO_2

19. a. Cyanic acid HOCN has a $K_a = 3.5 \times 10^{-4}$, what is the K_b for the cyanate ion OCN^-?

    b. Phenol is a relatively weak acid, $K_a = 1.3 \times 10^{-10}$. How does the strength of its conjugate base compare with the strength of ammonia, the acetate ion, and sodium hydroxide?

20. Calculate the equilibrium constant for the neutralization of hydrocyanic acid by ammonia:

    $$HCN(aq) + NH_3(aq) \rightleftharpoons NH_4^+(aq) + CN^-(aq)$$

    K_a for hydrocyanic acid = 4.0×10^{-10} at 25°C

    K_b for ammonia = 1.8×10^{-5} at 25°C

21. Is the solution that results from the neutralization of hydrocyanic acid by ammonia basic or acidic?

22. Calculate the pH of a 0.35 M solution of potassium cyanide. K_a for HCN = 4.0×10^{-10}.

23. a. What is the pH of a 0.80 M solution of sulfurous acid?

    b. What is the concentration of sulfite ion in a 0.80 M solution of sulfurous acid?

    c. What happens to the concentration of sulfite ion SO_3^{2-} if the concentration of sulfurous acid is halved, to 0.40 M?

24. Identify the Lewis acid and the Lewis base in the following reactions:

    a. Boron trichloride reacts with chloride ion to produce $[BCl_4]^-$.

    b. Nickel reacts with carbon monoxide to produce nickel tetracarbonyl $[Ni(CO)_4]$.

    c. Ammonia reacts with acetic acid to produce ammonium acetate.

    d. Sodium ions are solvated by water to produce $Na^+(aq)$.

The roots of education are bitter, but the fruit is sweet.

*Aristotle
(384–322BC)*

Answers to Study Questions and Problems

1. | | | |
    |---|---|---|
    | Molecular acid: | nitric acid | HNO_3 |
    | Cationic acid: | ammonium ion | NH_4^+ |
    | Anionic acid: | dihydrogen phosphate ion | $H_2PO_4^-$ |
    | Anionic base: | chloride | OH^- |
    | Molecular base: | ammonia | NH_3 |

2. | | | |
    |---|---|---|
    | Monoprotic acid: | hydrochloric acid | HCl |
    | Diprotic acid: | carbonic acid | H_2CO_3 |
    | Triprotic acid: | phosphorous acid | H_3PO_3 |

3. a. $NH_3(aq)$ + $H_2O(l)$ $\rightleftharpoons$ $NH_4^+(aq)$ + $OH^-(aq)$

    base weaker acid   acid stronger base

    b. $HCN(aq)$ + $H_2O(l)$ $\rightleftharpoons$ $H_3O^+(aq)$ + $CN^-(aq)$

    acid weaker base   acid stronger base

    c. $NH_4^+(aq)$ + $CO_3^-(aq)$ $\rightleftharpoons$ $NH_3(aq)$ + $HCO_3^-(aq)$

    acid stronger base   base weaker acid

4.   acid $\xrightarrow{\text{remove } H^+}$ conjugate base

     a. HNO_2 NO_2^- nitrite
     b. H_2SO_4 HSO_4^- bisulfate
     c. $H_2PO_4^-$ HPO_4^{2-} hydrogen phosphate
     d. HF F^- fluoride
     e. CH_3CO_2H $CH_3CO_2^-$ acetate
     f. $HOCl$ OCl^- hypochorite
     g. NH_4^+ NH_3 ammonia

5.   a. HSO_4^- + H_2O ⇌ H_3O^+ + SO_4^{2-}
           acid   base   acid   base

     b. NH_3 + H_2O ⇌ NH_4^+ + OH^-
           base   acid   acid   base

     c. CN^- + H_2O ⇌ HCN + OH^-
           base   acid   acid   base

     d. H^- + H_2O ⇌ H_2 + OH^-
           base   acid   acid   base

     e. $HClO_4$ + H_2O ⇌ H_3O^+ + ClO_4^-
           acid   base   acid   base

6. The HPO_4^{2-} ion is amphiprotic; it can donate or accept hydrogen ions:

         $H_2PO_4^-$ ⇌ HPO_4^{2-} ⇌ PO_4^{3-}
        conjugate acid   conjugate base

7. $CH_3CO_2H(aq)$ + $NH_3(aq)$ ⇌ $NH_4^+(aq)$ + $CH_3CO_2^-(aq)$

     $HF(aq)$ + $OH^-(aq)$ ⇌ $F^-(aq)$ + $H_2O(l)$

     $NH_4^+(aq)$ + $OH^-(aq)$ ⇌ $NH_3(aq)$ + $H_2O(l)$

     $H_3O^+(aq)$ + $HCO_3^-(aq)$ ⇌ $2H_2O(l)$ + $CO_2(g)$

     $HClO_2(aq)$ + $NH_3(aq)$ ⇌ $NH_4^+(aq)$ + $ClO_2^-(aq)$

     $HPO_4^{2-}(aq)$ + $CH_3CO_2H(aq)$ ⇌ $H_2PO_4^-(aq)$ + $CH_3CO_2^-(aq)$

Spectator ions are omitted—these are net ionic equations.

Each reaction involves the transfer of a proton from the acid to the base.

8.

$$HNO_3(aq) + H_2O(l) \rightleftharpoons H_3O^+(aq) + NO_3^-(aq) \quad K_a = \text{very large}$$

$$HSO_4^-(aq) + H_2O(l) \rightleftharpoons H_3O^+(aq) + SO_4^-(aq) \quad K_a = 1.2 \times 10^{-2}$$

$$HCN(aq) + H_2O(l) \rightleftharpoons H_3O^+(aq) + CN^-(aq) \quad K_a = 4.0 \times 10^{-10}$$

$$H_2CO_3(aq) + H_2O(l) \rightleftharpoons H_3O^+(aq) + CO_3^-(aq) \quad K_a = 4.2 \times 10^{-7}$$

$$NH_4^+(aq) + H_2O(l) \rightleftharpoons H_3O^+(aq) + NH_3(aq) \quad K_a = 5.6 \times 10^{-10}$$

$$HF(aq) + H_2O(l) \rightleftharpoons H_3O^+(aq) + F^-(aq) \quad K_a = 7.2 \times 10^{-4}$$

> The strongest acid is not necessarily a strong acid.

a. the strongest acid is HNO_3 (highest K_a).
b. the acid that produces the lowest concentration of hydronium ions per mole of acid is the weakest acid: HCN (lowest K_a).
c. the acid with the strongest conjugate base is the weakest acid: HCN.
d. the diprotic acid is H_2CO_3.
e. the strong acid is HNO_3.
f. the acid with the weakest conjugate base is the strongest acid: HNO_3.

9. a. HCl is a strong acid, so 0.0010 M HCl solution contains 0.0010 M H_3O^+. The pH = $-\log[H^+]$ = $-\log[0.0010]$ = 3.0.

b. KOH is a strong base, so 0.15 M KOH solution contains 0.15 M OH^- The pOH = $-\log[OH^-]$ = $-\log[0.15]$ = 0.82; pH = 13.2.

> The solution must be acidic, so the answer is not 8!
> The solution is slightly more acidic than pure water.
> There is always some H_3O^+ and OH^- in an aqueous solution due to the autoionization of water—usually insignificant but not in this case.

c. The total quantity of H^+ in the solution is initially 10^{-8} M from the HNO_3 plus 10^{-7} M from the water.
The total concentration of H^+ is approx. 1.1×10^{-7}. So the pH = 6.96.

10. In increasing acid strength from bottom to top:

HCl	very large
H_3O^+	1.0
H_2SO_3	1.2×10^{-2}
HCO_2H	1.8×10^{-4}
$[Cu(H_2O)_6]^{2+}$	1.6×10^{-7}
$H_2PO_4^-$	6.2×10^{-8}
NH_4^+	5.6×10^{-10}
HCN	4.0×10^{-10}
H_2O	1.0×10^{-14}
NH_3	very small

> For water at 25°C:
>
> $[H_3O^+][OH^-] = K_w = 10^{-14}$
>
> $pH + pOH = pK_w = 14$

11.

$[H_3O^+]$	$[OH^-]$	pH	pOH	acidic or basic
2.0×10^{-5}	5.0×10^{-10}	4.70	9.30	acidic
5.6×10^{-7}	1.8×10^{-8}	6.25	7.75	acidic
1.8×10^{-13}	5.6×10^{-2}	12.75	1.25	basic
1.6×10^{-5}	6.3×10^{-10}	4.80	9.20	acidic
8.7×10^{-10}	1.1×10^{-5}	9.06	4.94	basic

12. Sodium hydroxide is a strong base.
    Concentration of NaOH = 2.6 g/250 mL = 0.26 mol/L
    The concentration of OH^- ions is therefore the same = 0.26 M
    $pOH = -\log[OH] = 0.585$
    $pH = 13.4$

    Molar mass of NaOH = 40 g/mol

13. $pH = -\log[H^+] = 4.62$
    $[H^+] = 2.4 \times 10^{-5}$
    $[OH^-] = 4.2 \times 10^{-10}$

    $[OH^-]$ is much lower than $[H^+]$; the solution is acidic.

14. $pH = 4.26$ at 25°C
    $[H_3O^+] = 5.50 \times 10^{-5}$

    $K_a = \dfrac{[H_3O^+]^2}{0.12} = 2.52 \times 10^{-8}$.

    Learn how to take an antilog on your calculator. Your calculator may have a 10^x key, or an INV function key.

15. $K_b = 6.6 \times 10^{-9} = \dfrac{[OH^-]^2}{[NH_2OH]} = \dfrac{[OH^-]^2}{0.36}$

    $[OH^-] = 4.87 \times 10^{-5}$
    $pOH = 4.31$ and the $pH = 9.69$.

16.

		$C_6H_5CO_2H + H_2O \rightleftharpoons H_3O^+(aq) + C_6H_5CO_2^-(aq)$		
I	Initial	0.15	0	0
C	Change	$-x$	$+x$	$+x$
E	Equilibrium	0.15–x	x	x

K_a for benzoic acid $= 6.3 \times 10^{-5} = x^2/(0.15-x) = x^2/0.15$; x = 0.00307M

   a. the concentration of benzoic acid at equilibrium = 0.147M
   b. the concentration of hydronium ion = 0.0031 M
   c. the concentration of benzoate anion = 0.0031 M
   d. the pH of the solution = 2.51

(0.15–x) is approximately equal to 0.15. Actually 0.147.

Solving the quadratic yields a value for x = 0.00304.

17.
   a. sodium acetate — K_a for acetic acid = 1.8×10^{-5}; basic
   b. potassium chloride — strong acid : strong base : neutral solution
   c. sodium bisulfate — bisulfate ionizes ($K_a = 1.2 \times 10^{-2}$) lowest pH
   d. magnesium nitrate — strong acid : strong base : neutral solution
   e. potassium cyanide — K_a for HCN = 4.0×10^{-10}; basic

Determine the acid and base used to make the salt.
But look out for acid salts (the anions of polyprotic acids).

No calculations are necessary.

18.

a.	$NaNO_3$	strong acid	strong base	neutral
b.	NH_4I	strong acid	weak base	acidic
c.	$NaHCO_3$	weak acid	strong base	basic
d.	NH_4CN	weaker acid	weak base	slightly basic
e.	$NaOCl$	weak acid	strong base	basic
f.	KCH_3CO_2	weak acid	strong base	basic

Solutions continued on page 250

Equilibria
   —*a crossword puzzle*

Across:

3. In a titration, it lets you know when you have reached the equivalence point.

6. What the solution is when the equivalence point is reached in a strong acid - strong base titration.

8. When water produces *20 down* and *31 across* ions.

10. Solvation of ions involves an ion - *this* attraction.

12. Product concentrations divided by reactant concentrations, not necessarily at equilibrium.

13. It's assumed to be complete for a strong *14 across* in solution.

14. Weak or strong, it conducts an electrical current in solution.

17. The result of a Lewis acid-base interaction between a transition metal ion and a base.

18. Industrial manufacture of ammonia.

21. It transfers a hydrogen ion to form its conjugate base.

23. What happens to the salts of weak acids or weak bases in solution.

24. Normally from 0 to 14, an indication of hydronium ion concentration.

27. A process for which *9 down* is large.

31. The conjugate base of water; produced by Arrhenius bases in aqueous solution.

32. The idea that a system in equilibrium will adjust to accommodate any alteration in conditions.

33. Negative ion.

Down:

1. A species that acts as an acid in the presence of a base, and as a base in the presence of an acid.

2. The effect by which adjacent atoms, or groups of atoms, attract electrons from other parts of a molecule.

4. Base partner.

5. A solute that can either accept or donate a hydrogen ion.

7. Unchanging, except perhaps if the temperature changes.

9. Q at equilibrium.

11. A statement of the fact that the *9 down* is *7 down* regardless of how the masses of the components present are changed—developed by Guldberg & Waage.

15. He classified an acid as an electron pair acceptor and a base as an electron pair donor.

16. Sulfuric acid, oxalic acid, phosphoric acid, carbonic acid, for example.

19. Negative this of the concentration of *20 down* is pH.

20. Ion produced by the protonation of a water molecule.

21. This increases the hydroxide ion concentration...

22. ...whereas this increases the hydronium ion concentration in aqueous solution.

25. If the reaction is reversed, then the new equilibrium constant is this of the original.

26. His was the first set of definitions describing an acid and base in aqueous solution.

28. Acetylsalicylic acid.

29. One name for what is produced when a Lewis acid and a Lewis base react, forming a coordinate bond.

30. An electrolyte only partially ionized in solution.

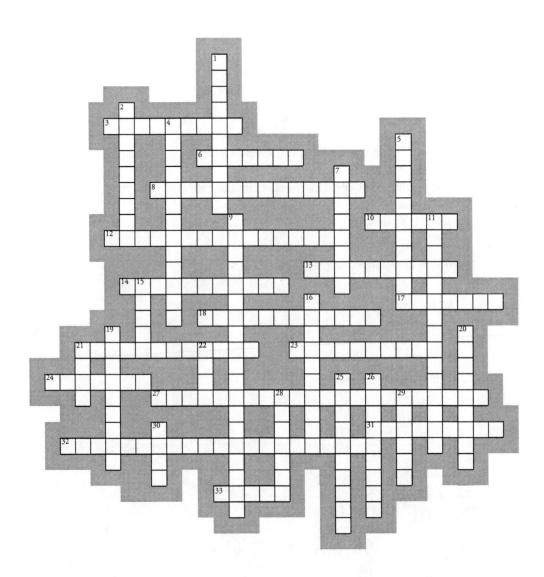

19. a. K_a for the acid and K_b for the conjugate base are related:

$K_a \times K_b = K_w$.

If $K_a = 3.5 \times 10^{-4}$ for cyanic acid HOCN,
then K_b for cyanate $= 10^{-14}/3.5 \times 10^{-4} = 2.86 \times 10^{-11}$.

b. Phenol is a relatively weak acid, $K_a = 1.3 \times 10^{-10}$.
K_b for its conjugate base $= 10^{-14}/1.3 \times 10^{-10} = 7.7 \times 10^{-5}$.

For comparison:
ammonia $K_b = 1.8 \times 10^{-5}$ (about the same)
acetate $K_b = 5.6 \times 10^{-10}$ (much weaker)
sodium hydroxide K_b = very large   (much stronger).

20. The equilibrium constant for the neutralization of any weak acid by any weak base is given by the expression:

$$K_{neut} = \frac{K_a \times K_b}{K_w}$$

which in this case $= (4.0 \times 10^{-10})(1.8 \times 10^{-5})/(1 \times 10^{-14}) = 0.72$

21. K_a for hydrocyanic acid $= 4.0 \times 10^{-10}$ at 25°C

K_b for ammonia $= 1.8 \times 10^{-5}$ at 25°C

The base is stronger than the acid, so the equivalence point will be slightly basic.

22. CN^-*(aq)* + H_2O*(l)* $\rightleftharpoons$ HCN*(aq)* + OH^-*(aq)*

$K_b = \dfrac{[HCN][OH^-]}{[CN^-]} = \dfrac{[OH^-]^2}{[CN^-]} = \dfrac{[OH^-]^2}{0.35} = \dfrac{1.0 \times 10^{-14}}{4.0 \times 10^{-10}}$

$[OH^-] = 2.96 \times 10^{-3}$
$pOH = 2.53$
$pH = 11.47$

Solve the quadratic to obtain the hydronium ion concentration.

23. a. $K_{a1} = \dfrac{[H_3O^+][HSO_3^-]}{[H_2SO_3]} = \dfrac{[H_3O^+]^2}{[H_2SO_3]} = 1.7 \times 10^{-2}$ $[H_3O^+] = 0.108$
$pH = 0.97$

b. $[SO_3^{2-}] = K_{a2} = 6.4 \times 10^{-8}$

c. Nothing; the $[SO_3^{2-}]$ is independent of $[H_2SO_3]$.

The Lewis base donates the electron pair; the Lewis acid accepts the electron pair.

24. a. Boron trichloride (acid) accepts a pair of electrons from chloride (base).

b. Nickel (acid) accepts a pair of electrons from carbon monoxide (base).

c. Ammonia (base) donates a pair of electrons to the proton (acid) from acetic acid.

d. Sodium ions (acid) are solvated by water (base).

SOLUTIONS

Contents

1   **Answers to Examinations**

2   **Answers to Crosswords**

Examination 1 (Page 95)

True–false questions

1.   **T**   All atoms of an element have the same atomic number regardless of the isotope. Isotopes have different mass numbers.

2.   **F**   Iodine is a halogen (Group 7A or 17).

3.   **T**   This is the law of conservation of mass. A chemical reaction is just a rearrangement of atoms; atoms are neither created nor destroyed.

4.   **T**   Heat capacity (JK^{-1}) = specific heat capacity $(JK^{-1}g^{-1})$ × mass (g).

5.   **T**   A Celsius degree interval is equal in magnitude to a Kelvin degree interval.

6.   **F**   The base SI unit for temperature is the Kelvin (K).

7.   **T** ΔH is an extensive property, if heat is liberated in one direction, heat will be absorbed in the reverse direction. For example, breaking bonds is endothermic, making bonds is exothermic.

8.   **T**   The prefix milli– means $\times 10^{-3}$.

9.   **T**   A compound must consist of two or more different elements—otherwise it wouldn't be a compound.

10.   **T**   Neon–22 has 12 neutrons in its nucleus (mass number 22, atomic number 10; difference 12 neutrons).

11.   **T**   An empirical formula is the simplest possible integer ratio.

12.   **T**   Energy = power × time (J = Ws) or Power = energy/time (W = Js^{-1}).

13.   **T**   Volume, pressure, and temperature are all state functions.

14.   T   Perchloric acid $HClO_4$ is one of the strong acids. Chlorous acid $HClO_2$ is not.

15.   F   Some molecules are elements. For example H_2, O_2 and O_3, Br_2, P_4, S_8, C_{60}.

16.   F   The pH of a solution at the equivalence point depends upon the acid and base involved. For example, a titration of a strong acid and a weak base produces an acidic solution.

17.   T   Bromine in its standard state is a liquid, so $\Delta H°_f (Br_2(l))$ = zero but $\Delta H°_f (Br_2(g))$ does not equal zero; energy is required to vaporize the liquid.

18.   T   The expression is correct; moles/liter $\times$ liter = moles.

19.   T   Melting always requires energy; bonds must be broken.

20.   T   The oxidizing agent is an oxidizing agent because it accepts electrons.

21.   F   An exothermic reaction is often product-favored, but not always. Some spontaneous reactions are endothermic.

22.   F   Boiling water is a physical change, the substance remains water. A chemical reaction is required to decompose water to hydrogen and oxygen.

23.   T   An allotrope is one form of an element. There are three allotropes of carbon: diamond, graphite, and the fullerenes.

24.   T   Lead sulfate is one of three insoluble sulfates (lead, barium, and strontium).

25.   T   Non-metal oxides produce acidic solutions when dissolved in water. For example, sulfur dioxide dissolves in water to produce sulfurous acid H_2SO_3.

Multiple Choice

1.   e.   Steam condensing is a physical change.

2.   d.   It is the number of protons (the atomic number) that identifies the element.

3.   e.   Calcium phosphate is $Ca_3(PO_4)_2$.

4.   e.   Area = $(8.00 \times 12.00$ inch$^2) \times (2.54$ cm / 1 inch$)^2$ = 619 cm^2.

5.   d.   40 grams of calcium = 1 mole of calcium atoms.
           19 grams of fluorine contains 1 mole of F atoms.

6.   b.   The formula for sodium sulfate is Na_2SO_4
           molar mass = $(2 \times 22.99) + 32.07 + (4 \times 16.00)$ = 142.05g.

7.   e.   bromine (halogen); iron (transition metal); beryllium (alkaline earth metal); helium (noble gas).

8.   c.   Molar mass of SO_2 = 64.07 g mol^{-1}; this is the mass of Avogadro's number of molecules. Average mass of one molecule = 64.07 / 6.022 × 10^{23} = 1.06 × 10^{-22}.

9.   e.   Mass / molar mass = moles.

10.   d.   volume; the only one that depends upon how much substance is present.

11.   g.   The atomic mass is approximately equal to the weighted average of the mass numbers of the isotope masses; at least sufficiently near to calculate the mass numbers of the isotopes:

Atomic number = 29; mass number of first isotope = 29 + 34 = 63
If mass number of second isotope = x
(0.71 × 63) + (0.29 × x) = 63.55
(0.29 × x) = 63.55 − 44.73 = 18.82
x = 64.9, so the mass number of the second isotope is 65.

12.   e.   The empirical formula is SN, the percentage of S is (32.07 / (32.07 + 14.01)) × 100 = 69.6%.

13.   d.   Convert mass to moles and then apply the stoichiometry shown in the balanced equation:

$$4.0 \text{ grams NaOH} \times \frac{1.0 \text{ mole NaOH}}{40 \text{ grams NaOH}} \times \frac{2 \text{ moles } H_2O}{4 \text{ moles NaOH}} \times \frac{18 \text{ grams } H_2O}{1 \text{ mole } H_2O} = 0.90 \text{ grams } H_2O$$

14.   c.   Add the atomic masses of the constituent molecules to obtain the molar mass
= (2 × 12) + (6 × 1) + (1 × 16) = 46 grams/mol — this is the mass of one mole.
Six moles have a mass six times the molar mass:
6 mol × 46 g/mol = 276 grams.

15.   d.   The easy way to determine the limiting reactant is to divide the molar amounts by the stoichiometric coefficient. For boron, this is 5/2 = 2.5; for hydrogen, it is 8/3 = 2.67, so boron is the limiting reactant. 5 moles of boron require 5 × (3/2) moles of hydrogen, which equals 7.5 moles. So 0.5 mole of hydrogen remains unused.

16.   b.   The mass of phosphorus can be obtained by subtracting 56.36 g from 100 g:

	P	O
mass ratio:	43.64 g	56.36 g
divide by molar mass:	/30.97	/16.00
	= 1.409	= 3.523
convert to integers by dividing by the smaller:	= 1	= 2.5
and then multiplying by 2:	= 2	= 5

The mole ratio must be 2:5 and P_4O_{10} is the only molecular formula that fits this requirement.

17.   c.   The balanced equation is CH_3CO_2H + $2O_2$ → $2CO_2$ + $2H_2O$

18.   e. $2N_2H_4 \; + \; 1N_2O_4 \; \rightarrow \; 3N_2 \; + \; 4H_2O$

19.   d.   The mass of water driven off = 5.29 – 3.38 g = 1.91 g

	$CuSO_4$	H_2O
mass ratio:	3.38 g	1.91 g
divide by molar mass:	/159.6	/18.02
	= 0.0212	= 0.106
convert to integers by dividing by the smaller:	= 1	= 5

The hydrated salt is $CuSO_4 \cdot 5H_2O$.

20.   f.

	carbon	hydrogen	oxygen
mass % ratio:	26.7%	2.2%	71.1%
divide by molar mass:	/12.011	/1.008	/16.00
	= 2.22	= 2.18	= 4.44
convert to integers by dividing by the smallest:	= 1	= 1	= 2

The empirical formula is CHO_2, with an empirical mass of 45 g. The only molecular formula that fits these data is oxalic acid $(CO_2H)_2$.

21.   h.   nitric acid is a strong acid.

22.   g.   potassium hydroxide is a strong base.

23.   f.   sugar is a nonelectrolyte, it does not ionize in solution.

24.   f.   S   oxidation number is +6.

25.   b.   Kr   oxidation number is +2.

26.   f.   Cr   oxidation number is +6.

27.   f.   Molarity = moles /liter = 1.5 moles / 0.200 L = 7.5 M.

28.   c.   *dilute solution*   *concentrated solution*
molarity × volume   =   molarity × volume
7.5   × volume   =   0.15   ×   1
volume = 0.020 liter = 20 mL

29.   g.   57 kJ goes into the system; 32 kJ goes out; the net gain is 25 kJ.
Or $\Delta E = q + w = +57 - 32 = +25$ kJ.

30. b. $C_2H_4(g) + H_2(g) \rightarrow C_2H_6(g)$

        $2C(s) + 3H_2(g) \rightarrow C_2H_6(g)$ $\Delta H° = -84.7$ kJ

        $2C(s) + 2H_2(g) \rightarrow C_2H_4(g)$ $\Delta H° = +52.3$ kJ

The second equation must be reversed and added to the first equation, so the sign must be changed for the second equation:

        $2C(s) + 3H_2(g) \rightarrow C_2H_6(g)$ $\Delta H° = -84.7$ kJ

        $C_2H_4(g) \rightarrow 2C(s) + 2H_2(g)$ $\Delta H° = -52.3$ kJ

        $C_2H_4(g) + H_2(g) \rightarrow C_2H_6(g)$ $\Delta H° = -137.0$ kJ

31. c. $CH_4 + 2O_2 \rightarrow CO_2 + 2H_2O$ $\Delta H° = -890$ kJ

In this reaction, two moles of water are produced. This is $2 \times 18 = 36$ grams.

If only 9.0 grams of water is produced, then 1/4 the amount of heat is released = $1/4 \times 890$ kJ = 222 kJ.

32. b. Acetic acid is a weak acid and should be written in the molecular form.
Silver chloride is a precipitate and should be written as the formula unit $AgCl(s)$.

Both silver acetate and hydrochloric acid are strong electrolytes and are written in the ionic form.

$Ag^+(aq) + CH_3CO_2^-(aq) + H^+(aq) + Cl^-(aq) \rightarrow AgCl(s) + CH_3CO_2H(aq)$

33. g. Divide the units $J\ K^{-1}\ mol^{-1}$ by the units $J\ K^{-1}\ g^{-1}$ to obtain the units $g\ mol^{-1}$:

$24.9\ J\ K^{-1}\ mol^{-1} / 0.446\ J\ K^{-1}\ g^{-1} = 55.8\ g\ mol^{-1}$.

34. e. Heat = specific heat × mass × temperature change

Heat = $0.446\ J\ K^{-1}\ g^{-1} \times 30\ g \times 25K = 335$ J

Note that the temperature *change* can be in °C or K, they are the same.

Examination 2 (Page 151)

True–false questions

1. **T** Red light has a lower frequency (less energy per photon).

2. **T** Allowed values for m_ℓ run from $+\ell$ to $-\ell$.

3. **F** Paramagnetic materials are drawn into a magnetic field.

4. **F** Fluorine is the smallest of the 2nd Period elements (except perhaps Ne) due to the large effective nuclear charge.

5. **T** There are $(2\ell+1)$ orbitals in a subshell, therefore $2(2\ell+1)$ electrons.

6. **F** The most stable ion of sodium is the Na^+ ion (although Na^- does exist).

7. **T** A lone pair of electrons is a nonbonding pair of electrons.

8. **T** This is how the bond order is determined in valence bond theory.

9. **T** Electronegativity is a property of an atom *in a compound*; it measures how strongly the atom attracts electrons.

10. **F** This would be a metallic bond.

11. **T** The see-saw molecular geometry is derived from the trigonal bipyramidal arrangement where there is one lone pair of electrons.

12. **F** Bonding pairs of electrons repel each other less than nonbonding pairs of electrons.

13. **F** A triple bond indicates that three pairs of electrons are shared in the bond.

14. **T** There's always some overlap of orbitals and some covalent contribution to the bond.

15. **F** Many ions are nonpolar (they are symmetrical in structure).

16. **T** The geometry of a set of sp hybrid orbitals is linear.

17. **T** The number of hybrid orbitals always equals the number of atomic orbitals used.

18. **F** Cis-trans isomerism is impossible about a triple bond; and it is impossible about a double bond in which the two groups at one end of the bond are both the same.

19.   T   It depends upon their orientation.

20.   F   The three π bonding pairs of electrons are shared by all carbon atoms in the ring. The electrons are delocalized around the ring. The bond order of each bond is 1.5.

21.   T   Resonance is required in VB theory for a satisfactory picture of the bonding.

22.   T   A single bond is a σ bond.

Multiple Choice

1.   a.   Radio waves have the lowest frequency and the longest wavelength.

2.   b.   γ-radiation is the highest frequency electromagnetic radiation, and its photons have the highest energy ($E = h\nu$).

3.   e.   5.

4.   d.   energy, shape, and orientation.

5.   b.   If $\ell = 1$, then the orbital must be a p orbital, and n = 4 so the orbital is 4p.

6.   a.   If $\ell = 0$, then the orbital must be an s orbital which can only accommodate 2 electrons, regardlesss of the value of n.

7.   h.   7s; follow the rows in the Periodic Table, left to right.

8.   f.   Ge.

9.   d.   the 3p set cannot hold more than 6 electrons, so $3p^8$ is impossible.

10.   e.   Iron, Fe, has a ground electron configuration $4s^2\, 3d^6$. The 6 electrons in the d orbitals are spread out as much as possible (Hund's rule). Only one of the d orbitals has a pair of electrons, the other four have just a single electron.

11.   a. $E = h\nu$, where ν is the frequency of the radiation and E is the energy of a single photon. and $\lambda \times \nu = c$, so $E = hc/\lambda$. There are 10^9 nm in one m.

E = $6.626 \times 10^{-34} \times 3.0 \times 10^8\,/\,450 \times 10^{-9}$ J.
E = 4.42×10^{-19} J.

12.   g.   P at the top right.

13.   g.   P at the top right.

14.   g.   P at the top right.

15.   c.   In at the bottom left.

16.   b.   Polar covalent; the electrons are shared, but shared unequally.

17.   c.   4 pairs, an octet of electrons.

18.   b.   Total valence electrons = 8 + 6 + (2 × 7) = 28.
             Therefore 3 bonding pairs and 2 lone pairs, a total of 5 pairs.
             Therefore trigonal bipyramidal arrangement.

19.   f.   Total valence electrons = 7 + (4 × 7) − 1 = 34.
             Therefore 4 bonding pairs and 1 lone pair, a total of 5 pairs.
             Therefore trigonal bipyramidal arrangement.
             The lone pair goes in the trigonal plane (equatorial).
             The shape is see-saw.

20.   c.   Four pairs of electrons in the valence shell.
             Therefore sp^3.

21.   e.   Any one of the three Lewis structures for the carbonate ion has two single bonds and one double
             bond around the carbon atom, an octet of electrons. The average bond order is (1 + 1 + 2)/3 = 4/3
             = 1.33.

22.   d. ClO_3^- is trigonal pyramidal in shape, and is polar. All the other ions are symmetrical in structure.

23.   f.   The two p_π orbitals must lie off the internuclear axis (i.e. p_x or p_y), and be parallel to one another.
             The only possibility is p_y and p_y. The d_{xy} orbital in choice g is not aligned correctly to form a π
             bond.   The only d orbitals with the correct orientation to form a π bond along the z axis are the d_{xz}
             and the d_{yz} orbitals.

24.   f.   Six electrons or three pairs.

25.   b.   Formal charge on the N: 3 lone pairs + half-share in 1 bonding pair = (3 × 2) + 1 = 7.
             To be neutral, N should have 5 electrons in its valence shell.
             Therefore a formal charge of 5 − 7 = −2

$$:O \equiv C - \overset{\cdot\cdot}{\underset{\cdot\cdot}{N}}:$$
$$\quad 1 \quad 0 \quad -2$$

26.   f.   Resonance indicates the true distribution of electrons in a molecule. In molecular orbital theory, the
             electron pair(s) is(are) delocalized in orbital(s) that extend over the entire molecule.

27.   g.   Write the equation for the formation of methane from its constituent elements:

             $C(s)$ + $2H_2(g)$ → $CH_4(g)$ ΔH_f° ?

             The process involves breaking up the carbon solid, breaking up two hydrogen molecules, and forming
             four C–H bonds. The total energy involved is

             716 + (2 × 436) − (4 × 413) kJ = −64 kJ

28. b. Orbital hybridization is the combination of atomic orbitals to form a new set of orbitals with directional properties more appropriate for bonding.

29. b. sp^2, with one p orbital left on each carbon atom for the π bonding.

Examination 3 (Page 199)

True–false questions

1.   T   All gases are real; although most behave ideally at ordinary temperatures and pressures.

2.   T   At constant volume, the pressure is directly porportional to temperature.

3.   T   A useful thing to know in gas law calculations.

4.   F   The average kinetic energy of all gases at the same temperature must be the same, so a larger molecule (greater molar mass) moves more slowly.

5.   F   There are exactly 100 kPa in one bar.

6.   T   The principal reason for deviation from ideal behavior is intermolecular attraction.

7.   F   The number of moles of gases decreases (from 4 to 2 moles) so the pressure decreases.

8.   T   This is the significance of the rms speed.

9.   F   Some gases are colored (for example Cl_2, Br_2, NO_2).

10. T   Both are condensed states of matter.

11. T   The strongest van der Waals intermolecular force, for molecules of comaparble size, is the hydrogen bond. Next strongest is dipole-dipole attraction, followed by dispersion forces.

12. F   Even for polar molecules, dispersion forces often contribute more to the intermolecular attraction.

13. T   Doubly–charged metal ions are more strongly solvated than singly–charged metal ions.

14. F   Ethanol, like all alcohols, contains the –O–H functional group and can hydrogen bond.

15. F   HF has the highest boiling point due to intermolecular hydrogen bonding.

16. F   Very few are; water is the most common example.

17. T   The heat of vaporization parallels the boiling point; in fact the ratio of the two for many compounds is a constant number called Trouton's constant.

18. T   The liquid and vapor cannot be distinguished beyond the critical point.

19. F   The surface tension is due to attraction between molecules in the liquid.

20. T   There are only seven crystal systems.

21. F One system has four associated crystal lattices, some only one.

22. F There are only 2 structural units within a bcc unit cell and 4 within a fcc unit cell. Molecules at the edge of a unit cell are shared with adjacent unit cells.

23. T Molality is a temperature-independent concentration unit; molarity changes with temperature.

24. F Supersaturated solutions exist; they are however thermodynamically unstable.

25. T Gases usually dissolve exothermically due to the formation of solute-solvent bonds.

26. F Solution processes are usually entropy-driven; many have a positive ΔH.

27. T According to Raoult's law, the vapor pressure of the solvent depends on the mole fraction of the solvent in the solution. Addition of any solute reduces that mole fraction.

28. F The freezing point depression has nothing to do with the reduction in vapor pressure. Both are due to the increase in disorder of the liquid phase when a solute is added.

29. T The van't Hoff factor i is an integer only in an extremely-dilute solution; association between ions occurs in concentrated solutions.

30. F Immiscible means that the liquids don't mix.

Multiple choice questions

1. e. The SI derived unit for pressure is the pascal Pa.

2. b. An ideal gas law problem (just make sure the units are correct).
        $P = 380/760$ atm $= 0.50$ atm; $V = 2.5$ L, $R = 0.08206$ L atm K^{-1} mol^{-1}; $T = 283.15$K,
        so, from $PV = nRT$, $n = 0.054$ mol.

3. b. The pressure increases from 760 torr to 1013 torr (an increase of one-third or by a factor of 4/3). The volume must decrease in the same ratio; ie. to 3/4 of the initial volume.

4. c. $$C_3H_8(g) + 5O_2(g) \rightarrow 3CO_2(g) + 4H_2O(l)$$
        One mole of any gas at STP has a volume of 22.4 liters.
        The molar mass of propane is 44 g, so 2.20 grams of propane is 2.2/44 moles = 0.050 moles.
        According to the stoichiometry of the reaction one mole of propane requires five moles of oxygen; so $0.050 \times 5 = 0.25$ mol of oxygen are required in this reaction.
        0.25 mol of oxygen occupies 22.4×0.25 liters $= 5.60$ liters.

5. b. Partial pressure of hydrogen = 1 atm pressure $\times (2.0/6.0) = 1/3$ atm
        Partial pressure of nitrogen = 1.5 atm pressure $\times (4.0/6.0) = 1$ atm
        Therefore the total pressure = $1/3 + 1$ atm = 1.33 atm

6.   i.   Initial partial pressure of H_2S = 2.0 atm × (2/5) = 4/5 atm.
Initial partial pressure of F_2 = 3.0 atm × (3/5) = 9/5 atm.

7.   a.   The limiting reactant is F_2, and it's all used up.

8.   b.   Initial partial pressure of H_2S = 4/5 atm.
Amount of H_2S used = (9/5) × (1/3) = 3/5 atm.
Amount of H_2S remaining unused = 4/5 atm − 3/5 atm = 1/5 atm.

9.   g.   Amount of HF formed = (9/5) × (2/3) = 6/5 atm.

10.   j.   Total pressure at end = sum of partial pressures = 1/5 + 0 + 6/5 + 3/5 atm = 10/5 atm = 2.0 atm.

11.   e.   Relative rates of diffusion are proportional to the inverse of the square roots of the molar masses (Graham's law). The molar mass of nitrogen gas is 28 g mol^{-1}. (Note that the answer has to be greater than 2, which limits your choice.) Rate = 2.0 × $\sqrt{(40/28)}$ = 2.4.

12.   e.   copper (metallic), graphite (covalent network), lithium fluoride (ionic), methane (intermolecular).

13.   e.   In a cubic lattice, a structural unit at the corner of a unit cell contributes 1/8:

14.   c.   Volume of one unit cell = $(362)^3$ pm^3 = 4.74 × 10^{-23} cm^3
Mass of one unit cell = volume × density = 4.24 × 10^{-22} g
Mass of one copper atom = 63.546 g / 6.022 × 10^{23} = 1.055 × 10^{-22} g

Number of atoms per unit cell = $\dfrac{\text{mass of one unit cell}}{\text{mass of one copper atom}} = \dfrac{4.24 \times 10^{-22}\,\text{g}}{1.055 \times 10^{-22}\,\text{g}} = 4$

15.   c.   Calcium = (8 × 1/8) + 1 = 2
Carbon = (8 × 1/4) + 2 = 4
Therefore CaC_2

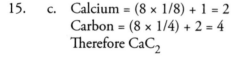

16.   b.   methylamine; note the –NH_2 group.

17.   d.   Some molecules in a liquid have sufficient energy to escape intermolecular attraction.

18.   a. b. c.   Any phase change that requires breaking bonds is endothermic:
melting, vaporization, sublimation.

19.   d.   The lines represent the conditions under which two phases coexist in equilibrium.

20.   b.   The metal ion most strongly solvated is the one with the largest charge and the smallest size.

21.   a.   It triples; Henry's law states that the solubility of a gas depends upon the partial pressure of that gas above the solvent.

22. b. the partial vapor pressure of acetone = 0.50×176 torr = 88 torr
the partial vapor pressure of ethanol = 0.50×50 torr = 25 torr
total vapor pressure = 113 torr.
According to Dalton's law of partial pressures, the mole fraction of ethanol = 25/113 = 0.22.
(Ethanol is the less volatile of the two solvents.)

23. d. Molality is the number of moles / 1000 g solvent, so in 200 g of solvent, we need 0.03 moles of NaOH. The molar mass is 40 g mol^{-1}.

24. d. 20% methanol means 20 g of methanol in 100 g solution, or 20 g methanol in 80 g ethanol.
The concentration of methanol is therefore 250 g /kg ethanol.
The molar mass of methanol is 32 g mol^{-1}.
Number of moles = 250 g / 32 g mol^{-1} = 7.8 mol.
Molality = 7.8 m.

25. a. $\Delta T = k_b \times m \times i = -3.0 \times 2.0 \times 1 = -6.0°C$, so the boiling point of pure acetic acid is 118°C.

26. c. $\Pi = cRT$; remember to use the correct units.
$\Pi = 9.8 / 760$ atm; R = 0.08206 L atm K^{-1} mol^{-1}; T = 293.15K; so c = 5.36×10^{-4} mol/L.
Number of moles in 25 mL = 1.34×10^{-5} mol; this is the number of moles in the 50 mg sample.
Molar mass = 0.050 g / 1.34×10^{-5} mol = 3730 g mol^{-1}.

27. a. An aerosol is a colloidal dispersion of a liquid or solid in a gas.

28. f. $\Delta T = k_b \times m \times i$. Look for the highest product $m \times i$. Colligative properties depend upon the concentration of particles, not their identity. For Na_2SO_4, $m \times i = 0.040 \times 3 = 0.120$.

29. d. The temperature of the phase change = $\Delta H_v / \Delta S_v$
= 38000 J mol^{-1} / 113 JK^{-1} mol^{-1}
= 336 K
= 63°C.

30. c. The rate of movement between the liquid and vapor states depends upon the surface area. For example, water spilled on the floor evaporates more quickly than the same water in a glass. When water boils, bubbles form in the liquid and the surface area increases dramatically.

31. e. Dalton's law: the partial pressure depends upon the mole fraction in the vapor = 3/4 of the total pressure, or a contribution 3 times that of gas B.

32. d. Raoult's law: vapor pressure due to a component in a solution = mole fraction of that component in the solution × vapor pressure of the component in the pure state. The mole fraction of A in the solution is 3/4 or 75%.

80 Elements (Page 26)

—solution

Across:

3. Its oxide is pitchblende, and radioactive.
6. A penny from Cyprus.
7. Named for Vanadis, the Norse goddess of beauty.
8. It plumbs the depths, this heavy metal.
10. Its oxide emits brilliant white light when heated.
13. Named for Greek stone.
14. Make a meal of it to see inside.
16. Brimstone...
19. ...and the element below.
20. ...and old lace, Capra's macabre farce.
24. Discovered by Priestley, but named by Lavoisier.
26. Its plate is shiny.
28. Discovered in 1839 in Sweden by Mosander.
29. Filled the first vacant space in Mendeleev's Table.
30. From a mineral hauled by 20 mules.
33. Dark red emission led to its discovery.
36. This one melts in your hand.
37. Beneath *13 across*, its lamps are yellow.
38. Argentum.
41. Noble origin of the man of steel?
43. A rose by this name would be as red.
44. The metal on galvanized iron.
45. The liquid halogen.
46. Produces iridescent colors.
49. But there's no W anywhere in the name!
50. Albert's in his element.
52. The most abundant metal in the earth's crust.
53. For the originator of the table.
55. For the German goblin.
57. America's element for smoke detectors.
59. With *6 across* it's bronze.
63. The most abundant gas in the atmosphere.
64. For the thief of fire.
65. Symbol from latin kalium, arabic al-kali.
67. Moisson received the Nobel Prize for isolating this.
68. A colored sign.
70. Halfway across the Lanthanides.
71. For the daughter of *23 down*.
72. For the Latin name for Copenhagen.
73. Its disulfide is slippery.

Down:

1. Its allotropes are white, red, and black.
2. For Madame Marie, two Nobel Prizes...
4. ...one for the discovery of this element.
5. Not alone, according to its name in Greek.
9. Is it the first of the actinides?
10. With or without the T, it's found where *42 down* is.
11. Its silicate is diamond–like.
12. Discovered with *46 across* and named for its smell.
15. Quicksilver, winged messenger.
17. Radioactive alkali metal.
18. A silent basement killer.
21. A semiconductor from the valley in California.
22. Between *59 across* and *66 down*.
23. Tantalizing element.
25. The goal of the alchemists.
27. A transition metal sometimes mistaken for *56 down*.
30. For the site of Seaborg's laboratory.
31. Named for the 8th planet from the sun.
32. The metal in cisplatin, the antitumor drug.
33. So many R's: Ra, Rb, Re, Rf, Rh, Rn, this one's Ru.
34. Its tincture is antiseptic.
35. Essential for bones...
38. ...and below, Dalton's symbol for it was ⊙.
39. For Lise, who explained nuclear fission in 1939.
40. The last of the nonradioactive elements.
42. Source and symbol initially Ytterby in Sweden.
47. A ferrous metal first cast as pigs.
48. Named for the Titans, symbolic of strength.
51. An essential element of living things.
54. Isolated from *58 down* and named for Europe.
55. Halogen used in water purification.
56. The milk of its hydroxide settles the stomach.
58. Isolated from a mineral named for Col. Samarskite.
60. Idle gas...
61. ...and the stranger below.
62. The largest Group 3 metal.
65. Named for the native land of *2 down*.

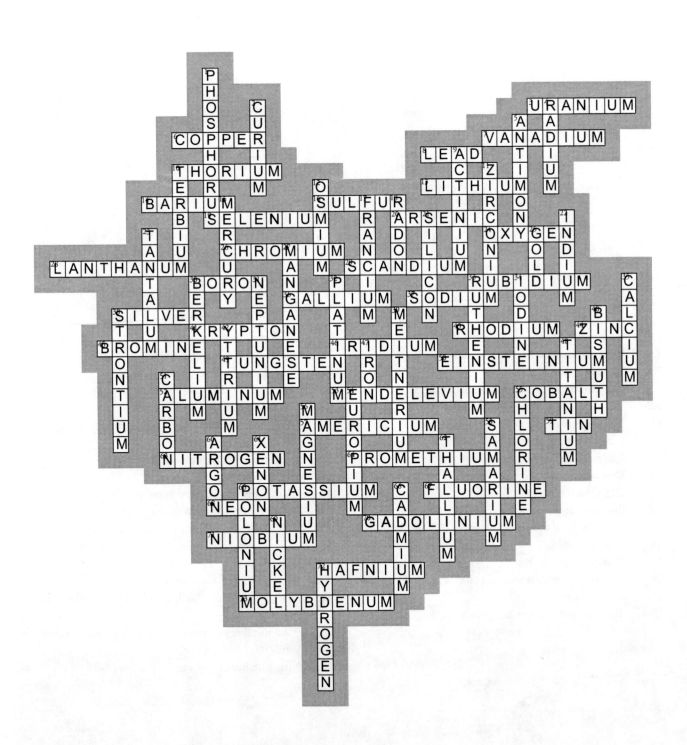

Numbers (Page 43)

—solution

Across:

1.   Molar mass of copper.
4.   The year Antoine Lavoisier lost his head.
7   Neptune's number.
8.   The most recently detected element (Jan '99).
10. The exponent of Avogadro's number.
11. The number of inches in one foot...
13. ...and the number of sq. in in one sq.ft.
15. The molar mass of oxygen atoms.
16. One atmosphere pressure in torr.
17. 273°C in K.
18. The mass of the empirical formula for 9 down.
19. The volume of one mole of a gas at 0°C and 1 atm.
21. Niobe's number.
23. Three moles of carbon.
25. The ignition temperature of paper in °F.
27. The molar mass of methane CH_4.
28. The first four digits of Avogadro's number.

Down:

1.   Lithium's mass.
2.   The atomic number of arsenic...
3.   ...and that of the element under it.
4.   Radioactive carbon isotope used in dating.
5.   The atomic number of 20 down.
6.   The group numbers of silicon, aluminum, nitrogen, and sulfur, respectively.
9.   The mass of four moles of acetylene C_2H_2.
12. It's freezing in K.
13. A number for the prize-giver.
14. The number of grams in one pound.
15. The number of cubic cm in one cubic inch.
18. The mass of a proton divided by the mass of an electron.
20. The isotope of uranium used in nuclear reactors.
22. The year Linus Pauling won his second Nobel Prize.
24. The number of carbon atoms in a common fuller-ene.
25. The number of neutrons in 2 down's isotope–75.

People (Page 112)

—solution

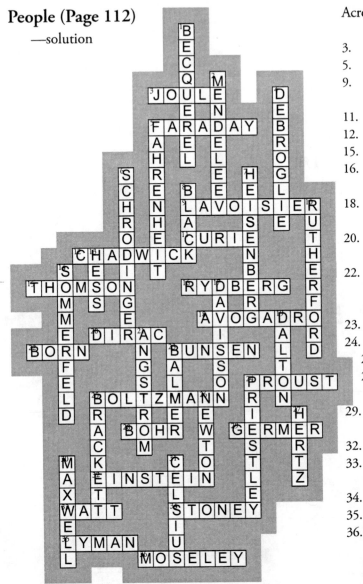

Across:

3. A man of energy, a student of *19 down*.
5. Wrote the laws of electrolysis in 1833.
9. Proposed the law of conservation of matter, then lost his head.
11. Discovered polonium, named after her native land.
12. Discovered the neutron in 1932.
15. Suggested the presence of electrons in all matter.
16. Developed an equation used to predict the lines in the emission spectrum of hydrogen.
18. An Italian whose ideas were a long time in being accepted—his is the number.
20. Incorporated Einstein's relativity into Schrödinger's equation.
22. Suggested that φ^2 should be interpreted as the probability of finding the electron at any point about the nucleus.
23. His burner was used to obtain emission spectra.
24. Proposed the law of constant composition.
25. His constant k is R/N_A.
28. Incorporated the quantization of energy into a model for the electronic structure of an H atom.
29. With *17 down*, he established the wave-particle duality of an electron beam.
32. He explained the photoelectric effect in 1905.
33. What was his name, the unit for power? A student of *14 down*.
34. He named the electron.
35. His series is in the UV region.
36. He determined that elements in the Periodic Table should be arranged by atomic number, not mass.

Down:

1. He discovered radioactivity.
2. Russian who discovered periodicity in the properties of elements and designed the first Periodic Table.
4. Proposed wave–particle duality.
5. His degree is smaller than that of Celsius.
6. Used the assertion of *4 down* to write a wave equation for the electron in a hydrogen atom.
7. A man of some uncertainty.
8. Distinguished heat, temperature, and heat capacity.
10. Proposed the nuclear model for the atom.
13. Developed the law of constant heat summation.
14. Made elliptical orbits from Bohr's circular ones.
17. With *28 across*, he established the wave-particle duality of an electron beam.
19. Forcefully revived the idea of atoms in 1803.
21. His unit is 100 pm in length.
23. His series is in the visible region.
24. He prepared and isolated oxygen—named by *9 across*.
25. The electrons fall to n=4 in his series.
26. The SI unit for force is named after him.
27. Proved the existence of electromagnetic radiation.
30. Described radiation in terms of electric and magnetic waves.

People of this chapter and their States (Page 170)

—solution

Across:

3. He was concerned with probabilities and distributions...
6. ...and his country.
8. Jacques, the hydrogen-balloonist.
11. Country of *1 down*.
12. He is remembered by his number.
15. His law states that the total pressure is the sum of the partial pressures.
16. Country of *8 across* and *2 down*, amongst others.
17. Country of *12 across* and *10 down*.
18. A sceptical chemist, his was the first gas law.

Down:

1. His was the absolute temperature scale.
2. He formulated the law of combining volumes.
4. Country of the scientist ...
5. ...who developed a gas law for real gases.
7. Mathematician for whom the SI unit of pressure is named.
9. Joseph and Etienne, who designed the first balloon.
10. He invented the mercury barometer in 1643.
13. Another Frenchman, he discovered the relationship between pressure and temperature.
14. Country of *15 across*.

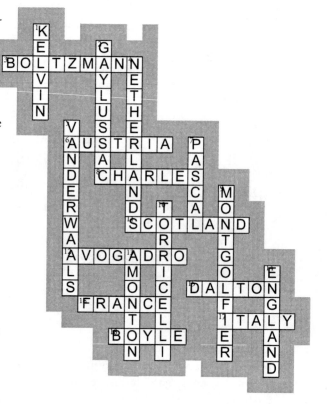

Equilibria (Page 248)
   —solution

Across:

3.   In a titration, it lets you know when you have reached the equivalence point.

6.   What the solution is when the equivalence point is reached in a strong acid - strong base titration.

8.   When water produces *20 down* and *31 across* ions.

10.   Solvation of ions involves an ion - *this* attraction.

12.   Product concentrations divided by reactant concentrations, not necessarily at equilibrium.

13.   It's assumed to be complete for a strong *14 across* in solution.

14.   Weak or strong, it conducts an electrical current in solution.

17.   The result of a Lewis acid-base interaction between a transition metal ion and a base.

18.   Industrial manufacture of ammonia.

21.   It transfers a hydrogen ion to form its conjugate base.

23.   What happens to the salts of weak acids or weak bases in solution.

24.   Normally from 0 to 14, an indication of hydronium ion concentration.

27.   A process for which *9 down* is large.

31.   The conjugate base of water; produced by Arrhenius bases in aqueous solution.

32.   The idea that a system in equilibrium will adjust to accommodate any alteration in conditions.

33.   Negative ion.

Down:

1.   A species that acts as an acid in the presence of a base, and as a base in the presence of an acid.

2.   The effect by which adjacent atoms, or groups of atoms, attract electrons from other parts of a molecule.

4.   Base partner.

5.   A solute that can either accept or donate a hydrogen ion.

7.   Unchanging, except perhaps if the temperature changes.

9.   Q at equilibrium.

11.   A statement of the fact that the *9 down* is *7 down* regardless of how the masses of the components present are changed—developed by Guldberg & Waage.

15.   He classified an acid as an electron pair acceptor and a base as an electron pair donor.

16.   Sulfuric acid, oxalic acid, phosphoric acid, carbonic acid, for example.

19.   Negative this of the concentration of *20 down* is pH.

20.   Ion produced by the protonation of a water molecule.

21.   This increases the hydroxide ion concentration...

22.   ...whereas this increases the hydronium ion concentration in aqueous solution.

25.   If the reaction is reversed, then the new equilibrium constant is this of the original.

26.   His was the first set of definitions describing an acid and base in aqueous solution.

28.   Acetylsalicylic acid.

29.   One name for what is produced when a Lewis acid and a Lewis base react, forming a coordinate bond.

30.   An electrolyte only partially ionized in solution.

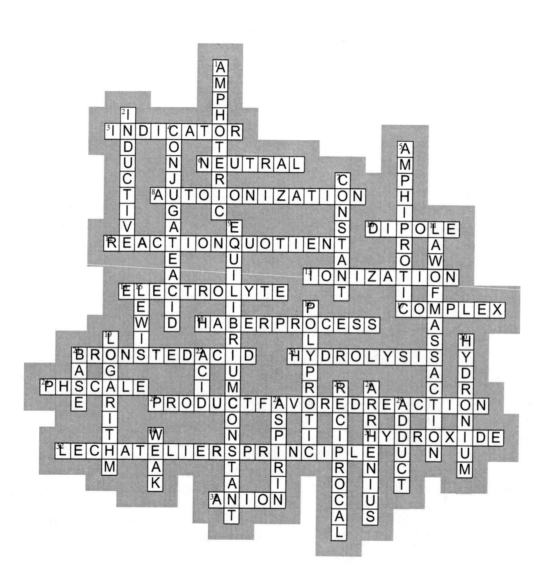